LOVE and HEART

6

OSE KAIDO

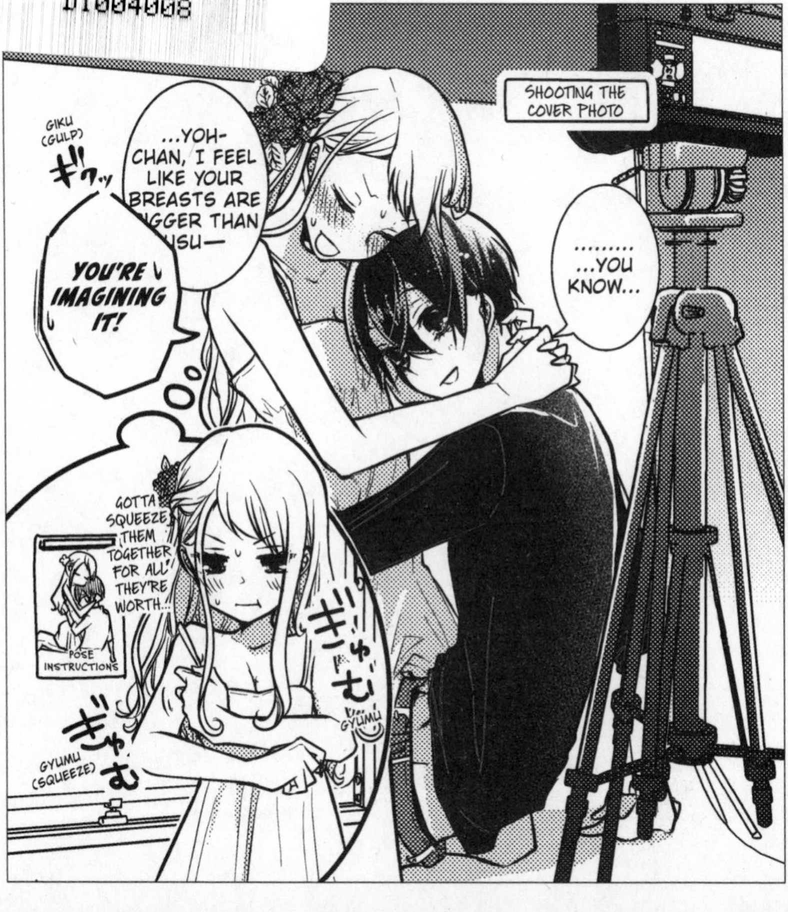
SHOOTING THE COVER PHOTO
....YOU KNOW...
...YOH-CHAN, I FEEL LIKE YOUR BREASTS ARE IGGER THAN USU—
GIKU (GULP)
YOU'RE IMAGINING IT!
GYUMU
GOTTA SQUEEZE THEM TOGETHER FOR ALL THEY'RE WORTH...
POSE INSTRUCTIONS
GYUMU (SQUEEZE)

CONTENTS

84 —————— 003

85 —————— 011

86 —————— 019

87 —————— 027

88 —————— 035

89 —————— 043

90 —————— 051

91 —————— 059

92 —————— 067

93 —————— 075

94 —————— 083

95 —————— 091

96 —————— 099

97 —————— 107

98 —————— 115

99 —————— 123

100 —————— 131

101 —————— 139

BONUS —————— 147

LOVE AND HEART

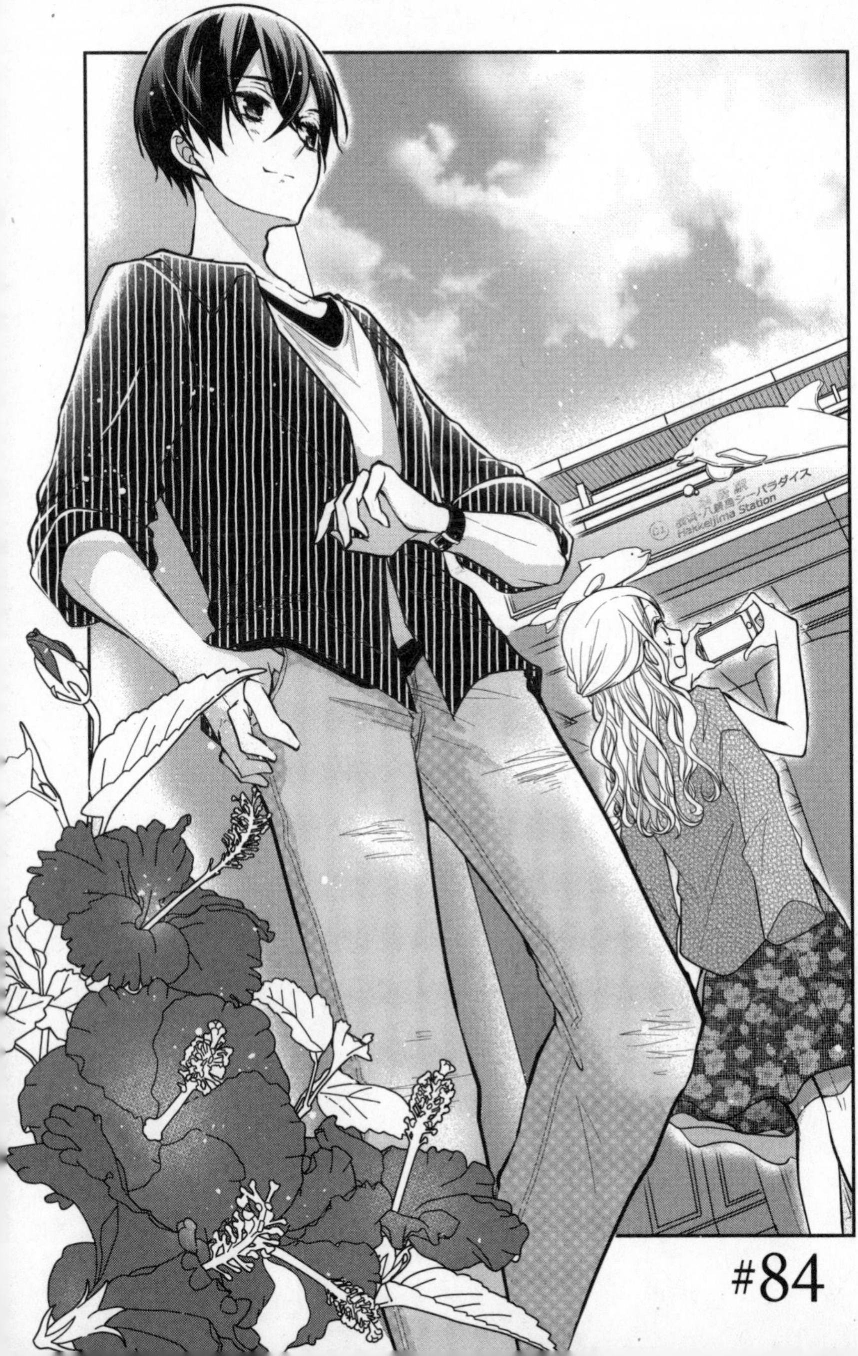
シーパラダイス
Hakkeijima Station

#84

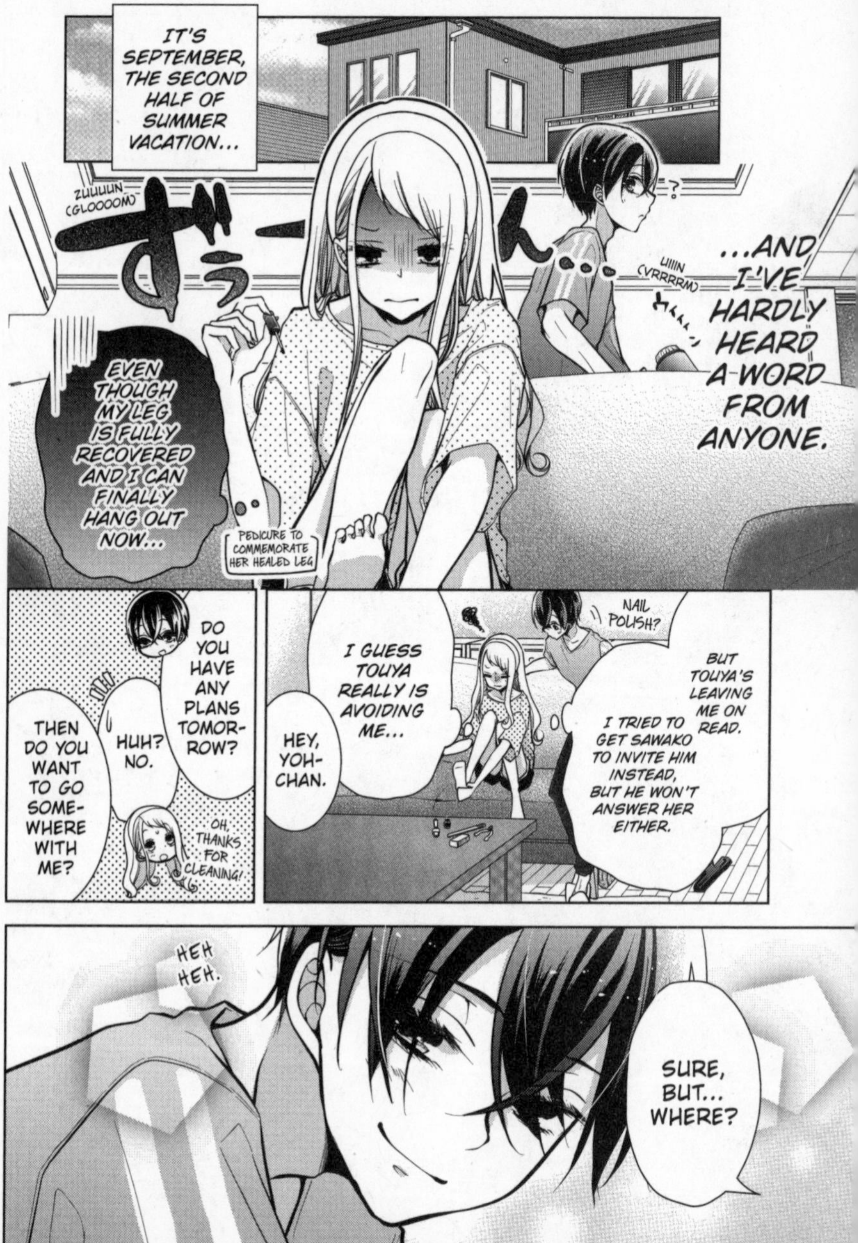
IT'S SEPTEMBER, THE SECOND HALF OF SUMMER VACATION...
?
UIIIN (VRRRRM)
...AND I'VE HARDLY HEARD A WORD FROM ANYONE.
ZUUUUN (GLOOOOM)
EVEN THOUGH MY LEG IS FULLY RECOVERED AND I CAN FINALLY HANG OUT NOW...
PEDICURE TO COMMEMORATE HER HEALED LEG
NAIL POLISH?
BUT TOUYA'S LEAVING ME ON READ.
I TRIED TO GET SAWAKO TO INVITE HIM INSTEAD, BUT HE WON'T ANSWER HER EITHER.
I GUESS TOUYA REALLY IS AVOIDING ME...
HEY, YOH-CHAN.
DO YOU HAVE ANY PLANS TOMORROW?
HUH? NO.
OH, THANKS FOR CLEANING!
THEN DO YOU WANT TO GO SOMEWHERE WITH ME?
SURE, BUT... WHERE?
HEH HEH.

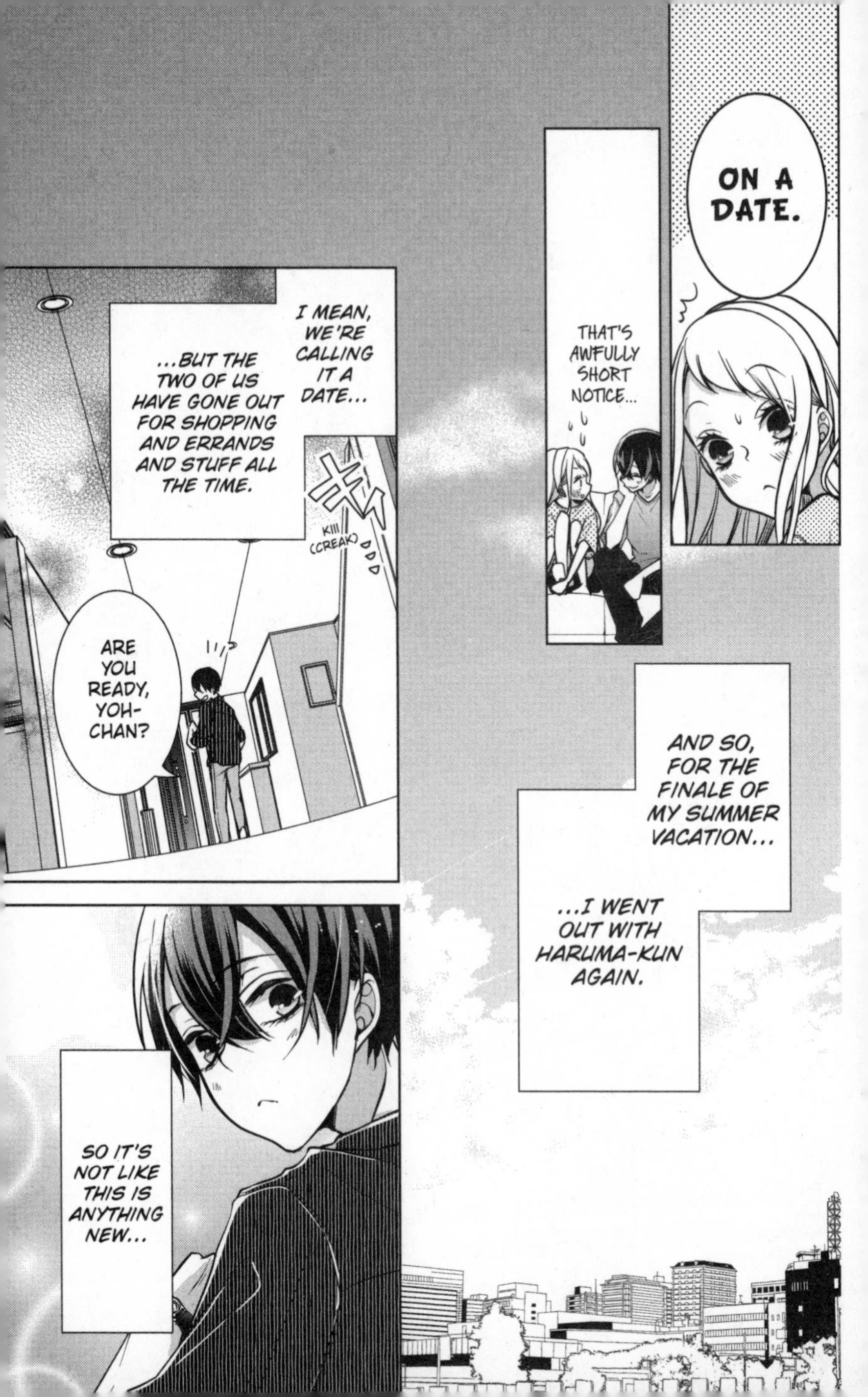
ON A DATE.
THAT'S AWFULLY SHORT NOTICE...
AND SO, FOR THE FINALE OF MY SUMMER VACATION...
...I WENT OUT WITH HARUMA-KUN AGAIN.
I MEAN, WE'RE CALLING IT A DATE...
...BUT THE TWO OF US HAVE GONE OUT FOR SHOPPING AND ERRANDS AND STUFF ALL THE TIME.
KIII (CREAK)
ARE YOU READY, YOH-CHAN?
SO IT'S NOT LIKE THIS IS ANYTHING NEW...

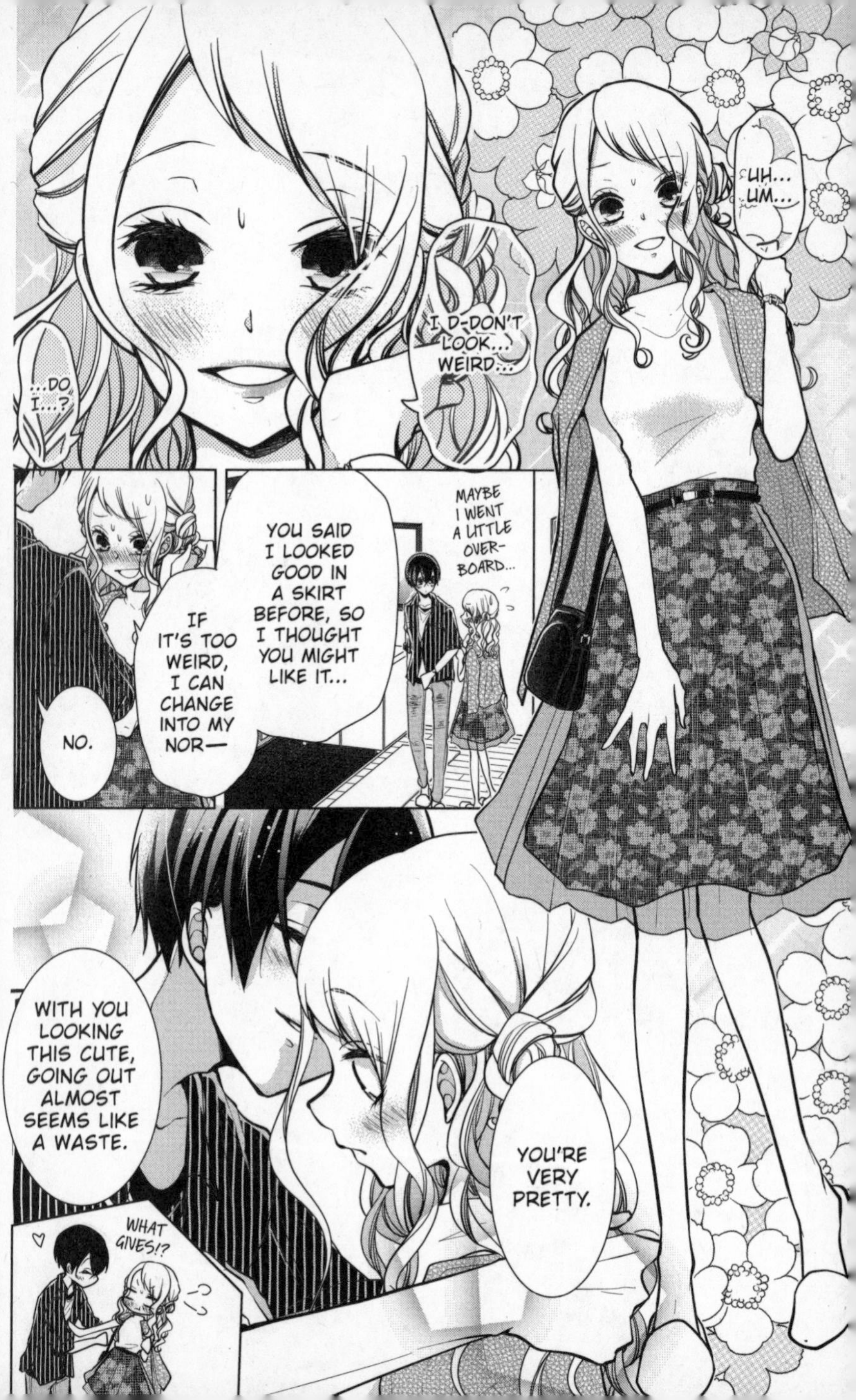
UH... UM...
I D-DON'T LOOK... WEIRD...
...DO I...?
MAYBE I WENT A LITTLE OVER-BOARD...
YOU SAID I LOOKED GOOD IN A SKIRT BEFORE, SO I THOUGHT YOU MIGHT LIKE IT...
IF IT'S TOO WEIRD, I CAN CHANGE INTO MY NOR—
NO.
YOU'RE VERY PRETTY.
WITH YOU LOOKING THIS CUTE, GOING OUT ALMOST SEEMS LIKE A WASTE.
WHAT GIVES!?

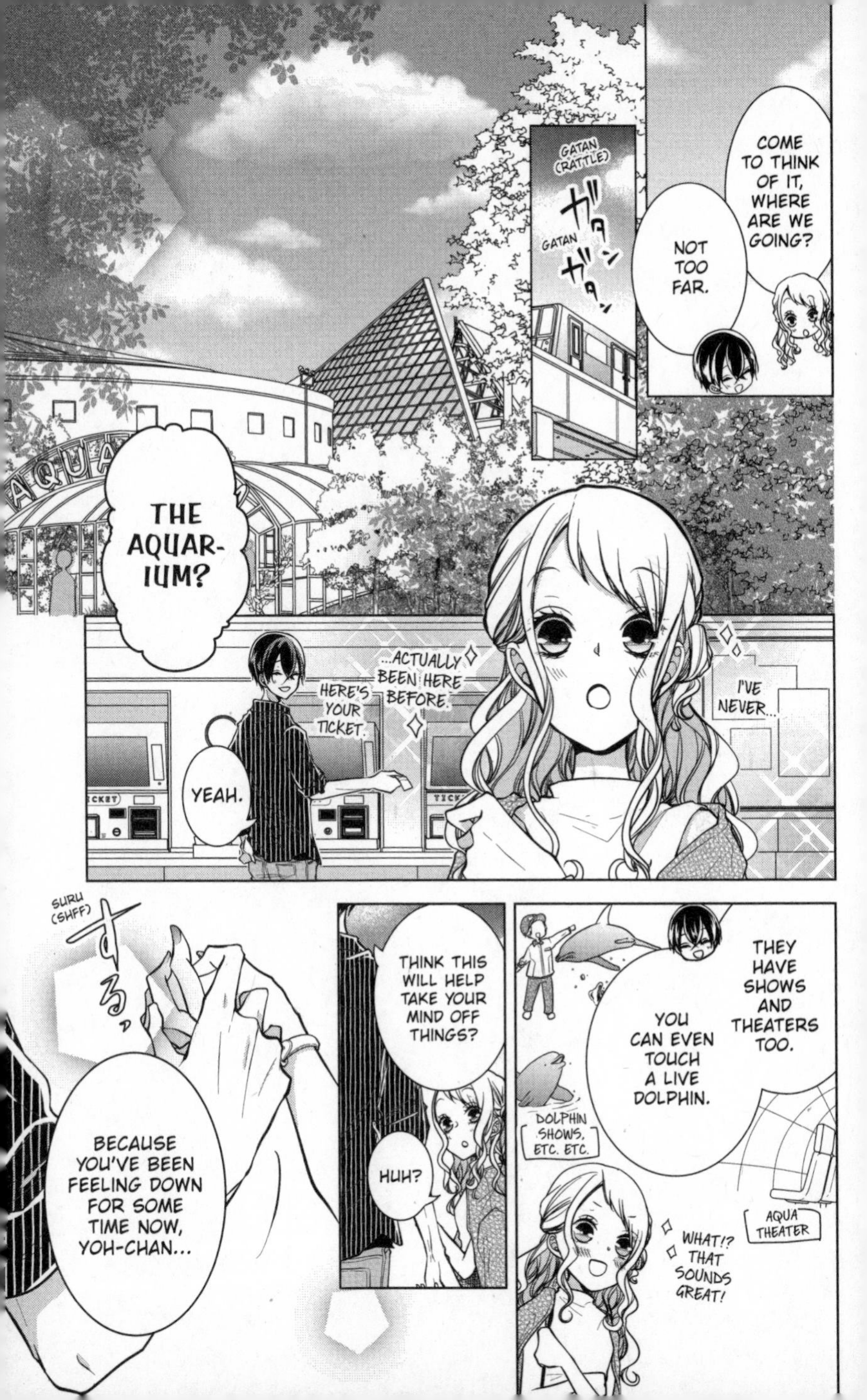
COME TO THINK OF IT, WHERE ARE WE GOING?
NOT TOO FAR.
GATAN (RATTLE)
GATAN
THE AQUARIUM?
I'VE NEVER...
...ACTUALLY BEEN HERE BEFORE.
HERE'S YOUR TICKET.
YEAH.
THEY HAVE SHOWS AND THEATERS TOO.
YOU CAN EVEN TOUCH A LIVE DOLPHIN.
DOLPHIN SHOWS, ETC. ETC.
AQUA THEATER
WHAT!? THAT SOUNDS GREAT!
THINK THIS WILL HELP TAKE YOUR MIND OFF THINGS?
HUH?
SURU (SHFF)
BECAUSE YOU'VE BEEN FEELING DOWN FOR SOME TIME NOW, YOH-CHAN...

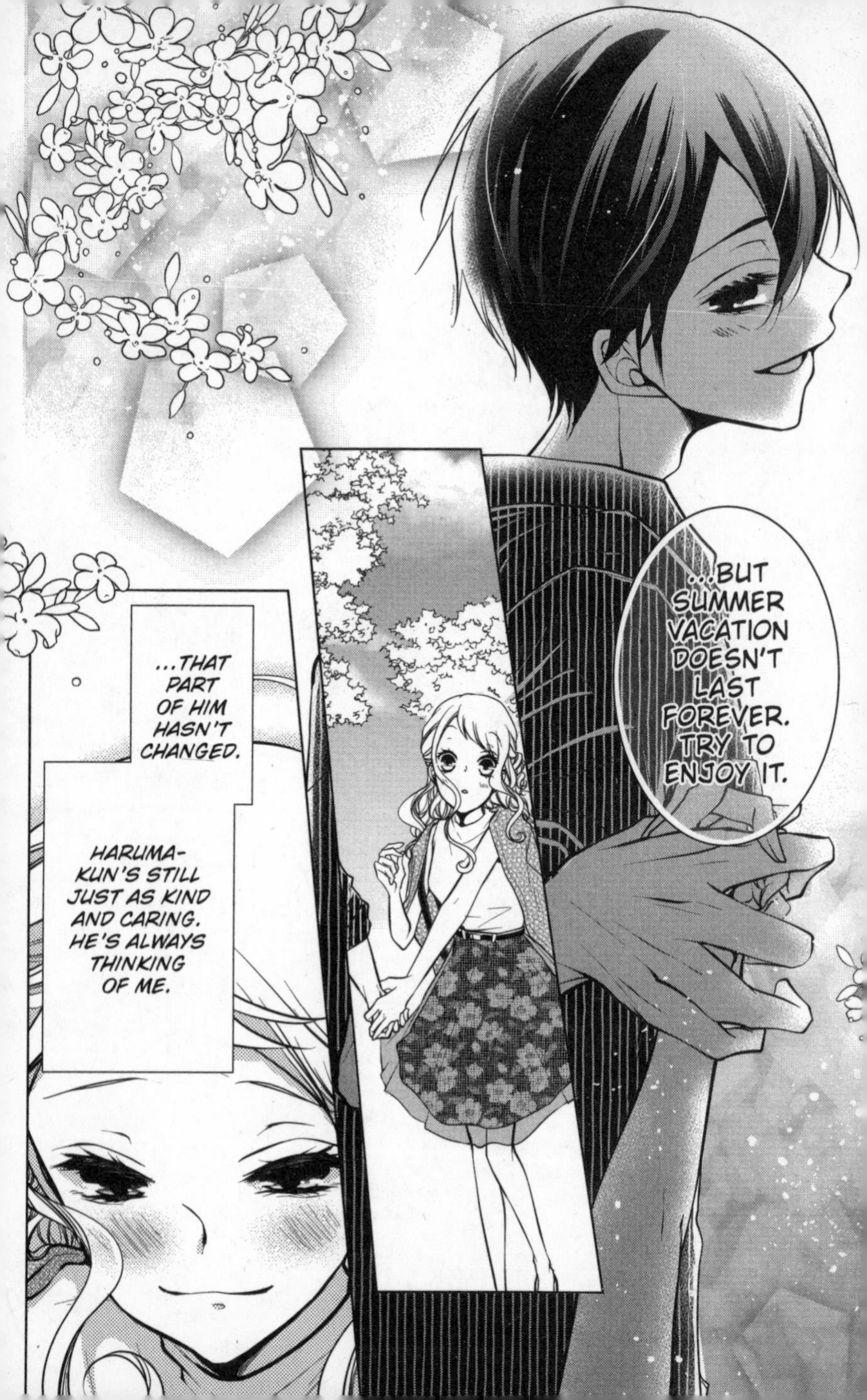
...BUT SUMMER VACATION DOESN'T LAST FOREVER. TRY TO ENJOY IT.
...THAT PART OF HIM HASN'T CHANGED.
HARUMA-KUN'S STILL JUST AS KIND AND CARING. HE'S ALWAYS THINKING OF ME.

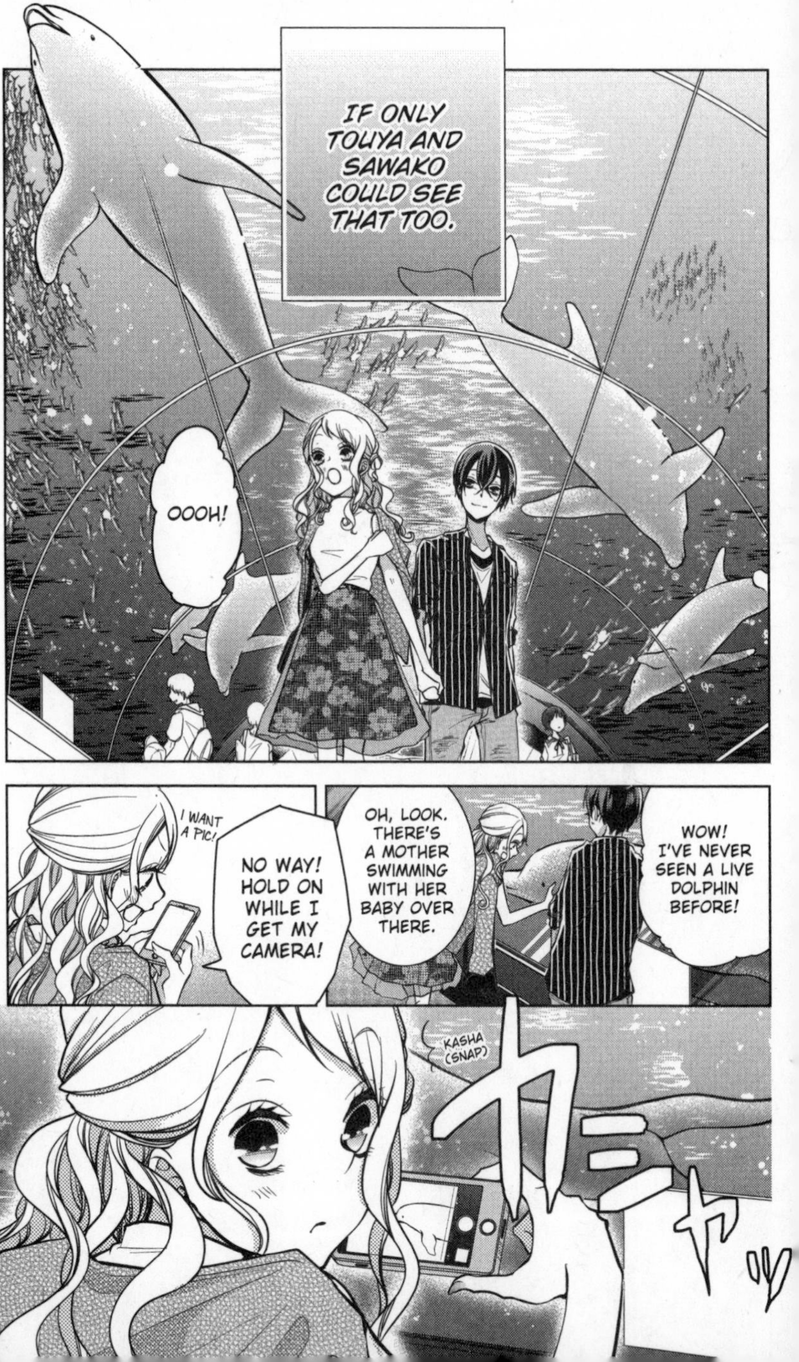

IF ONLY TOUYA AND SAWAKO COULD SEE THAT TOO.
OOOH!
WOW! I'VE NEVER SEEN A LIVE DOLPHIN BEFORE!
OH, LOOK. THERE'S A MOTHER SWIMMING WITH HER BABY OVER THERE.
NO WAY! HOLD ON WHILE I GET MY CAMERA!
I WANT A PIC!
KASHA (SNAP)

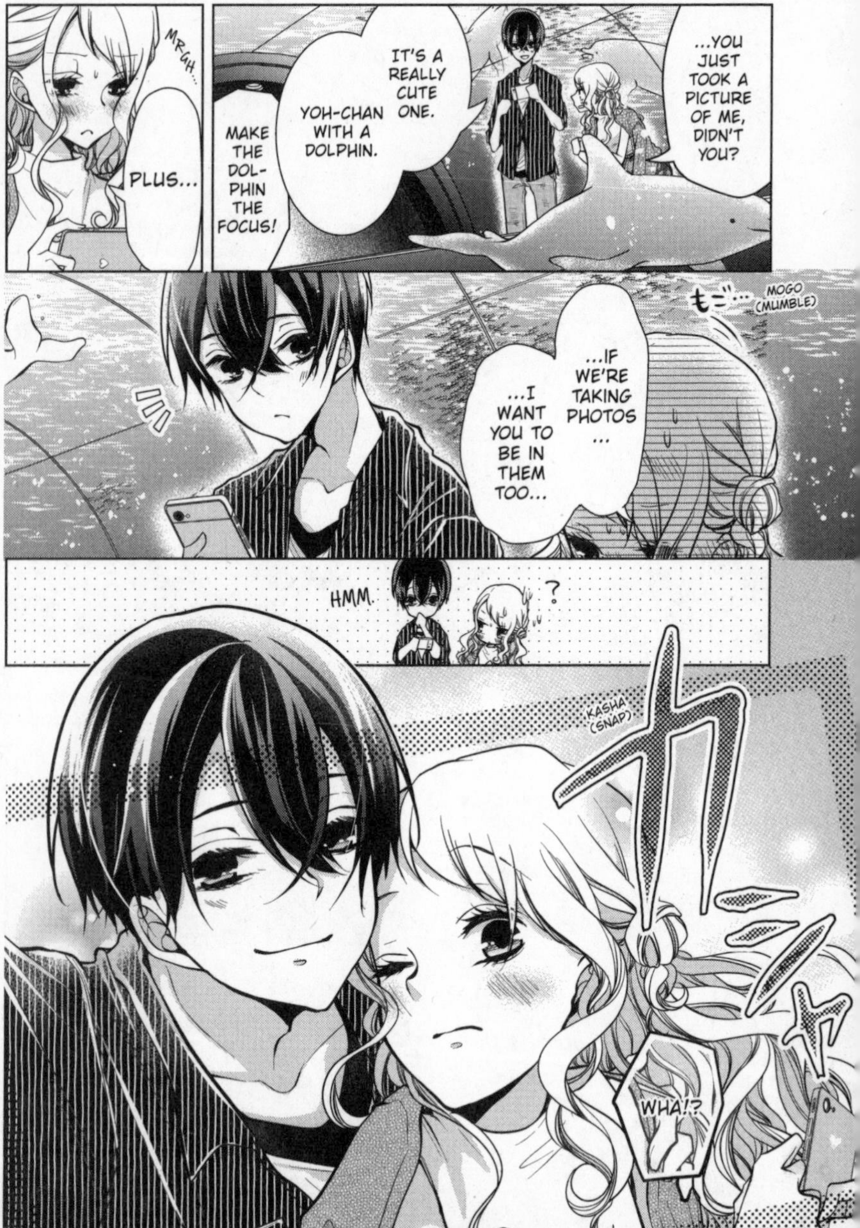
...YOU JUST TOOK A PICTURE OF ME, DIDN'T YOU?
IT'S A REALLY CUTE ONE.
YOH-CHAN WITH A DOLPHIN.
MAKE THE DOLPHIN THE FOCUS!
MRGH...
PLUS...
もご…
MOGO (MUMBLE)
...IF WE'RE TAKING PHOTOS...
...I WANT YOU TO BE IN THEM TOO...
?
HMM.
KASHA (SNAP)
WHA!?

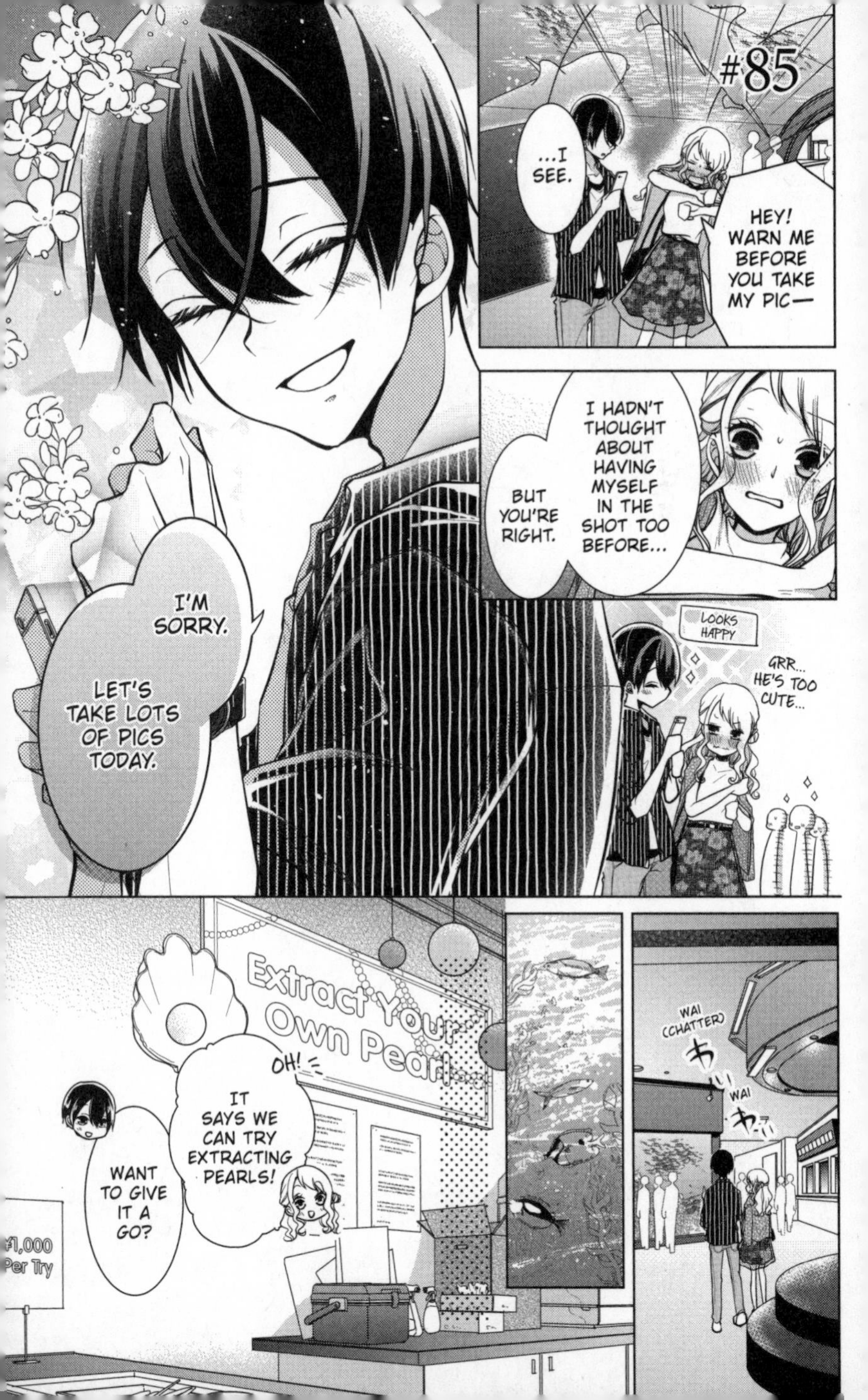
#85
HEY! WARN ME BEFORE YOU TAKE MY PIC—
...I SEE.
I HADN'T THOUGHT ABOUT HAVING MYSELF IN THE SHOT TOO BEFORE...
BUT YOU'RE RIGHT.
GRR... HE'S TOO CUTE...
LOOKS HAPPY
I'M SORRY.
LET'S TAKE LOTS OF PICS TODAY.
WAI (CHATTER)
WAI
Extract Your Own Pearl
OH!
IT SAYS WE CAN TRY EXTRACTING PEARLS!
WANT TO GIVE IT A GO?
¥1,000 Per Try

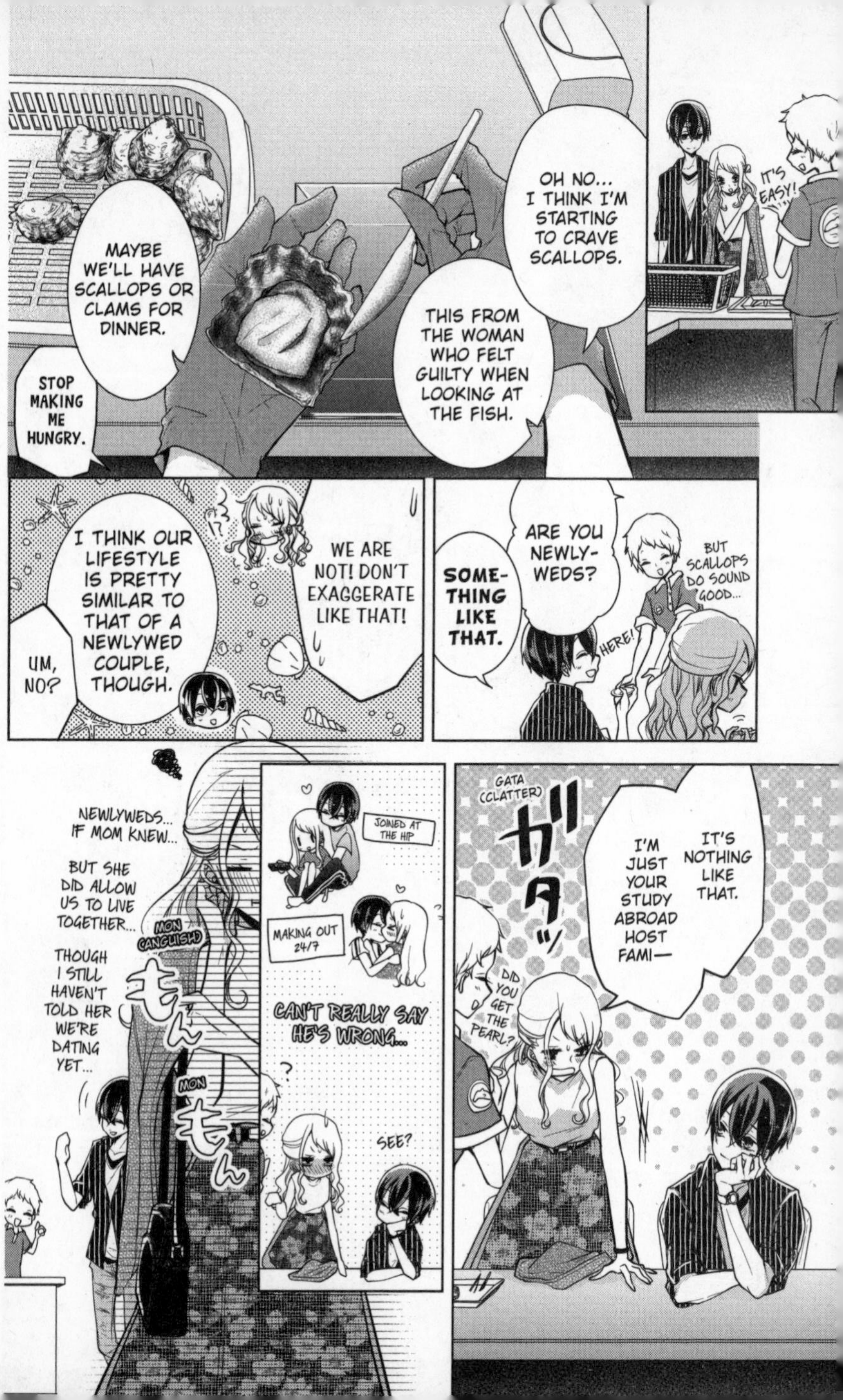
IT'S EASY!
OH NO... I THINK I'M STARTING TO CRAVE SCALLOPS.
THIS FROM THE WOMAN WHO FELT GUILTY WHEN LOOKING AT THE FISH.
MAYBE WE'LL HAVE SCALLOPS OR CLAMS FOR DINNER.
STOP MAKING ME HUNGRY.
BUT SCALLOPS DO SOUND GOOD...
ARE YOU NEWLY-WEDS?
HERE!
SOME-THING LIKE THAT.
WE ARE NOT! DON'T EXAGGERATE LIKE THAT!
I THINK OUR LIFESTYLE IS PRETTY SIMILAR TO THAT OF A NEWLYWED COUPLE, THOUGH.
UM, NO?
GATA (CLATTER)
IT'S NOTHING LIKE THAT.
I'M JUST YOUR STUDY ABROAD HOST FAMI—
DID YOU GET THE PEARL?
JOINED AT THE HIP
MAKING OUT 24/7
CAN'T REALLY SAY HE'S WRONG...
SEE?
NEWLYWEDS... IF MOM KNEW...
BUT SHE DID ALLOW US TO LIVE TOGETHER...
MON (ANGUISH)
THOUGH I STILL HAVEN'T TOLD HER WE'RE DATING YET...
MON

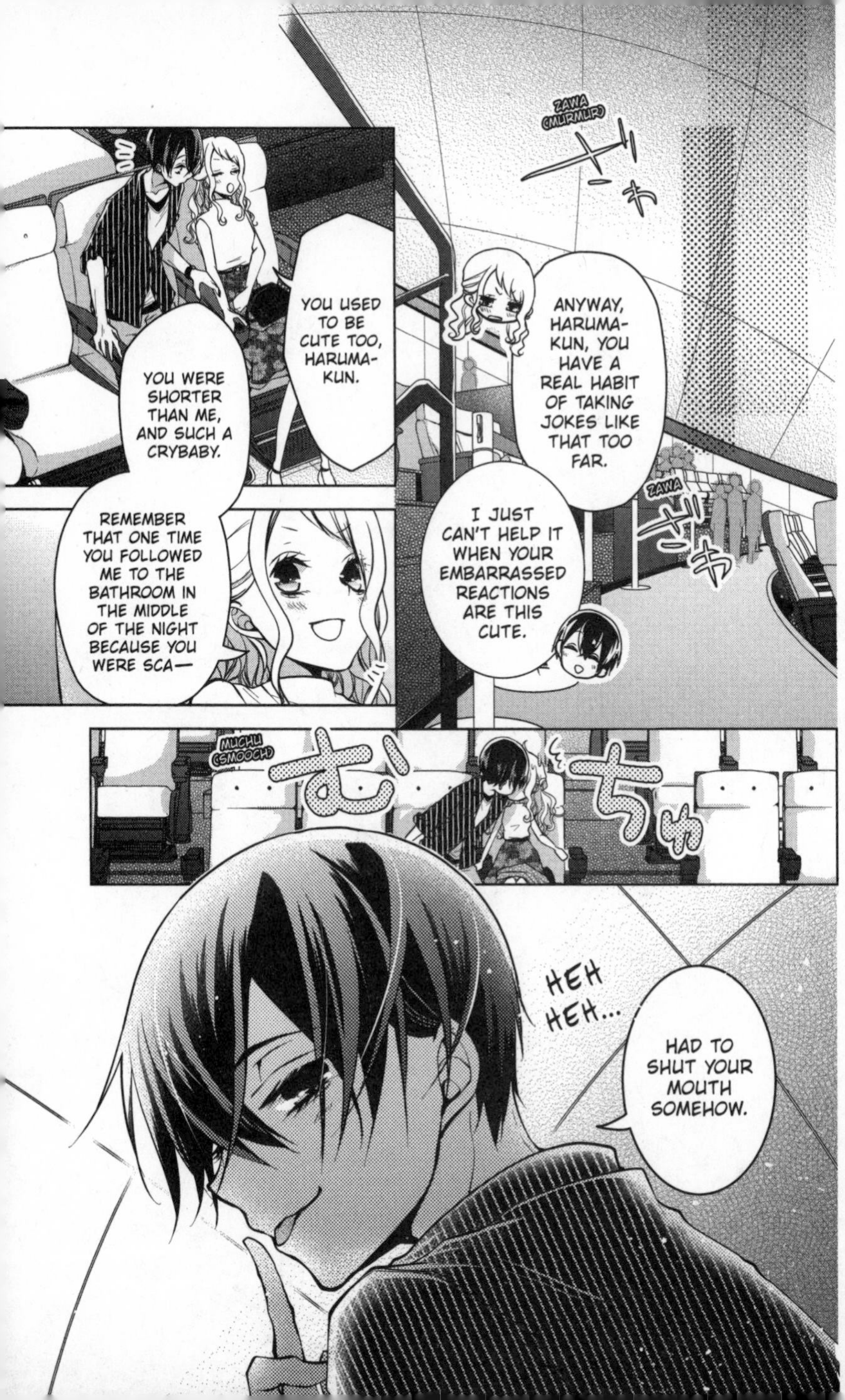
ZAWA (MURMUR)
ANYWAY, HARUMA-KUN, YOU HAVE A REAL HABIT OF TAKING JOKES LIKE THAT TOO FAR.
ZAWA
I JUST CAN'T HELP IT WHEN YOUR EMBARRASSED REACTIONS ARE THIS CUTE.
YOU USED TO BE CUTE TOO, HARUMA-KUN.
YOU WERE SHORTER THAN ME, AND SUCH A CRYBABY.
REMEMBER THAT ONE TIME YOU FOLLOWED ME TO THE BATHROOM IN THE MIDDLE OF THE NIGHT BECAUSE YOU WERE SCA—
MUCHU (SMOOCH)
HEH HEH...
HAD TO SHUT YOUR MOUTH SOMEHOW.

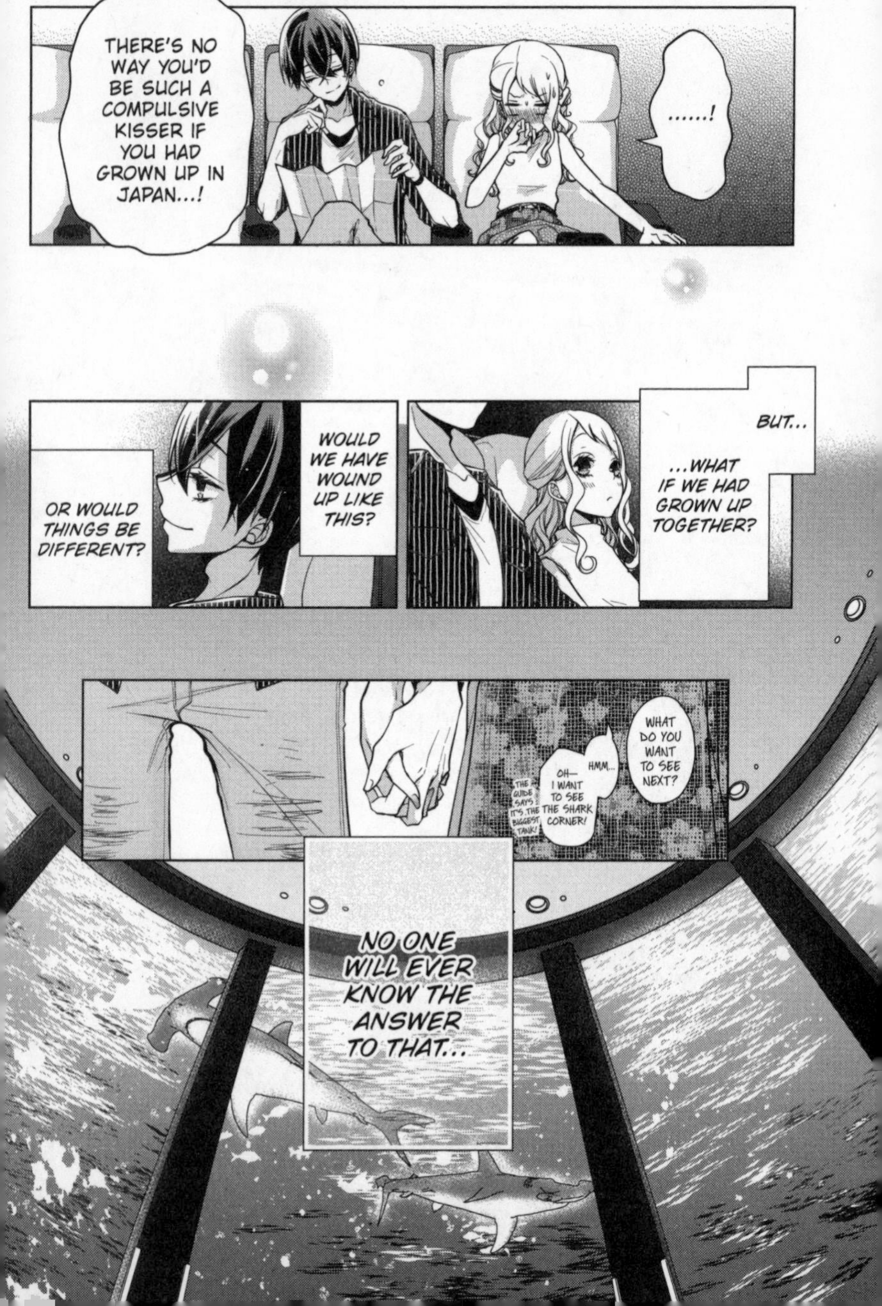
THERE'S NO WAY YOU'D BE SUCH A COMPULSIVE KISSER IF YOU HAD GROWN UP IN JAPAN...!
......!
BUT...
...WHAT IF WE HAD GROWN UP TOGETHER?
WOULD WE HAVE WOUND UP LIKE THIS?
OR WOULD THINGS BE DIFFERENT?
WHAT DO YOU WANT TO SEE NEXT?
HMM...
OH— I WANT TO SEE THE SHARK CORNER!
THE GUIDE SAYS IT'S THE BIGGEST TANK!
NO ONE WILL EVER KNOW THE ANSWER TO THAT...

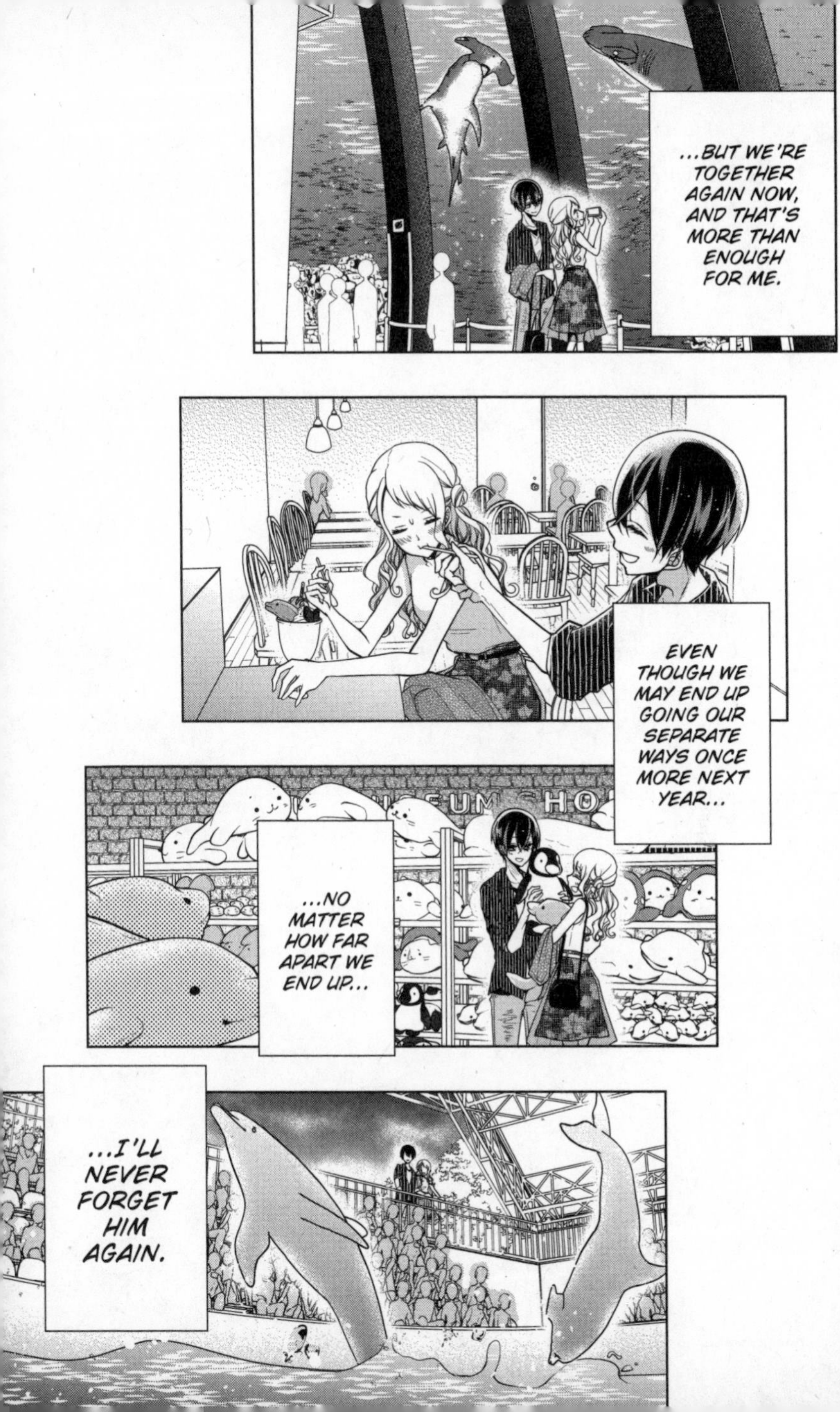
...BUT WE'RE TOGETHER AGAIN NOW, AND THAT'S MORE THAN ENOUGH FOR ME.
EVEN THOUGH WE MAY END UP GOING OUR SEPARATE WAYS ONCE MORE NEXT YEAR...
...NO MATTER HOW FAR APART WE END UP...
...I'LL NEVER FORGET HIM AGAIN.

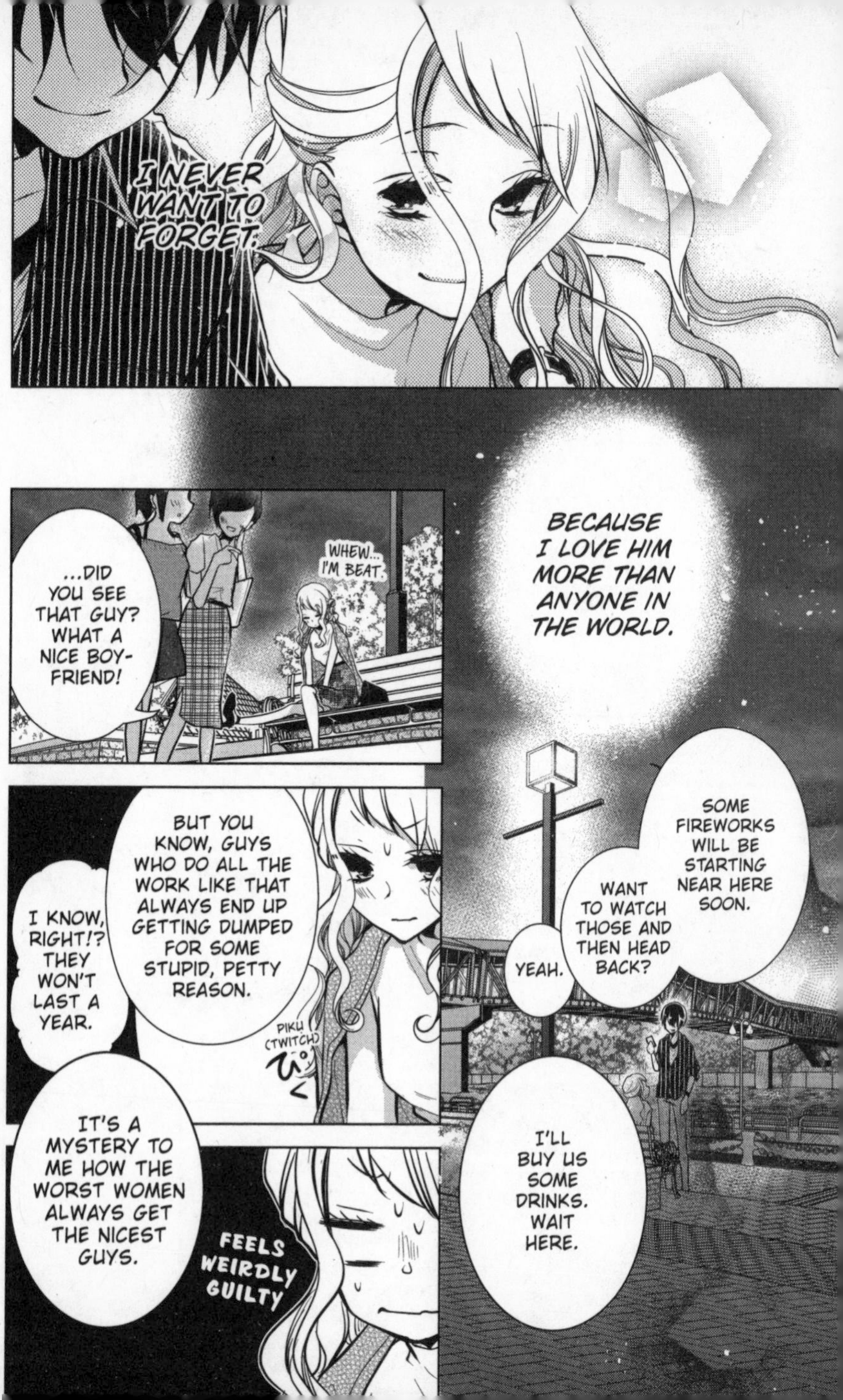
I NEVER WANT TO FORGET.
BECAUSE I LOVE HIM MORE THAN ANYONE IN THE WORLD.
SOME FIREWORKS WILL BE STARTING NEAR HERE SOON.
WANT TO WATCH THOSE AND THEN HEAD BACK?
YEAH.
I'LL BUY US SOME DRINKS. WAIT HERE.
WHEW... I'M BEAT.
...DID YOU SEE THAT GUY? WHAT A NICE BOY-FRIEND!
BUT YOU KNOW, GUYS WHO DO ALL THE WORK LIKE THAT ALWAYS END UP GETTING DUMPED FOR SOME STUPID, PETTY REASON.
I KNOW, RIGHT!? THEY WON'T LAST A YEAR.
PIKU (TWITCH)
IT'S A MYSTERY TO ME HOW THE WORST WOMEN ALWAYS GET THE NICEST GUYS.
FEELS WEIRDLY GUILTY

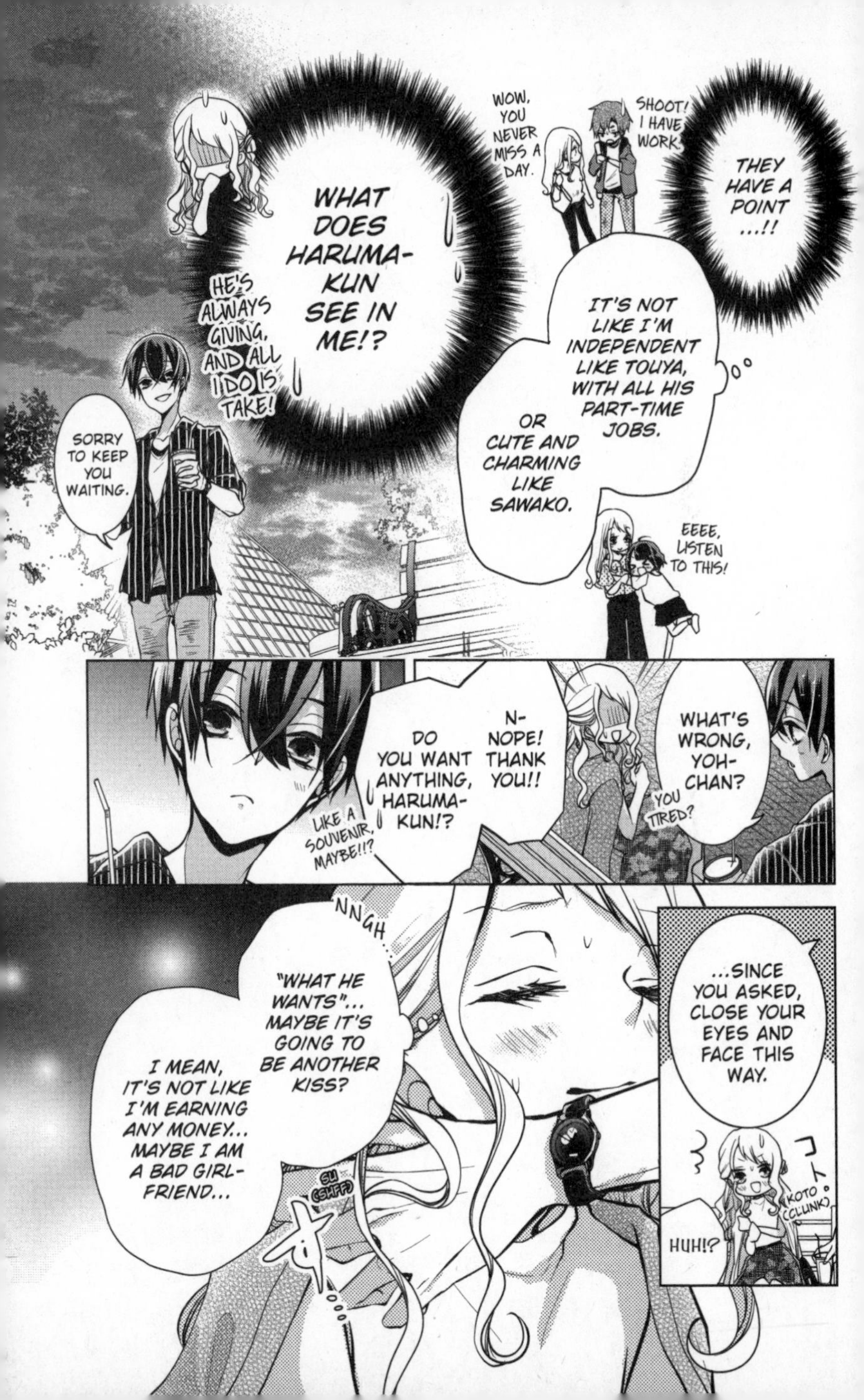
THEY HAVE A POINT ...!!
SHOOT! I HAVE WORK.
WOW, YOU NEVER MISS A DAY.
IT'S NOT LIKE I'M INDEPENDENT LIKE TOUYA, WITH ALL HIS PART-TIME JOBS.
OR CUTE AND CHARMING LIKE SAWAKO.
EEEE, LISTEN TO THIS!
WHAT DOES HARUMA-KUN SEE IN ME!?
HE'S ALWAYS GIVING, AND ALL I DO IS TAKE!
SORRY TO KEEP YOU WAITING.
WHAT'S WRONG, YOH-CHAN?
YOU TIRED?
N-NOPE! THANK YOU!!
DO YOU WANT ANYTHING, HARUMA-KUN!?
LIKE A SOUVENIR, MAYBE!!?
...SINCE YOU ASKED, CLOSE YOUR EYES AND FACE THIS WAY.
KOTO (CLUNK)
HUH!?
NNGH...
"WHAT HE WANTS"... MAYBE IT'S GOING TO BE ANOTHER KISS?
I MEAN, IT'S NOT LIKE I'M EARNING ANY MONEY... MAYBE I AM A BAD GIRL-FRIEND...
SU (SHFF)

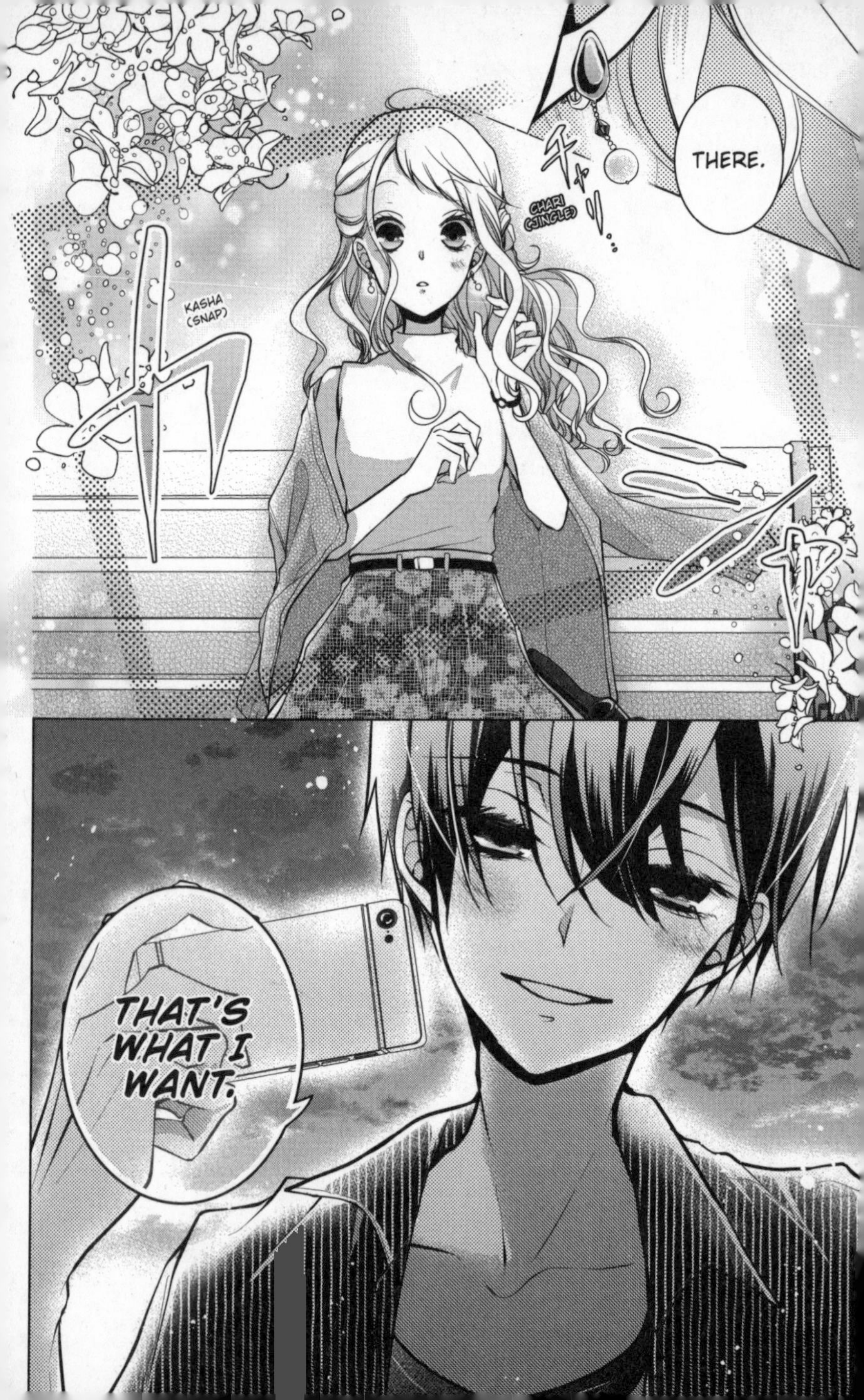
THERE.
チャリ…
CHARI (JINGLE)
KASHA (SNAP)
THAT'S WHAT I WANT.

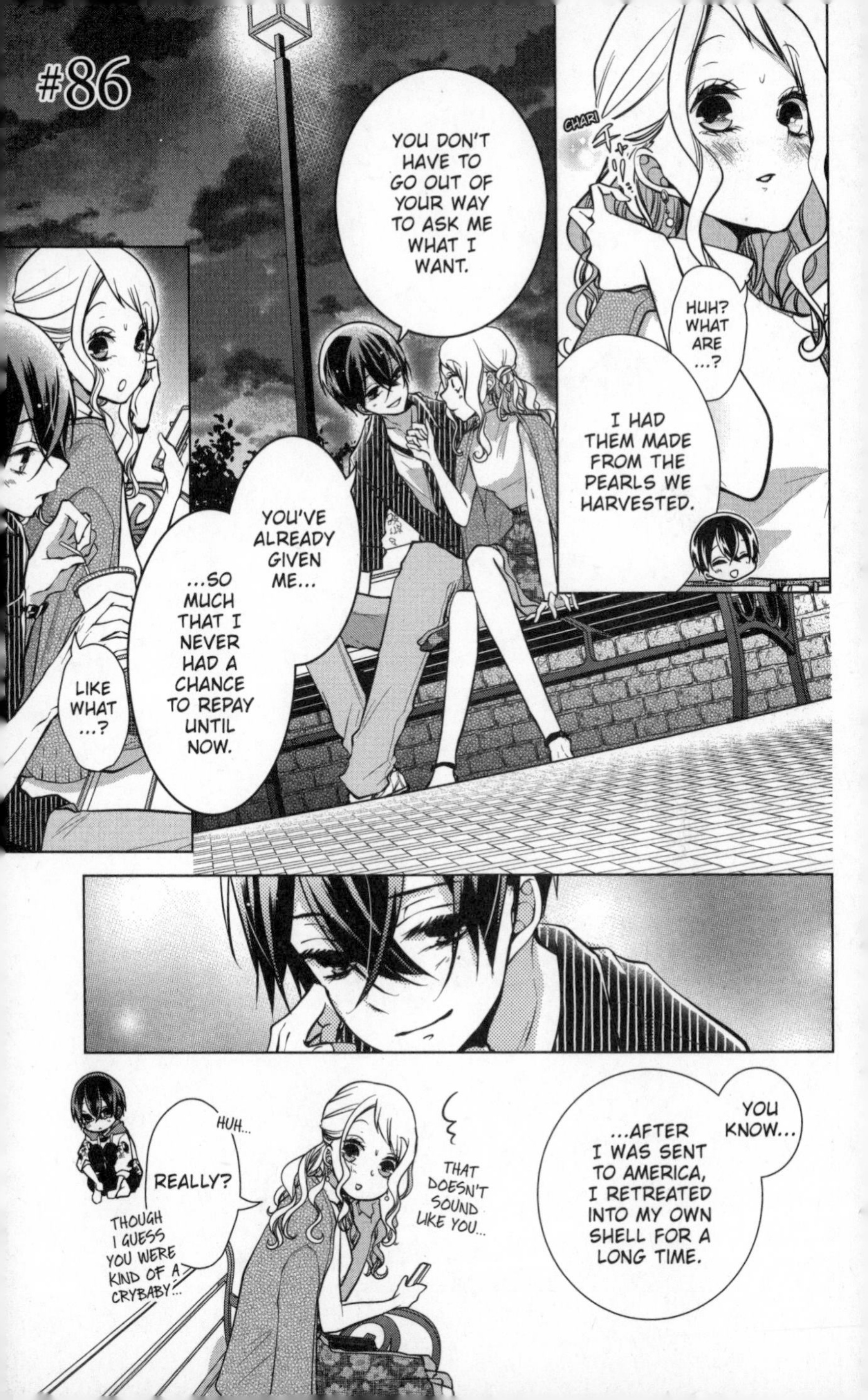
#86
CHARI
HUH? WHAT ARE ...?
I HAD THEM MADE FROM THE PEARLS WE HARVESTED.
YOU DON'T HAVE TO GO OUT OF YOUR WAY TO ASK ME WHAT I WANT.
YOU'VE ALREADY GIVEN ME...
...SO MUCH THAT I NEVER HAD A CHANCE TO REPAY UNTIL NOW.
LIKE WHAT ...?
YOU KNOW...
...AFTER I WAS SENT TO AMERICA, I RETREATED INTO MY OWN SHELL FOR A LONG TIME.
THAT DOESN'T SOUND LIKE YOU...
HUH...
REALLY?
THOUGH I GUESS YOU WERE KIND OF A CRYBABY...

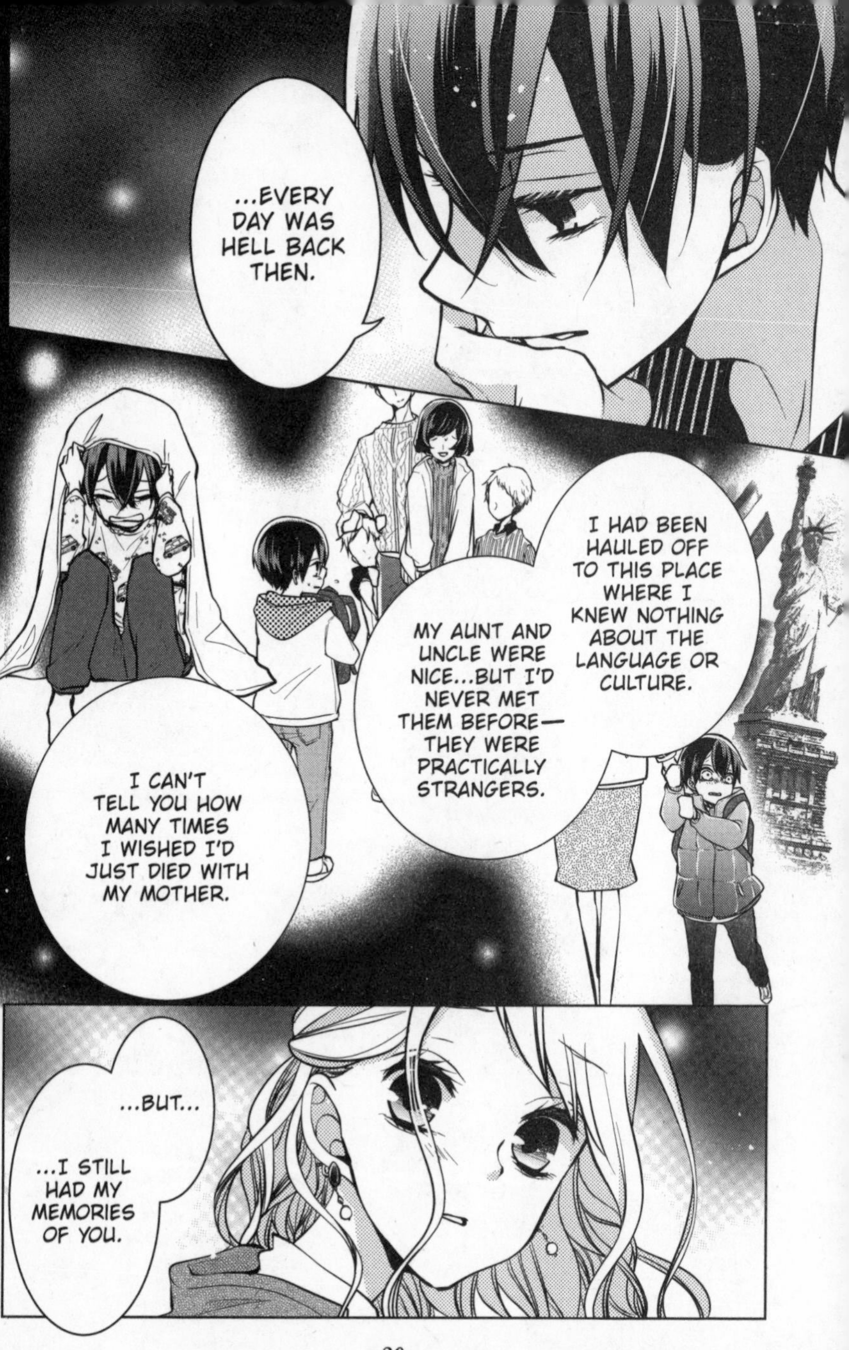
...EVERY DAY WAS HELL BACK THEN.
I HAD BEEN HAULED OFF TO THIS PLACE WHERE I KNEW NOTHING ABOUT THE LANGUAGE OR CULTURE.
MY AUNT AND UNCLE WERE NICE...BUT I'D NEVER MET THEM BEFORE—THEY WERE PRACTICALLY STRANGERS.
I CAN'T TELL YOU HOW MANY TIMES I WISHED I'D JUST DIED WITH MY MOTHER.
...BUT...
...I STILL HAD MY MEMORIES OF YOU.

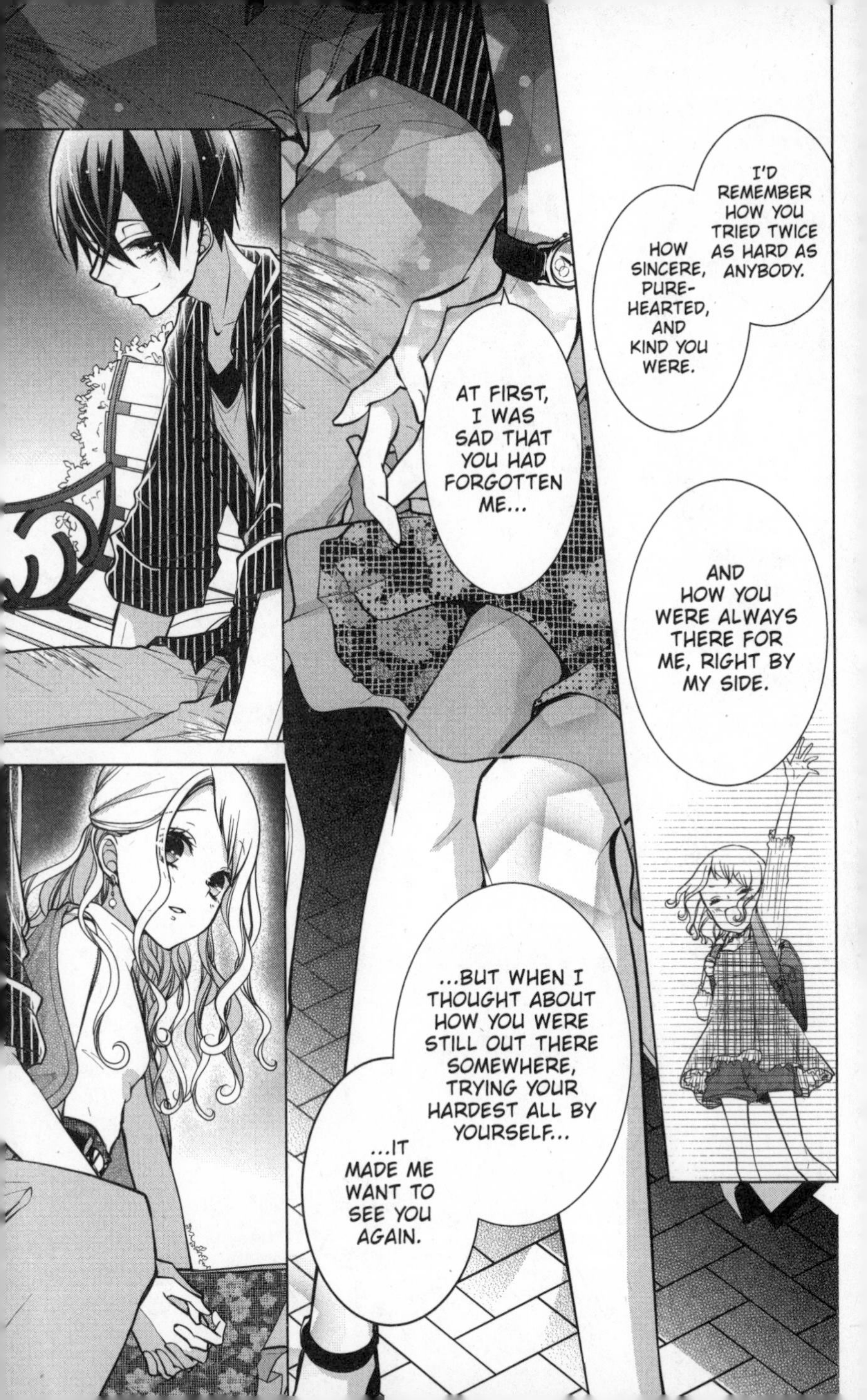
I'D REMEMBER HOW YOU TRIED TWICE AS HARD AS ANYBODY.
HOW SINCERE, PURE-HEARTED, AND KIND YOU WERE.
AND HOW YOU WERE ALWAYS THERE FOR ME, RIGHT BY MY SIDE.
AT FIRST, I WAS SAD THAT YOU HAD FORGOTTEN ME...
...BUT WHEN I THOUGHT ABOUT HOW YOU WERE STILL OUT THERE SOMEWHERE, TRYING YOUR HARDEST ALL BY YOURSELF...
...IT MADE ME WANT TO SEE YOU AGAIN.

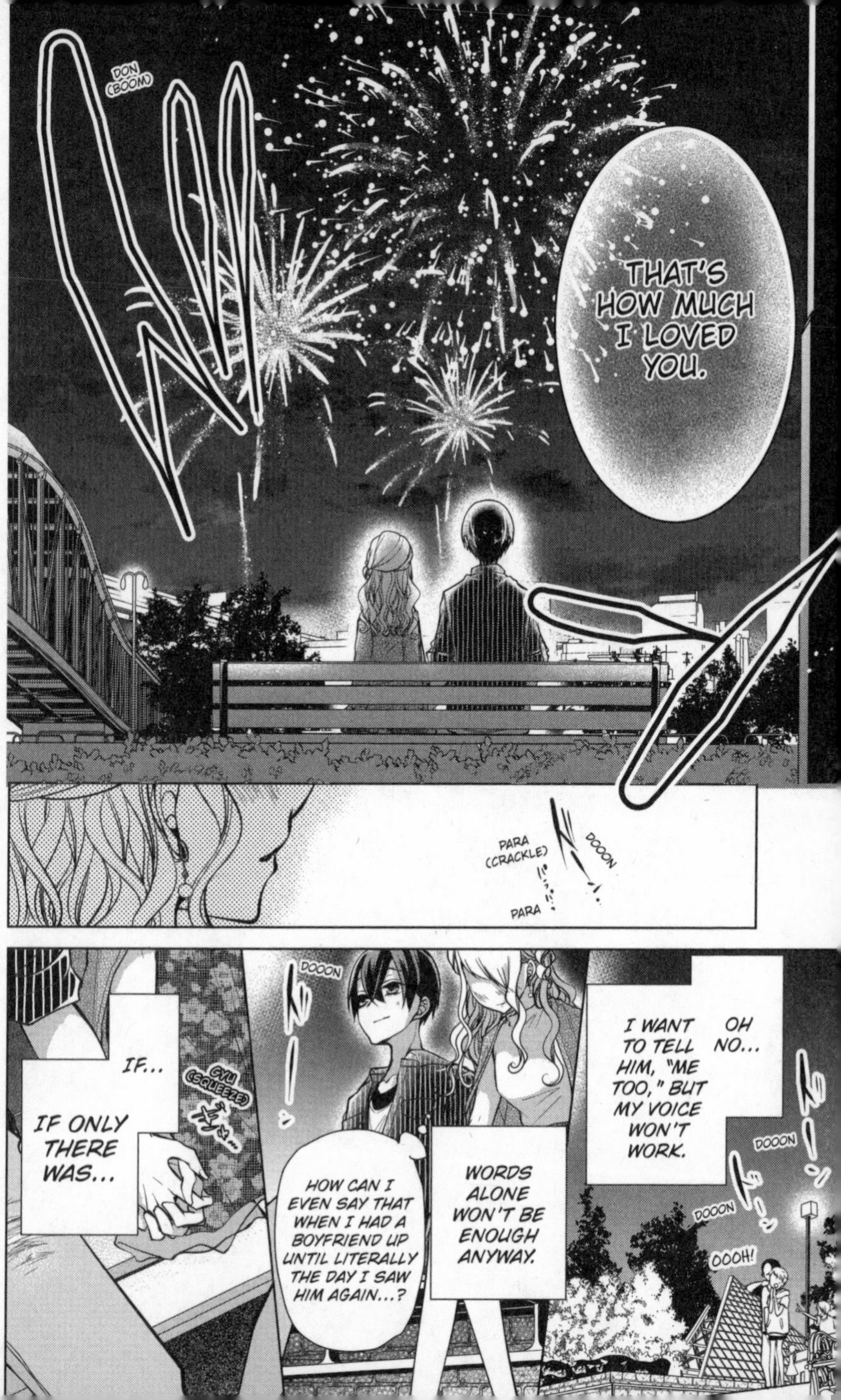
THAT'S HOW MUCH I LOVED YOU.
DON (BOOM)
DOOON
PARA (CRACKLE)
PARA
OH NO...
I WANT TO TELL HIM, "ME TOO," BUT MY VOICE WON'T WORK.
DOOON
DOOON
OOOH!
WORDS ALONE WON'T BE ENOUGH ANYWAY.
HOW CAN I EVEN SAY THAT WHEN I HAD A BOYFRIEND UP UNTIL LITERALLY THE DAY I SAW HIM AGAIN...?
DOOON
GYU (SQUEEZE)
IF...
IF ONLY THERE WAS...

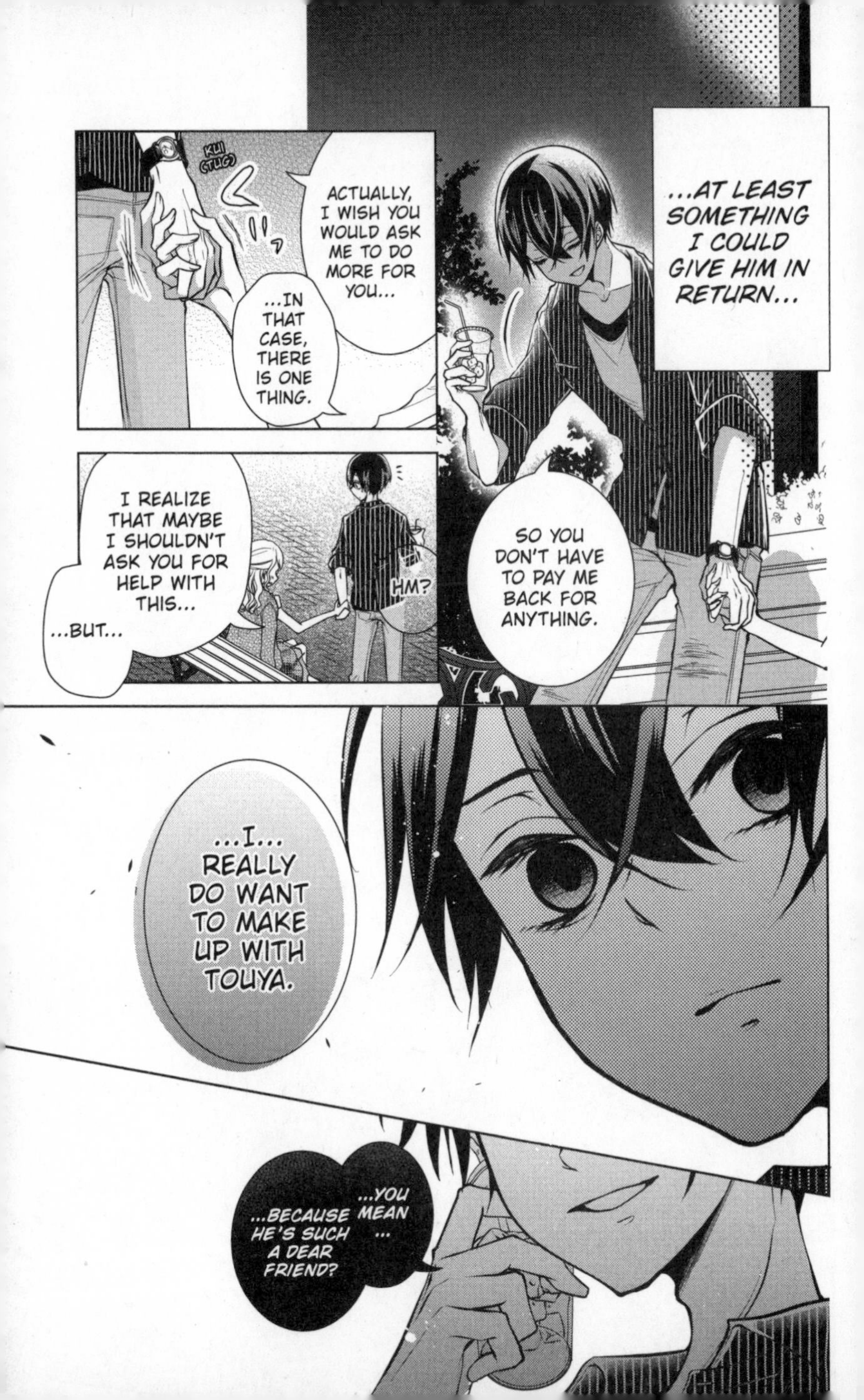
...AT LEAST SOMETHING I COULD GIVE HIM IN RETURN...
SO YOU DON'T HAVE TO PAY ME BACK FOR ANYTHING.
ACTUALLY, I WISH YOU WOULD ASK ME TO DO MORE FOR YOU...
KUI (TUG)
...IN THAT CASE, THERE IS ONE THING.
HM?
I REALIZE THAT MAYBE I SHOULDN'T ASK YOU FOR HELP WITH THIS...
...BUT...
...I... REALLY DO WANT TO MAKE UP WITH TOUYA.
...YOU MEAN ...
...BECAUSE HE'S SUCH A DEAR FRIEND?

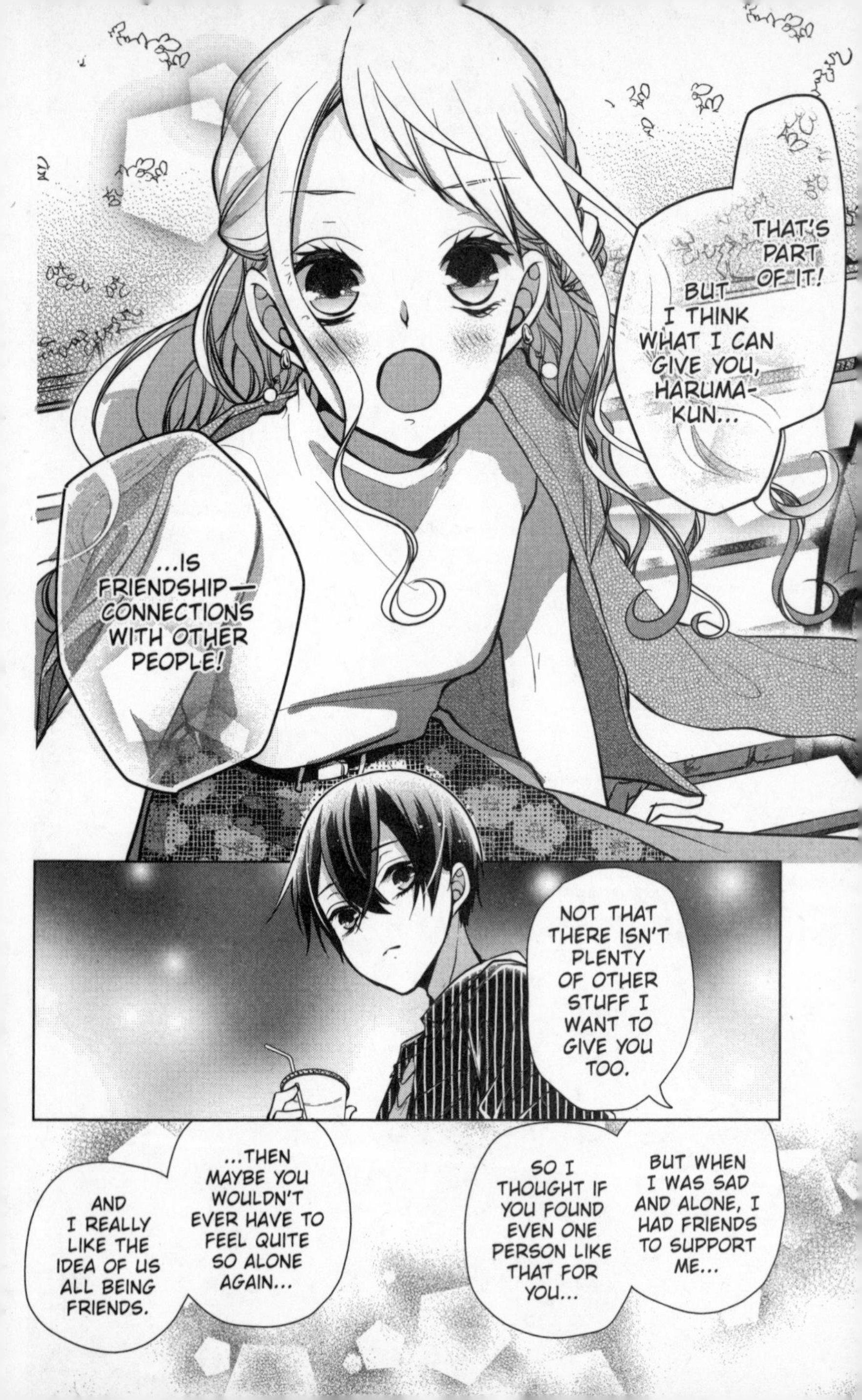
THAT'S PART OF IT!
BUT I THINK WHAT I CAN GIVE YOU, HARUMA-KUN...
...IS FRIENDSHIP—CONNECTIONS WITH OTHER PEOPLE!
NOT THAT THERE ISN'T PLENTY OF OTHER STUFF I WANT TO GIVE YOU TOO.
BUT WHEN I WAS SAD AND ALONE, I HAD FRIENDS TO SUPPORT ME...
SO I THOUGHT IF YOU FOUND EVEN ONE PERSON LIKE THAT FOR YOU...
...THEN MAYBE YOU WOULDN'T EVER HAVE TO FEEL QUITE SO ALONE AGAIN...
AND I REALLY LIKE THE IDEA OF US ALL BEING FRIENDS.

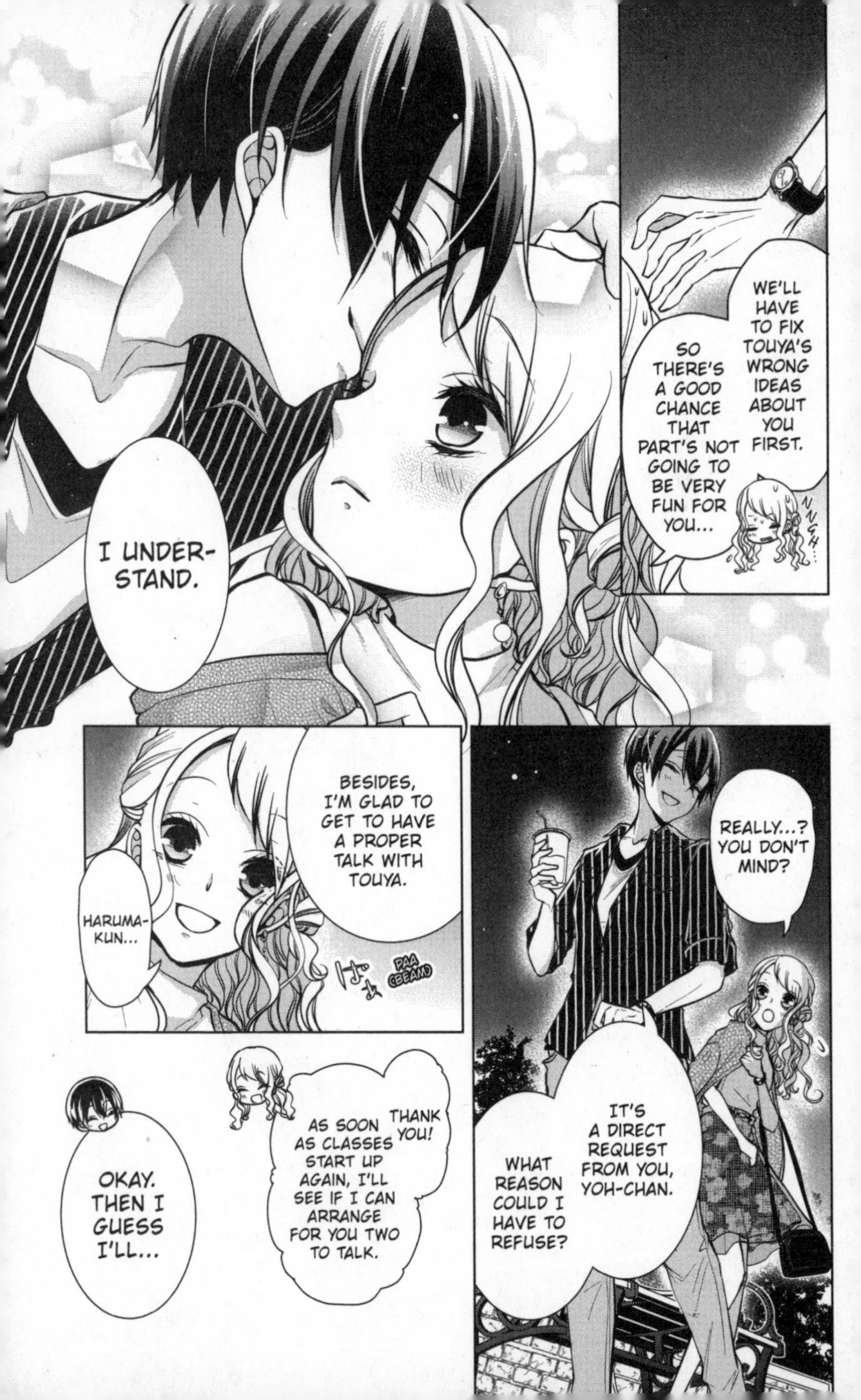

WE'LL HAVE TO FIX TOUYA'S WRONG IDEAS ABOUT YOU FIRST.
SO THERE'S A GOOD CHANCE THAT PART'S NOT GOING TO BE VERY FUN FOR YOU...
NNGH...
I UNDER-STAND.
REALLY...? YOU DON'T MIND?
IT'S A DIRECT REQUEST FROM YOU, YOH-CHAN.
WHAT REASON COULD I HAVE TO REFUSE?
BESIDES, I'M GLAD TO GET TO HAVE A PROPER TALK WITH TOUYA.
HARUMA-KUN...
PAA (BEAM)
THANK YOU!
AS SOON AS CLASSES START UP AGAIN, I'LL SEE IF I CAN ARRANGE FOR YOU TWO TO TALK.
OKAY. THEN I GUESS I'LL...

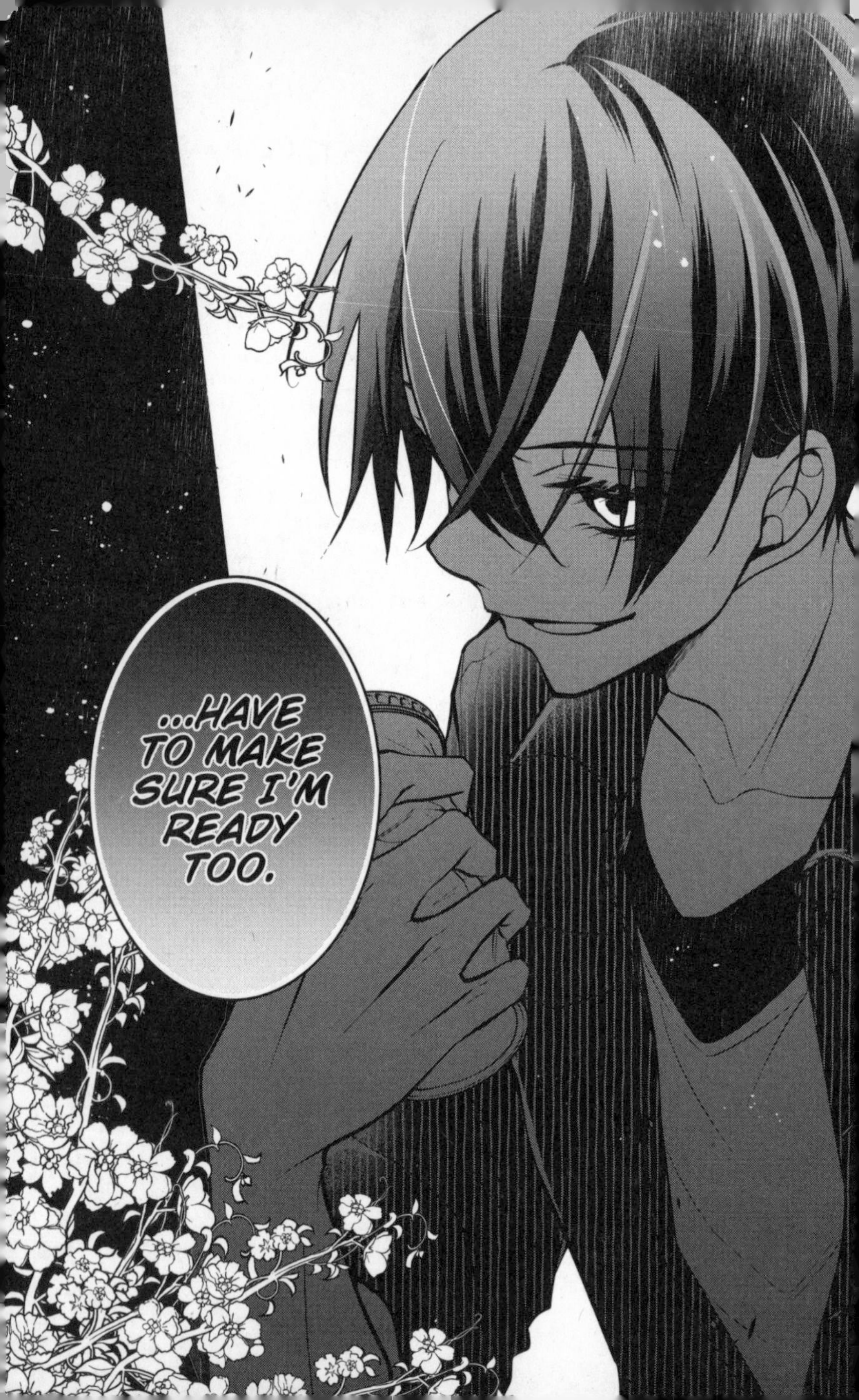
...HAVE TO MAKE SURE I'M READY TOO.

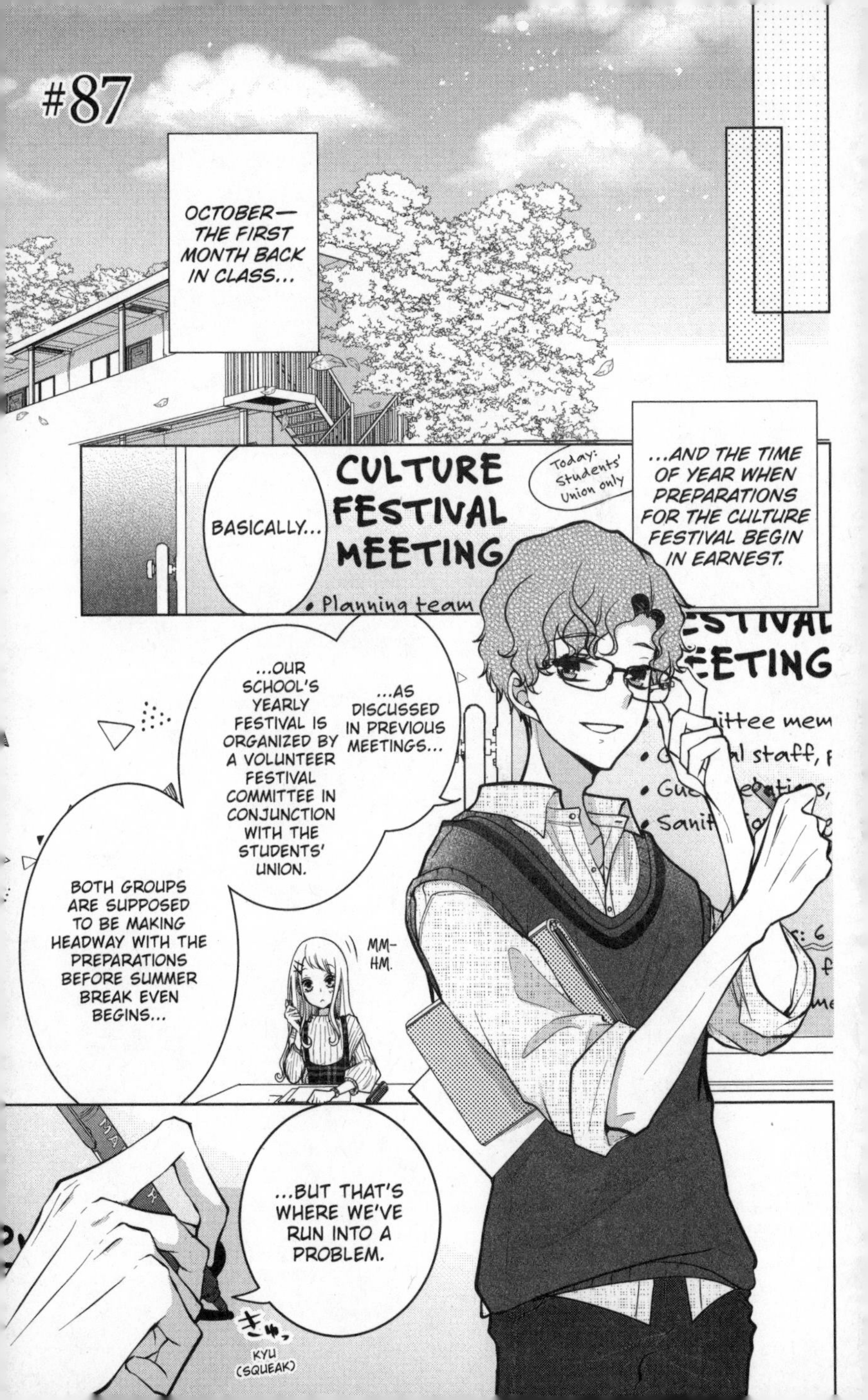
#87
OCTOBER—THE FIRST MONTH BACK IN CLASS...
...AND THE TIME OF YEAR WHEN PREPARATIONS FOR THE CULTURE FESTIVAL BEGIN IN EARNEST.
Today: Students' Union only
CULTURE FESTIVAL MEETING
• Planning team
BASICALLY...
...AS DISCUSSED IN PREVIOUS MEETINGS...
...OUR SCHOOL'S YEARLY FESTIVAL IS ORGANIZED BY A VOLUNTEER FESTIVAL COMMITTEE IN CONJUNCTION WITH THE STUDENTS' UNION.
BOTH GROUPS ARE SUPPOSED TO BE MAKING HEADWAY WITH THE PREPARATIONS BEFORE SUMMER BREAK EVEN BEGINS...
MM-HM.
...BUT THAT'S WHERE WE'VE RUN INTO A PROBLEM.
KYU (SQUEAK)

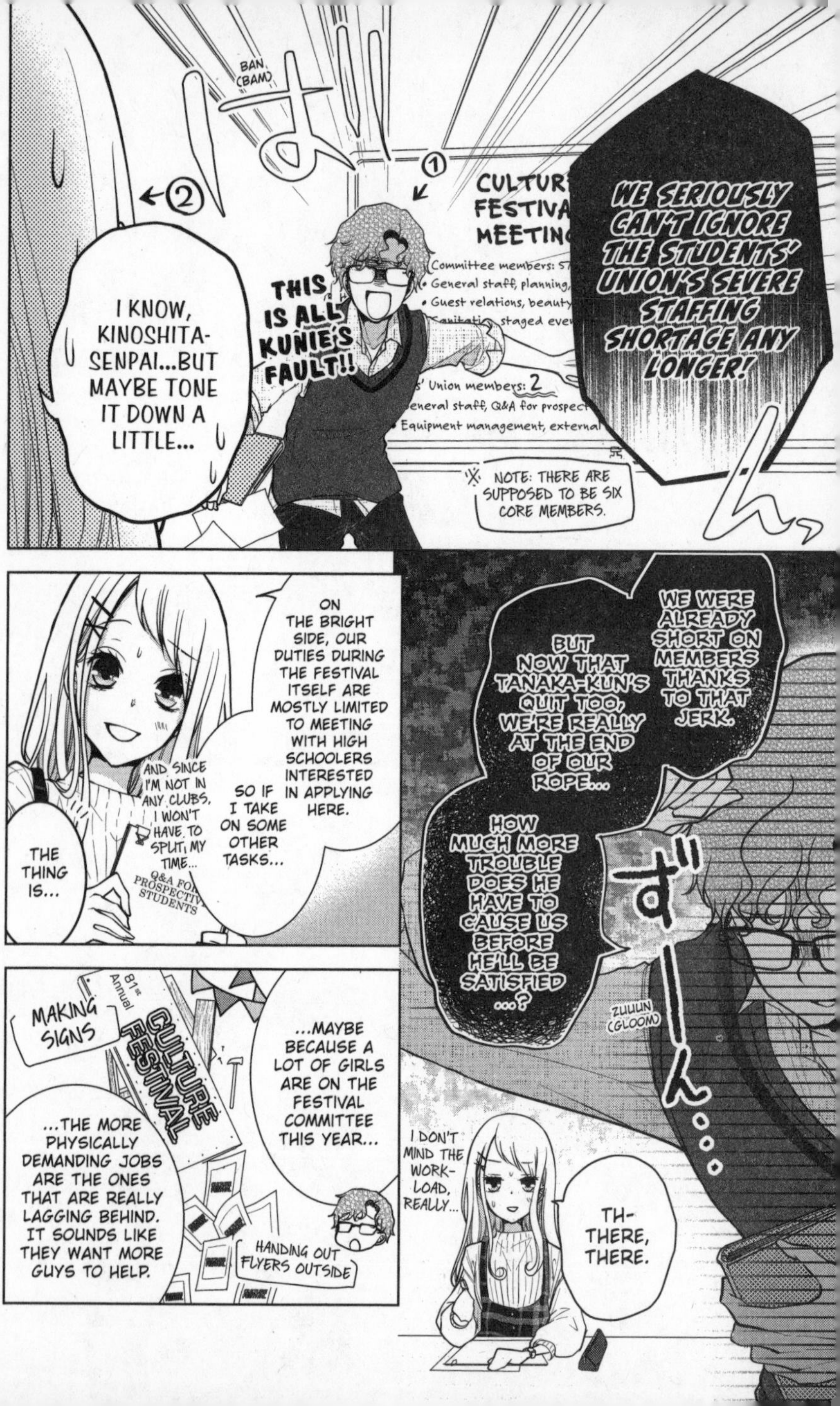
WE SERIOUSLY CAN'T IGNORE THE STUDENTS' UNION'S SEVERE STAFFING SHORTAGE ANY LONGER!
①
CULTUR FESTIVA MEETIN
Committee members: 57
• General staff, planning,
• Guest relations, beauty
staged even
s' Union members: 2
eneral staff, Q&A for prospect
• Equipment management, external
※ NOTE: THERE ARE SUPPOSED TO BE SIX CORE MEMBERS.
THIS IS ALL KUNIE'S FAULT!!
BAN (BAM)
②
I KNOW, KINOSHITA-SENPAI...BUT MAYBE TONE IT DOWN A LITTLE...
WE WERE ALREADY SHORT ON MEMBERS THANKS TO THAT JERK.
BUT NOW THAT TANAKA-KUN'S QUIT TOO, WE'RE REALLY AT THE END OF OUR ROPE...
HOW MUCH MORE TROUBLE DOES HE HAVE TO CAUSE US BEFORE HE'LL BE SATISFIED...?
ZUUUN (GLOOM)
TH-THERE, THERE.
I DON'T MIND THE WORK-LOAD, REALLY...
ON THE BRIGHT SIDE, OUR DUTIES DURING THE FESTIVAL ITSELF ARE MOSTLY LIMITED TO MEETING WITH HIGH SCHOOLERS INTERESTED IN APPLYING HERE.
SO IF I TAKE ON SOME OTHER TASKS...
AND SINCE I'M NOT IN ANY CLUBS, I WON'T HAVE TO SPLIT MY TIME...
Q&A FOR PROSPECTIVE STUDENTS
THE THING IS...
...MAYBE BECAUSE A LOT OF GIRLS ARE ON THE FESTIVAL COMMITTEE THIS YEAR...
81st Annual CULTURE FESTIVAL
MAKING SIGNS
...THE MORE PHYSICALLY DEMANDING JOBS ARE THE ONES THAT ARE REALLY LAGGING BEHIND. IT SOUNDS LIKE THEY WANT MORE GUYS TO HELP.
HANDING OUT FLYERS OUTSIDE

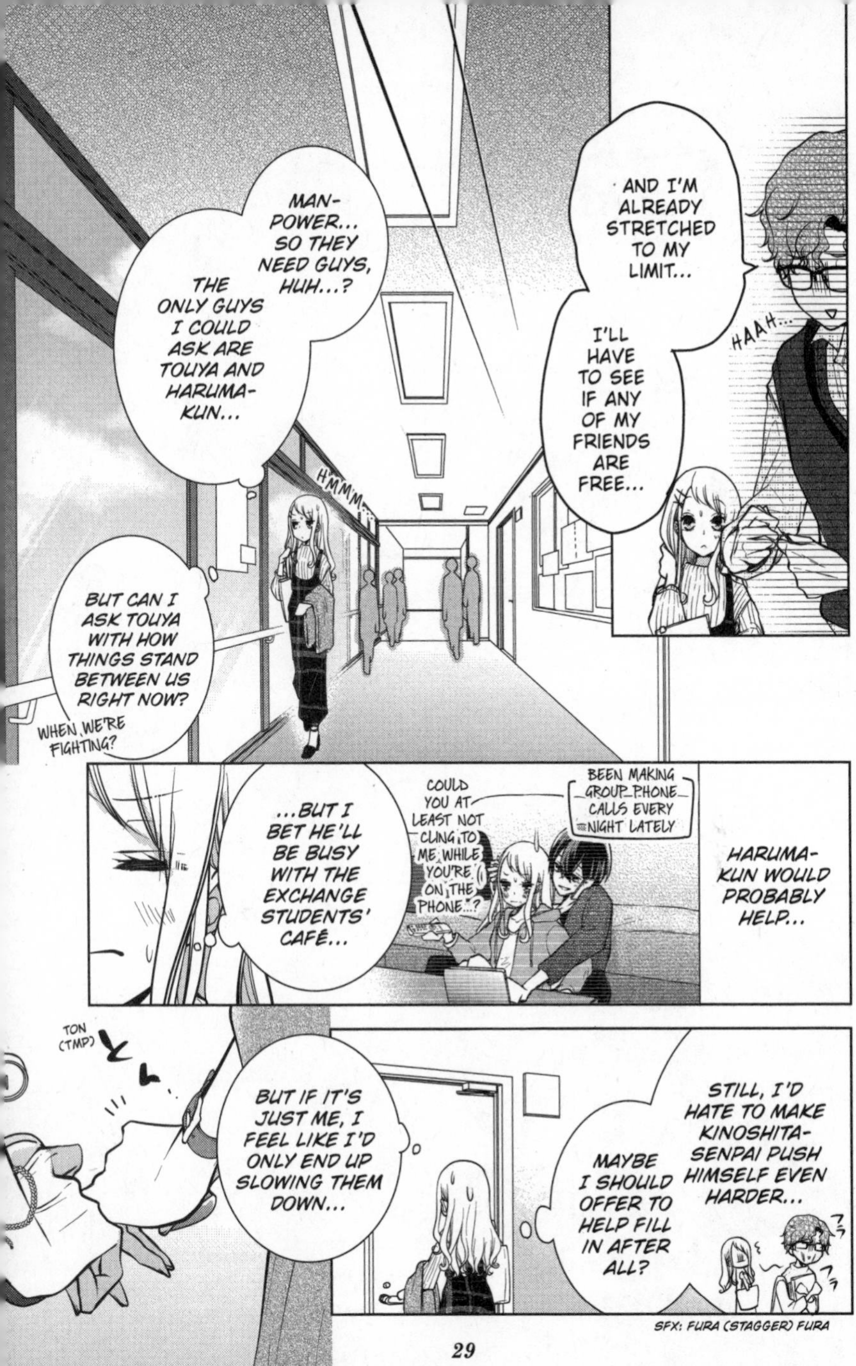
AND I'M ALREADY STRETCHED TO MY LIMIT...
I'LL HAVE TO SEE IF ANY OF MY FRIENDS ARE FREE...
HAAH...
MAN-POWER... SO THEY NEED GUYS, HUH...?
THE ONLY GUYS I COULD ASK ARE TOUYA AND HARUMA-KUN...
HMMM...
BUT CAN I ASK TOUYA WITH HOW THINGS STAND BETWEEN US RIGHT NOW?
WHEN WE'RE FIGHTING?
HARUMA-KUN WOULD PROBABLY HELP...
BEEN MAKING GROUP PHONE CALLS EVERY NIGHT LATELY
COULD YOU AT LEAST NOT CLING TO ME WHILE YOU'RE ON THE PHONE...?
...BUT I BET HE'LL BE BUSY WITH THE EXCHANGE STUDENTS' CAFÉ...
STILL, I'D HATE TO MAKE KINOSHITA-SENPAI PUSH HIMSELF EVEN HARDER...
MAYBE I SHOULD OFFER TO HELP FILL IN AFTER ALL?
BUT IF IT'S JUST ME, I FEEL LIKE I'D ONLY END UP SLOWING THEM DOWN...
TON (TMP)
SFX: FURA (STAGGER) FURA

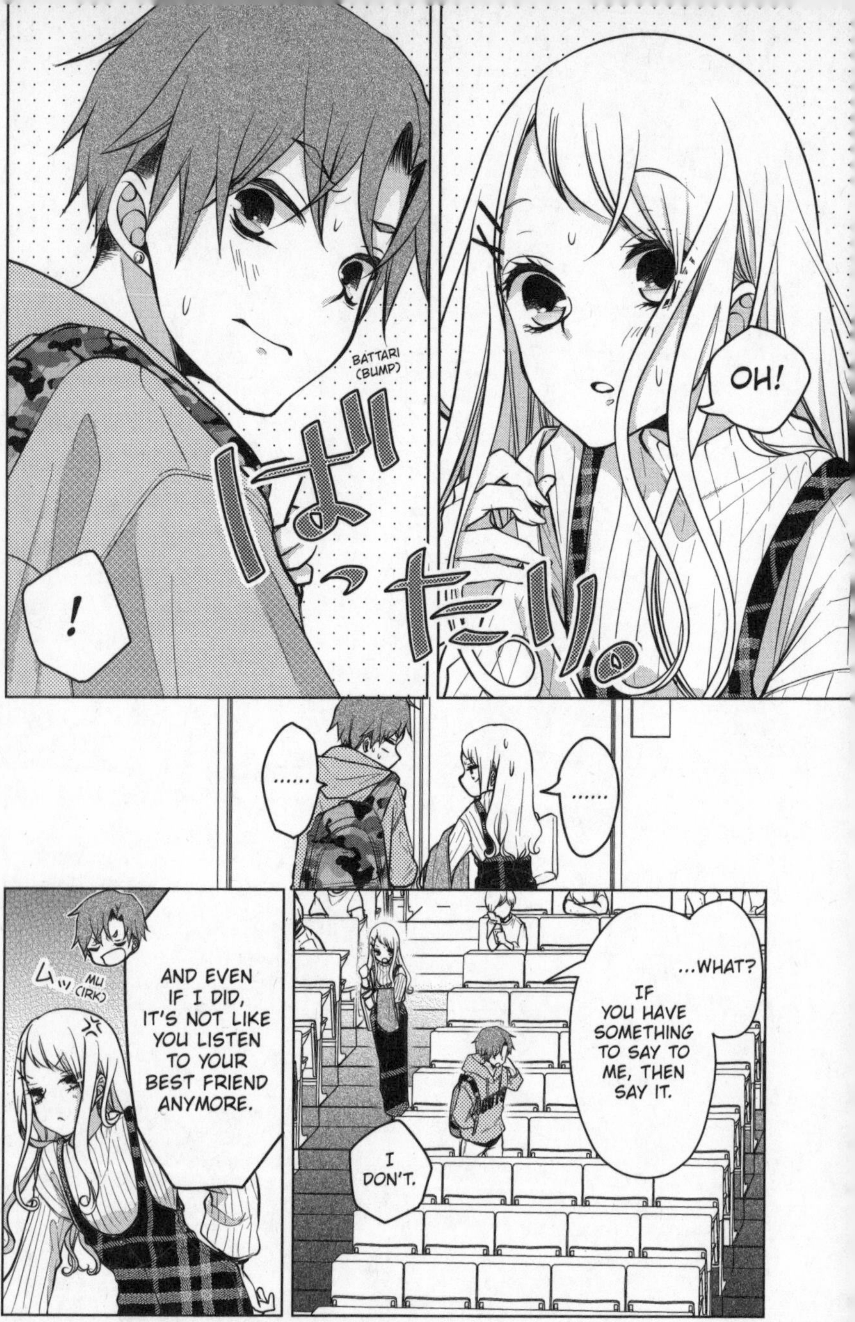
OH!
ばったり
BATTARI (BUMP)
!
......
......
...WHAT?
IF YOU HAVE SOMETHING TO SAY TO ME, THEN SAY IT.
I DON'T.
ムッ
MU (IRK)
AND EVEN IF I DID, IT'S NOT LIKE YOU LISTEN TO YOUR BEST FRIEND ANYMORE.

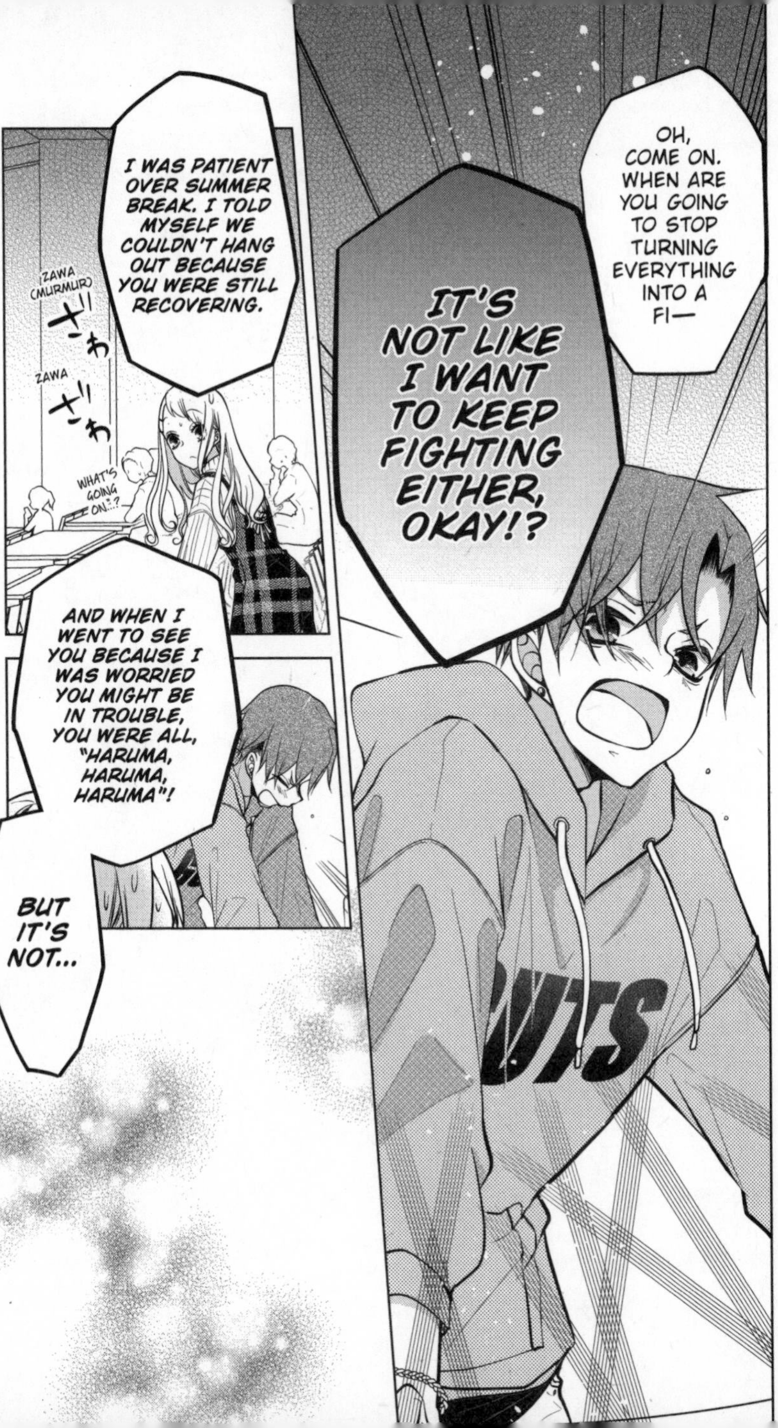
OH, COME ON. WHEN ARE YOU GOING TO STOP TURNING EVERYTHING INTO A FI—
IT'S NOT LIKE I WANT TO KEEP FIGHTING EITHER, OKAY!?
I WAS PATIENT OVER SUMMER BREAK. I TOLD MYSELF WE COULDN'T HANG OUT BECAUSE YOU WERE STILL RECOVERING.
ZAWA (MURMUR)
ZAWA
WHAT'S GOING ON...?
AND WHEN I WENT TO SEE YOU BECAUSE I WAS WORRIED YOU MIGHT BE IN TROUBLE, YOU WERE ALL, "HARUMA, HARUMA, HARUMA"!
BUT IT'S NOT...

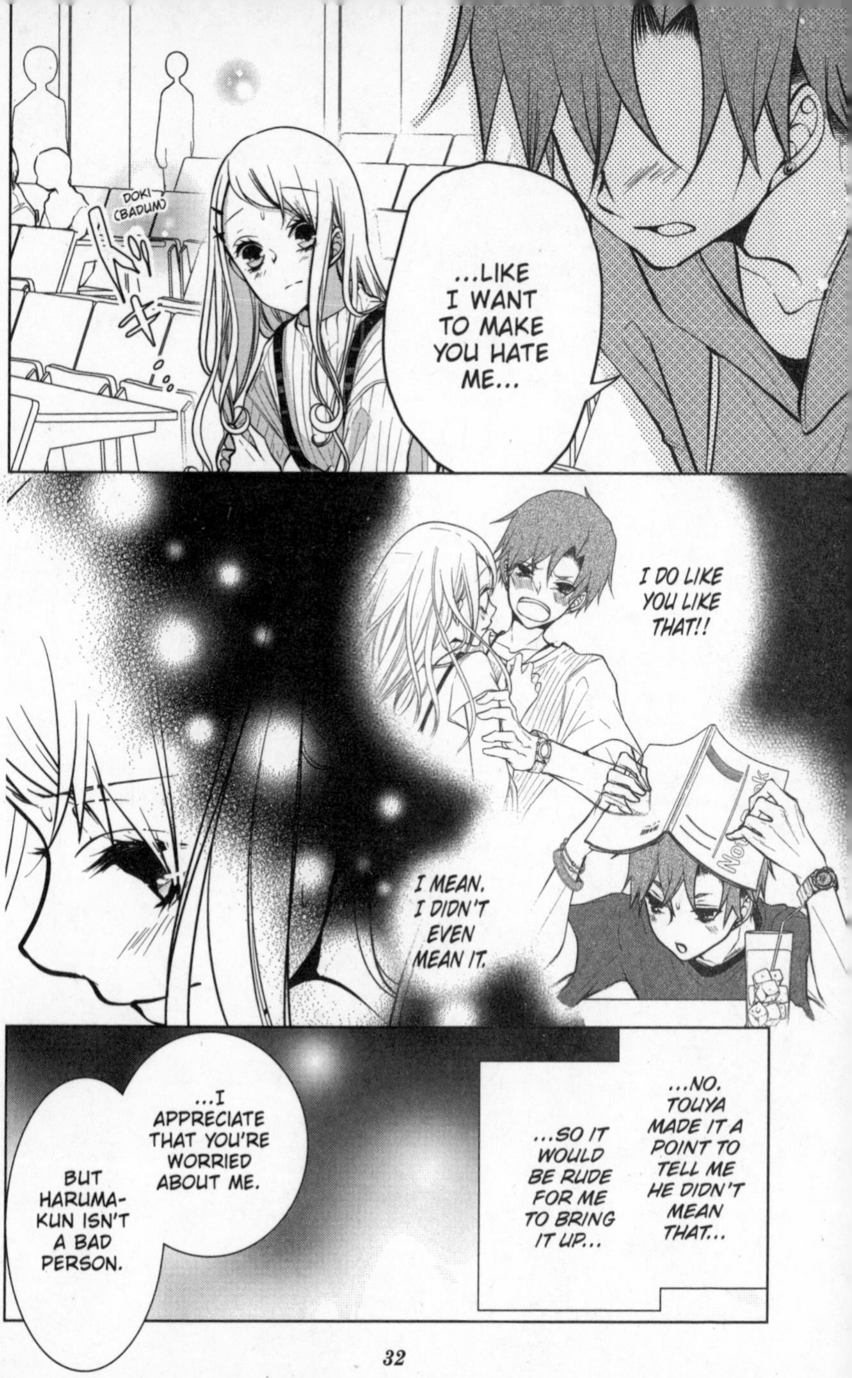

...LIKE I WANT TO MAKE YOU HATE ME...
DOKI (BADUM)
I DO LIKE YOU LIKE THAT!!
I MEAN. I DIDN'T EVEN MEAN IT.
...NO. TOUYA MADE IT A POINT TO TELL ME HE DIDN'T MEAN THAT...
...SO IT WOULD BE RUDE FOR ME TO BRING IT UP...
...I APPRECIATE THAT YOU'RE WORRIED ABOUT ME.
BUT HARUMA-KUN ISN'T A BAD PERSON.

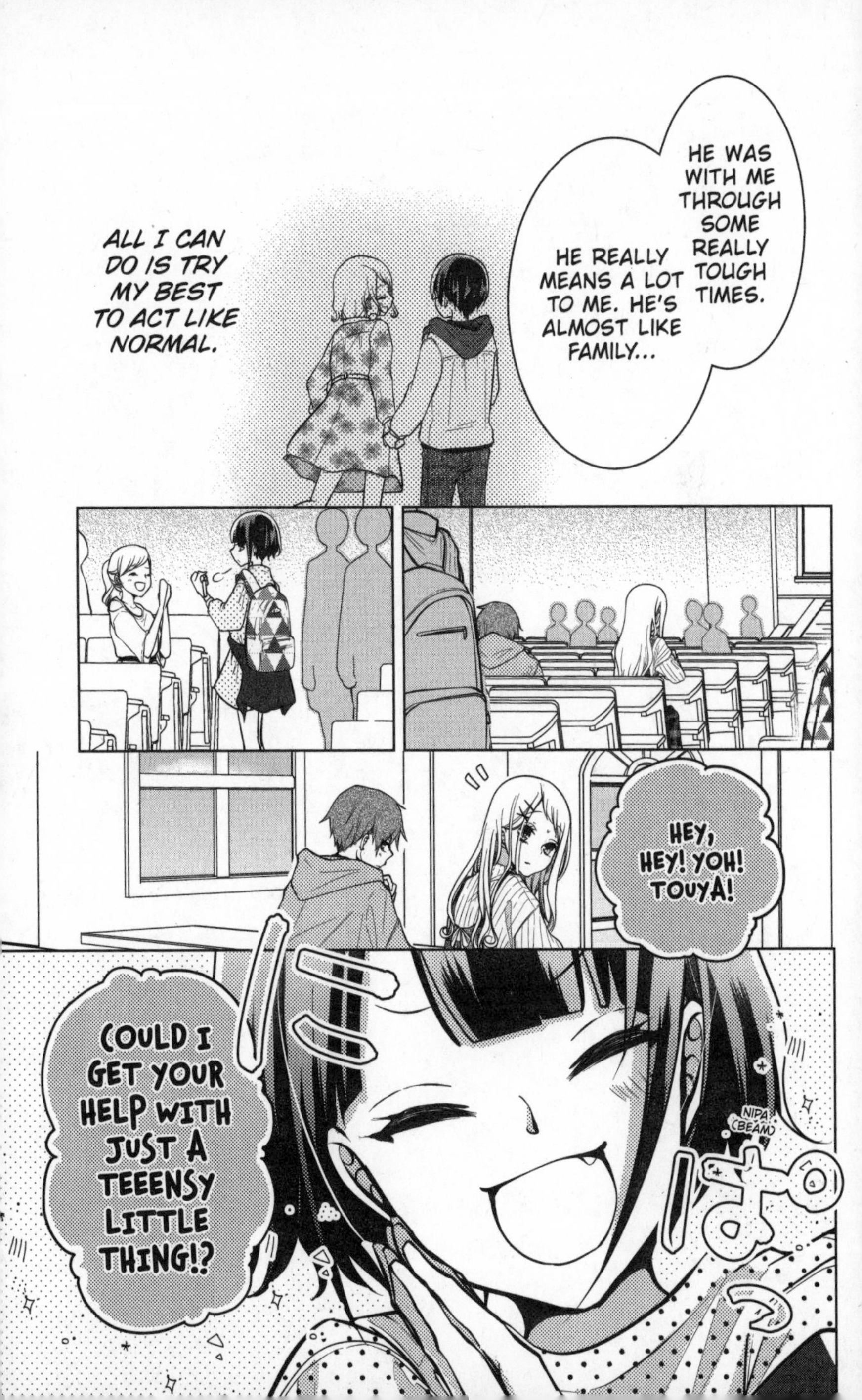
HE WAS WITH ME THROUGH SOME REALLY TOUGH TIMES.
HE REALLY MEANS A LOT TO ME. HE'S ALMOST LIKE FAMILY...
ALL I CAN DO IS TRY MY BEST TO ACT LIKE NORMAL.
HEY, HEY! YOH! TOUYA!
NIPA! (BEAM)
COULD I GET YOUR HELP WITH JUST A TEEENSY LITTLE THING!?

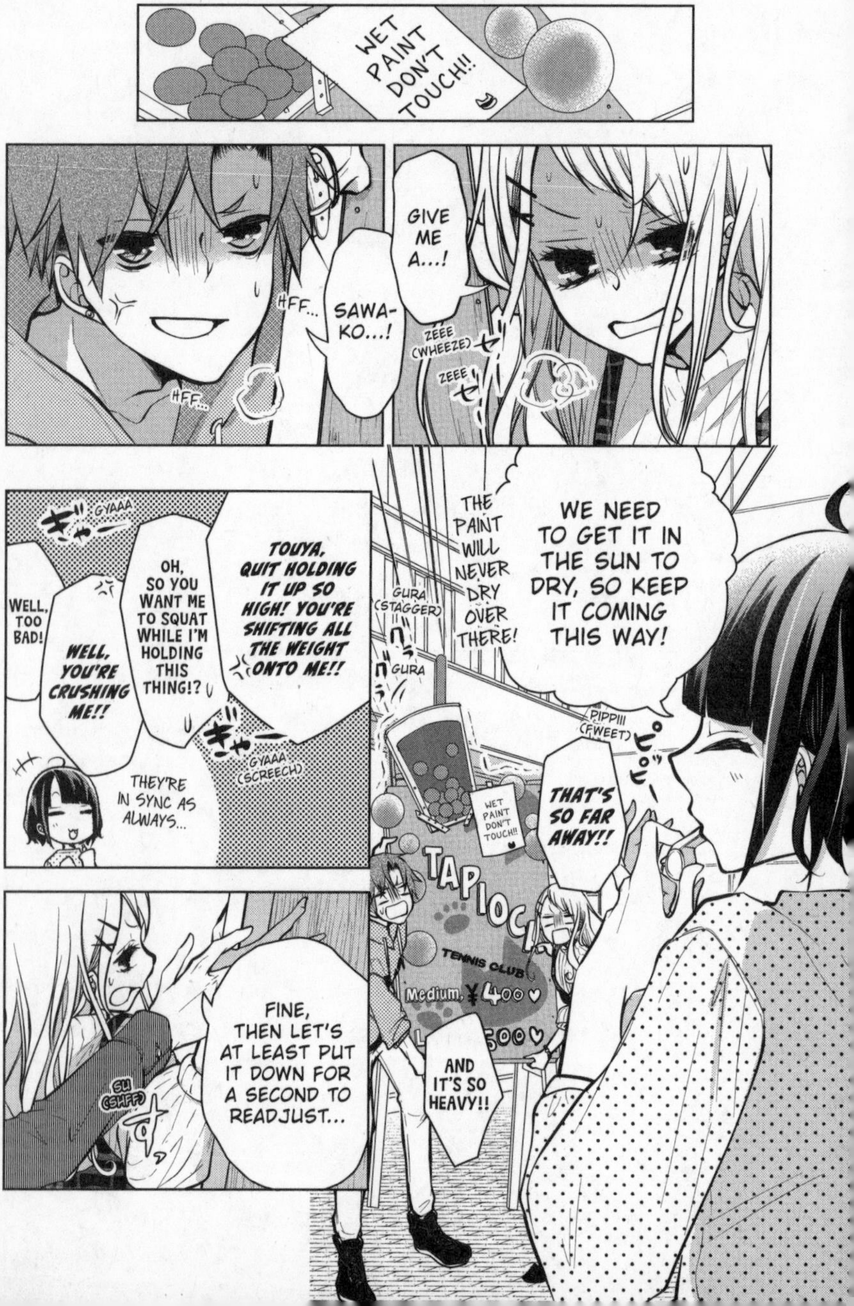
WET PAINT DON'T TOUCH!!
GIVE ME A...!
SAWAKO...!
ZEEE (WHEEZE)
ZEEE
HFF...
HFF...
WE NEED TO GET IT IN THE SUN TO DRY, SO KEEP IT COMING THIS WAY!
THE PAINT WILL NEVER DRY OVER THERE!
PIPPIII (FWEET)
THAT'S SO FAR AWAY!!
GURA (STAGGER)
GURA
WET PAINT DON'T TOUCH!!
TAPIOCA
TENNIS CLUB
Medium ¥400
AND IT'S SO HEAVY!!
GYAAA
TOUYA, QUIT HOLDING IT UP SO HIGH! YOU'RE SHIFTING ALL THE WEIGHT ONTO ME!!
OH, SO YOU WANT ME TO SQUAT WHILE I'M HOLDING THIS THING!?
WELL, YOU'RE CRUSHING ME!!
WELL, TOO BAD!
GYAAA (SCREECH)
THEY'RE IN SYNC AS ALWAYS...
FINE, THEN LET'S AT LEAST PUT IT DOWN FOR A SECOND TO READJUST...
SU (SHFF)

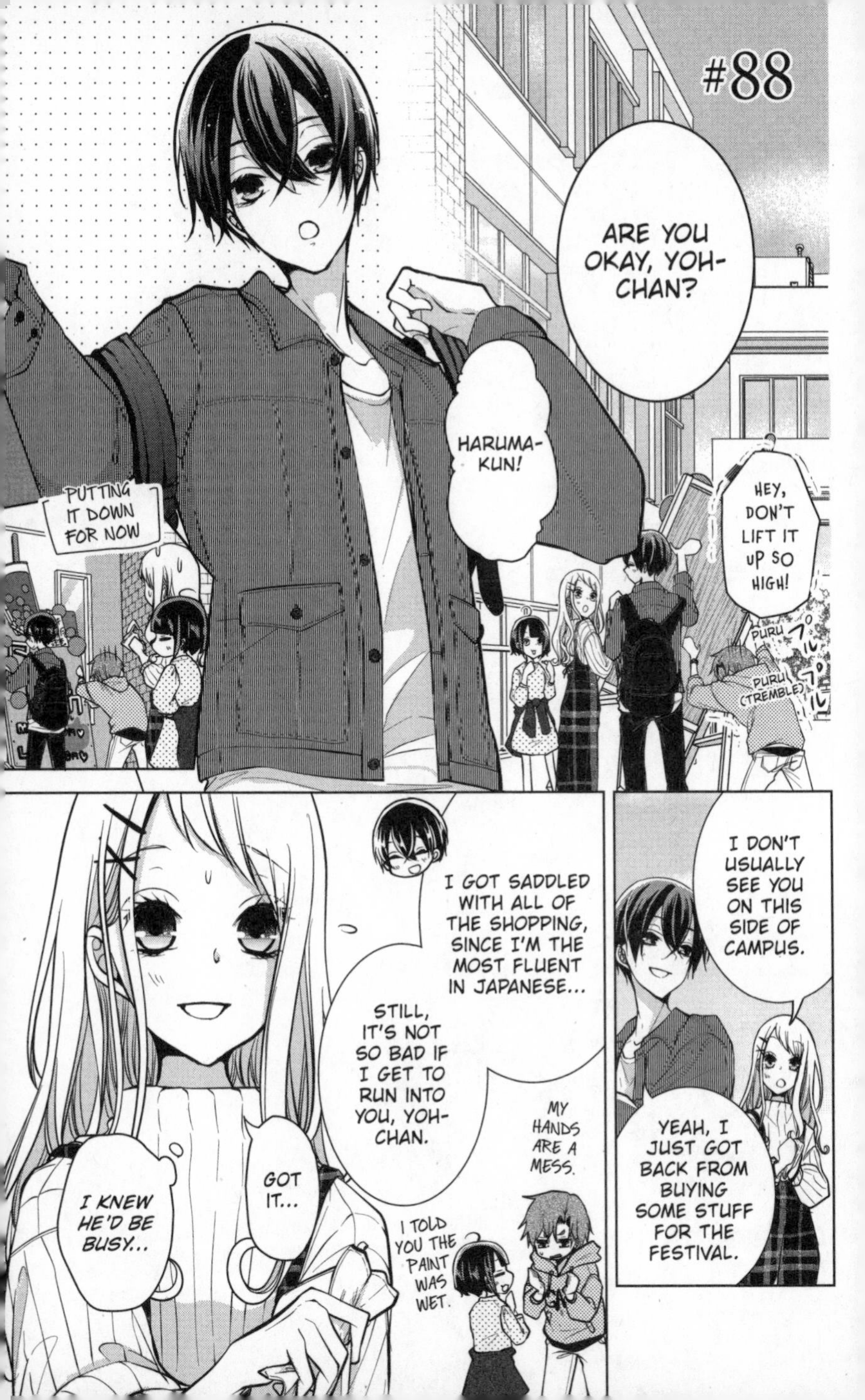
#88
ARE YOU OKAY, YOH-CHAN?
HARUMA-KUN!
HEY, DON'T LIFT IT UP SO HIGH!
PURU
PURU (TREMBLE)
PUTTING IT DOWN FOR NOW
I DON'T USUALLY SEE YOU ON THIS SIDE OF CAMPUS.
YEAH, I JUST GOT BACK FROM BUYING SOME STUFF FOR THE FESTIVAL.
I GOT SADDLED WITH ALL OF THE SHOPPING, SINCE I'M THE MOST FLUENT IN JAPANESE...
STILL, IT'S NOT SO BAD IF I GET TO RUN INTO YOU, YOH-CHAN.
MY HANDS ARE A MESS.
GOT IT...
I KNEW HE'D BE BUSY...
I TOLD YOU THE PAINT WAS WET.

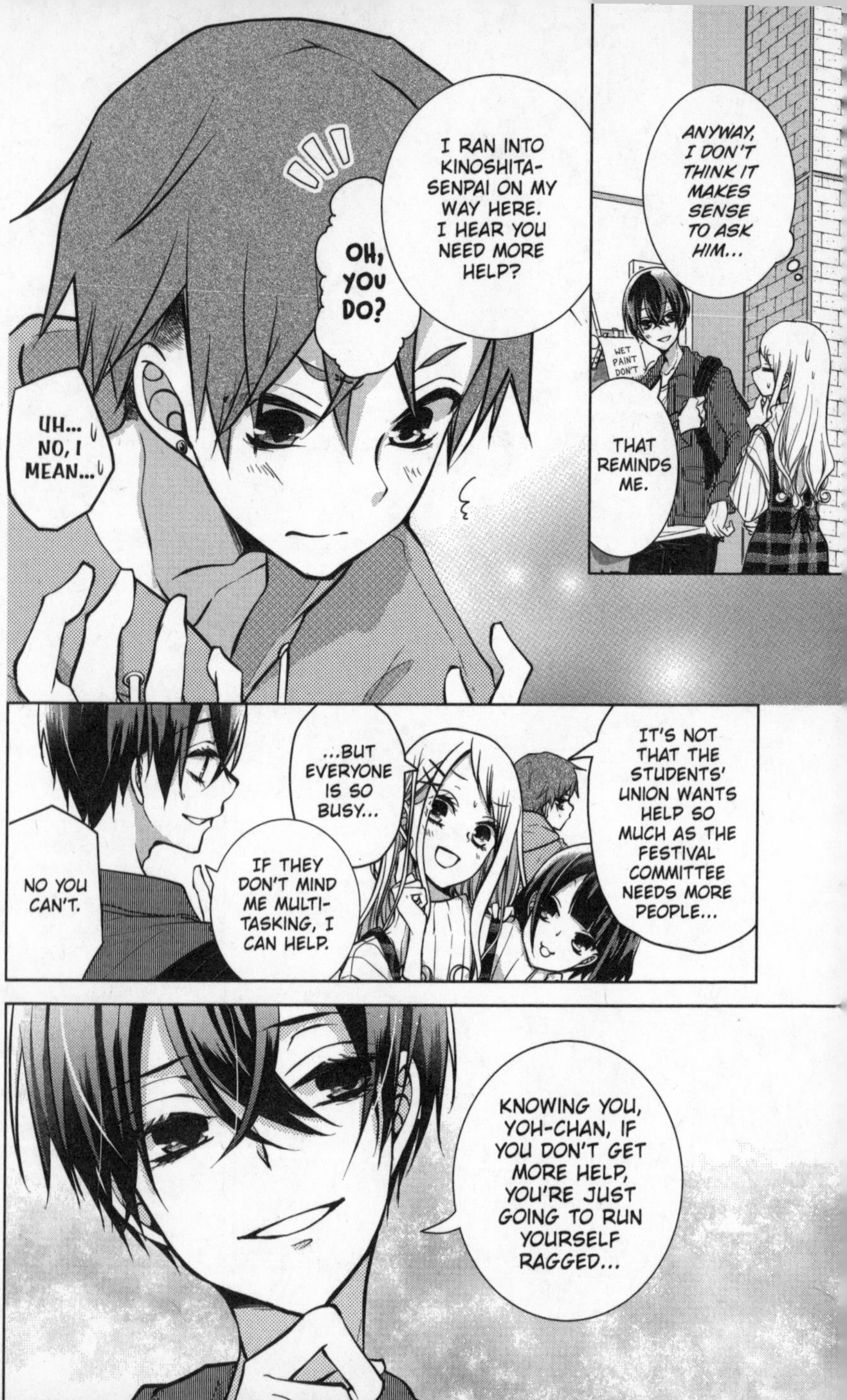
ANYWAY, I DON'T THINK IT MAKES SENSE TO ASK HIM...
WET PAINT DON'T
THAT REMINDS ME.
I RAN INTO KINOSHITA-SENPAI ON MY WAY HERE. I HEAR YOU NEED MORE HELP?
OH, YOU DO?
UH... NO, I MEAN...
IT'S NOT THAT THE STUDENTS' UNION WANTS HELP SO MUCH AS THE FESTIVAL COMMITTEE NEEDS MORE PEOPLE...
...BUT EVERYONE IS SO BUSY...
IF THEY DON'T MIND ME MULTI-TASKING, I CAN HELP.
NO YOU CAN'T.
KNOWING YOU, YOH-CHAN, IF YOU DON'T GET MORE HELP, YOU'RE JUST GOING TO RUN YOURSELF RAGGED...

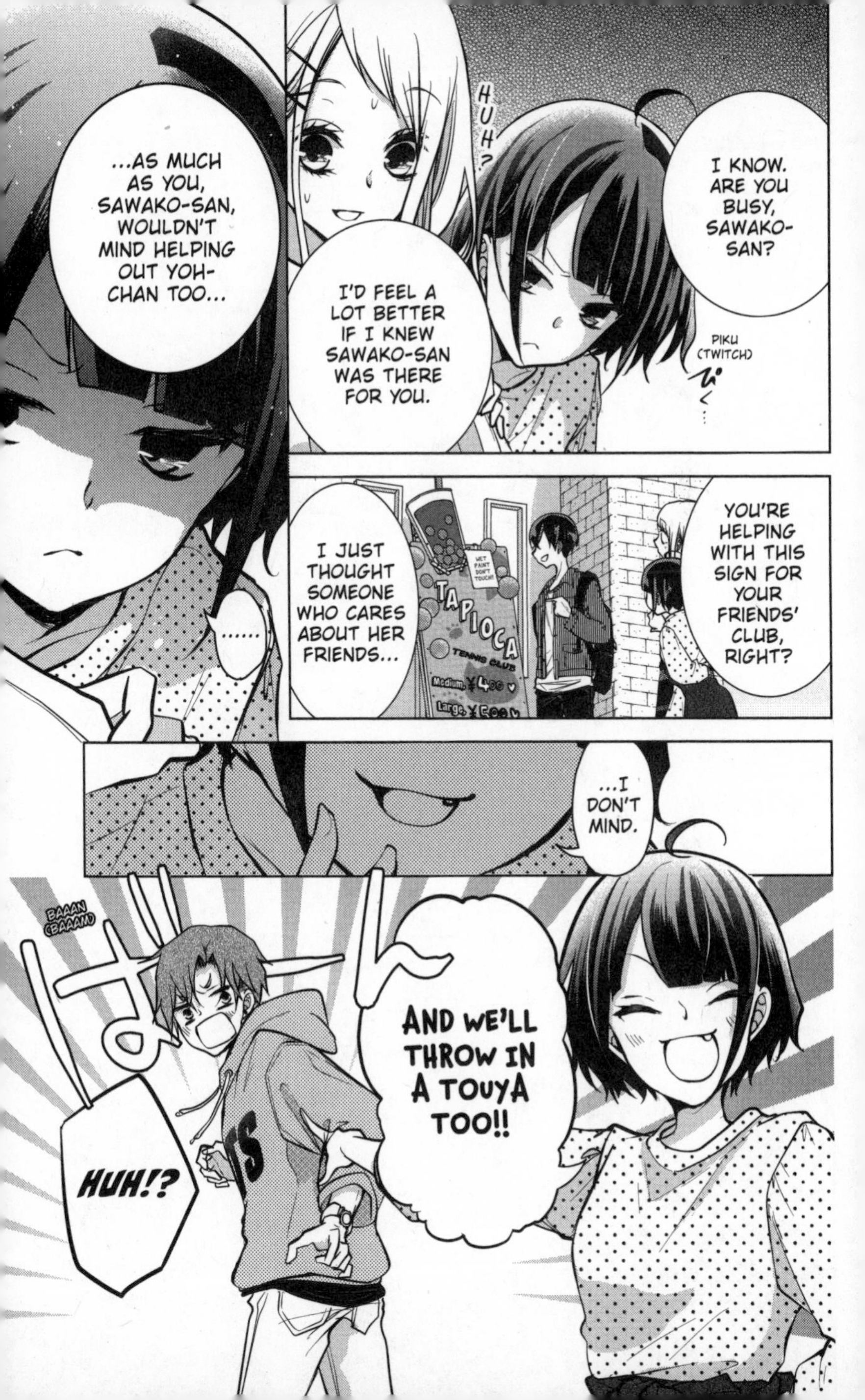
I KNOW. ARE YOU BUSY, SAWAKO-SAN?
PIKU (TWITCH)
HUH?
I'D FEEL A LOT BETTER IF I KNEW SAWAKO-SAN WAS THERE FOR YOU.
YOU'RE HELPING WITH THIS SIGN FOR YOUR FRIENDS' CLUB, RIGHT?
WET PAINT DON'T TOUCH!
TAPIOCA
TENNIS CLUB
Medium ¥400
I JUST THOUGHT SOMEONE WHO CARES ABOUT HER FRIENDS...
...AS MUCH AS YOU, SAWAKO-SAN, WOULDN'T MIND HELPING OUT YOH-CHAN TOO...
......
...I DON'T MIND.
AND WE'LL THROW IN A TOUYA TOO!!
BAAAN (BAAAM)
HUH!?

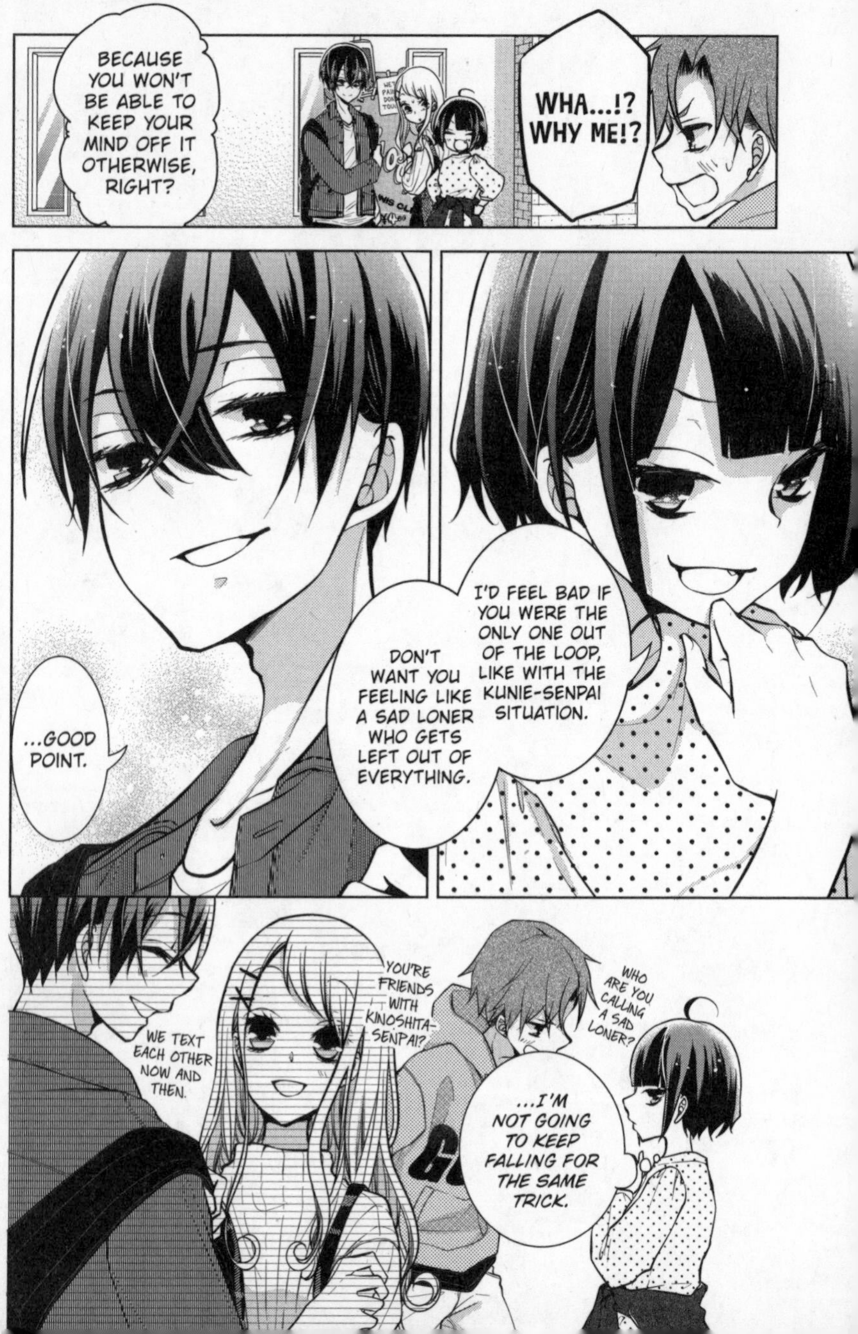
WHA...!? WHY ME!?
BECAUSE YOU WON'T BE ABLE TO KEEP YOUR MIND OFF IT OTHERWISE, RIGHT?
I'D FEEL BAD IF YOU WERE THE ONLY ONE OUT OF THE LOOP, LIKE WITH THE KUNIE-SENPAI SITUATION.
DON'T WANT YOU FEELING LIKE A SAD LONER WHO GETS LEFT OUT OF EVERYTHING.
...GOOD POINT.
WHO ARE YOU CALLING A SAD LONER?
...I'M NOT GOING TO KEEP FALLING FOR THE SAME TRICK.
YOU'RE FRIENDS WITH KINOSHITA-SENPAI?
WE TEXT EACH OTHER NOW AND THEN.

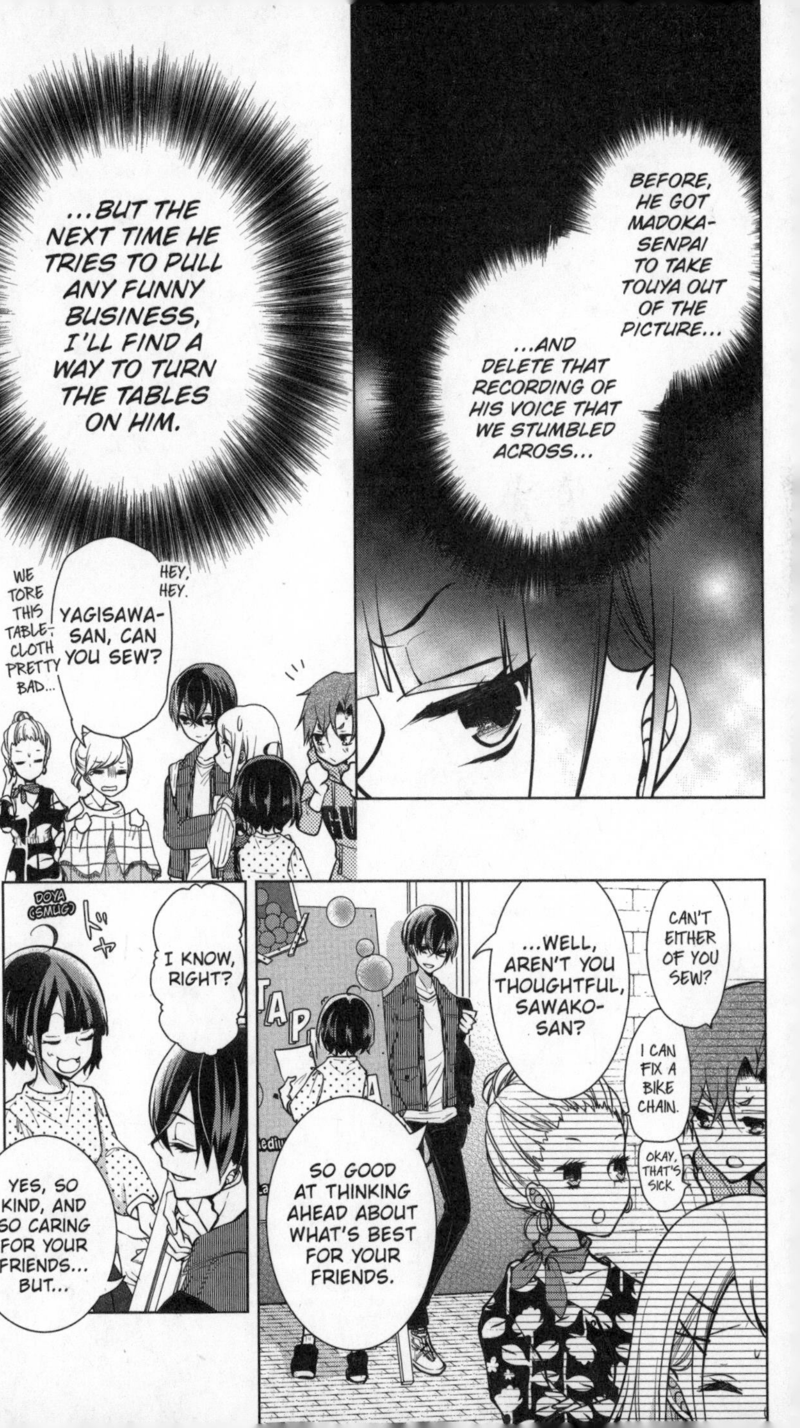
BEFORE, HE GOT MADOKA-SENPAI TO TAKE TOUYA OUT OF THE PICTURE...
...AND DELETE THAT RECORDING OF HIS VOICE THAT WE STUMBLED ACROSS...
...BUT THE NEXT TIME HE TRIES TO PULL ANY FUNNY BUSINESS, I'LL FIND A WAY TO TURN THE TABLES ON HIM.
HEY, HEY.
YAGISAWA-SAN, CAN YOU SEW?
WE TORE THIS TABLE-CLOTH PRETTY BAD...
CAN'T EITHER OF YOU SEW?
I CAN FIX A BIKE CHAIN.
OKAY, THAT'S SICK.
...WELL, AREN'T YOU THOUGHTFUL, SAWAKO-SAN?
SO GOOD AT THINKING AHEAD ABOUT WHAT'S BEST FOR YOUR FRIENDS.
DOYA (SMUG)
I KNOW, RIGHT?
YES, SO KIND, AND SO CARING FOR YOUR FRIENDS... BUT...

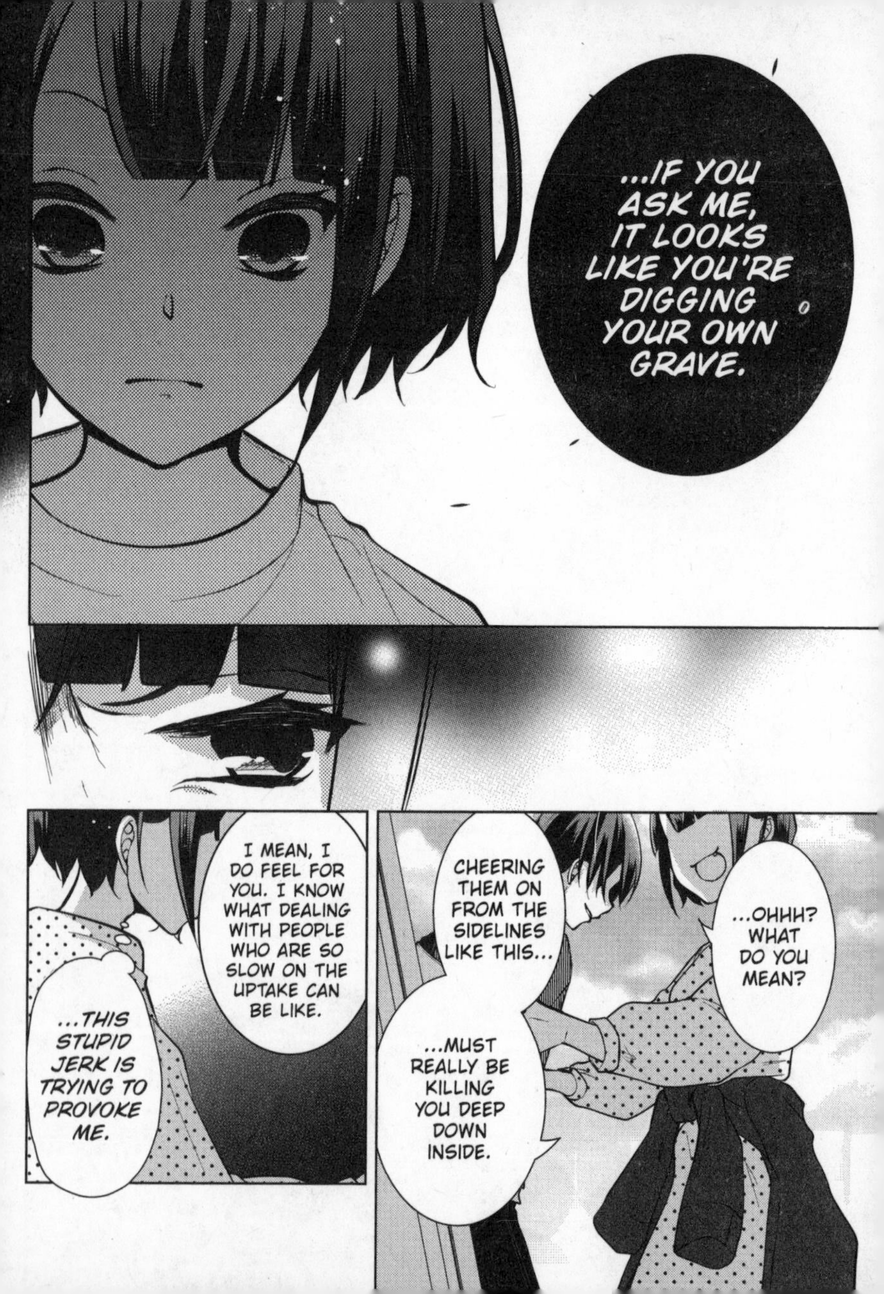
...IF YOU ASK ME, IT LOOKS LIKE YOU'RE DIGGING YOUR OWN GRAVE.
...OHHH? WHAT DO YOU MEAN?
CHEERING THEM ON FROM THE SIDELINES LIKE THIS...
...MUST REALLY BE KILLING YOU DEEP DOWN INSIDE.
I MEAN, I DO FEEL FOR YOU. I KNOW WHAT DEALING WITH PEOPLE WHO ARE SO SLOW ON THE UPTAKE CAN BE LIKE.
...THIS STUPID JERK IS TRYING TO PROVOKE ME.

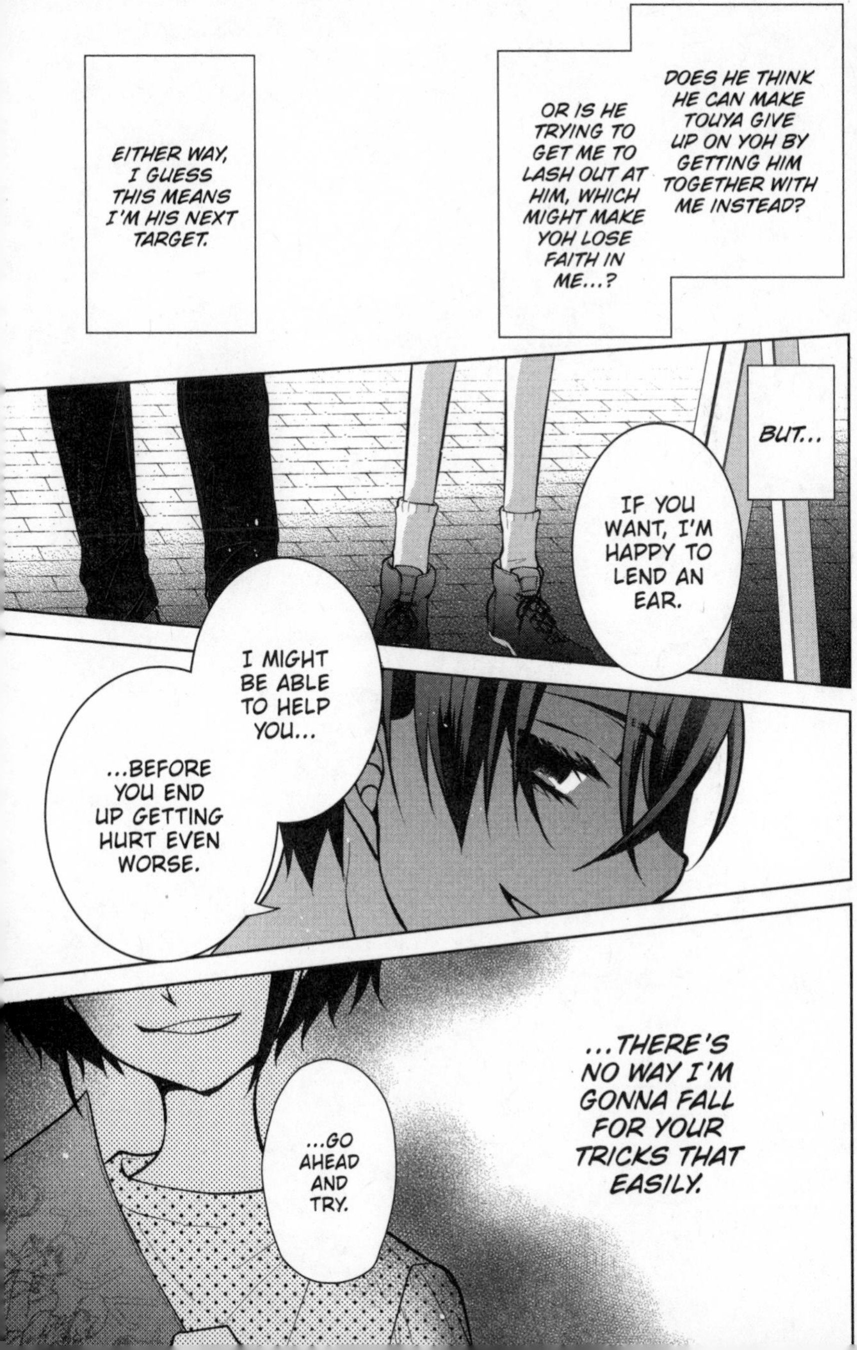
DOES HE THINK HE CAN MAKE TOUYA GIVE UP ON YOH BY GETTING HIM TOGETHER WITH ME INSTEAD?
OR IS HE TRYING TO GET ME TO LASH OUT AT HIM, WHICH MIGHT MAKE YOH LOSE FAITH IN ME...?
EITHER WAY, I GUESS THIS MEANS I'M HIS NEXT TARGET.
BUT...
IF YOU WANT, I'M HAPPY TO LEND AN EAR.
I MIGHT BE ABLE TO HELP YOU...
...BEFORE YOU END UP GETTING HURT EVEN WORSE.
...THERE'S NO WAY I'M GONNA FALL FOR YOUR TRICKS THAT EASILY.
...GO AHEAD AND TRY.

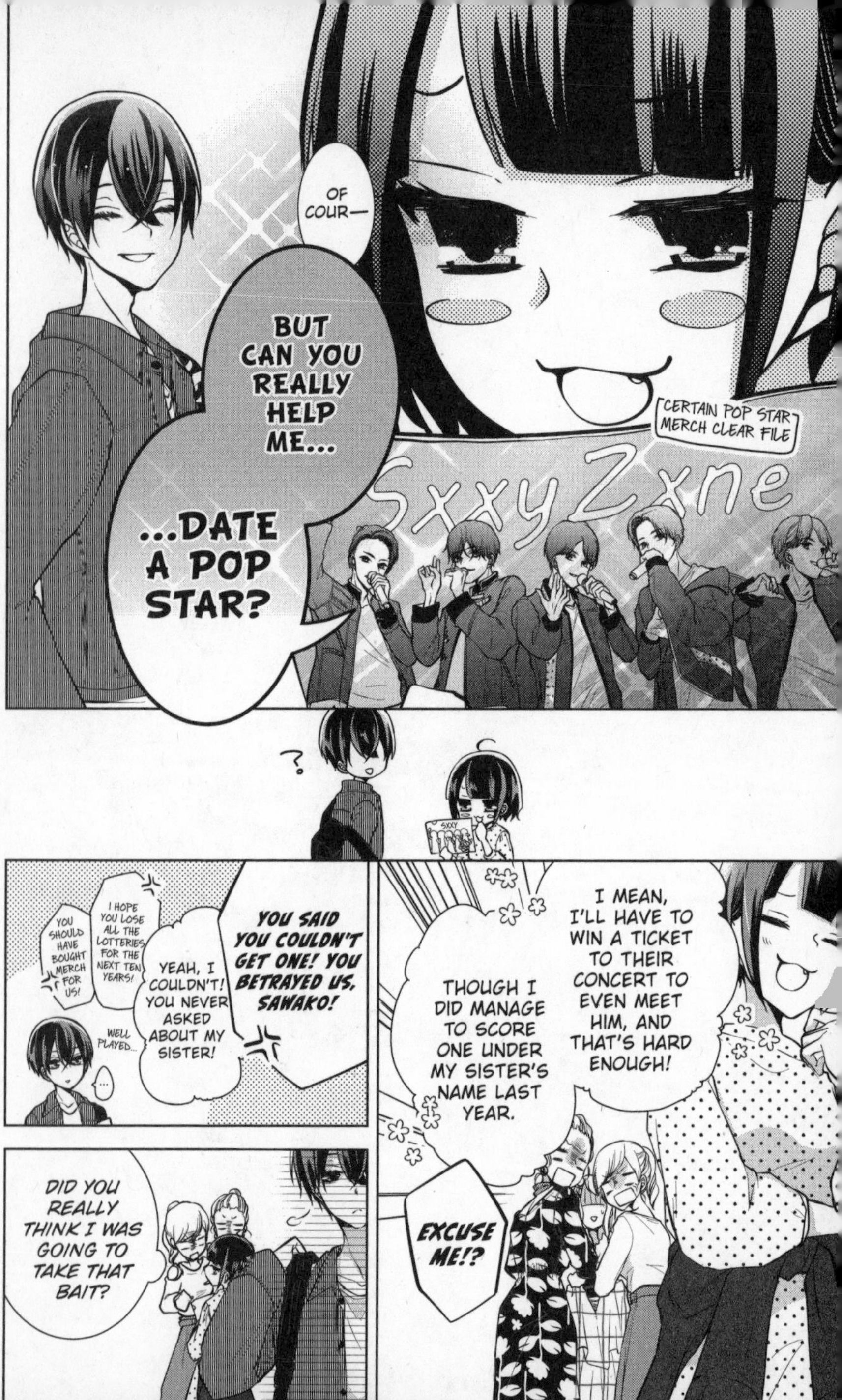
OF COUR—
BUT CAN YOU REALLY HELP ME...
...DATE A POP STAR?
CERTAIN POP STAR MERCH CLEAR FILE
Sxxy Zxne
?
I MEAN, I'LL HAVE TO WIN A TICKET TO THEIR CONCERT TO EVEN MEET HIM, AND THAT'S HARD ENOUGH!
THOUGH I DID MANAGE TO SCORE ONE UNDER MY SISTER'S NAME LAST YEAR.
EXCUSE ME!?
YOU SAID YOU COULDN'T GET ONE! YOU BETRAYED US, SAWAKO!
YEAH, I COULDN'T! YOU NEVER ASKED ABOUT MY SISTER!
I HOPE YOU LOSE ALL THE LOTTERIES FOR THE NEXT TEN YEARS!
YOU SHOULD HAVE BOUGHT MERCH FOR US!
WELL PLAYED...
...
DID YOU REALLY THINK I WAS GOING TO TAKE THAT BAIT?

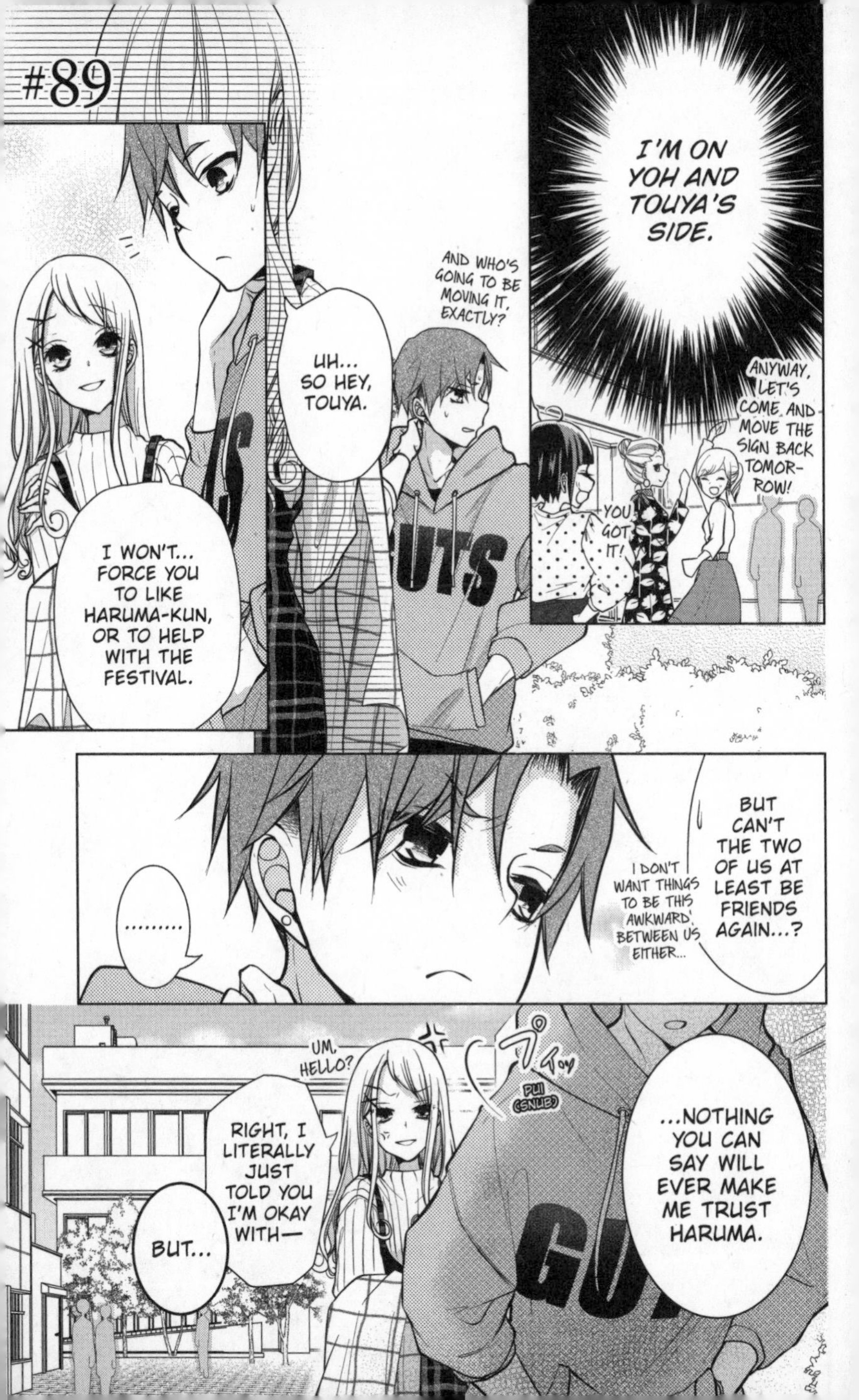
#89
I'M ON YOH AND TOUYA'S SIDE.
ANYWAY, LET'S COME AND MOVE THE SIGN BACK TOMORROW!
YOU GOT IT!
AND WHO'S GOING TO BE MOVING IT, EXACTLY?
UH... SO HEY, TOUYA.
I WON'T... FORCE YOU TO LIKE HARUMA-KUN, OR TO HELP WITH THE FESTIVAL.
BUT CAN'T THE TWO OF US AT LEAST BE FRIENDS AGAIN...?
I DON'T WANT THINGS TO BE THIS AWKWARD BETWEEN US EITHER...
....
...NOTHING YOU CAN SAY WILL EVER MAKE ME TRUST HARUMA.
プイッ
PUI (SNUB)
UM, HELLO?
RIGHT, I LITERALLY JUST TOLD YOU I'M OKAY WITH—
BUT...

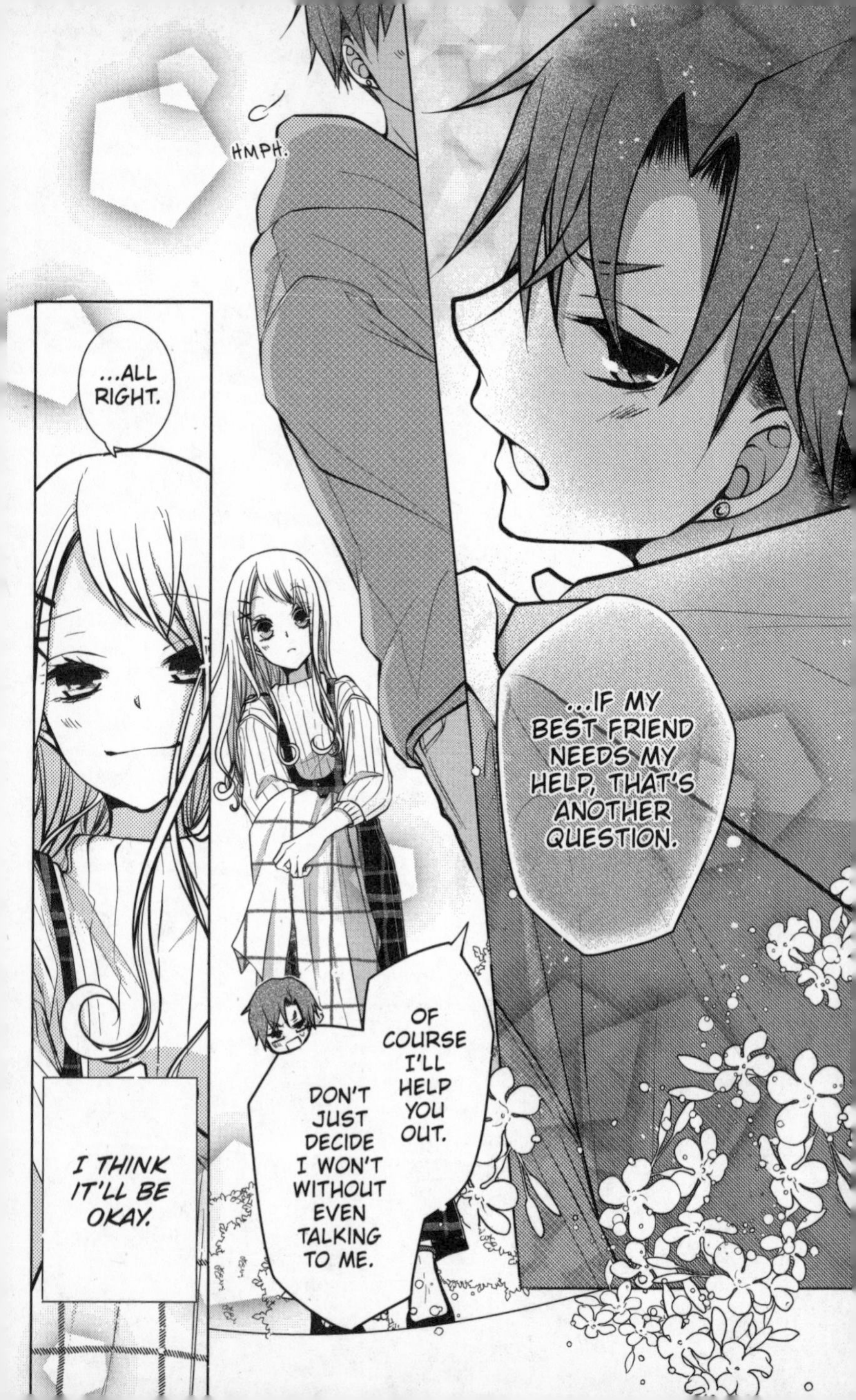
HMPH.
...IF MY BEST FRIEND NEEDS MY HELP, THAT'S ANOTHER QUESTION.
OF COURSE I'LL HELP YOU OUT.
DON'T JUST DECIDE I WON'T WITHOUT EVEN TALKING TO ME.
...ALL RIGHT.
I THINK IT'LL BE OKAY.

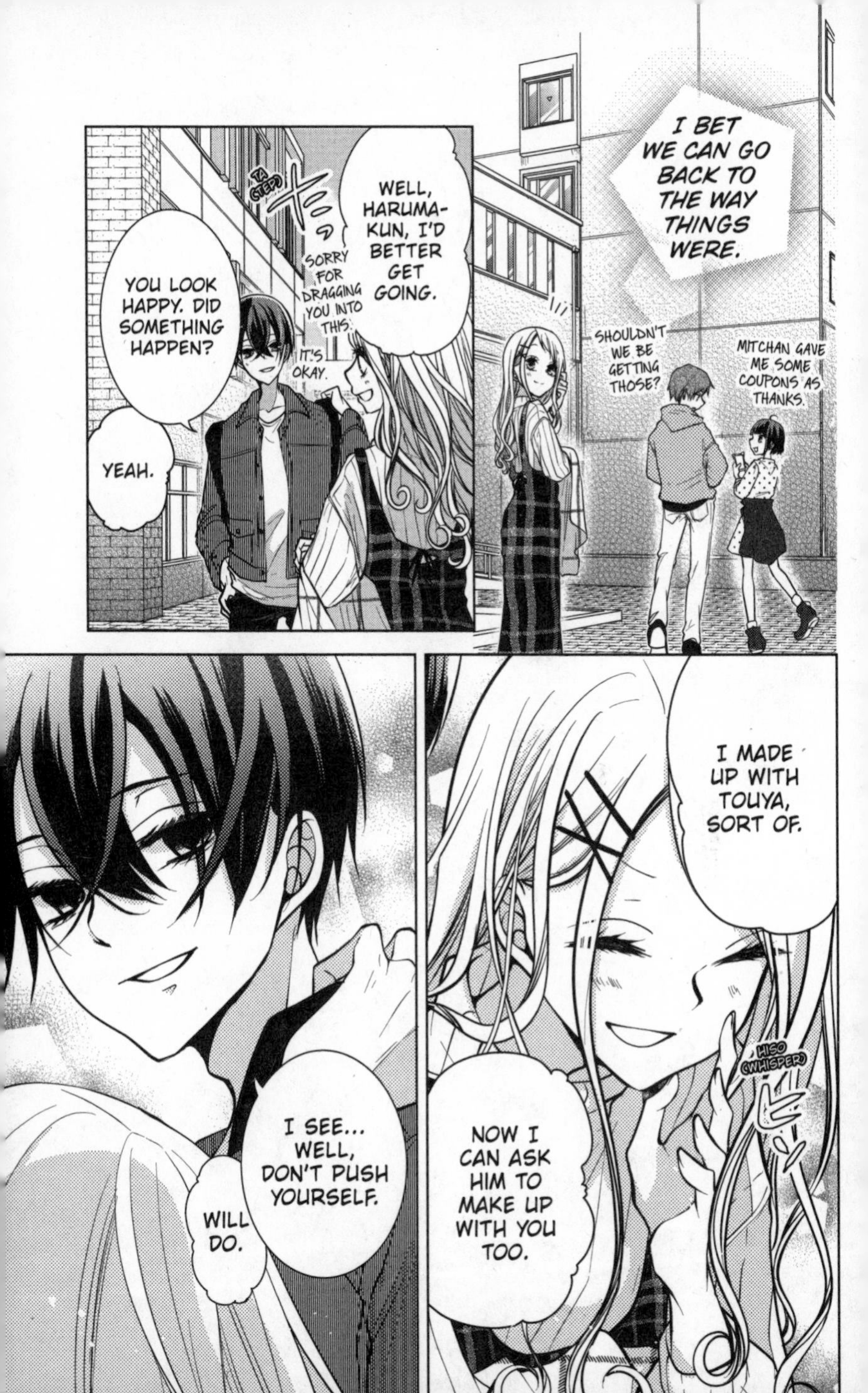
I BET WE CAN GO BACK TO THE WAY THINGS WERE.
MITCHAN GAVE ME SOME COUPONS AS THANKS.
SHOULDN'T WE BE GETTING THOSE?
WELL, HARUMA-KUN, I'D BETTER GET GOING.
TA (STEP)
SORRY FOR DRAGGING YOU INTO THIS.
IT'S OKAY.
YOU LOOK HAPPY. DID SOMETHING HAPPEN?
YEAH.
I MADE UP WITH TOUYA, SORT OF.
HISO (WHISPER)
NOW I CAN ASK HIM TO MAKE UP WITH YOU TOO.
I SEE... WELL, DON'T PUSH YOURSELF.
WILL DO.

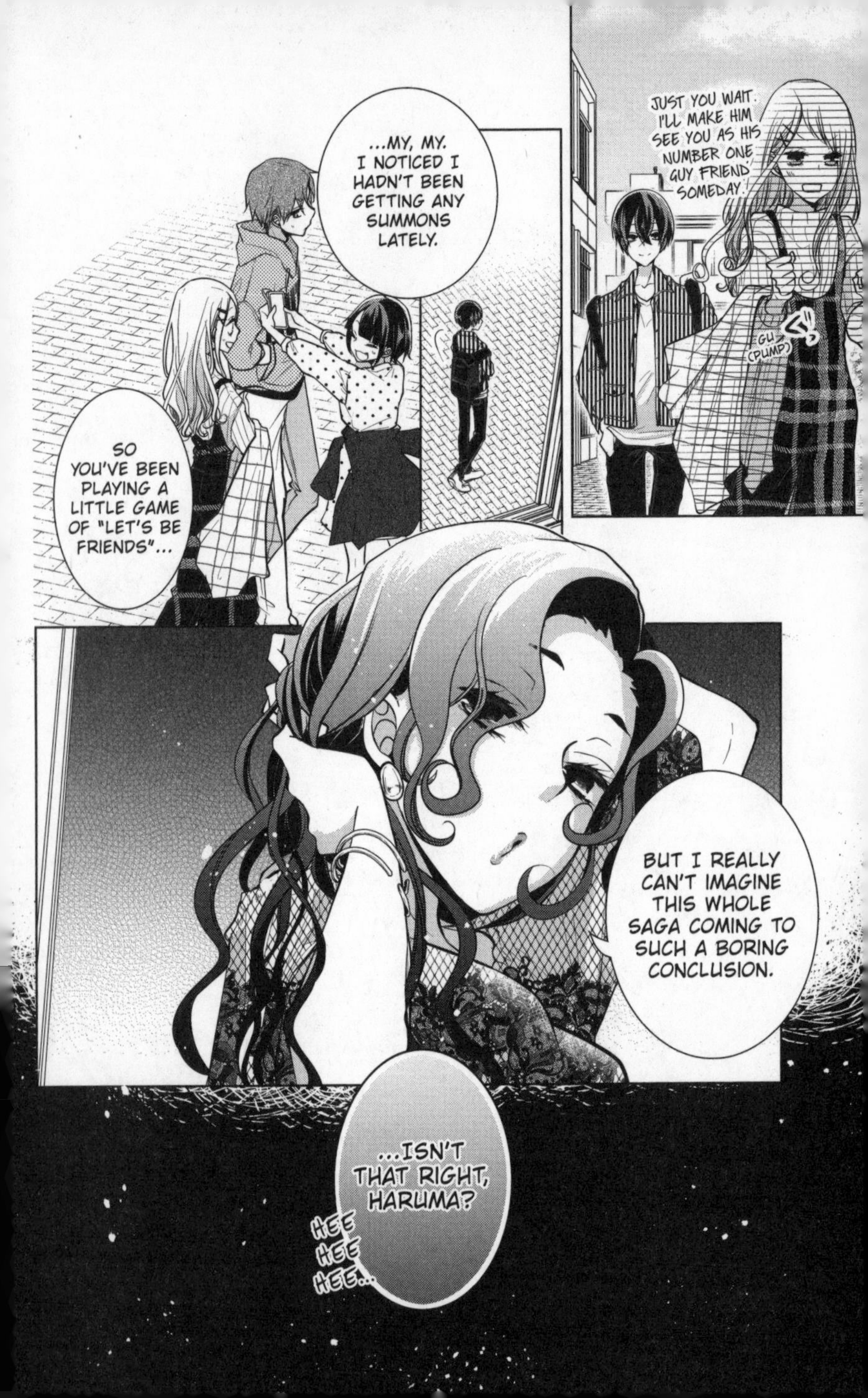
JUST YOU WAIT. I'LL MAKE HIM SEE YOU AS HIS NUMBER ONE GUY FRIEND SOMEDAY.
GU (PUMP)
...MY, MY. I NOTICED I HADN'T BEEN GETTING ANY SUMMONS LATELY.
SO YOU'VE BEEN PLAYING A LITTLE GAME OF "LET'S BE FRIENDS"...
BUT I REALLY CAN'T IMAGINE THIS WHOLE SAGA COMING TO SUCH A BORING CONCLUSION.
...ISN'T THAT RIGHT, HARUMA?
HEE HEE HEE...

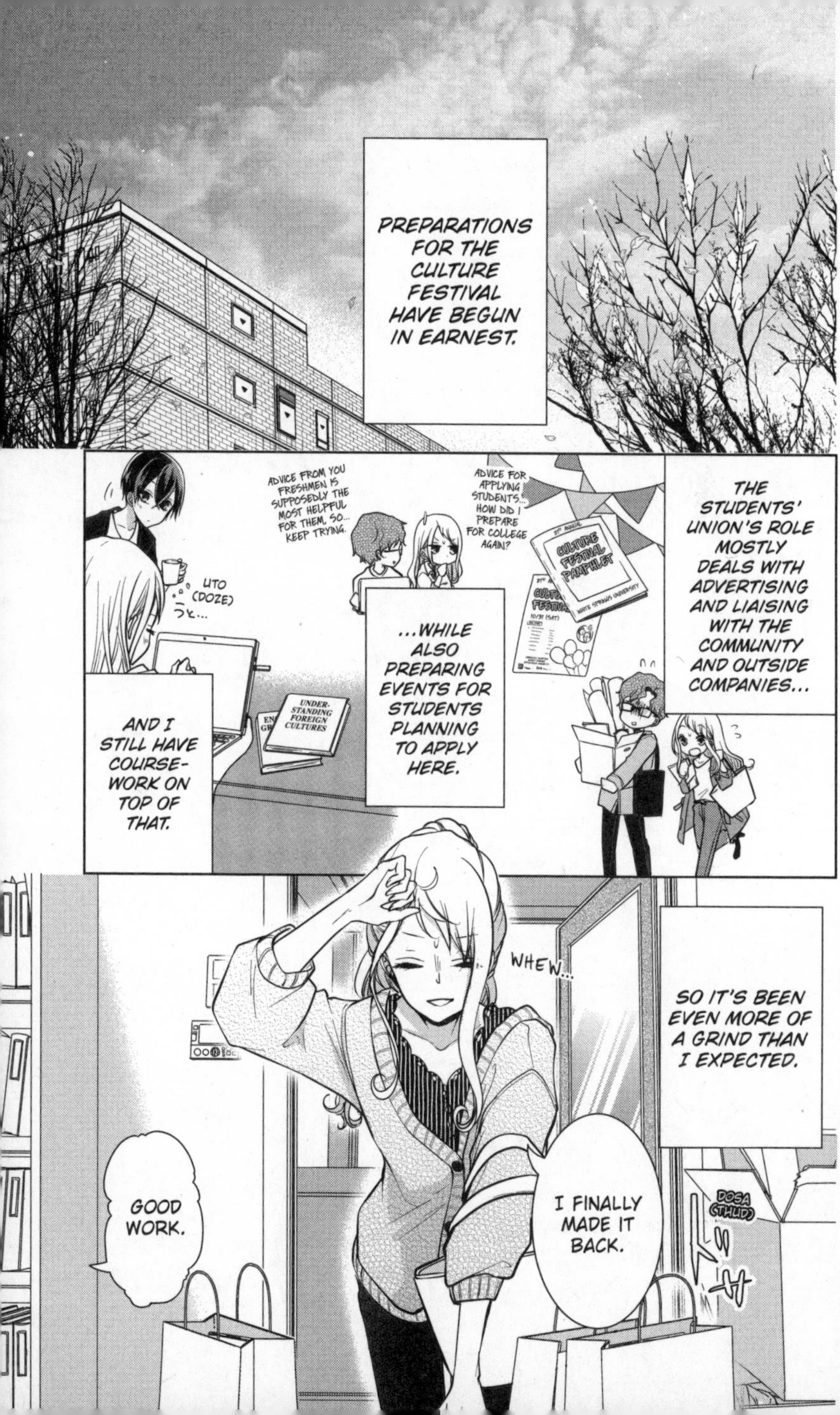
PREPARATIONS FOR THE CULTURE FESTIVAL HAVE BEGUN IN EARNEST.
THE STUDENTS' UNION'S ROLE MOSTLY DEALS WITH ADVERTISING AND LIAISING WITH THE COMMUNITY AND OUTSIDE COMPANIES...
CULTURE FESTIVAL PAMPHLET
WHITE SPRINGS UNIVERSITY
CULTURE FESTIVAL
10/31 (SAT)
ADVICE FOR APPLYING STUDENTS... HOW DID I PREPARE FOR COLLEGE AGAIN?
ADVICE FROM YOU FRESHMEN IS SUPPOSEDLY THE MOST HELPFUL FOR THEM, SO... KEEP TRYING.
...WHILE ALSO PREPARING EVENTS FOR STUDENTS PLANNING TO APPLY HERE.
UTO (DOZE)
うと...
UNDERSTANDING FOREIGN CULTURES
AND I STILL HAVE COURSEWORK ON TOP OF THAT.
SO IT'S BEEN EVEN MORE OF A GRIND THAN I EXPECTED.
DOSA (THUD)
WHEW...
I FINALLY MADE IT BACK.
GOOD WORK.

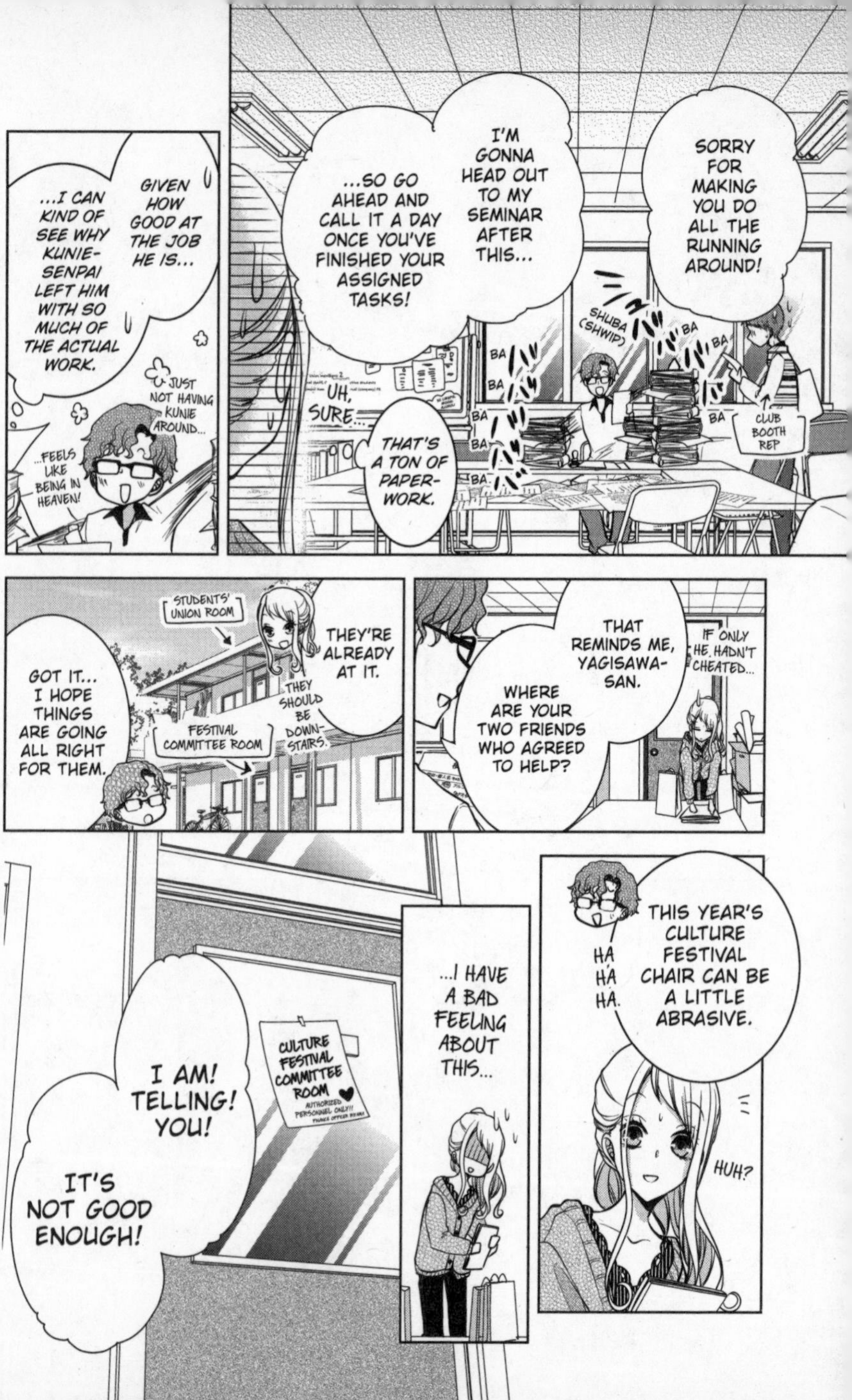
SORRY FOR MAKING YOU DO ALL THE RUNNING AROUND!
I'M GONNA HEAD OUT TO MY SEMINAR AFTER THIS...
...SO GO AHEAD AND CALL IT A DAY ONCE YOU'VE FINISHED YOUR ASSIGNED TASKS!
SHUBA (SHWIP)
BA BA BA BA BA BA BA BA
CLUB BOOTH REP
UH, SURE...
THAT'S A TON OF PAPERWORK.
GIVEN HOW GOOD AT THE JOB HE IS...
...I CAN KIND OF SEE WHY KUNIE-SENPAI LEFT HIM WITH SO MUCH OF THE ACTUAL WORK.
JUST NOT HAVING KUNIE AROUND...
...FEELS LIKE BEING IN HEAVEN!
THAT REMINDS ME, YAGISAWA-SAN.
WHERE ARE YOUR TWO FRIENDS WHO AGREED TO HELP?
IF ONLY HE HADN'T CHEATED...
THEY'RE ALREADY AT IT.
THEY SHOULD BE DOWNSTAIRS.
STUDENTS' UNION ROOM
FESTIVAL COMMITTEE ROOM
GOT IT... I HOPE THINGS ARE GOING ALL RIGHT FOR THEM.
THIS YEAR'S CULTURE FESTIVAL CHAIR CAN BE A LITTLE ABRASIVE.
HA HA HA.
HUH?
...I HAVE A BAD FEELING ABOUT THIS...
CULTURE FESTIVAL COMMITTEE ROOM
AUTHORIZED PERSONNEL ONLY!!
I AM! TELLING! YOU!
IT'S NOT GOOD ENOUGH!

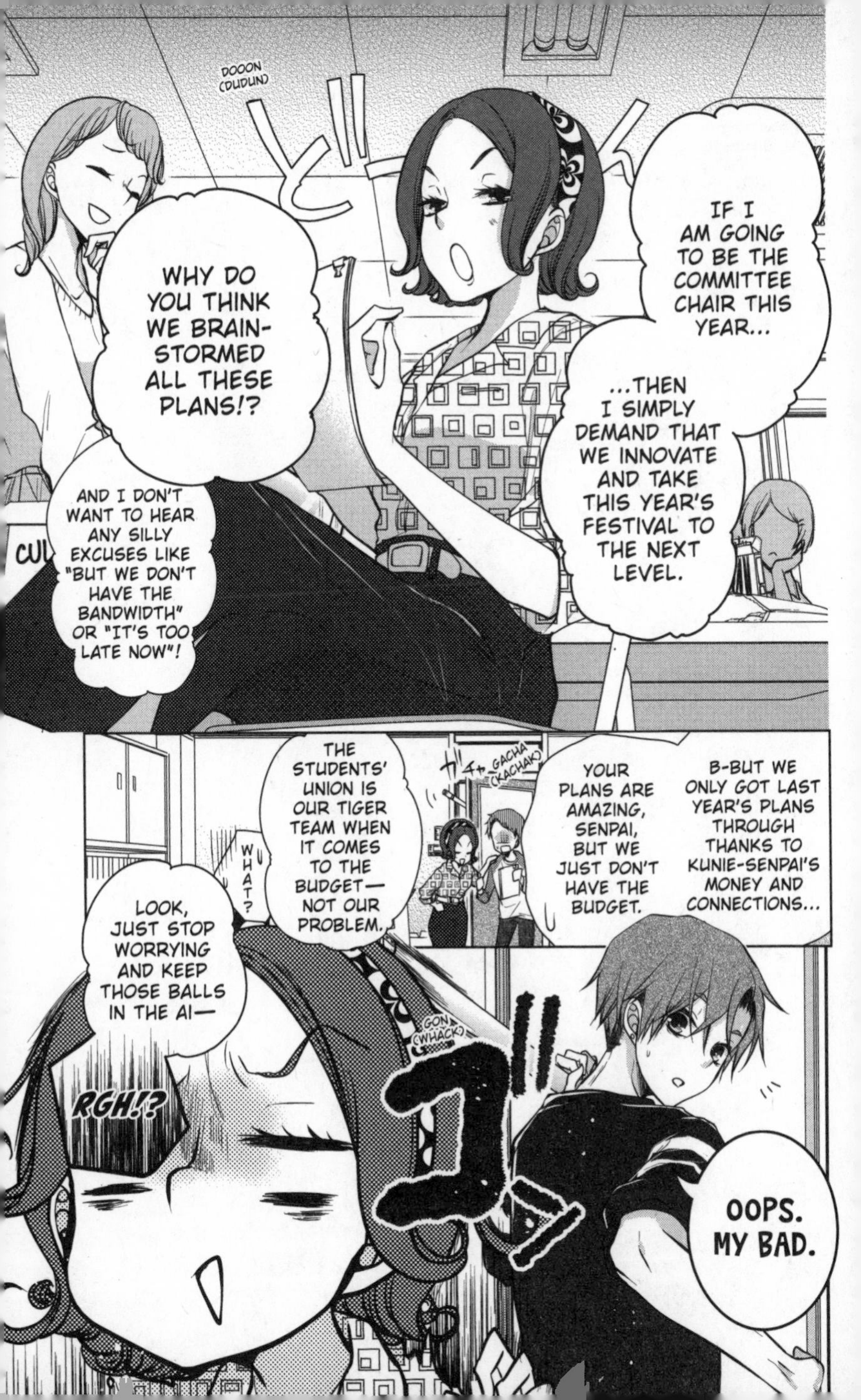
IF I AM GOING TO BE THE COMMITTEE CHAIR THIS YEAR...
...THEN I SIMPLY DEMAND THAT WE INNOVATE AND TAKE THIS YEAR'S FESTIVAL TO THE NEXT LEVEL.
DOOON (DUDUN)
WHY DO YOU THINK WE BRAIN-STORMED ALL THESE PLANS!?
AND I DON'T WANT TO HEAR ANY SILLY EXCUSES LIKE "BUT WE DON'T HAVE THE BANDWIDTH" OR "IT'S TOO LATE NOW"!
B-BUT WE ONLY GOT LAST YEAR'S PLANS THROUGH THANKS TO KUNIE-SENPAI'S MONEY AND CONNECTIONS...
YOUR PLANS ARE AMAZING, SENPAI, BUT WE JUST DON'T HAVE THE BUDGET.
GACHA (KACHAK)
THE STUDENTS' UNION IS OUR TIGER TEAM WHEN IT COMES TO THE BUDGET— NOT OUR PROBLEM.
WHAT?
LOOK, JUST STOP WORRYING AND KEEP THOSE BALLS IN THE AI—
GON (WHACK)
OOPS. MY BAD.
RGH!?

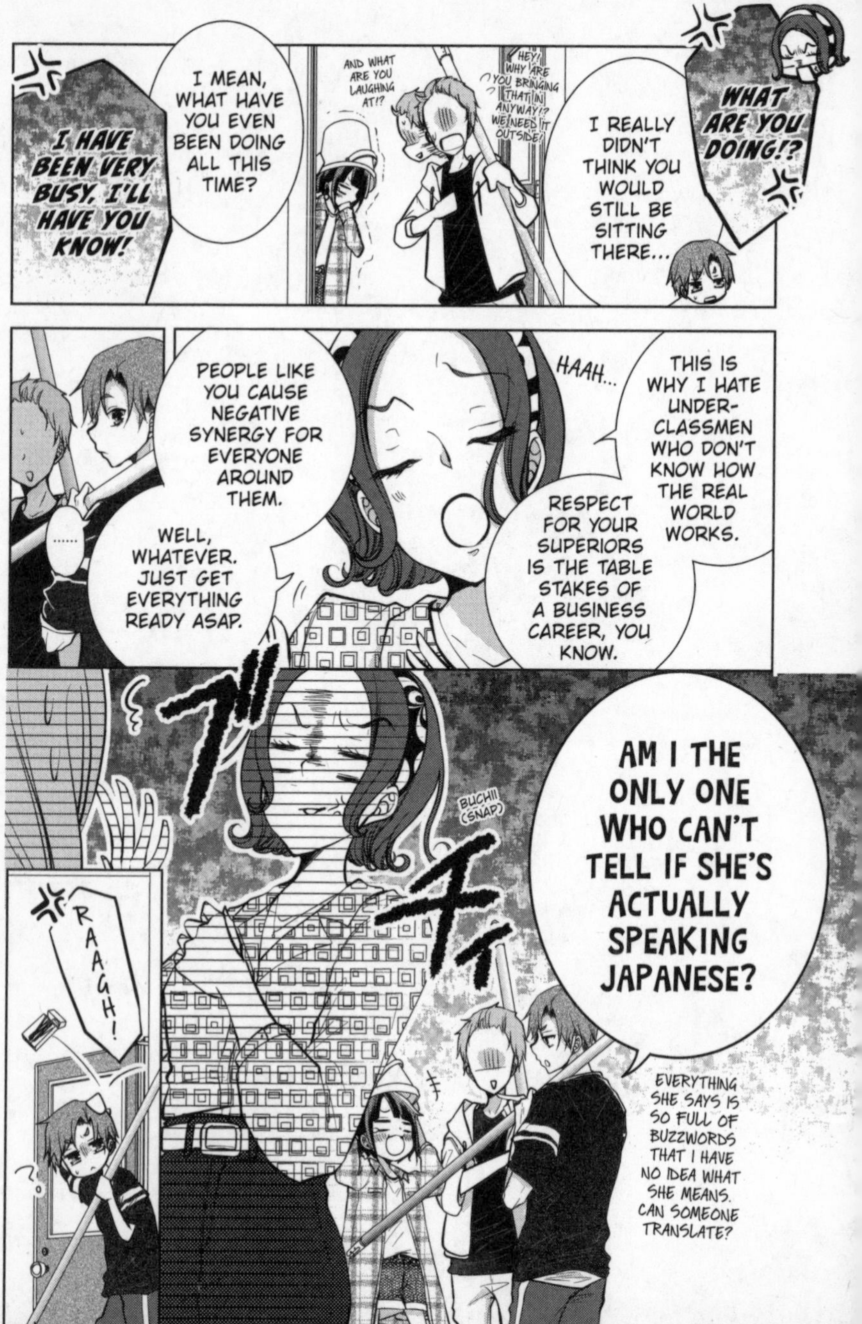
WHAT ARE YOU DOING!?
I REALLY DIDN'T THINK YOU WOULD STILL BE SITTING THERE...
HEY! WHY ARE YOU BRINGING THAT IN ANYWAY!? WE NEED IT OUTSIDE!
AND WHAT ARE YOU LAUGHING AT!?
I MEAN, WHAT HAVE YOU EVEN BEEN DOING ALL THIS TIME?
I HAVE BEEN VERY BUSY, I'LL HAVE YOU KNOW!
HAAH...
THIS IS WHY I HATE UNDER-CLASSMEN WHO DON'T KNOW HOW THE REAL WORLD WORKS.
RESPECT FOR YOUR SUPERIORS IS THE TABLE STAKES OF A BUSINESS CAREER, YOU KNOW.
PEOPLE LIKE YOU CAUSE NEGATIVE SYNERGY FOR EVERYONE AROUND THEM.
WELL, WHATEVER. JUST GET EVERYTHING READY ASAP.
......
BUCHI! (SNAP)
AM I THE ONLY ONE WHO CAN'T TELL IF SHE'S ACTUALLY SPEAKING JAPANESE?
EVERYTHING SHE SAYS IS SO FULL OF BUZZWORDS THAT I HAVE NO IDEA WHAT SHE MEANS. CAN SOMEONE TRANSLATE?
RAAGH!

#90

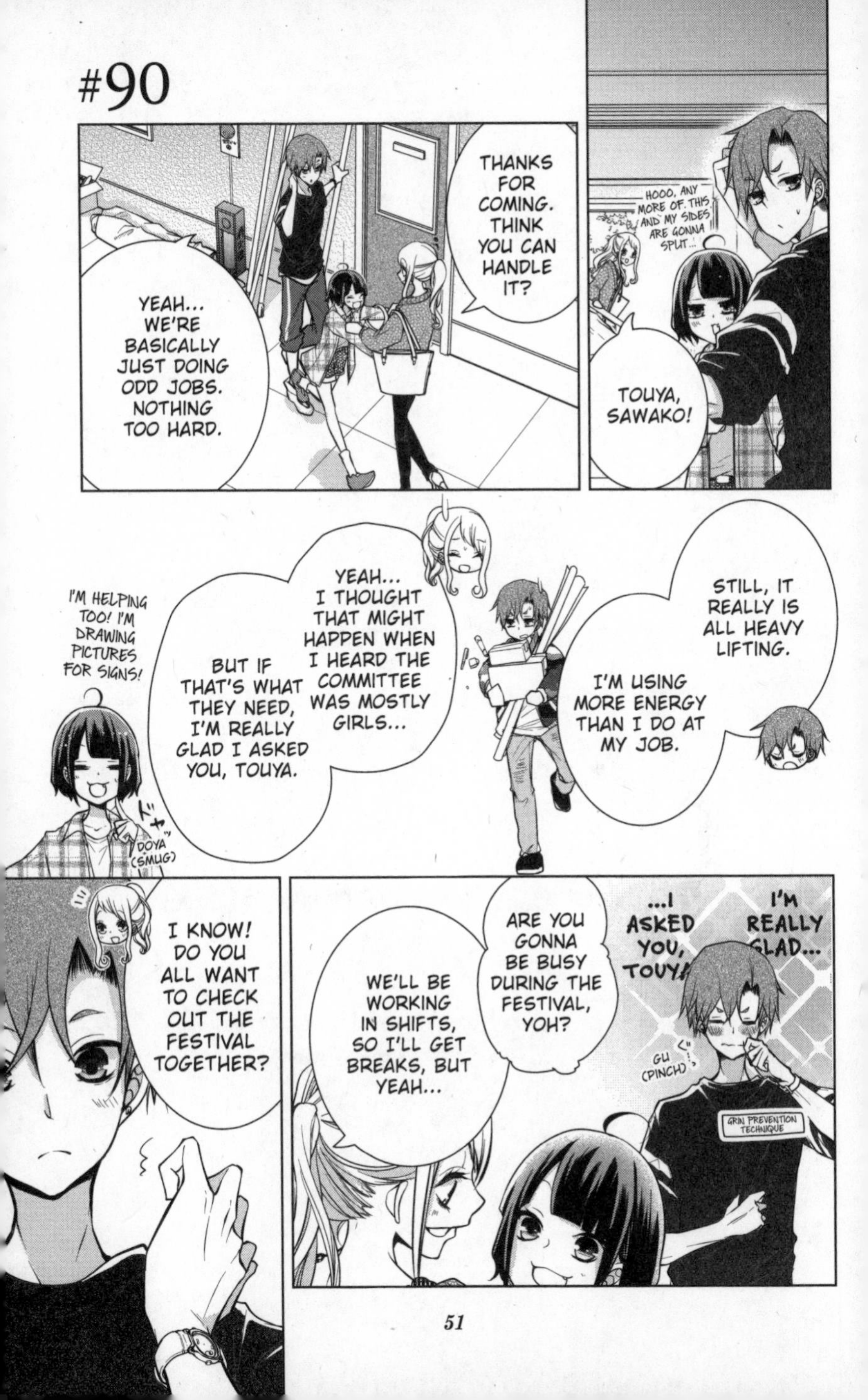
HOOO, ANY MORE OF THIS AND MY SIDES ARE GONNA SPLIT...
TOUYA, SAWAKO!
THANKS FOR COMING. THINK YOU CAN HANDLE IT?
YEAH... WE'RE BASICALLY JUST DOING ODD JOBS. NOTHING TOO HARD.
STILL, IT REALLY IS ALL HEAVY LIFTING.
I'M USING MORE ENERGY THAN I DO AT MY JOB.
YEAH... I THOUGHT THAT MIGHT HAPPEN WHEN I HEARD THE COMMITTEE WAS MOSTLY GIRLS...
BUT IF THAT'S WHAT THEY NEED, I'M REALLY GLAD I ASKED YOU, TOUYA.
I'M HELPING TOO! I'M DRAWING PICTURES FOR SIGNS!
DOYA (SMUG)
I'M REALLY GLAD...
...I ASKED YOU, TOUYA
ARE YOU GONNA BE BUSY DURING THE FESTIVAL, YOH?
GU (PINCH)
GRIN PREVENTION TECHNIQUE
WE'LL BE WORKING IN SHIFTS, SO I'LL GET BREAKS, BUT YEAH...
I KNOW! DO YOU ALL WANT TO CHECK OUT THE FESTIVAL TOGETHER?

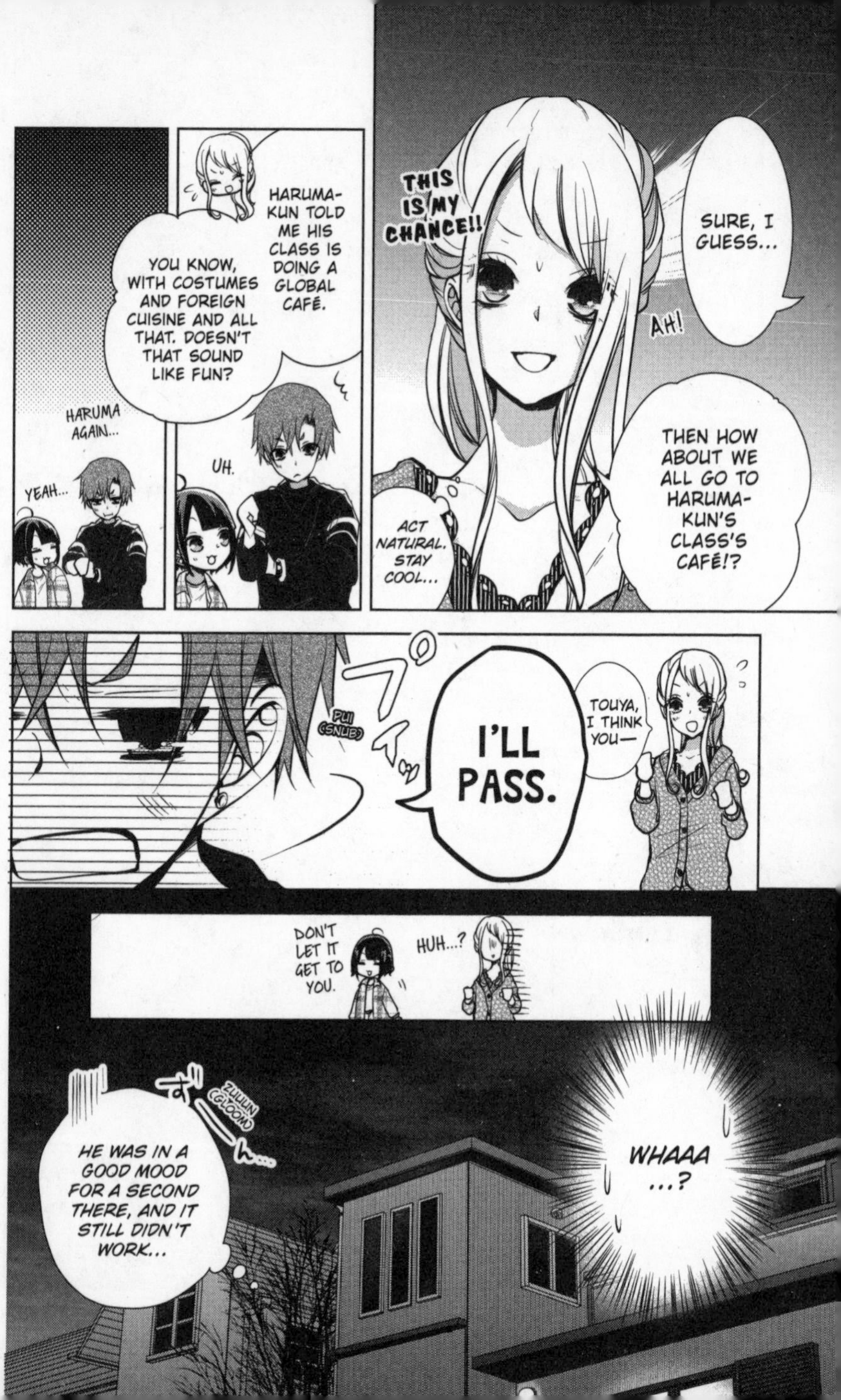
SURE, I GUESS...
THIS IS MY CHANCE!!
AH!
THEN HOW ABOUT WE ALL GO TO HARUMA-KUN'S CLASS'S CAFÉ!?
ACT NATURAL. STAY COOL...
HARUMA-KUN TOLD ME HIS CLASS IS DOING A GLOBAL CAFÉ.
YOU KNOW, WITH COSTUMES AND FOREIGN CUISINE AND ALL THAT. DOESN'T THAT SOUND LIKE FUN?
UH.
HARUMA AGAIN...
YEAH...
TOUYA, I THINK YOU—
I'LL PASS.
PUI (SNUB)
HUH...?
DON'T LET IT GET TO YOU.
WHAAA ...?
ZUUUN (GLOOM)
HE WAS IN A GOOD MOOD FOR A SECOND THERE, AND IT STILL DIDN'T WORK...

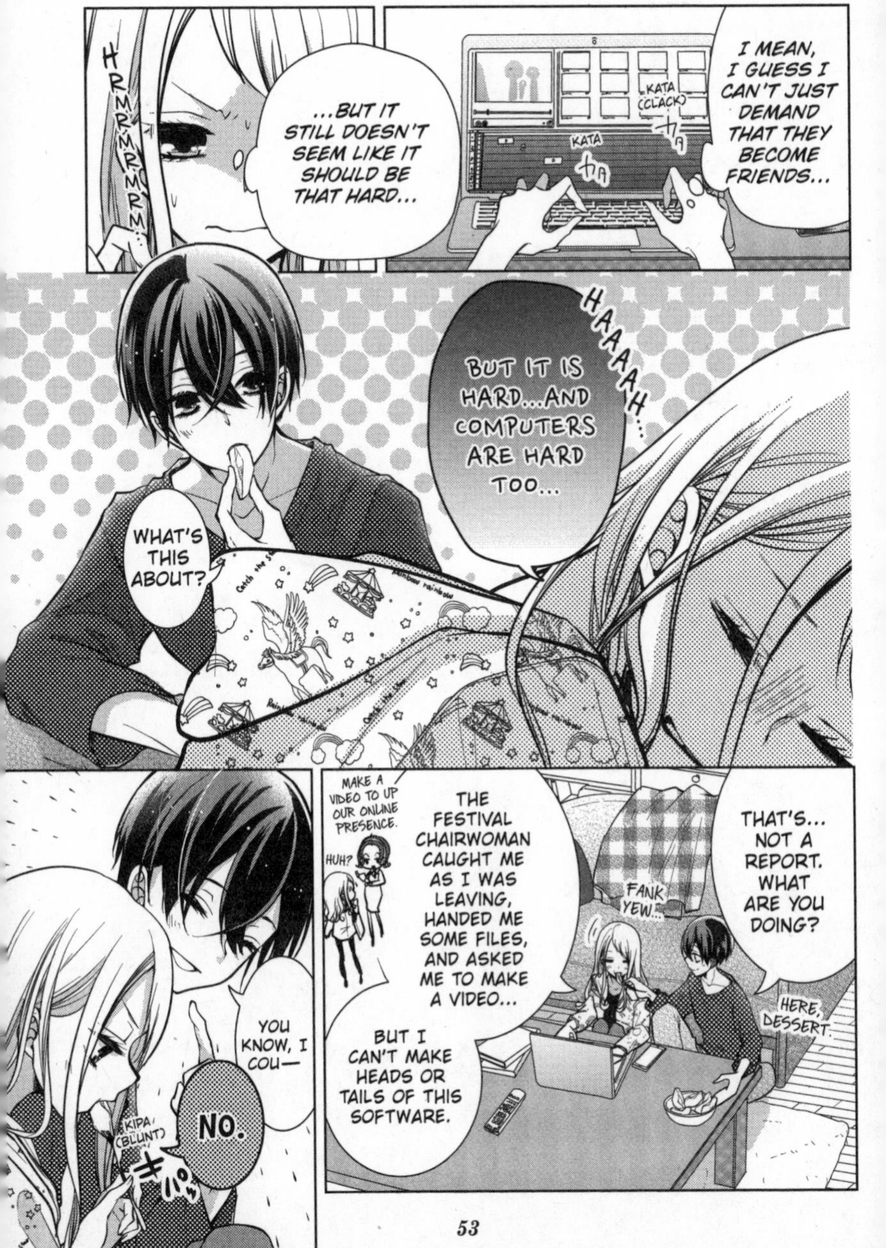
I MEAN, I GUESS I CAN'T JUST DEMAND THAT THEY BECOME FRIENDS...
KATA (CLACK)
KATA
...BUT IT STILL DOESN'T SEEM LIKE IT SHOULD BE THAT HARD...
HRMRMRMRM...
BUT IT IS HARD...AND COMPUTERS ARE HARD TOO...
HAAAAAH...
WHAT'S THIS ABOUT?
THAT'S... NOT A REPORT. WHAT ARE YOU DOING?
HERE, DESSERT.
FANK YEW...
THE FESTIVAL CHAIRWOMAN CAUGHT ME AS I WAS LEAVING, HANDED ME SOME FILES, AND ASKED ME TO MAKE A VIDEO...
MAKE A VIDEO TO UP OUR ONLINE PRESENCE.
HUH?
BUT I CAN'T MAKE HEADS OR TAILS OF THIS SOFTWARE.
YOU KNOW, I COU—
NO.
SKIPA (BLUNT)

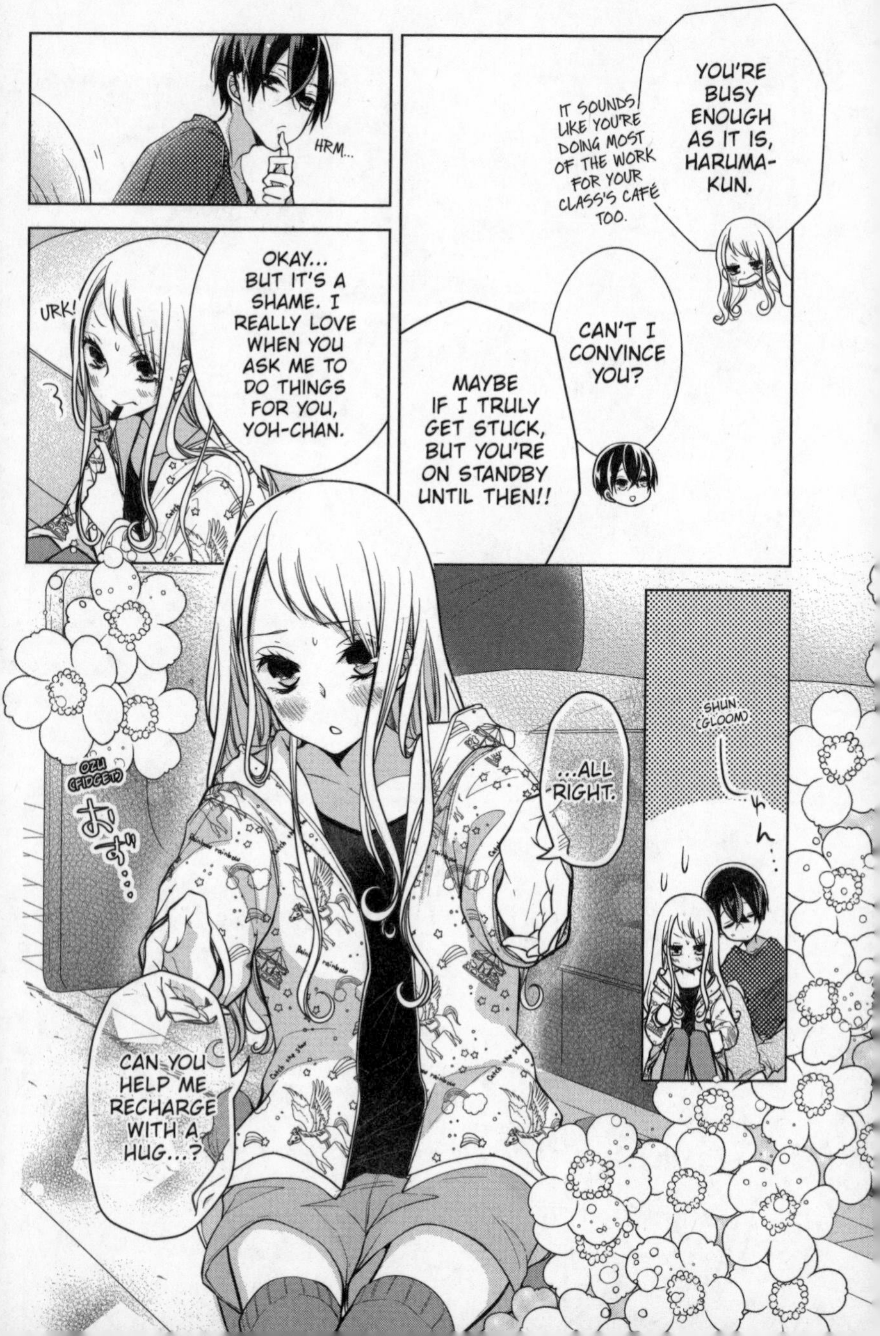
YOU'RE BUSY ENOUGH AS IT IS, HARUMA-KUN.
IT SOUNDS LIKE YOU'RE DOING MOST OF THE WORK FOR YOUR CLASS'S CAFÉ TOO.
CAN'T I CONVINCE YOU?
MAYBE IF I TRULY GET STUCK, BUT YOU'RE ON STANDBY UNTIL THEN!!
HRM...
URK!
OKAY... BUT IT'S A SHAME. I REALLY LOVE WHEN YOU ASK ME TO DO THINGS FOR YOU, YOH-CHAN.
SHUN (GLOOM)
しゅん…
...ALL RIGHT.
OZU (FIDGET)
おず…
CAN YOU HELP ME RECHARGE WITH A HUG...?

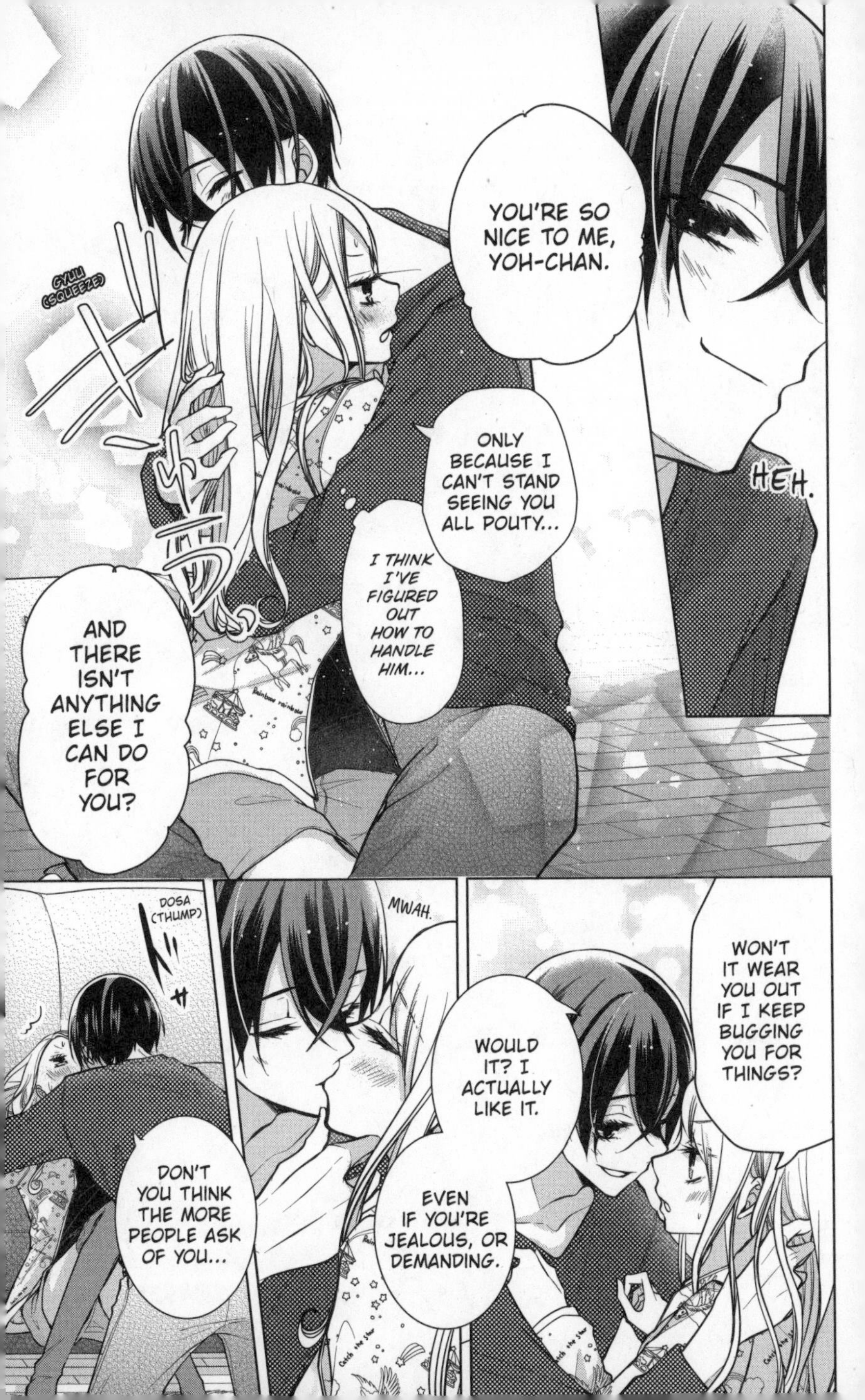
YOU'RE SO NICE TO ME, YOH-CHAN.
HEH.
GYUU (SQUEEZE)
ONLY BECAUSE I CAN'T STAND SEEING YOU ALL POUTY...
I THINK I'VE FIGURED OUT HOW TO HANDLE HIM...
AND THERE ISN'T ANYTHING ELSE I CAN DO FOR YOU?
WON'T IT WEAR YOU OUT IF I KEEP BUGGING YOU FOR THINGS?
WOULD IT? I ACTUALLY LIKE IT.
EVEN IF YOU'RE JEALOUS, OR DEMANDING.
MWAH.
DON'T YOU THINK THE MORE PEOPLE ASK OF YOU...
DOSA (THUMP)

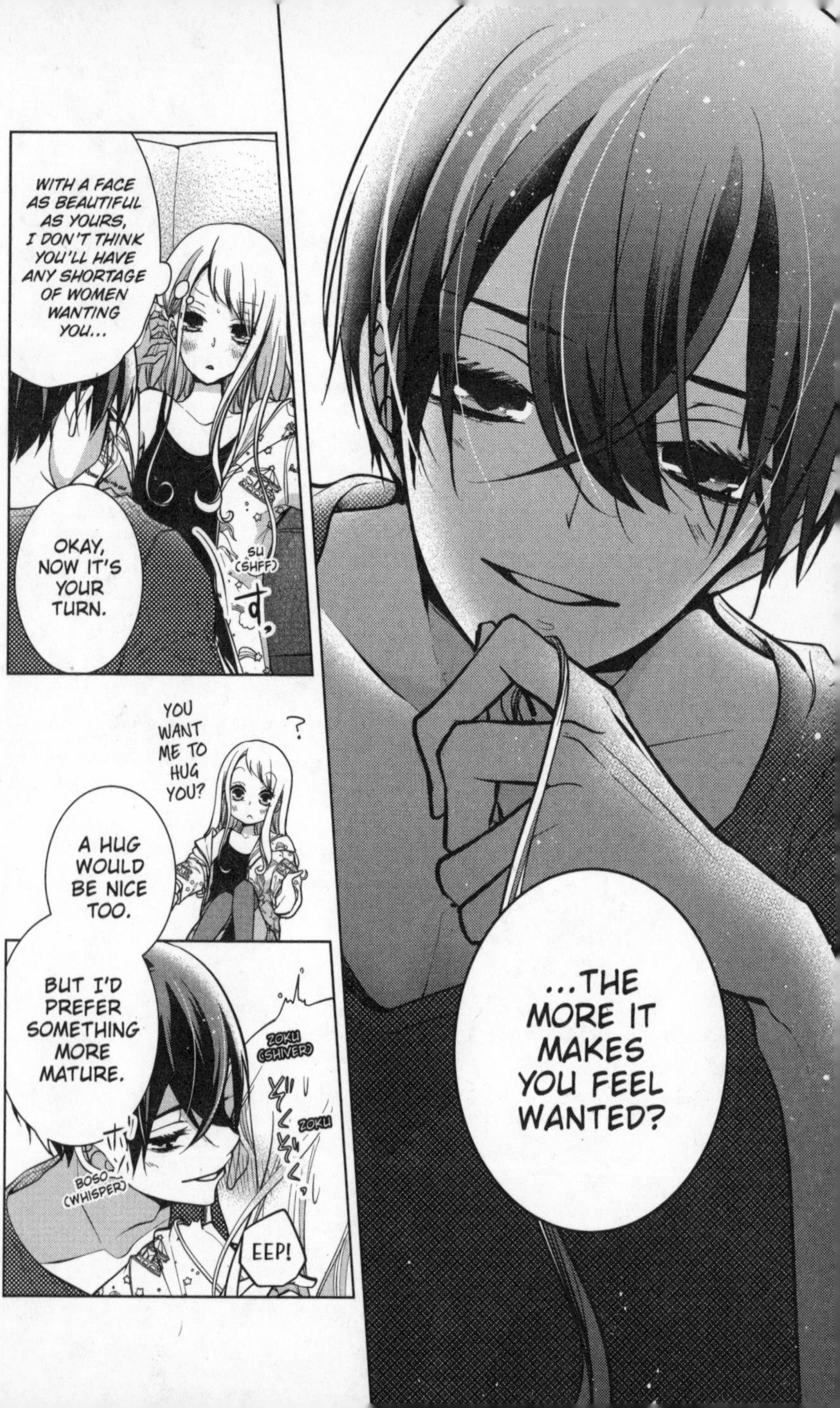
...THE MORE IT MAKES YOU FEEL WANTED?
WITH A FACE AS BEAUTIFUL AS YOURS, I DON'T THINK YOU'LL HAVE ANY SHORTAGE OF WOMEN WANTING YOU...
OKAY, NOW IT'S YOUR TURN.
SU (SHFF)
YOU WANT ME TO HUG YOU?
?
A HUG WOULD BE NICE TOO.
BUT I'D PREFER SOMETHING MORE MATURE.
ZOKU (SHIVER)
ZOKU
BOSO (WHISPER)
EEP!

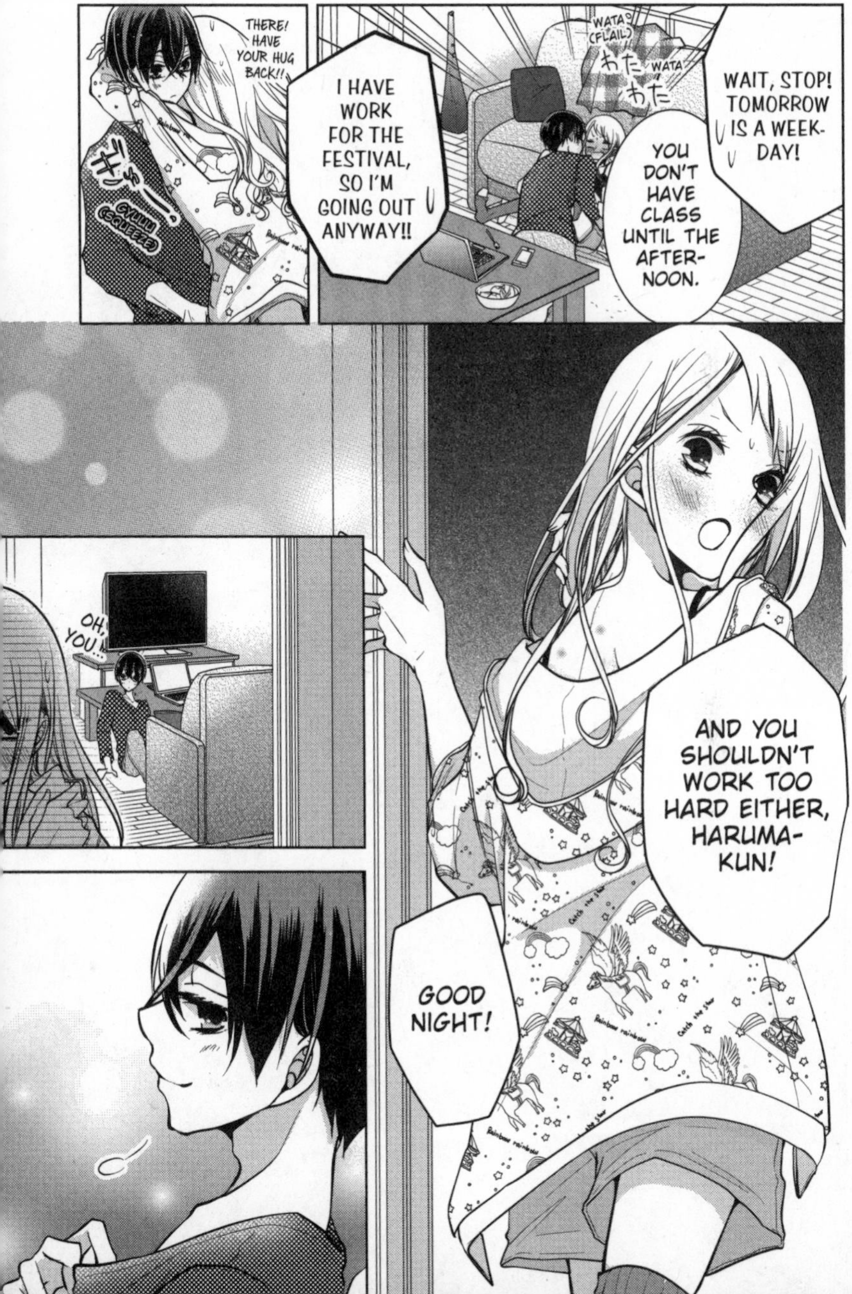

WAIT, STOP! TOMORROW IS A WEEK-DAY!
WATA (FLAIL) わた WATA わた
YOU DON'T HAVE CLASS UNTIL THE AFTER-NOON.
I HAVE WORK FOR THE FESTIVAL, SO I'M GOING OUT ANYWAY!!
THERE! HAVE YOUR HUG BACK!!
ギュー GYUUU (SQUEEZE)
AND YOU SHOULDN'T WORK TOO HARD EITHER, HARUMA-KUN!
GOOD NIGHT!
OH, YOU...!

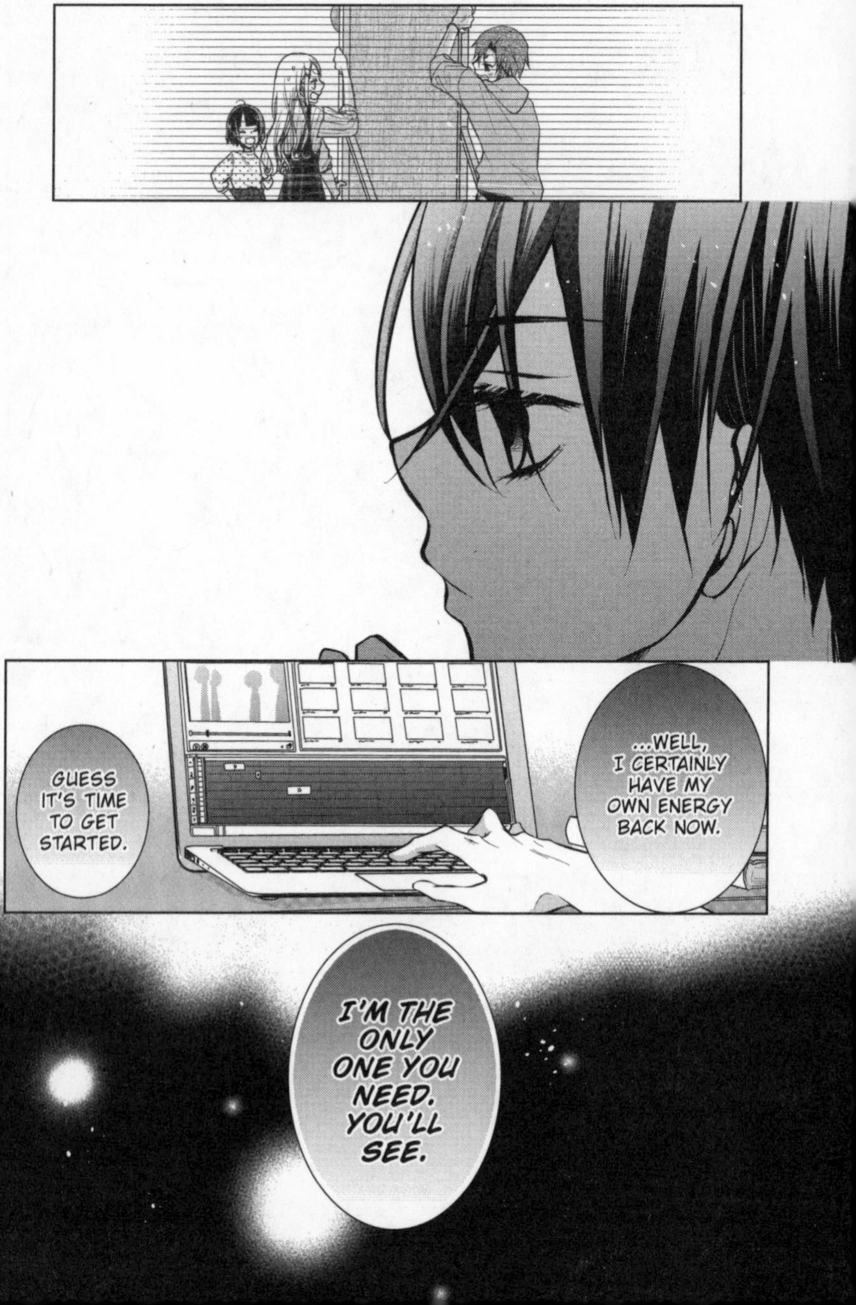
...WELL, I CERTAINLY HAVE MY OWN ENERGY BACK NOW.
GUESS IT'S TIME TO GET STARTED.
I'M THE ONLY ONE YOU NEED. YOU'LL SEE.

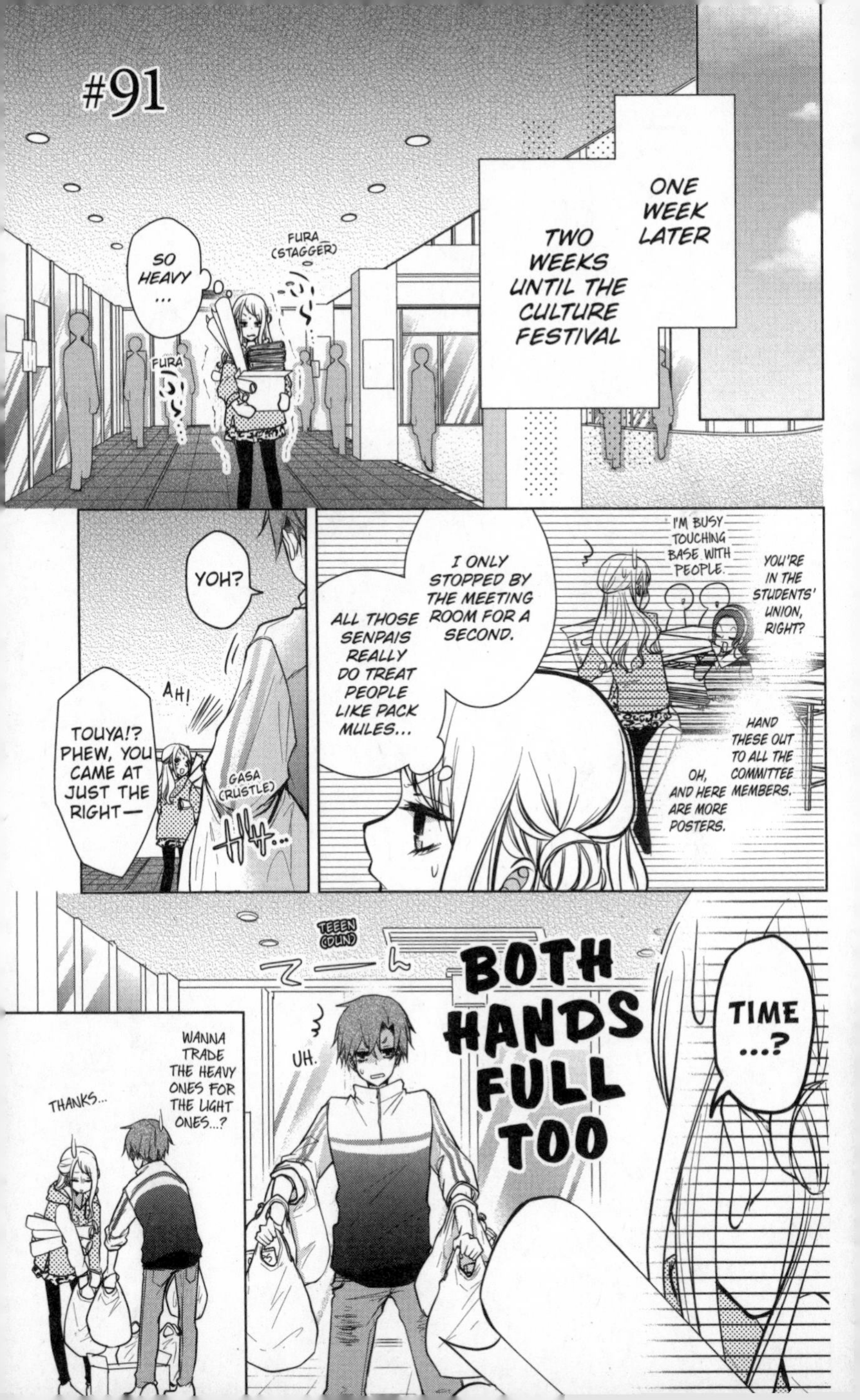
#91
ONE WEEK LATER
TWO WEEKS UNTIL THE CULTURE FESTIVAL
FURA (STAGGER)
SO HEAVY ...
FURA
YOU'RE IN THE STUDENTS' UNION, RIGHT?
I'M BUSY TOUCHING BASE WITH PEOPLE.
HAND THESE OUT TO ALL THE COMMITTEE MEMBERS.
OH, AND HERE ARE MORE POSTERS.
I ONLY STOPPED BY THE MEETING ROOM FOR A SECOND.
ALL THOSE SENPAIS REALLY DO TREAT PEOPLE LIKE PACK MULES...
YOH?
AH!
TOUYA!? PHEW, YOU CAME AT JUST THE RIGHT—
GASA (RUSTLE)
TIME ...?
TEEEN (DUN)
BOTH HANDS FULL TOO
UH.
WANNA TRADE THE HEAVY ONES FOR THE LIGHT ONES...?
THANKS...

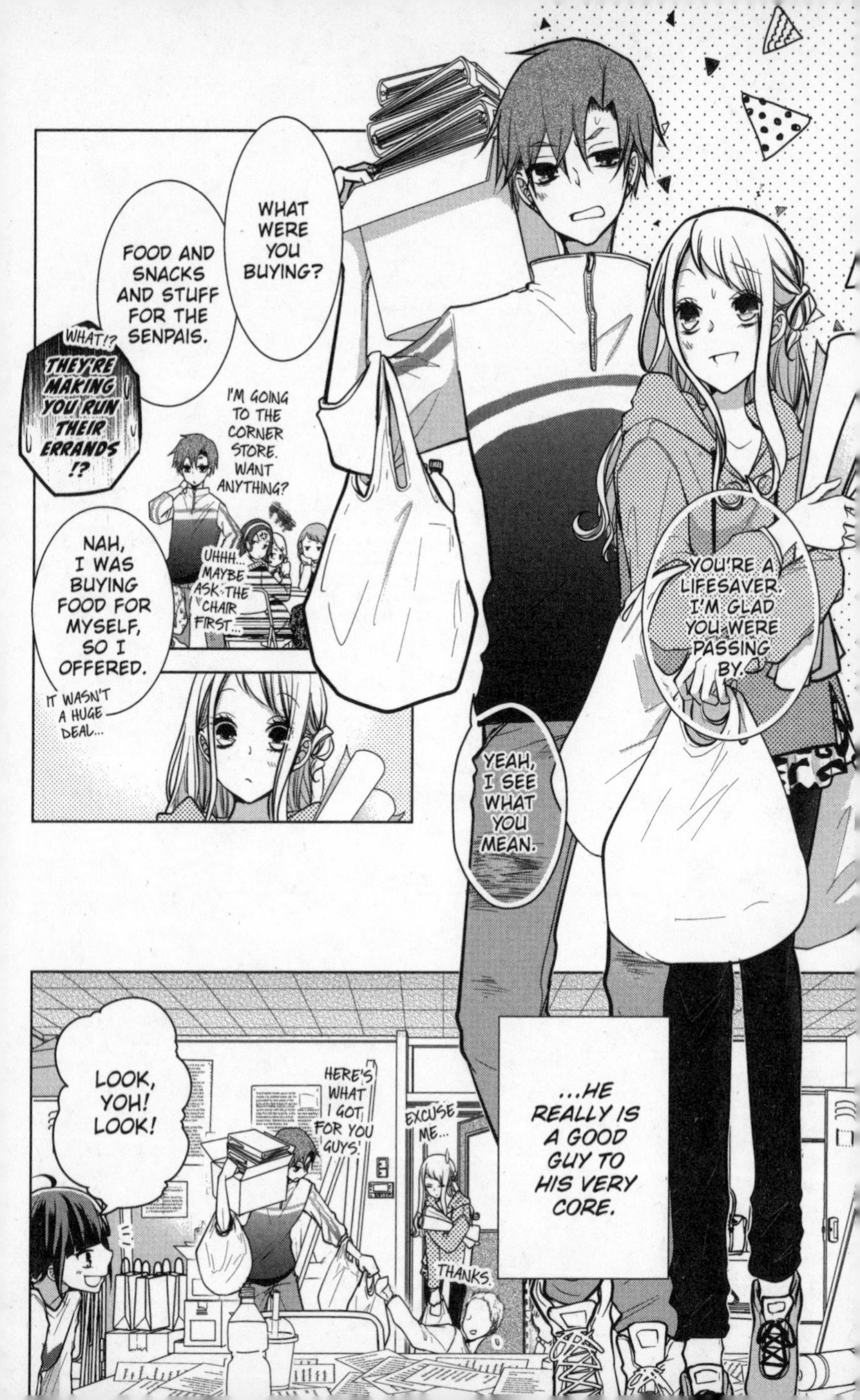
YOU'RE A LIFESAVER. I'M GLAD YOU WERE PASSING BY.
WHAT WERE YOU BUYING?
FOOD AND SNACKS AND STUFF FOR THE SENPAIS.
WHAT!?
THEY'RE MAKING YOU RUN THEIR ERRANDS !?
I'M GOING TO THE CORNER STORE. WANT ANYTHING?
UHHH... MAYBE ASK THE CHAIR FIRST...
NAH, I WAS BUYING FOOD FOR MYSELF, SO I OFFERED.
IT WASN'T A HUGE DEAL...
YEAH, I SEE WHAT YOU MEAN.
...HE REALLY IS A GOOD GUY TO HIS VERY CORE.
EXCUSE ME...
THANKS.
HERE'S WHAT I GOT FOR YOU GUYS!
LOOK, YOH! LOOK!

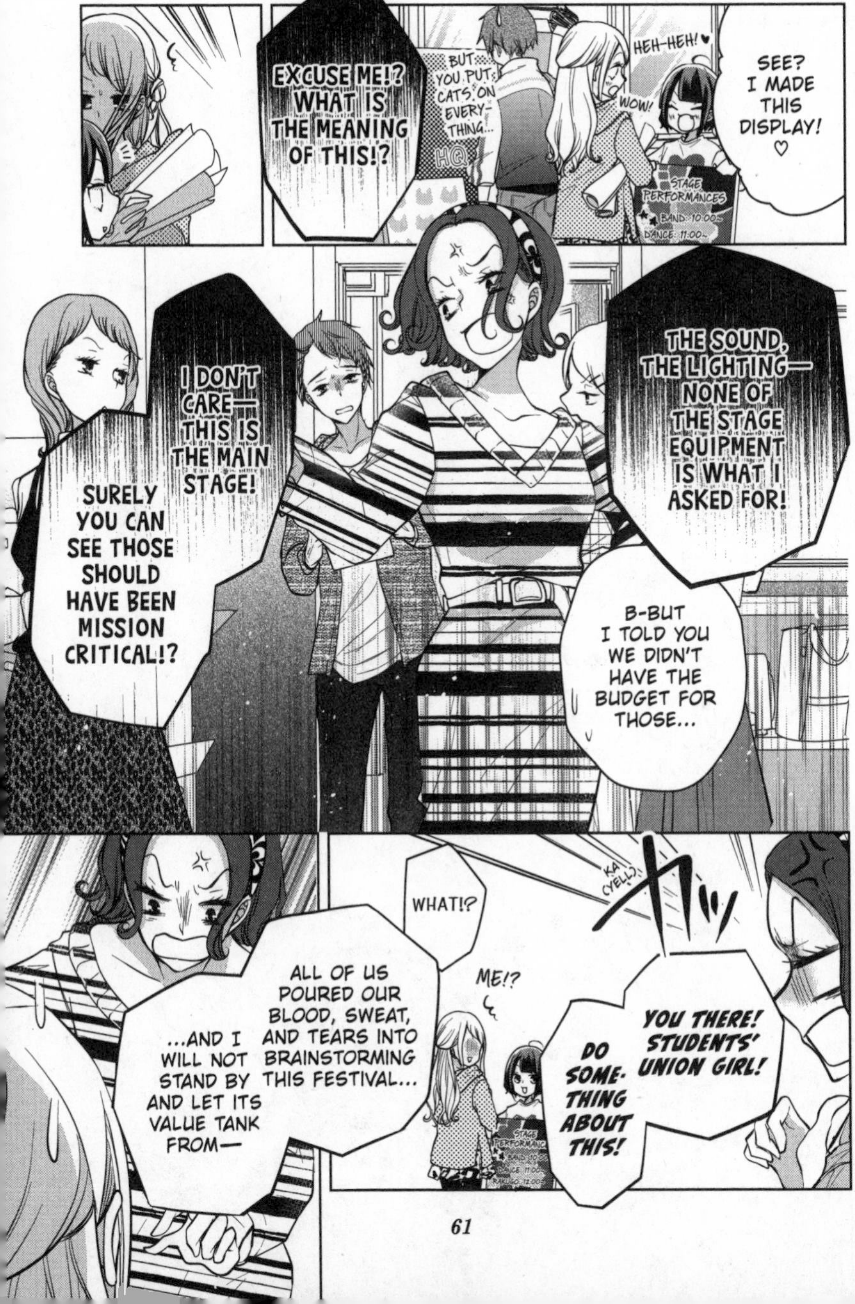
SEE? I MADE THIS DISPLAY! ♡
HEH-HEH! ♥
WOW!
STAGE PERFORMANCES
BAND: 10:00~
DANCE: 11:00~
BUT YOU PUT CATS ON EVERY-THING...
HQ
EXCUSE ME!? WHAT IS THE MEANING OF THIS!?
THE SOUND, THE LIGHTING—NONE OF THE STAGE EQUIPMENT IS WHAT I ASKED FOR!
B-BUT I TOLD YOU WE DIDN'T HAVE THE BUDGET FOR THOSE...
I DON'T CARE—THIS IS THE MAIN STAGE!
SURELY YOU CAN SEE THOSE SHOULD HAVE BEEN MISSION CRITICAL!?
KA (YELL)
YOU THERE! STUDENTS' UNION GIRL!
DO SOME-THING ABOUT THIS!
ME!?
WHAT!?
ALL OF US POURED OUR BLOOD, SWEAT, AND TEARS INTO BRAINSTORMING THIS FESTIVAL...
...AND I WILL NOT STAND BY AND LET ITS VALUE TANK FROM—

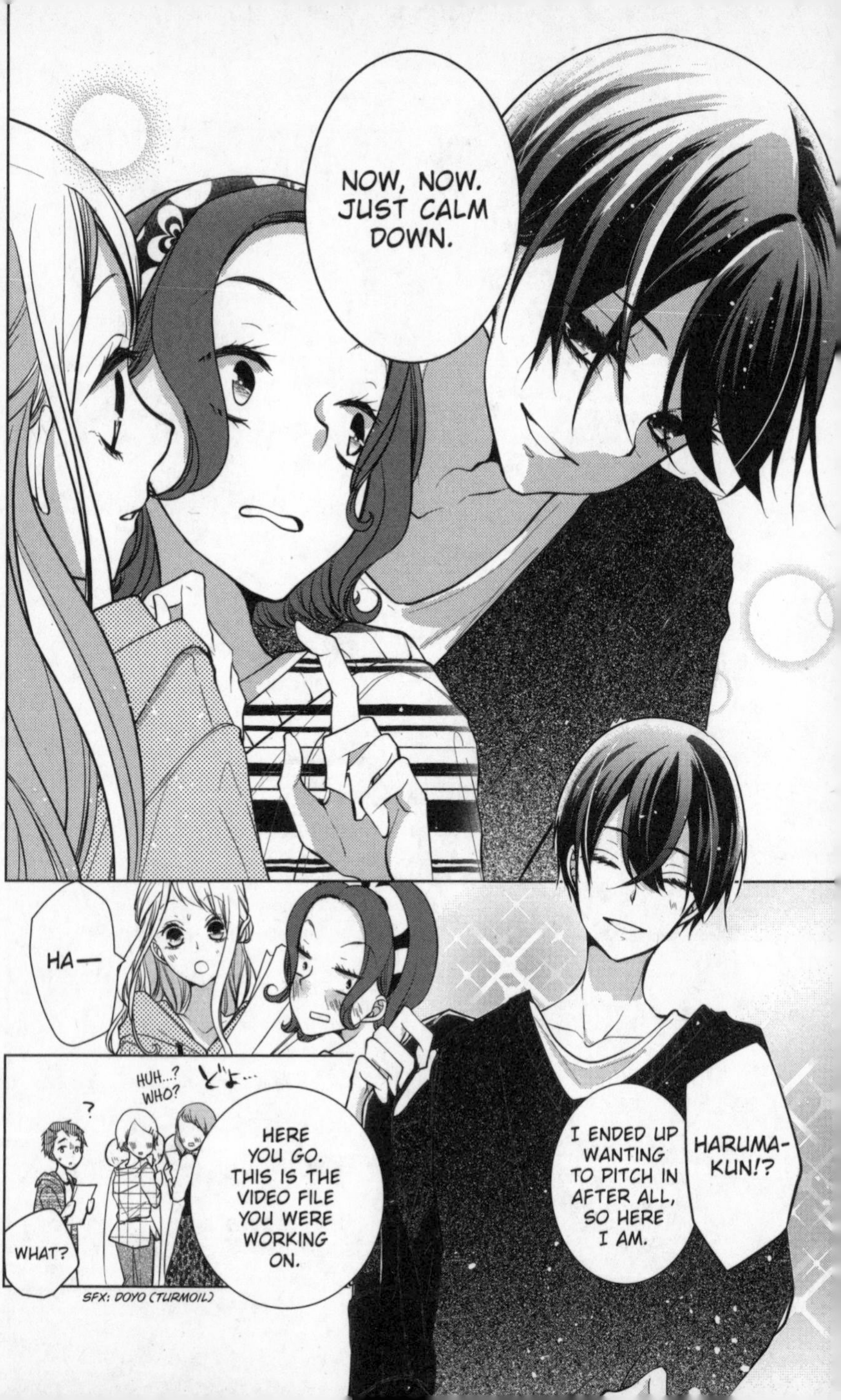
NOW, NOW. JUST CALM DOWN.
HA—
HARUMA-KUN!?
I ENDED UP WANTING TO PITCH IN AFTER ALL, SO HERE I AM.
HERE YOU GO. THIS IS THE VIDEO FILE YOU WERE WORKING ON.
HUH...? WHO?
どよ…
?
WHAT?
SFX: DOYO (TURMOIL)

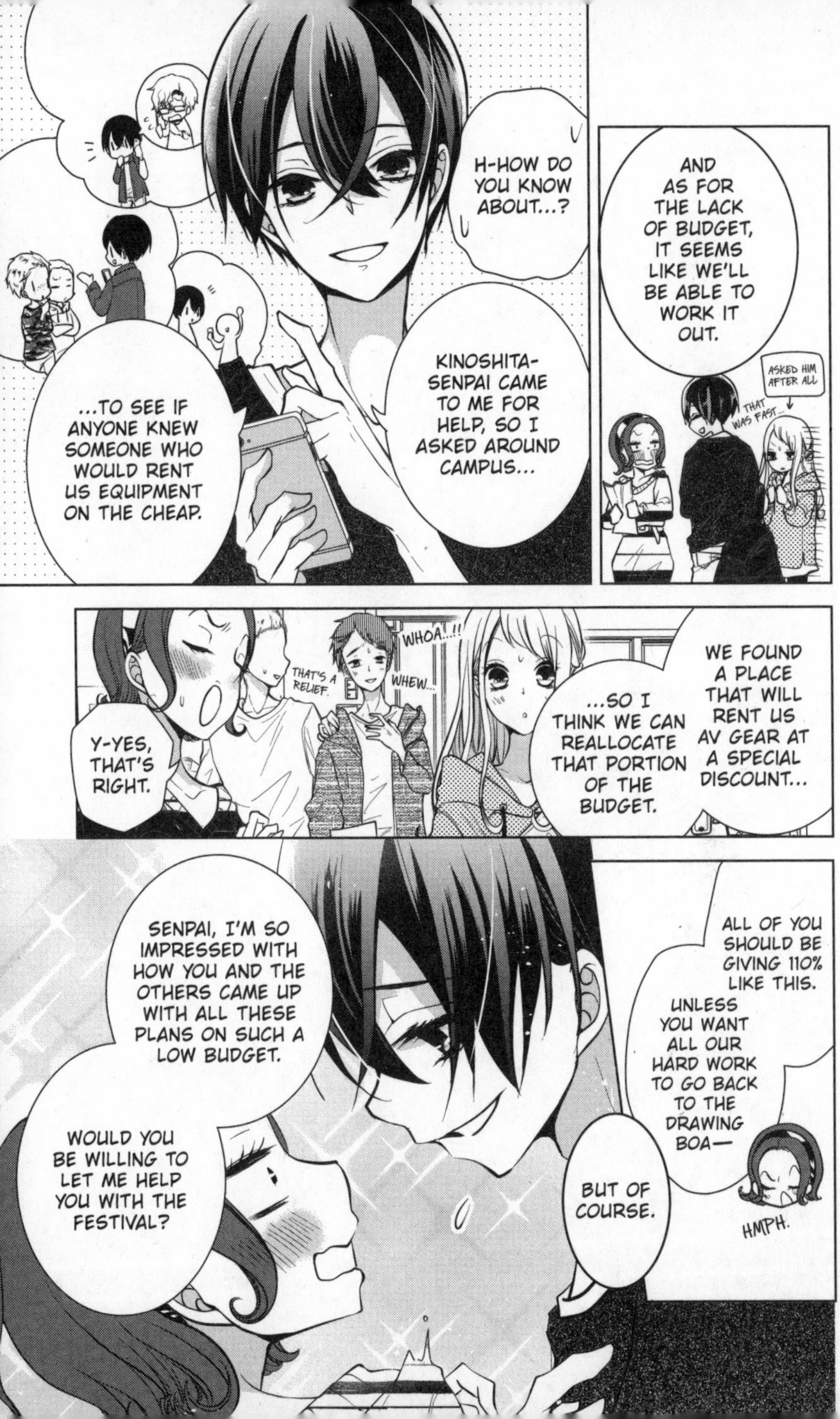
AND AS FOR THE LACK OF BUDGET, IT SEEMS LIKE WE'LL BE ABLE TO WORK IT OUT.
ASKED HIM AFTER ALL
THAT WAS FAST...
H-HOW DO YOU KNOW ABOUT...?
KINOSHITA-SENPAI CAME TO ME FOR HELP, SO I ASKED AROUND CAMPUS...
...TO SEE IF ANYONE KNEW SOMEONE WHO WOULD RENT US EQUIPMENT ON THE CHEAP.
WE FOUND A PLACE THAT WILL RENT US AV GEAR AT A SPECIAL DISCOUNT...
...SO I THINK WE CAN REALLOCATE THAT PORTION OF THE BUDGET.
WHOA...!!
WHEW...
THAT'S A RELIEF.
Y-YES, THAT'S RIGHT.
ALL OF YOU SHOULD BE GIVING 110% LIKE THIS.
UNLESS YOU WANT ALL OUR HARD WORK TO GO BACK TO THE DRAWING BOA—
HMPH.
BUT OF COURSE.
SENPAI, I'M SO IMPRESSED WITH HOW YOU AND THE OTHERS CAME UP WITH ALL THESE PLANS ON SUCH A LOW BUDGET.
WOULD YOU BE WILLING TO LET ME HELP YOU WITH THE FESTIVAL?

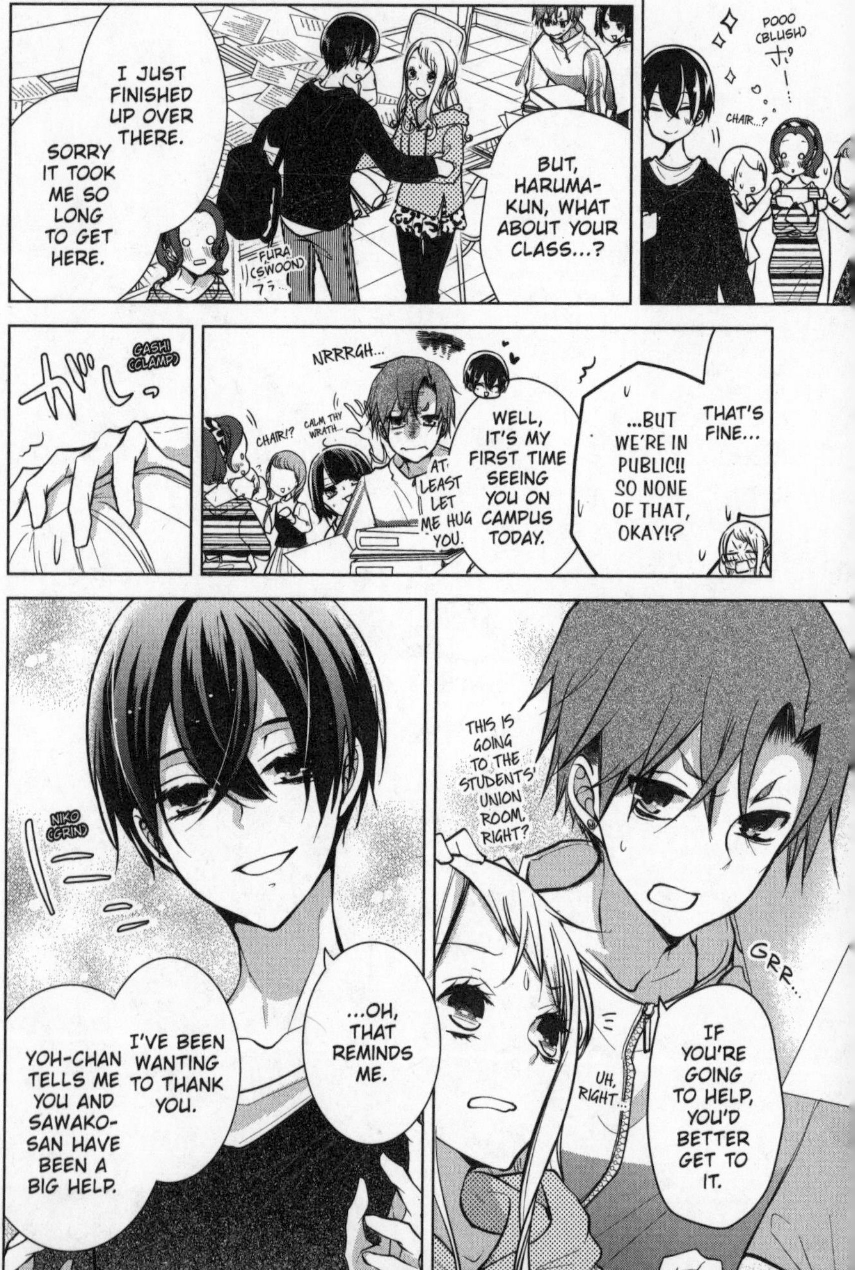
POOO (BLUSH)
CHAIR...?
BUT, HARUMA-KUN, WHAT ABOUT YOUR CLASS...?
I JUST FINISHED UP OVER THERE.
SORRY IT TOOK ME SO LONG TO GET HERE.
FURA (SWOON)
THAT'S FINE...
...BUT WE'RE IN PUBLIC!! SO NONE OF THAT, OKAY!?
WELL, IT'S MY FIRST TIME SEEING YOU ON CAMPUS TODAY.
AT LEAST LET ME HUG YOU.
NRRRGH...
CALM THY WRATH...
CHAIR!?
GASHI (CLAMP)
THIS IS GOING TO THE STUDENTS' UNION ROOM, RIGHT?
GRR...
IF YOU'RE GOING TO HELP, YOU'D BETTER GET TO IT.
UH, RIGHT...
...OH, THAT REMINDS ME.
I'VE BEEN WANTING TO THANK YOU.
YOH-CHAN TELLS ME YOU AND SAWAKO-SAN HAVE BEEN A BIG HELP.
NIKO (GRIN)

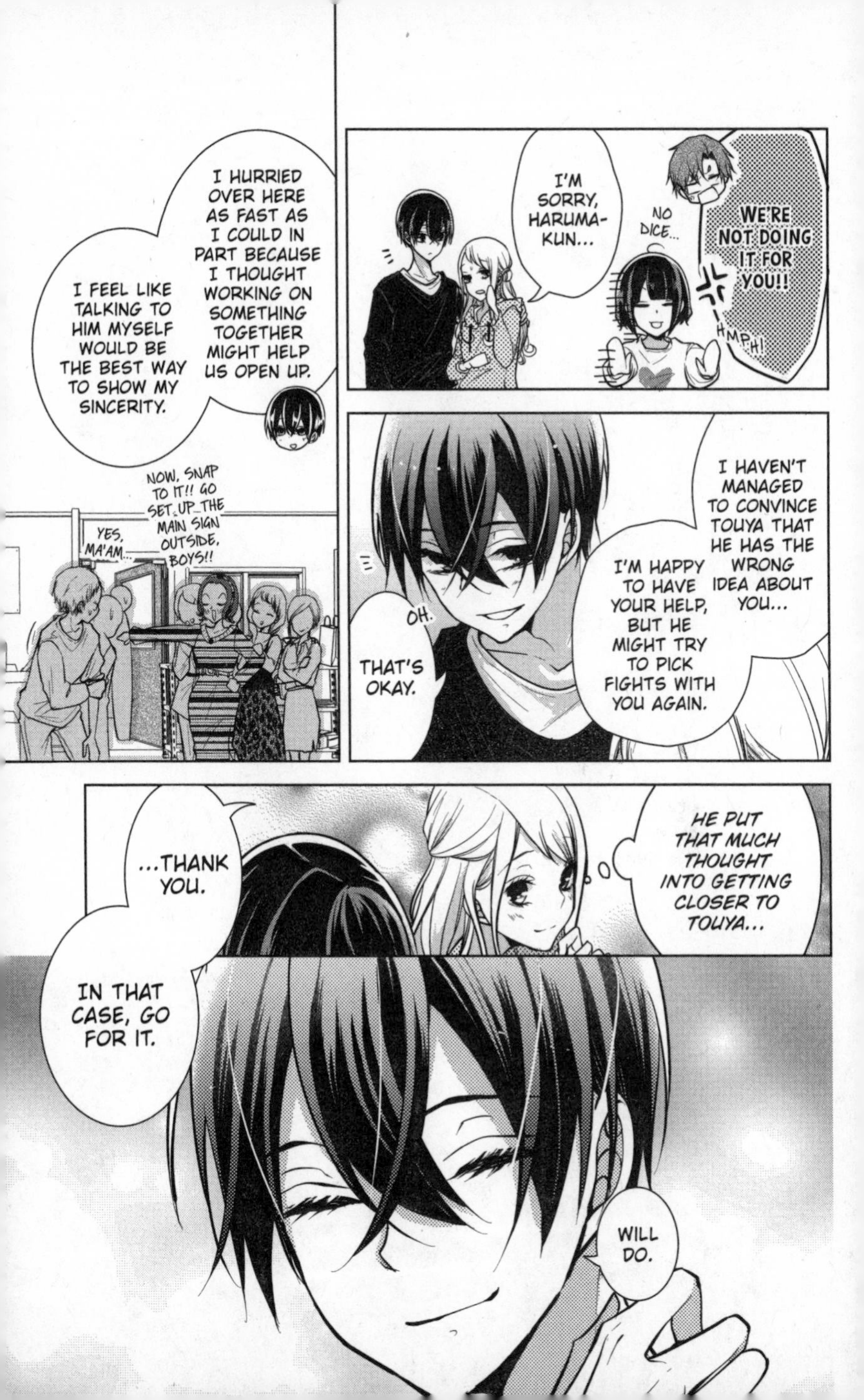
WE'RE NOT DOING IT FOR YOU!!
HMPH!
NO DICE...
I'M SORRY, HARUMA-KUN...
I HURRIED OVER HERE AS FAST AS I COULD IN PART BECAUSE I THOUGHT WORKING ON SOMETHING TOGETHER MIGHT HELP US OPEN UP.
I FEEL LIKE TALKING TO HIM MYSELF WOULD BE THE BEST WAY TO SHOW MY SINCERITY.
I HAVEN'T MANAGED TO CONVINCE TOUYA THAT HE HAS THE WRONG IDEA ABOUT YOU...
I'M HAPPY TO HAVE YOUR HELP, BUT HE MIGHT TRY TO PICK FIGHTS WITH YOU AGAIN.
OH.
THAT'S OKAY.
NOW, SNAP TO IT!! GO SET UP THE MAIN SIGN OUTSIDE, BOYS!!
YES, MA'AM...
HE PUT THAT MUCH THOUGHT INTO GETTING CLOSER TO TOUYA...
...THANK YOU.
IN THAT CASE, GO FOR IT.
WILL DO.

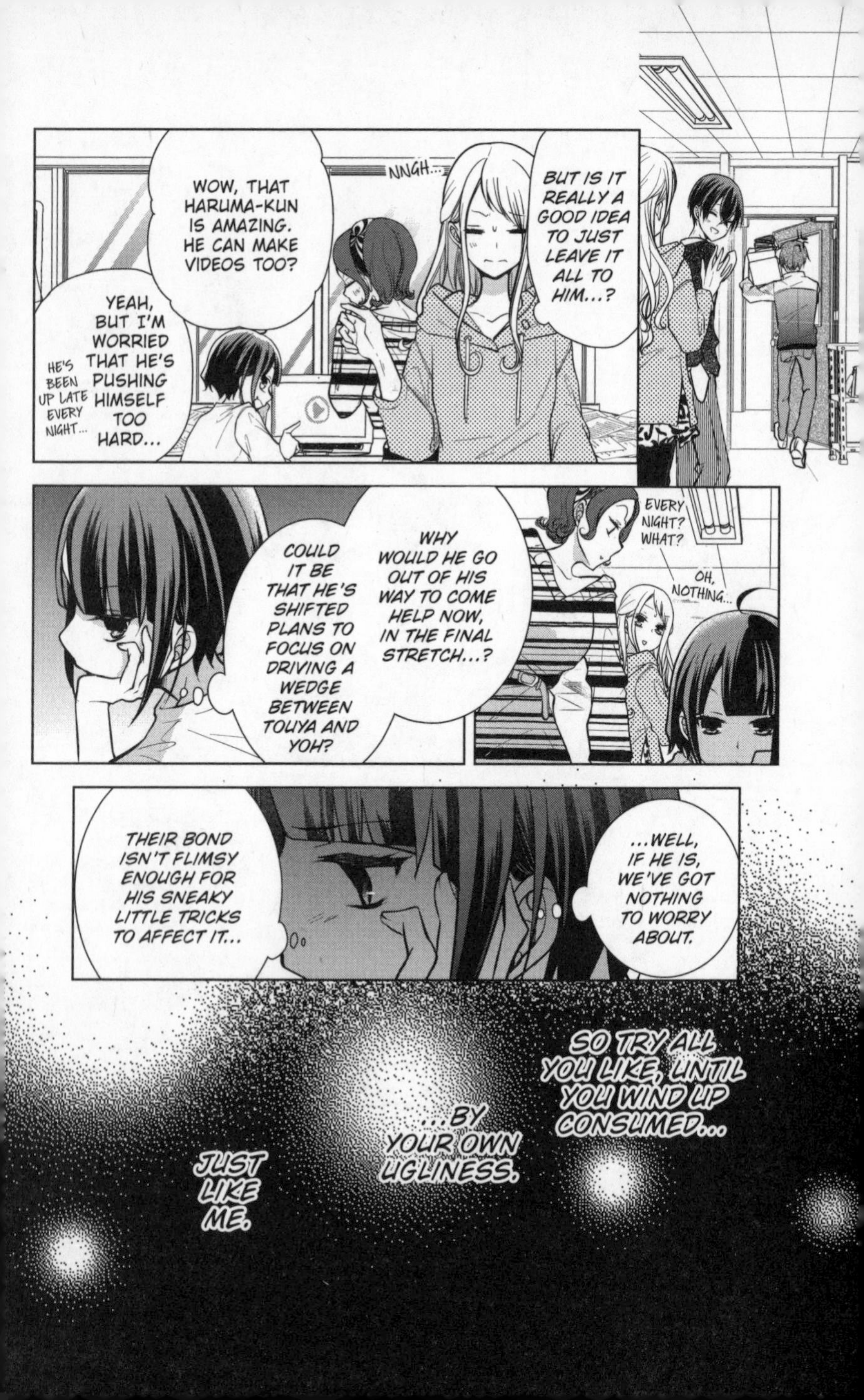
BUT IS IT REALLY A GOOD IDEA TO JUST LEAVE IT ALL TO HIM...?
NNGH...
WOW, THAT HARUMA-KUN IS AMAZING. HE CAN MAKE VIDEOS TOO?
YEAH, BUT I'M WORRIED THAT HE'S PUSHING HIMSELF TOO HARD...
HE'S BEEN UP LATE EVERY NIGHT...
EVERY NIGHT? WHAT?
OH, NOTHING...
WHY WOULD HE GO OUT OF HIS WAY TO COME HELP NOW, IN THE FINAL STRETCH...?
COULD IT BE THAT HE'S SHIFTED PLANS TO FOCUS ON DRIVING A WEDGE BETWEEN TOUYA AND YOH?
...WELL, IF HE IS, WE'VE GOT NOTHING TO WORRY ABOUT.
THEIR BOND ISN'T FLIMSY ENOUGH FOR HIS SNEAKY LITTLE TRICKS TO AFFECT IT...
SO TRY ALL YOU LIKE, UNTIL YOU WIND UP CONSUMED...
...BY YOUR OWN UGLINESS.
JUST LIKE ME.

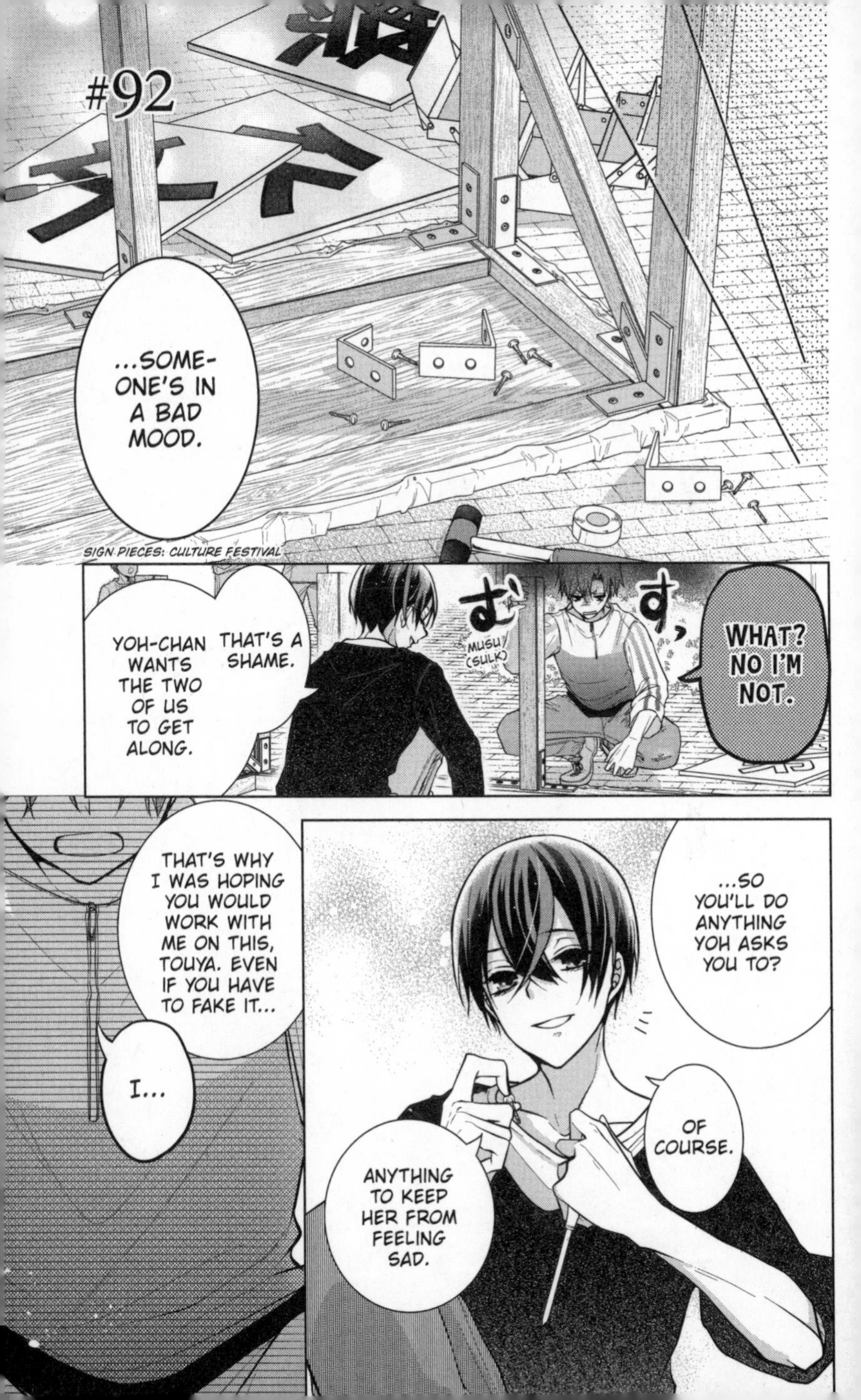
#92
...SOME-ONE'S IN A BAD MOOD.
SIGN PIECES: CULTURE FESTIVAL
WHAT? NO I'M NOT.
むす,
MUSU (SULK)
THAT'S A SHAME.
YOH-CHAN WANTS THE TWO OF US TO GET ALONG.
...SO YOU'LL DO ANYTHING YOH ASKS YOU TO?
OF COURSE.
ANYTHING TO KEEP HER FROM FEELING SAD.
THAT'S WHY I WAS HOPING YOU WOULD WORK WITH ME ON THIS, TOUYA. EVEN IF YOU HAVE TO FAKE IT...
I...

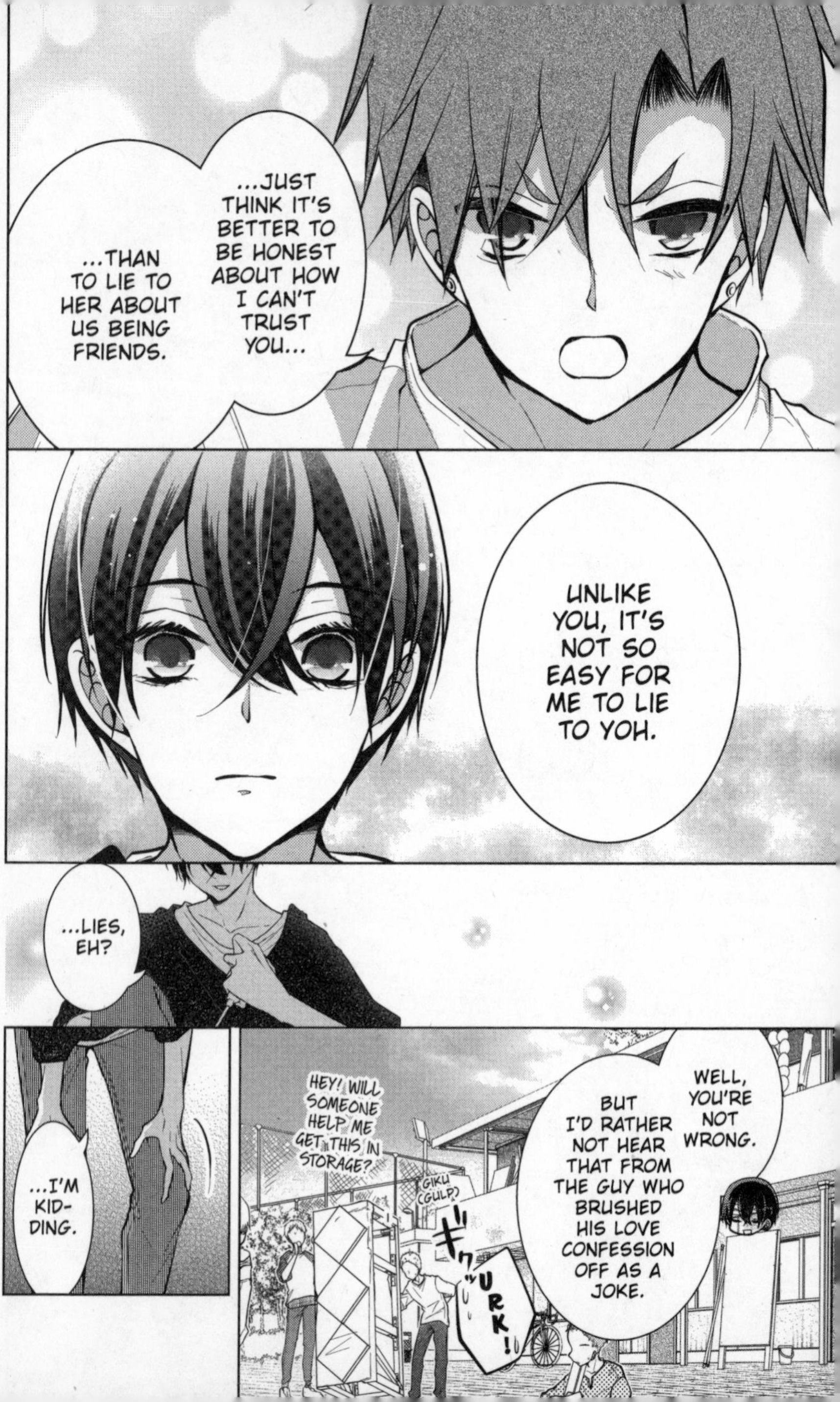
...JUST THINK IT'S BETTER TO BE HONEST ABOUT HOW I CAN'T TRUST YOU...
...THAN TO LIE TO HER ABOUT US BEING FRIENDS.
UNLIKE YOU, IT'S NOT SO EASY FOR ME TO LIE TO YOH.
...LIES, EH?
WELL, YOU'RE NOT WRONG.
BUT I'D RATHER NOT HEAR THAT FROM THE GUY WHO BRUSHED HIS LOVE CONFESSION OFF AS A JOKE.
HEY! WILL SOMEONE HELP ME GET THIS IN STORAGE?
GIKU (GULP)
URK!
...I'M KID-DING.

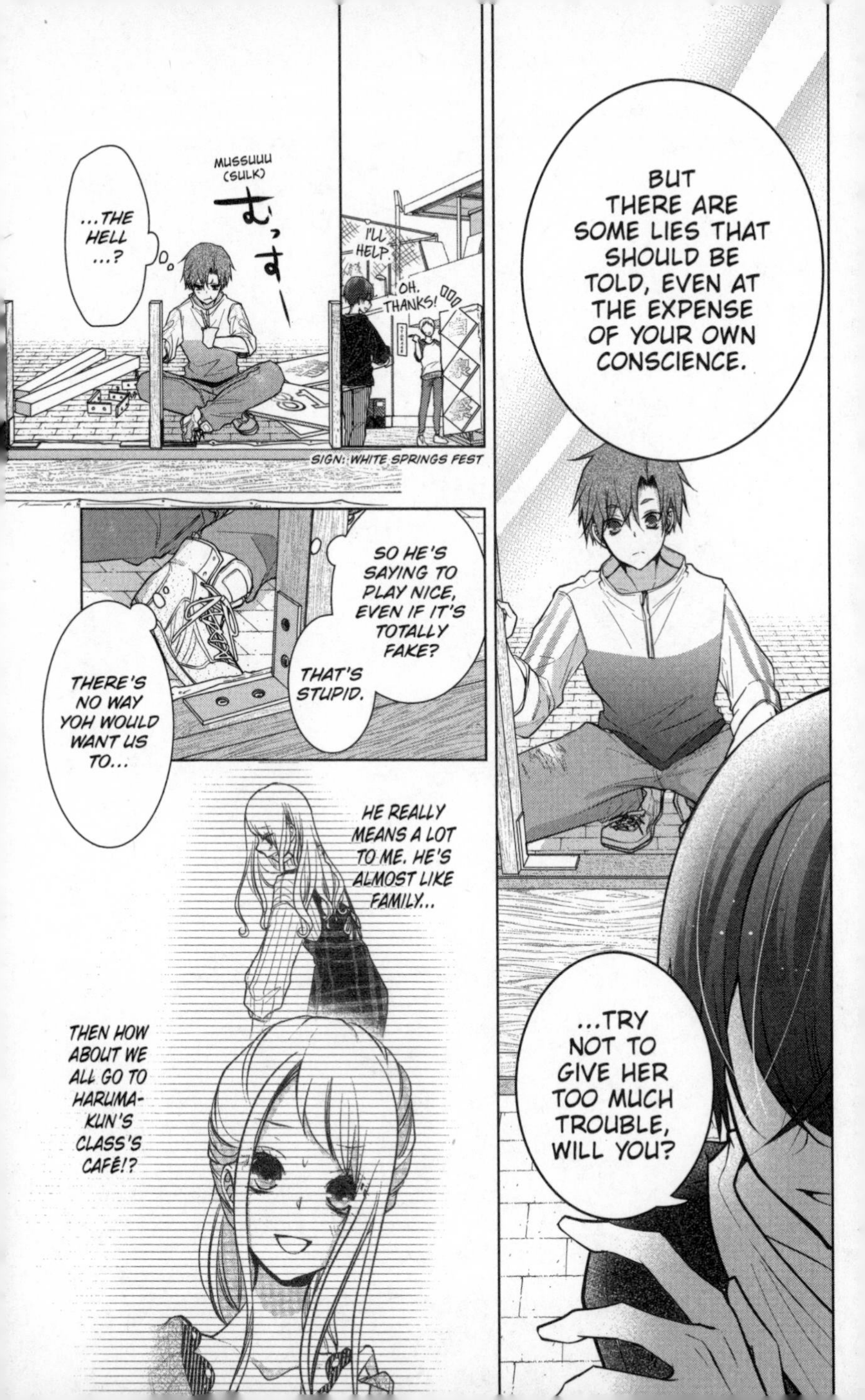
BUT THERE ARE SOME LIES THAT SHOULD BE TOLD, EVEN AT THE EXPENSE OF YOUR OWN CONSCIENCE.
...TRY NOT TO GIVE HER TOO MUCH TROUBLE, WILL YOU?
I'LL HELP.
OH. THANKS!
SIGN: WHITE SPRINGS FEST
MUSSUUU (SULK)
...THE HELL ...?
SO HE'S SAYING TO PLAY NICE, EVEN IF IT'S TOTALLY FAKE?
THAT'S STUPID.
THERE'S NO WAY YOH WOULD WANT US TO...
HE REALLY MEANS A LOT TO ME. HE'S ALMOST LIKE FAMILY...
THEN HOW ABOUT WE ALL GO TO HARUMA-KUN'S CLASS'S CAFÉ!?

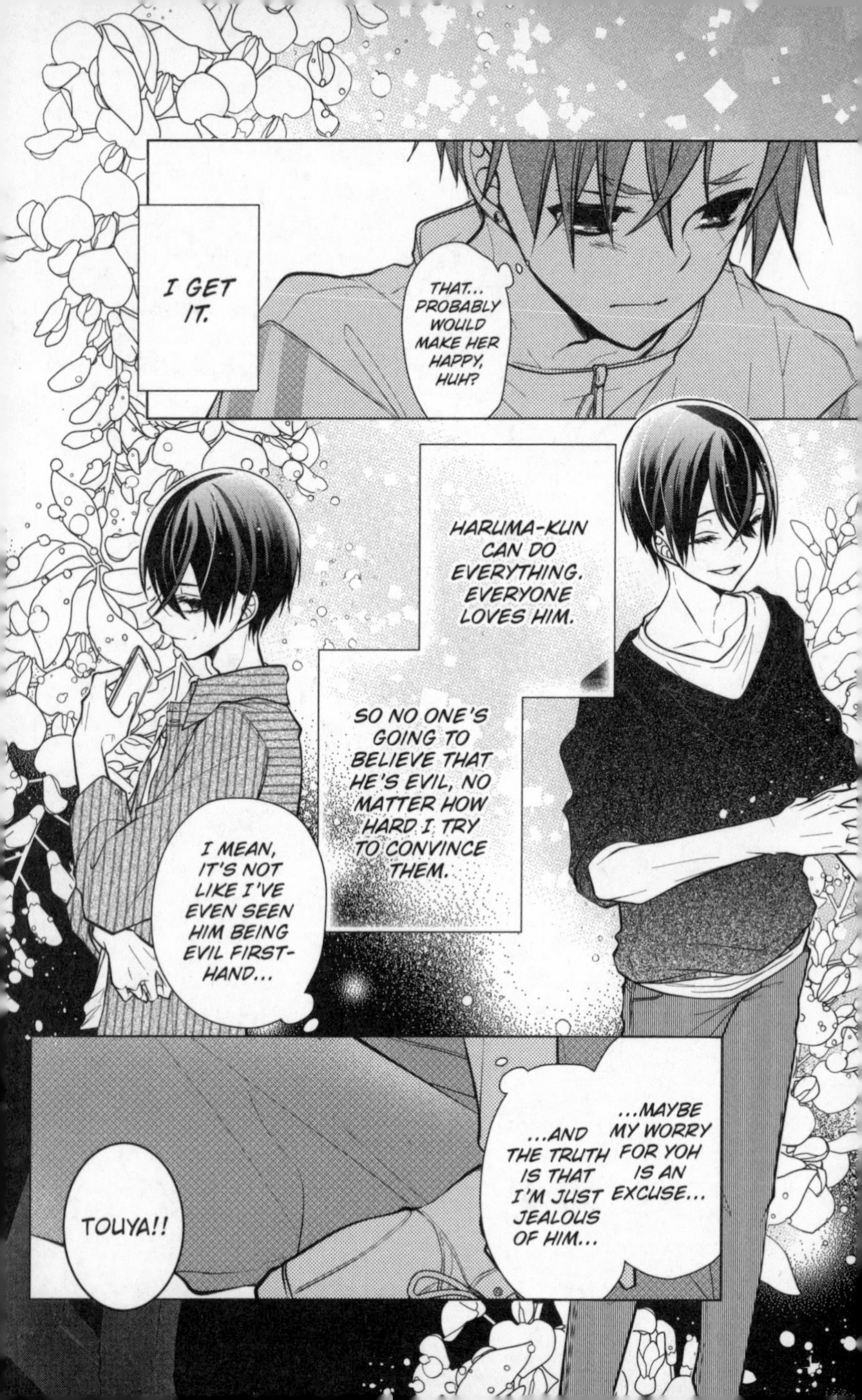
THAT... PROBABLY WOULD MAKE HER HAPPY, HUH?
I GET IT.
HARUMA-KUN CAN DO EVERYTHING. EVERYONE LOVES HIM.
SO NO ONE'S GOING TO BELIEVE THAT HE'S EVIL, NO MATTER HOW HARD I TRY TO CONVINCE THEM.
I MEAN, IT'S NOT LIKE I'VE EVEN SEEN HIM BEING EVIL FIRST-HAND...
...MAYBE MY WORRY FOR YOH IS AN EXCUSE...
...AND THE TRUTH IS THAT I'M JUST JEALOUS OF HIM...
TOUYA!!

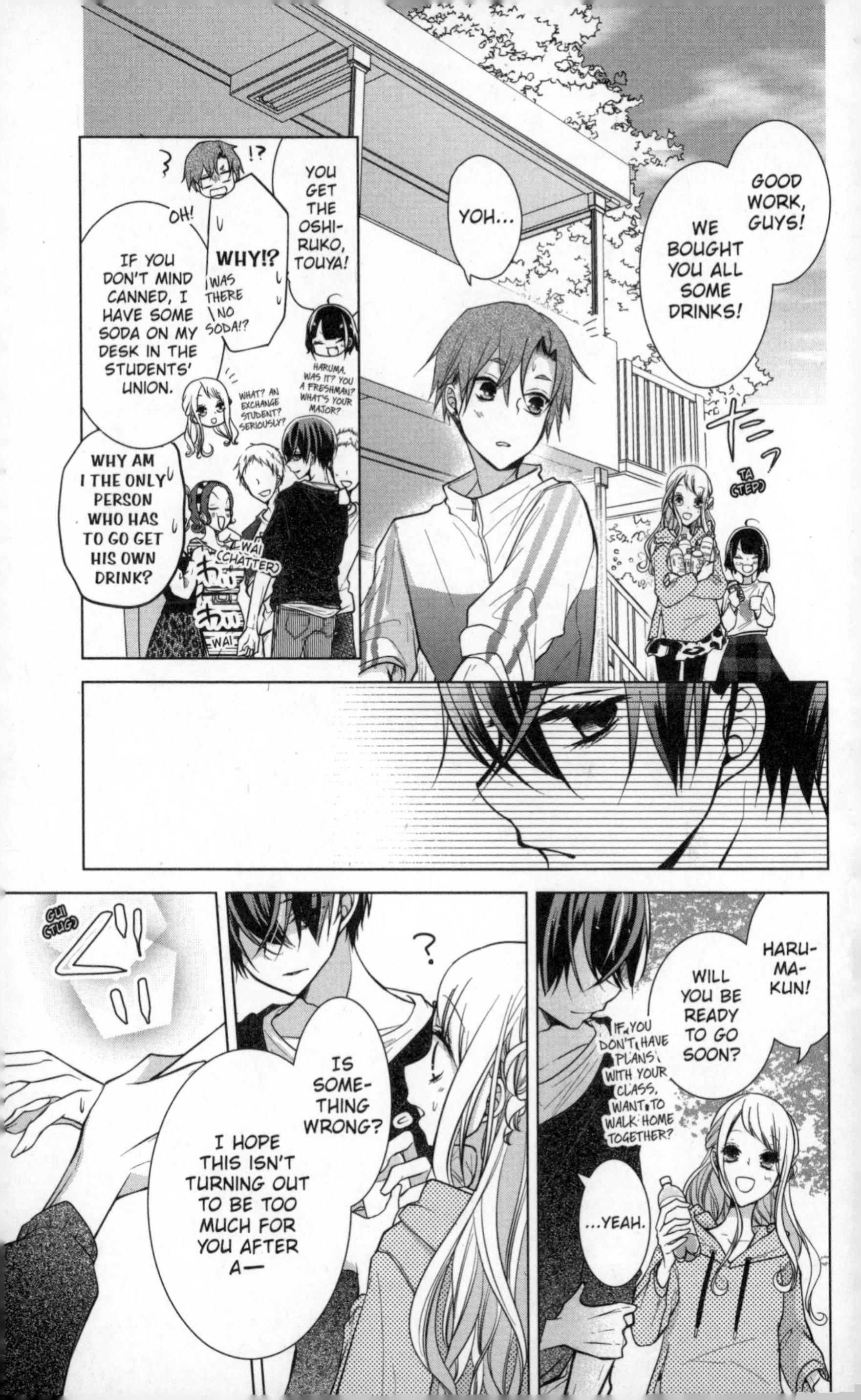

GOOD WORK, GUYS!
WE BOUGHT YOU ALL SOME DRINKS!
TA (STEP)
YOH...
YOU GET THE OSHIRUKO, TOUYA!
!?
WHY!? WAS THERE NO SODA!?
OH!
IF YOU DON'T MIND CANNED, I HAVE SOME SODA ON MY DESK IN THE STUDENTS' UNION.
HARUMA, WAS IT? YOU A FRESHMAN? WHAT'S YOUR MAJOR?
WHAT? AN EXCHANGE STUDENT? SERIOUSLY?
WHY AM I THE ONLY PERSON WHO HAS TO GO GET HIS OWN DRINK?
WAI (CHATTER)
WAI
HARUMA-KUN!
WILL YOU BE READY TO GO SOON?
IF YOU DON'T HAVE PLANS WITH YOUR CLASS, WANT TO WALK HOME TOGETHER?
...YEAH.
?
IS SOMETHING WRONG?
I HOPE THIS ISN'T TURNING OUT TO BE TOO MUCH FOR YOU AFTER A—
GUI (TUG)

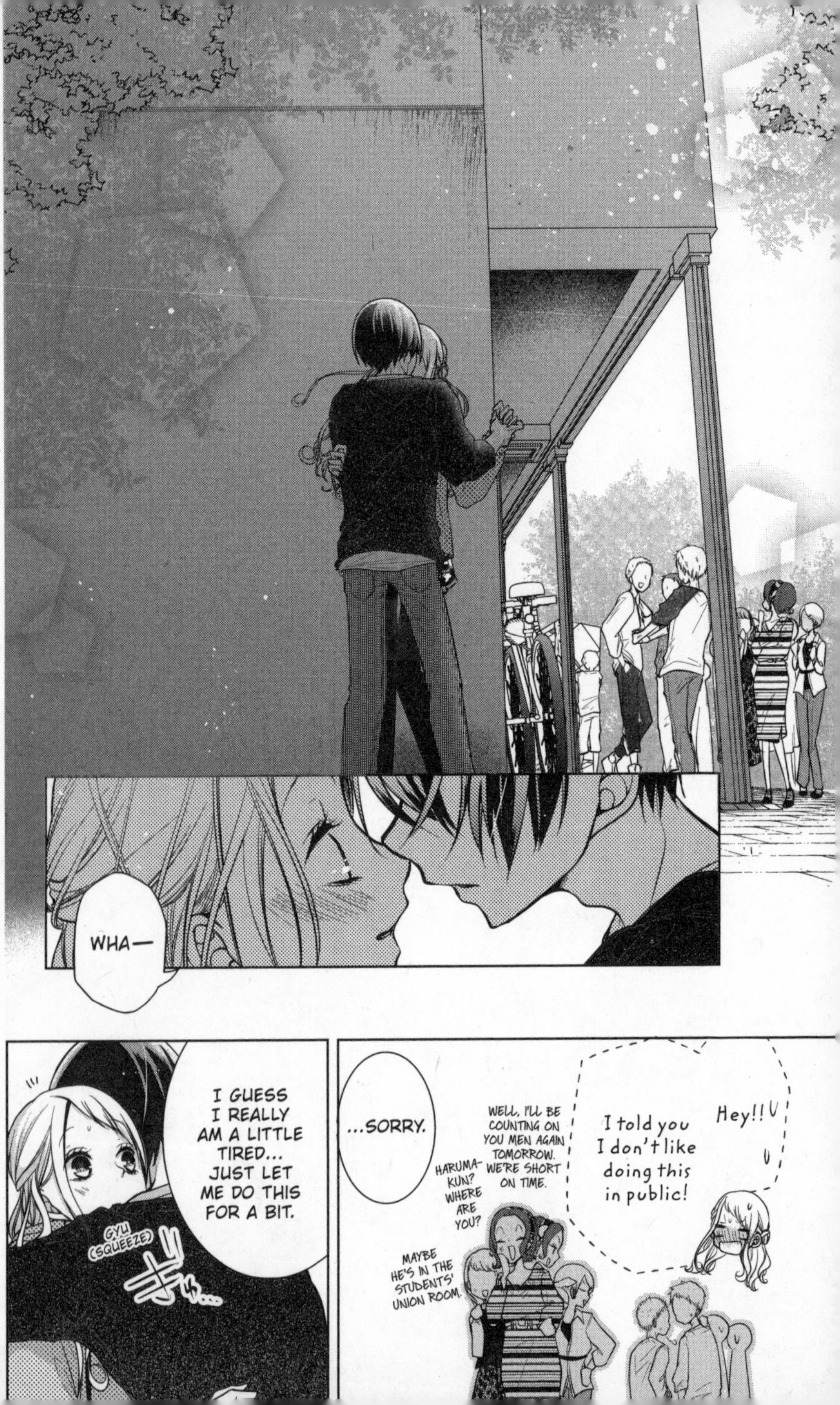
WHA—
Hey!!
I told you I don't like doing this in public!
WELL, I'LL BE COUNTING ON YOU MEN AGAIN TOMORROW. WE'RE SHORT ON TIME.
...SORRY.
HARUMA-KUN? WHERE ARE YOU?
MAYBE HE'S IN THE STUDENTS' UNION ROOM.
I GUESS I REALLY AM A LITTLE TIRED... JUST LET ME DO THIS FOR A BIT.
GYU (SQUEEZE)

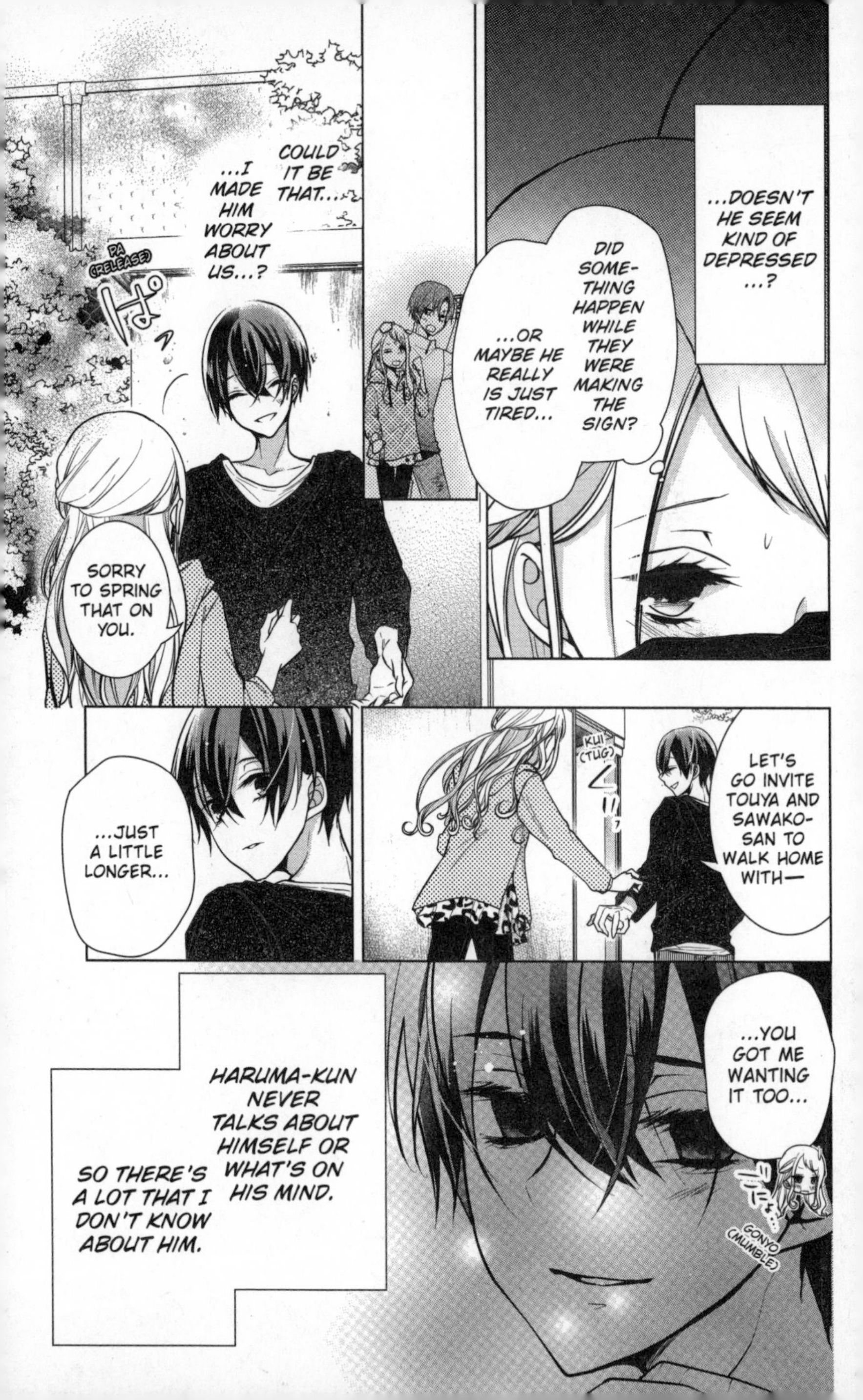
...DOESN'T HE SEEM KIND OF DEPRESSED ...?
DID SOME-THING HAPPEN WHILE THEY WERE MAKING THE SIGN?
...OR MAYBE HE REALLY IS JUST TIRED...
COULD IT BE THAT...
...I MADE HIM WORRY ABOUT US...?
PA (RELEASE)
SORRY TO SPRING THAT ON YOU.
LET'S GO INVITE TOUYA AND SAWAKO-SAN TO WALK HOME WITH—
KUI (TUG)
...JUST A LITTLE LONGER...
...YOU GOT ME WANTING IT TOO...
GONYO (MUMBLE)
HARUMA-KUN NEVER TALKS ABOUT HIMSELF OR WHAT'S ON HIS MIND.
SO THERE'S A LOT THAT I DON'T KNOW ABOUT HIM.

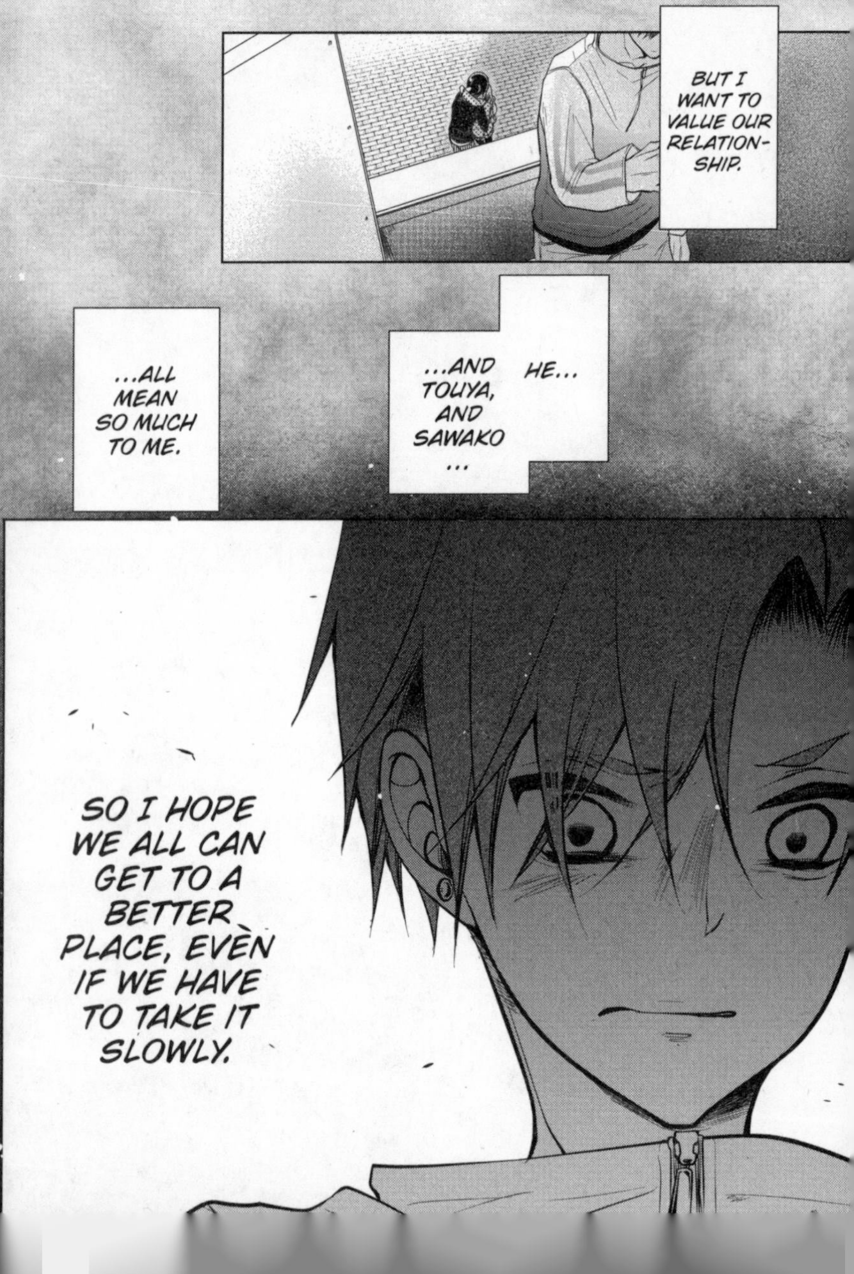
BUT I WANT TO VALUE OUR RELATION-SHIP.
HE...
...AND TOUYA, AND SAWAKO ...
...ALL MEAN SO MUCH TO ME.
SO I HOPE WE ALL CAN GET TO A BETTER PLACE, EVEN IF WE HAVE TO TAKE IT SLOWLY.

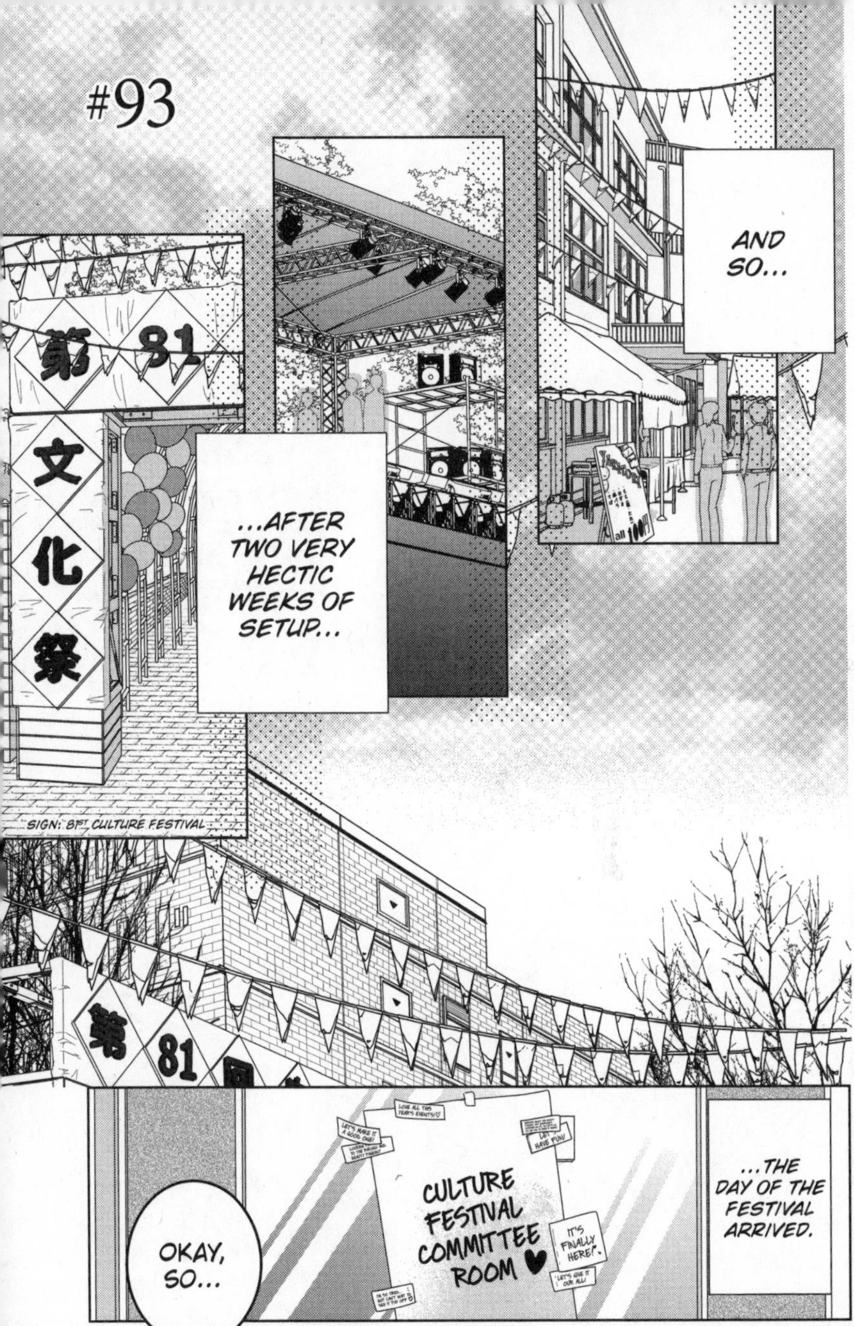
#93
AND SO...
...AFTER TWO VERY HECTIC WEEKS OF SETUP...
第 81
文化祭
SIGN: 81ST CULTURE FESTIVAL
第 81
...THE DAY OF THE FESTIVAL ARRIVED.
CULTURE FESTIVAL COMMITTEE ROOM
LOVE ALL THIS YEAR'S EVENTS!
LET'S MAKE IT A GOOD ONE!
LET'S HAVE FUN!
IT'S FINALLY HERE!
LET'S GIVE IT OUR ALL!
OKAY, SO...

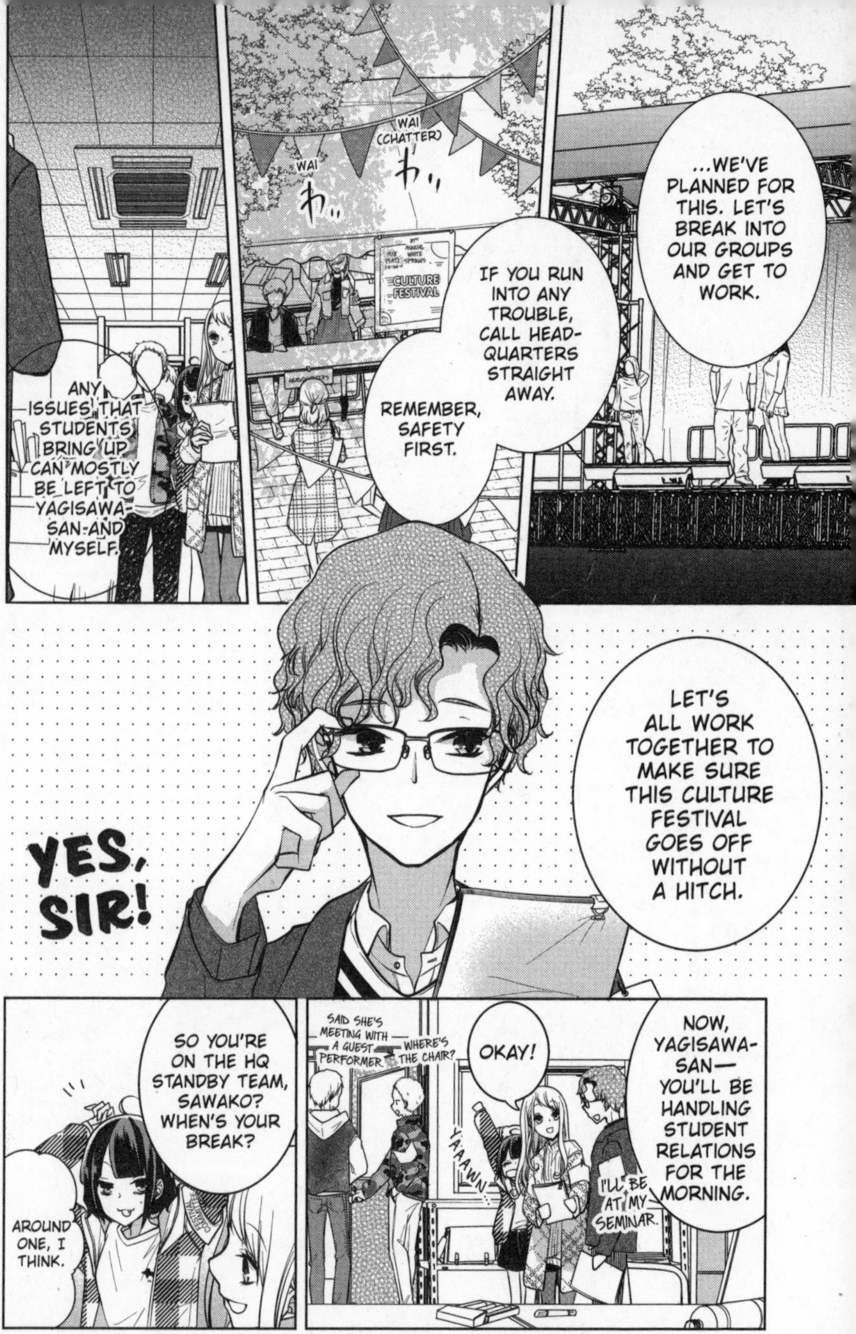
...WE'VE PLANNED FOR THIS. LET'S BREAK INTO OUR GROUPS AND GET TO WORK.
WAI (CHATTER)
WAI
CULTURE FESTIVAL
IF YOU RUN INTO ANY TROUBLE, CALL HEAD-QUARTERS STRAIGHT AWAY.
REMEMBER, SAFETY FIRST.
ANY ISSUES THAT STUDENTS BRING UP CAN MOSTLY BE LEFT TO YAGISAWA-SAN AND MYSELF.
LET'S ALL WORK TOGETHER TO MAKE SURE THIS CULTURE FESTIVAL GOES OFF WITHOUT A HITCH.
YES, SIR!
NOW, YAGISAWA-SAN—YOU'LL BE HANDLING STUDENT RELATIONS FOR THE MORNING.
I'LL BE AT MY SEMINAR.
OKAY!
YAAAWN...
WHERE'S THE CHAIR?
SAID SHE'S MEETING WITH A GUEST PERFORMER.
SO YOU'RE ON THE HQ STANDBY TEAM, SAWAKO? WHEN'S YOUR BREAK?
AROUND ONE, I THINK.

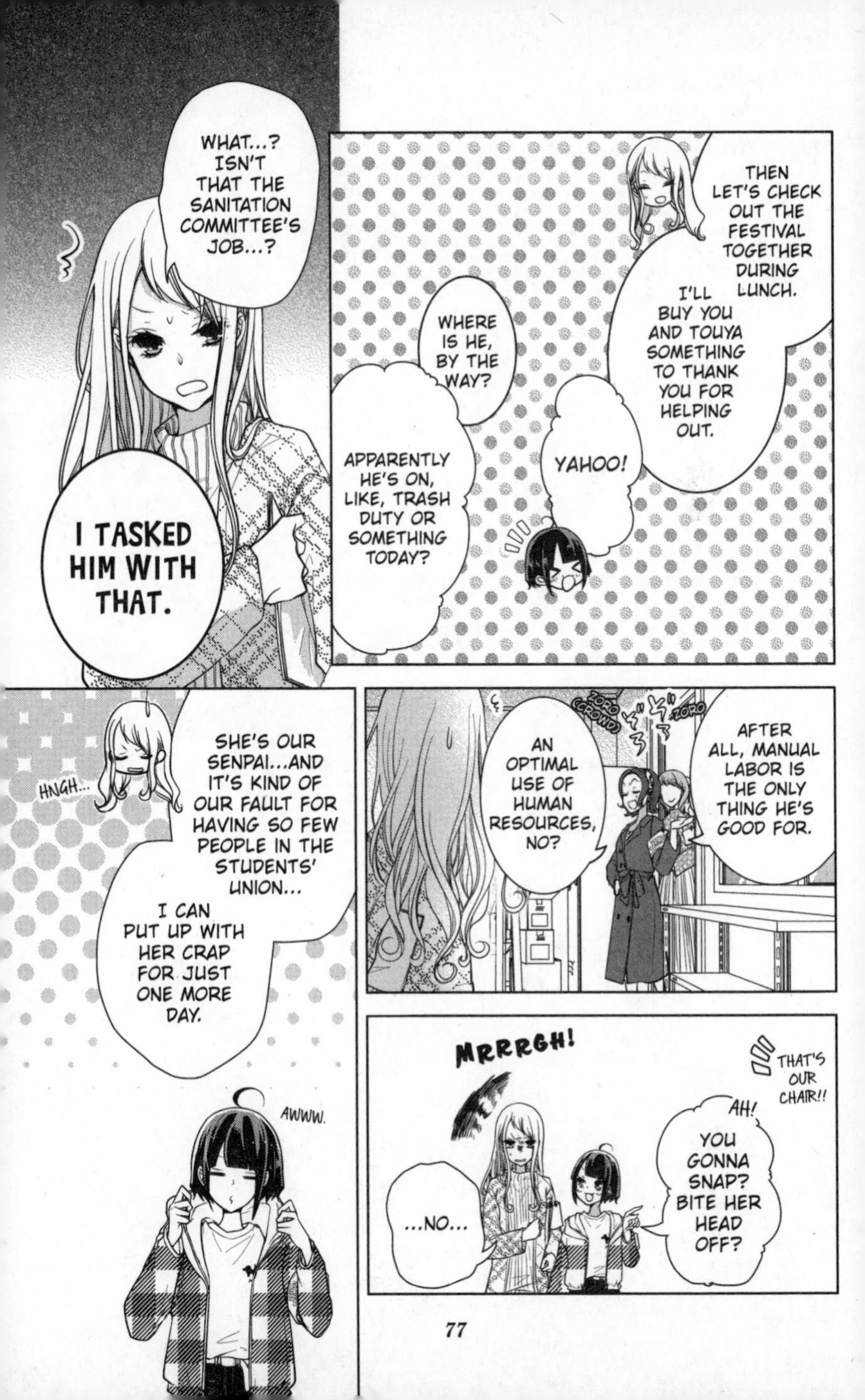
THEN LET'S CHECK OUT THE FESTIVAL TOGETHER DURING LUNCH.
I'LL BUY YOU AND TOUYA SOMETHING TO THANK YOU FOR HELPING OUT.
YAHOO!
WHERE IS HE, BY THE WAY?
APPARENTLY HE'S ON, LIKE, TRASH DUTY OR SOMETHING TODAY?
WHAT...? ISN'T THAT THE SANITATION COMMITTEE'S JOB...?
I TASKED HIM WITH THAT.
ZORO ZORO (CROWD)
AFTER ALL, MANUAL LABOR IS THE ONLY THING HE'S GOOD FOR.
AN OPTIMAL USE OF HUMAN RESOURCES, NO?
THAT'S OUR CHAIR!!
AH!
YOU GONNA SNAP? BITE HER HEAD OFF?
MRRRGH!
...NO...
HNGH...
SHE'S OUR SENPAI...AND IT'S KIND OF OUR FAULT FOR HAVING SO FEW PEOPLE IN THE STUDENTS' UNION...
I CAN PUT UP WITH HER CRAP FOR JUST ONE MORE DAY.
AWWW.

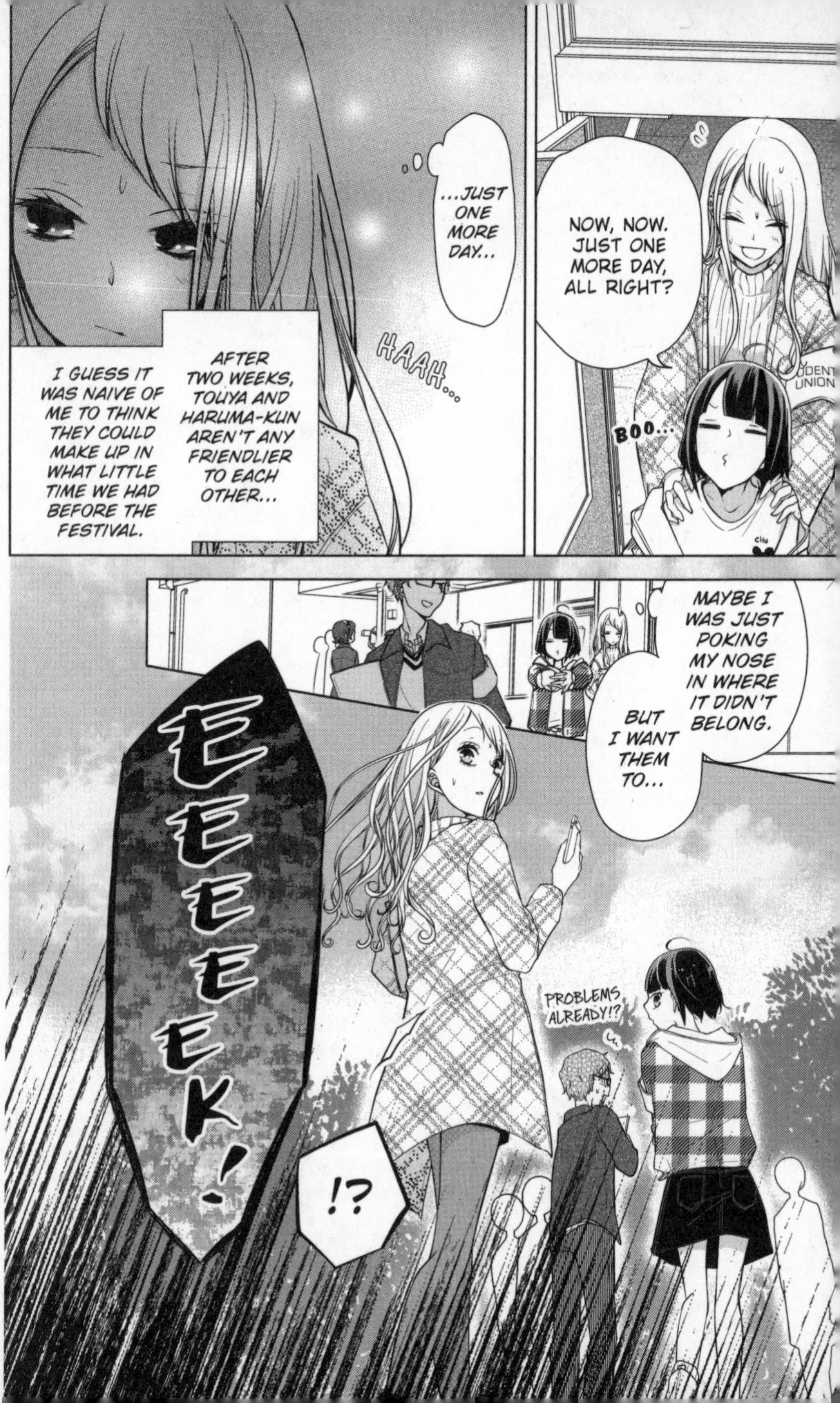
NOW, NOW. JUST ONE MORE DAY, ALL RIGHT?
BOO...
...JUST ONE MORE DAY...
HAAAH...
AFTER TWO WEEKS, TOUYA AND HARUMA-KUN AREN'T ANY FRIENDLIER TO EACH OTHER...
I GUESS IT WAS NAIVE OF ME TO THINK THEY COULD MAKE UP IN WHAT LITTLE TIME WE HAD BEFORE THE FESTIVAL.
MAYBE I WAS JUST POKING MY NOSE IN WHERE IT DIDN'T BELONG.
BUT I WANT THEM TO...
PROBLEMS ALREADY!?
EEEEEEK!
!?

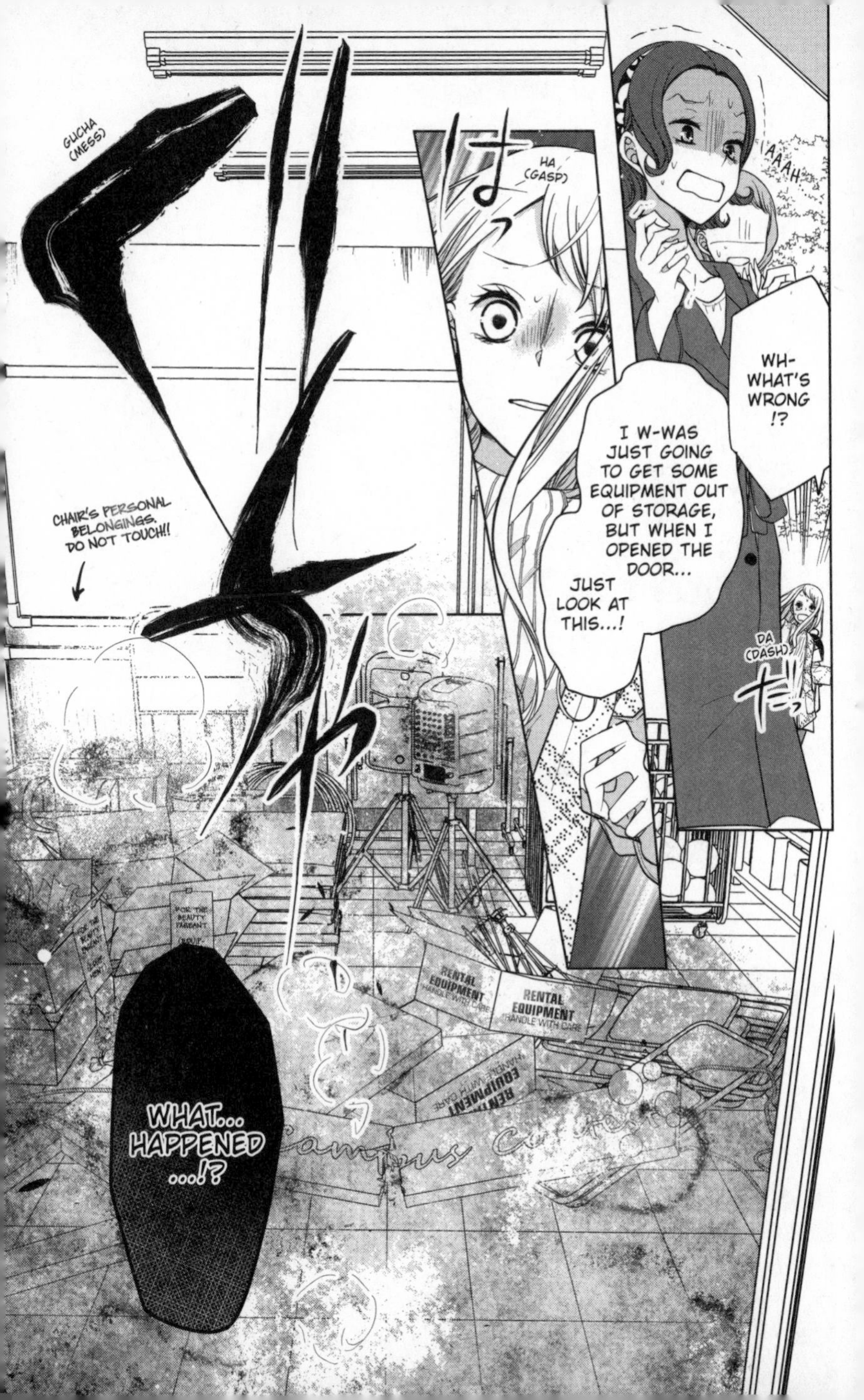
AAAH
WH- WHAT'S WRONG !?
HA (GASP)
I W-WAS JUST GOING TO GET SOME EQUIPMENT OUT OF STORAGE, BUT WHEN I OPENED THE DOOR...
JUST LOOK AT THIS...!
DA (DASH)
GUCHA (MESS)
CHAIR'S PERSONAL BELONGINGS. DO NOT TOUCH!!
RENTAL EQUIPMENT HANDLE WITH CARE
RENTAL EQUIPMENT HANDLE WITH CARE
WHAT... HAPPENED ...!?

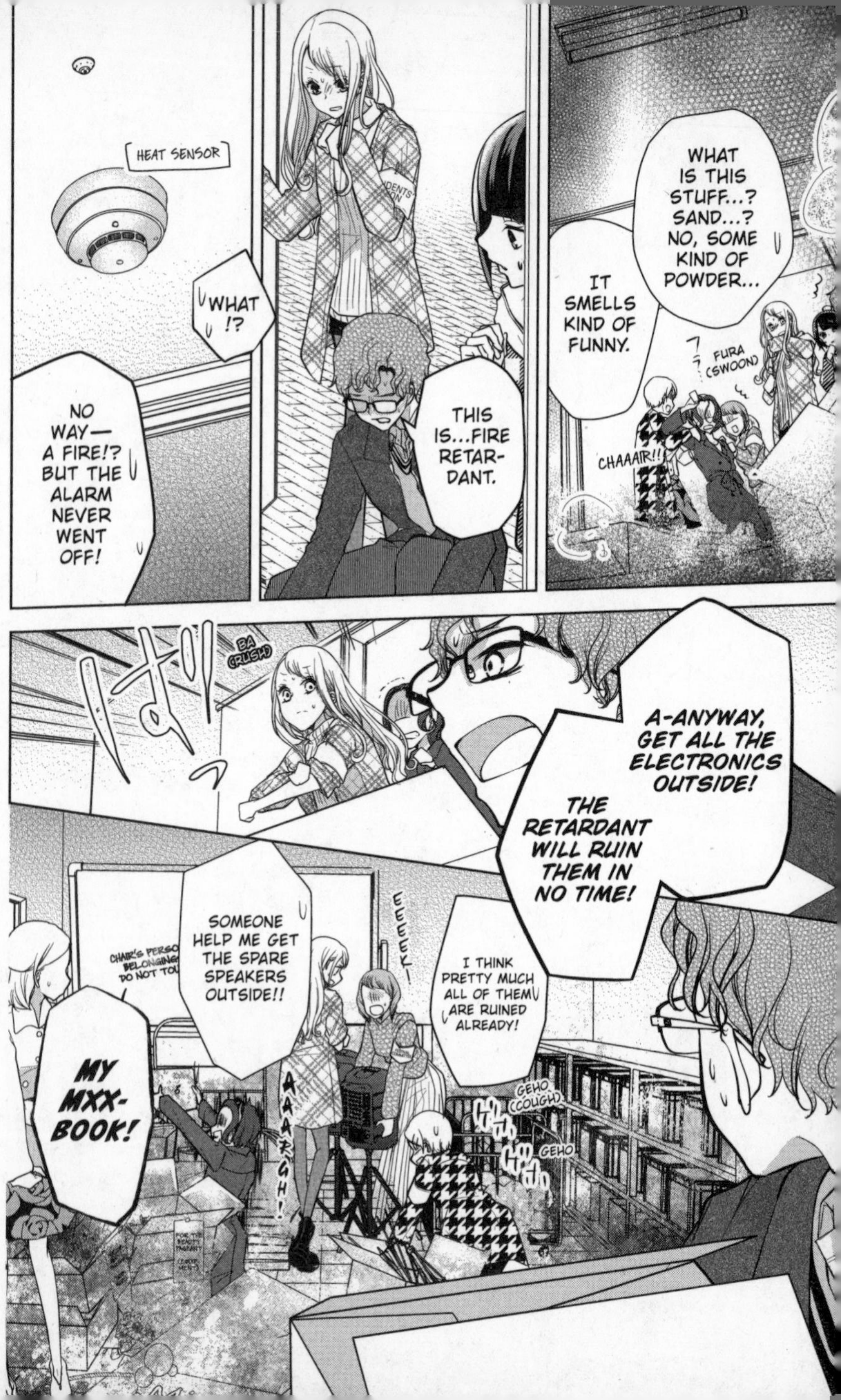
WHAT IS THIS STUFF...? SAND...? NO, SOME KIND OF POWDER...
IT SMELLS KIND OF FUNNY.
FURA (SWOON)
CHAAAIR!!
THIS IS...FIRE RETARDANT.
HEAT SENSOR
WHAT!?
NO WAY— A FIRE!? BUT THE ALARM NEVER WENT OFF!
BA (RUSH)
A-ANYWAY, GET ALL THE ELECTRONICS OUTSIDE!
THE RETARDANT WILL RUIN THEM IN NO TIME!
I THINK PRETTY MUCH ALL OF THEM ARE RUINED ALREADY!
EEEEK!
SOMEONE HELP ME GET THE SPARE SPEAKERS OUTSIDE!!
GEHO (COUGH)
GEHO
AAAARGH!
MY MXX-BOOK!

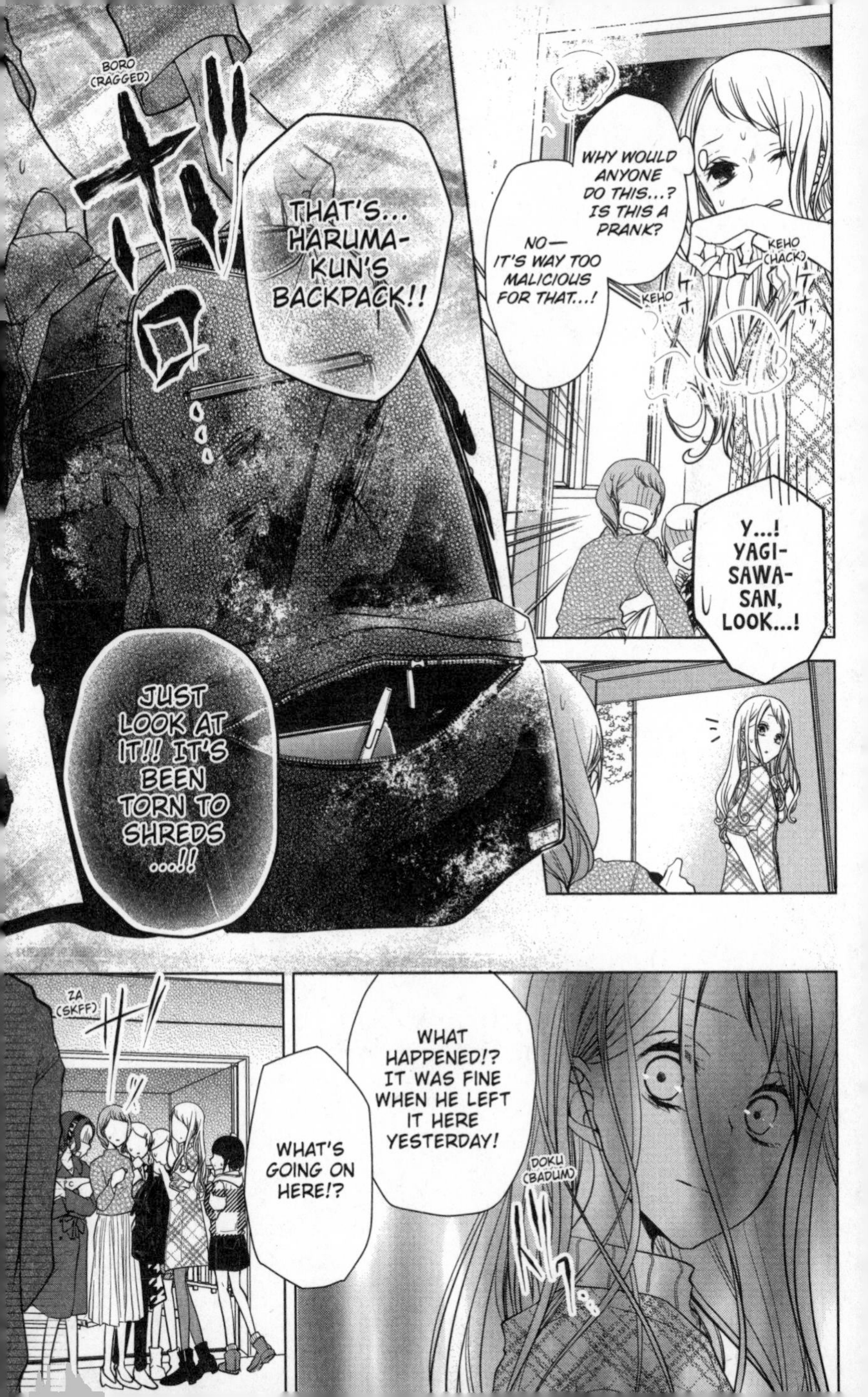
KEHO (HACK)
KEHO
WHY WOULD ANYONE DO THIS...? IS THIS A PRANK?
NO— IT'S WAY TOO MALICIOUS FOR THAT...!
Y...! YAGI-SAWA-SAN, LOOK...!
BORO (RAGGED)
THAT'S... HARUMA-KUN'S BACKPACK!!
JUST LOOK AT IT!! IT'S BEEN TORN TO SHREDS ...!!
WHAT HAPPENED!? IT WAS FINE WHEN HE LEFT IT HERE YESTERDAY!
DOKU (BADUM)
WHAT'S GOING ON HERE!?
ZA (SKFF)

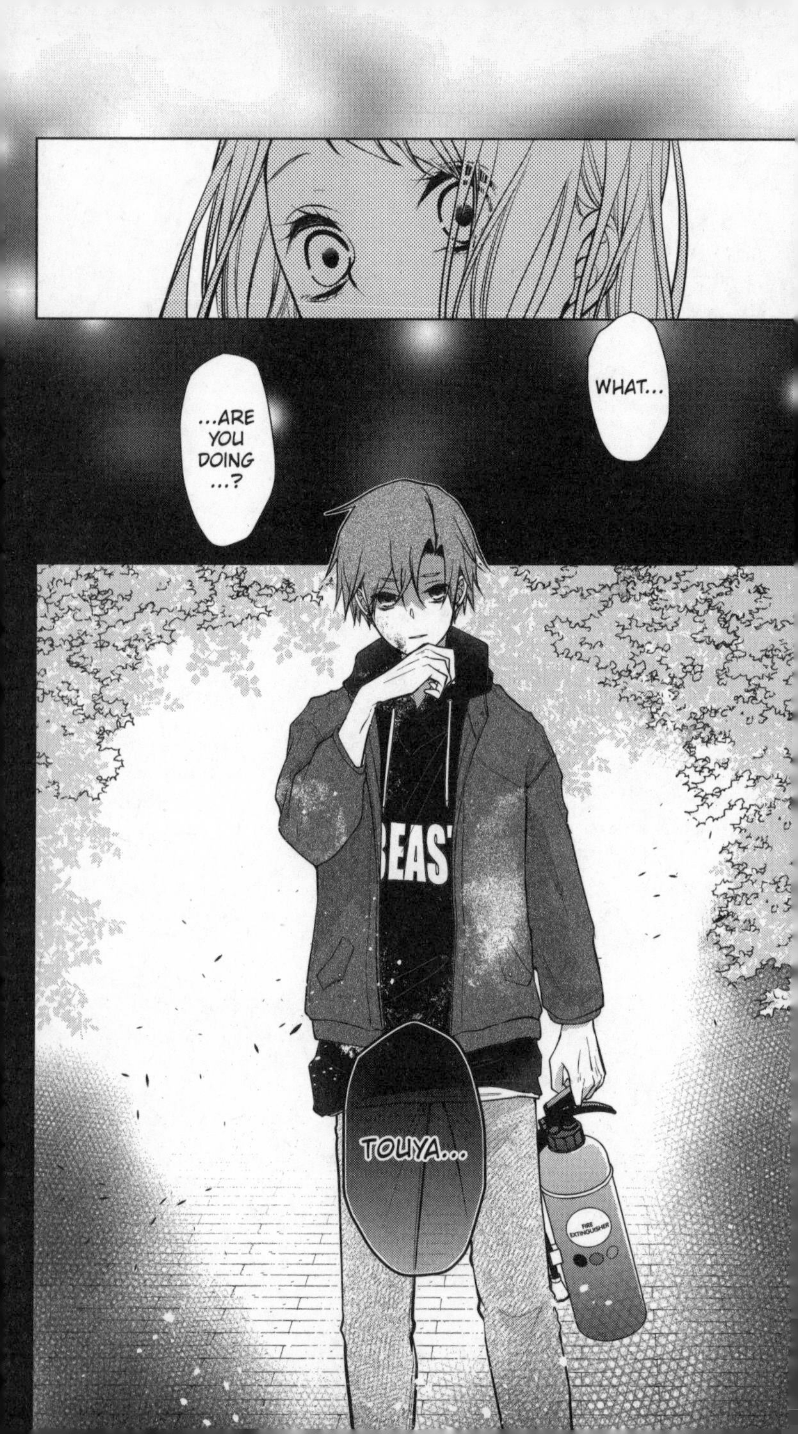
WHAT...
...ARE YOU DOING ...?
TOUYA...
FIRE EXTINGUISHER

#94

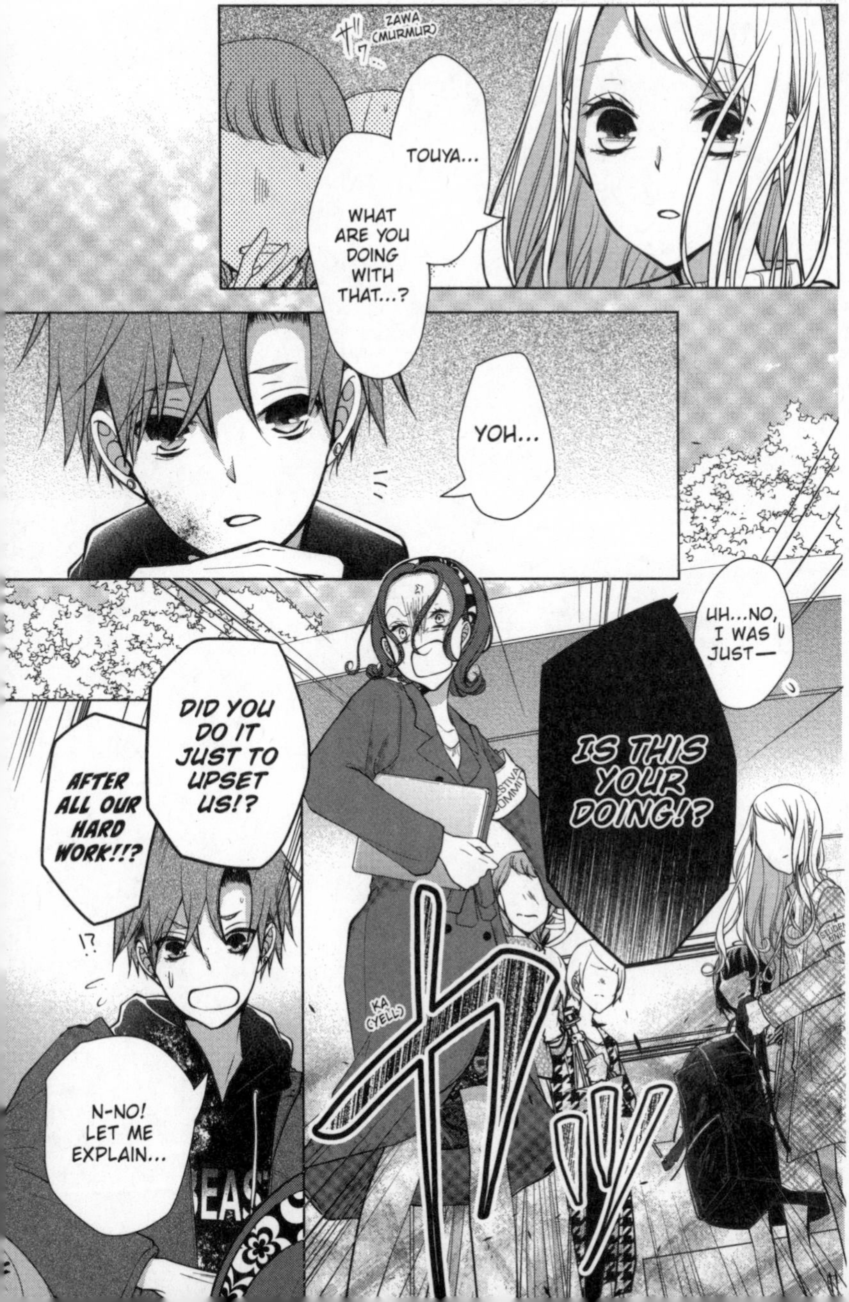
ZAWA (MURMUR)
TOUYA...
WHAT ARE YOU DOING WITH THAT...?
YOH...
UH...NO, I WAS JUST—
IS THIS YOUR DOING!?
KA (YELL)
DID YOU DO IT JUST TO UPSET US!?
AFTER ALL OUR HARD WORK!!?
!?
N-NO! LET ME EXPLAIN...

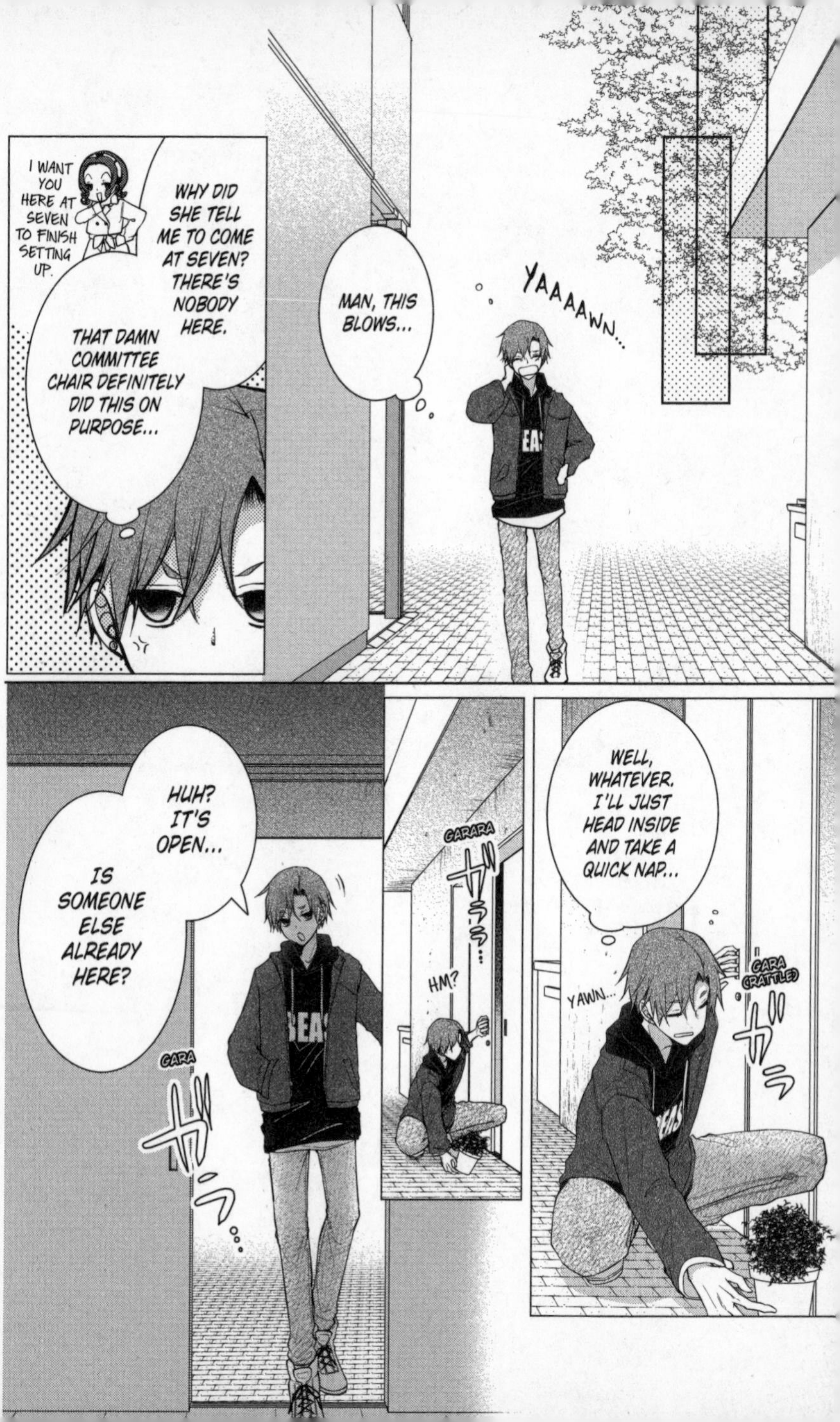
YAAAAWN...
MAN, THIS BLOWS...
WHY DID SHE TELL ME TO COME AT SEVEN? THERE'S NOBODY HERE.
I WANT YOU HERE AT SEVEN TO FINISH SETTING UP.
THAT DAMN COMMITTEE CHAIR DEFINITELY DID THIS ON PURPOSE...
WELL, WHATEVER. I'LL JUST HEAD INSIDE AND TAKE A QUICK NAP...
YAWN...
GARA (RATTLE)
GARARA
HM?
HUH? IT'S OPEN...
IS SOMEONE ELSE ALREADY HERE?
GARA

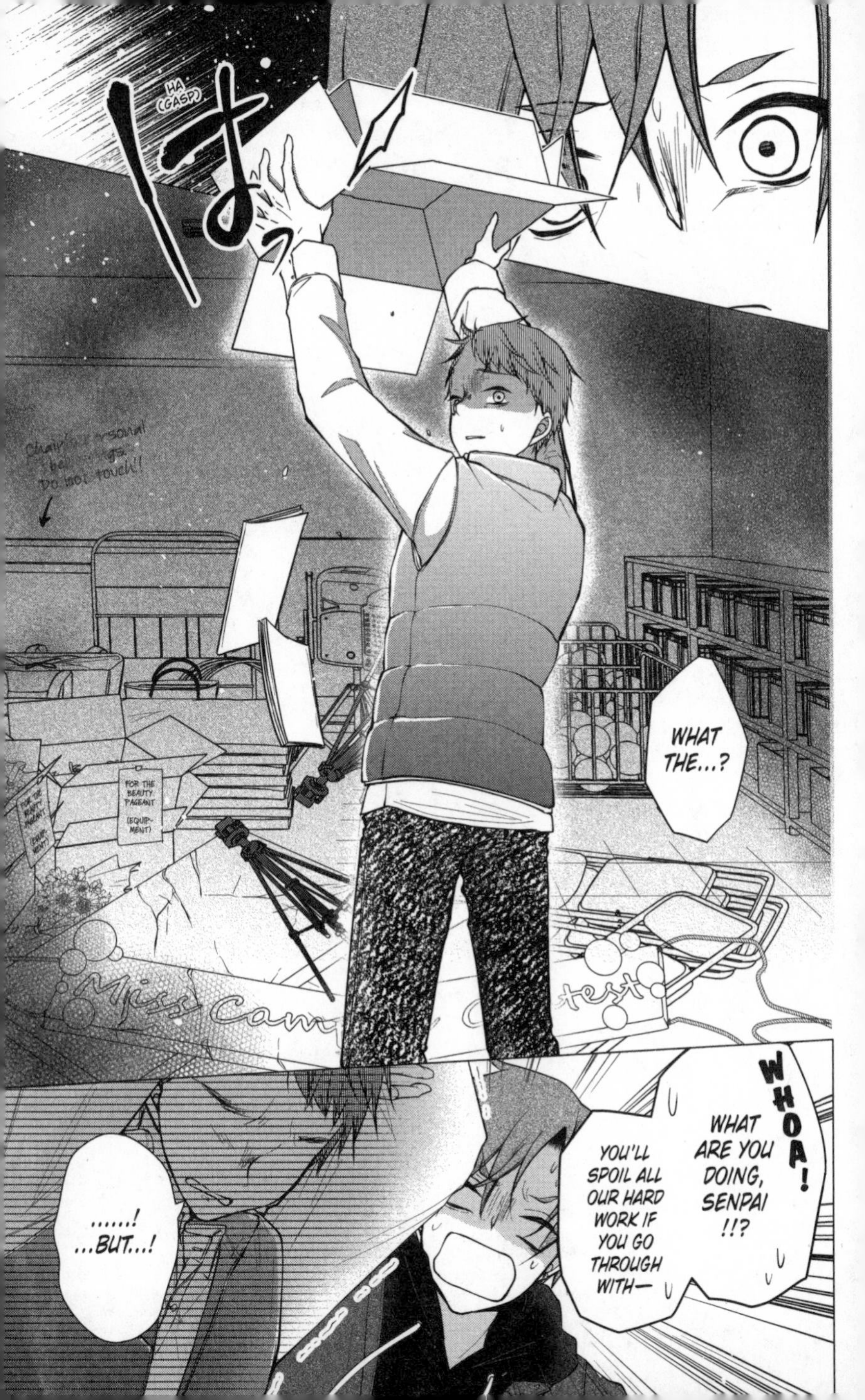
HA (GASP)
Do not touch!!
FOR THE BEAUTY PAGEANT (EQUIPMENT)
WHAT THE...?
WHOA!
WHAT ARE YOU DOING, SENPAI!!?
YOU'LL SPOIL ALL OUR HARD WORK IF YOU GO THROUGH WITH—
......! ...BUT...!

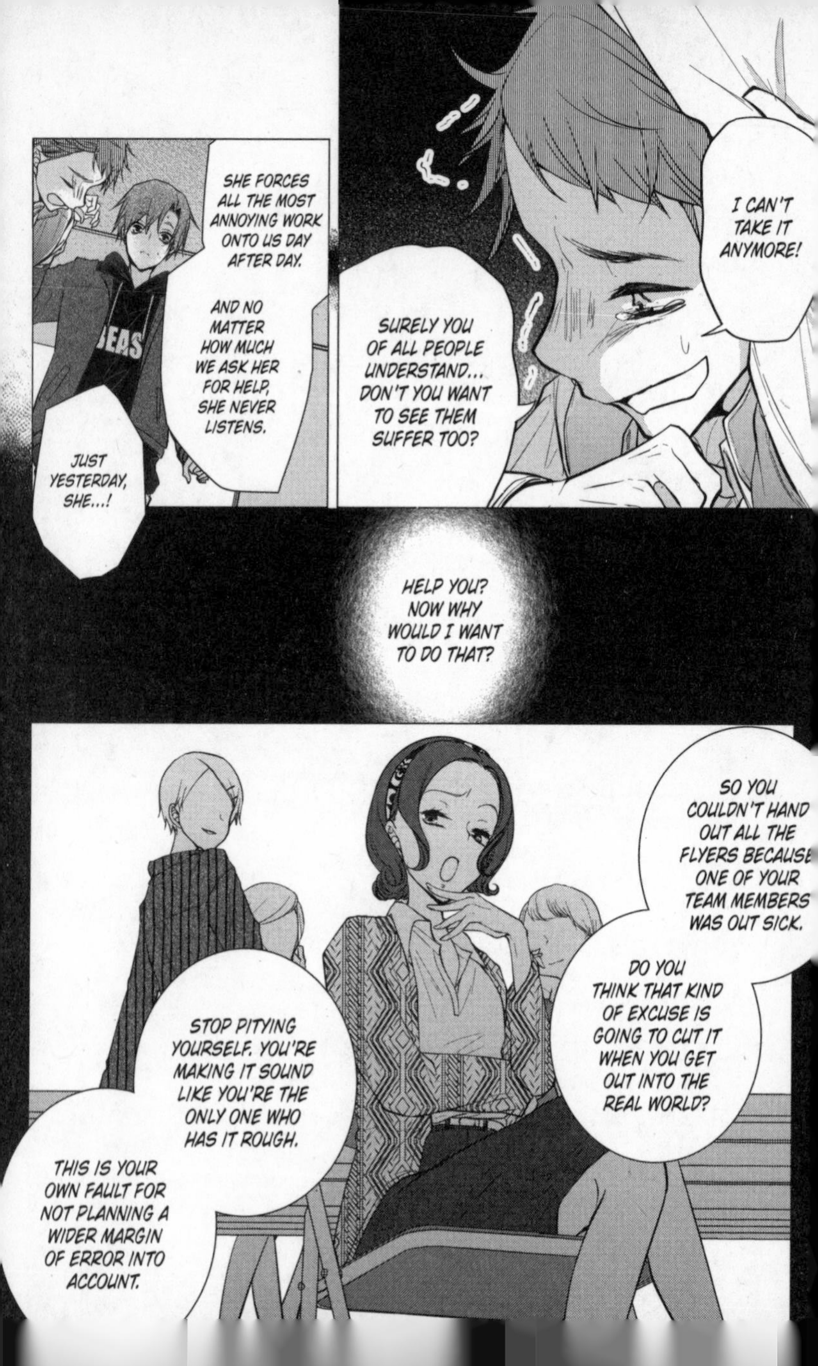
I CAN'T TAKE IT ANYMORE!
SURELY YOU OF ALL PEOPLE UNDERSTAND... DON'T YOU WANT TO SEE THEM SUFFER TOO?
SHE FORCES ALL THE MOST ANNOYING WORK ONTO US DAY AFTER DAY.
AND NO MATTER HOW MUCH WE ASK HER FOR HELP, SHE NEVER LISTENS.
JUST YESTERDAY, SHE...!
HELP YOU? NOW WHY WOULD I WANT TO DO THAT?
SO YOU COULDN'T HAND OUT ALL THE FLYERS BECAUSE ONE OF YOUR TEAM MEMBERS WAS OUT SICK.
DO YOU THINK THAT KIND OF EXCUSE IS GOING TO CUT IT WHEN YOU GET OUT INTO THE REAL WORLD?
STOP PITYING YOURSELF. YOU'RE MAKING IT SOUND LIKE YOU'RE THE ONLY ONE WHO HAS IT ROUGH.
THIS IS YOUR OWN FAULT FOR NOT PLANNING A WIDER MARGIN OF ERROR INTO ACCOUNT.

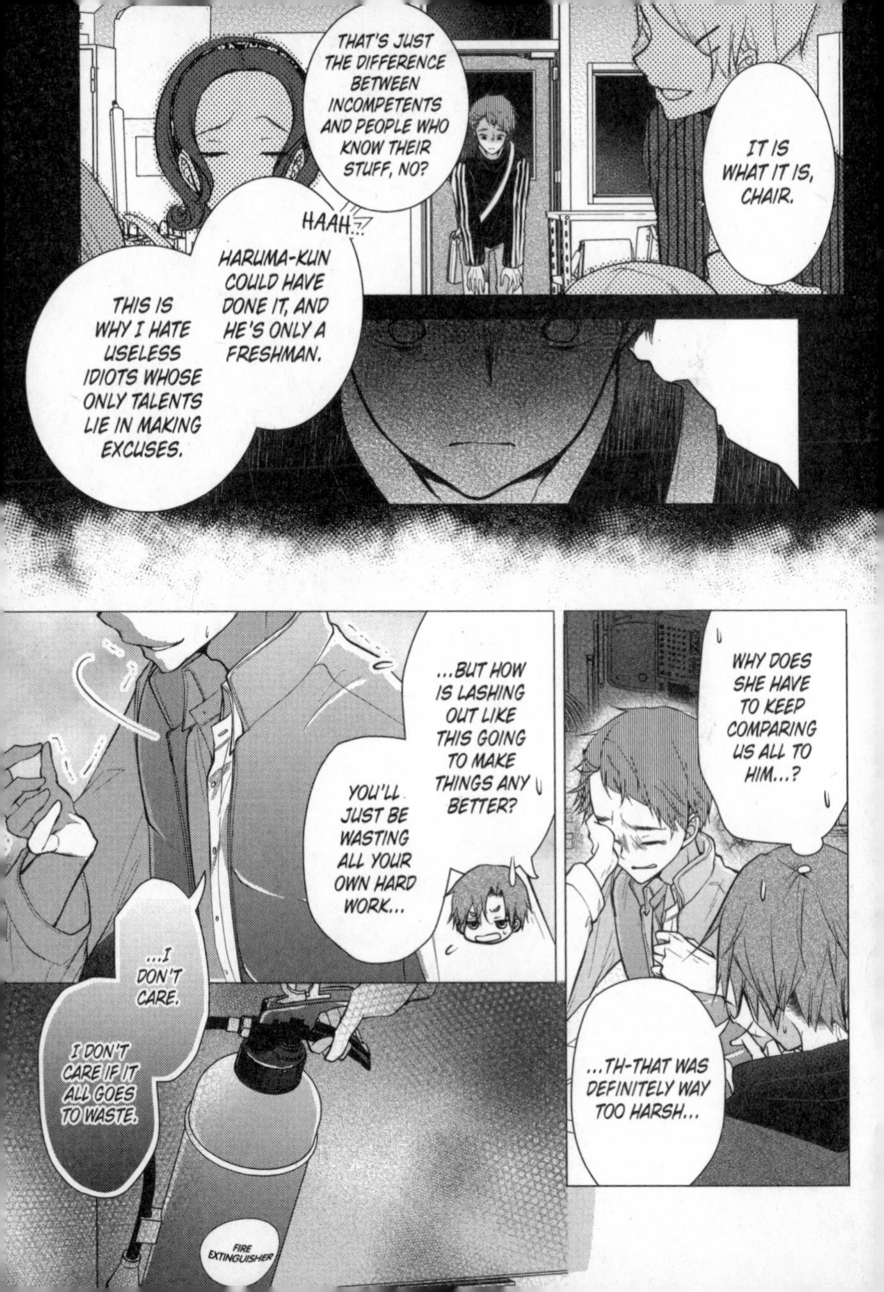
IT IS WHAT IT IS, CHAIR.
THAT'S JUST THE DIFFERENCE BETWEEN INCOMPETENTS AND PEOPLE WHO KNOW THEIR STUFF, NO?
HAAH...
HARUMA-KUN COULD HAVE DONE IT, AND HE'S ONLY A FRESHMAN.
THIS IS WHY I HATE USELESS IDIOTS WHOSE ONLY TALENTS LIE IN MAKING EXCUSES.
WHY DOES SHE HAVE TO KEEP COMPARING US ALL TO HIM...?
...TH-THAT WAS DEFINITELY WAY TOO HARSH...
...BUT HOW IS LASHING OUT LIKE THIS GOING TO MAKE THINGS ANY BETTER?
YOU'LL JUST BE WASTING ALL YOUR OWN HARD WORK...
...I DON'T CARE.
I DON'T CARE IF IT ALL GOES TO WASTE.
FIRE EXTINGUISHER

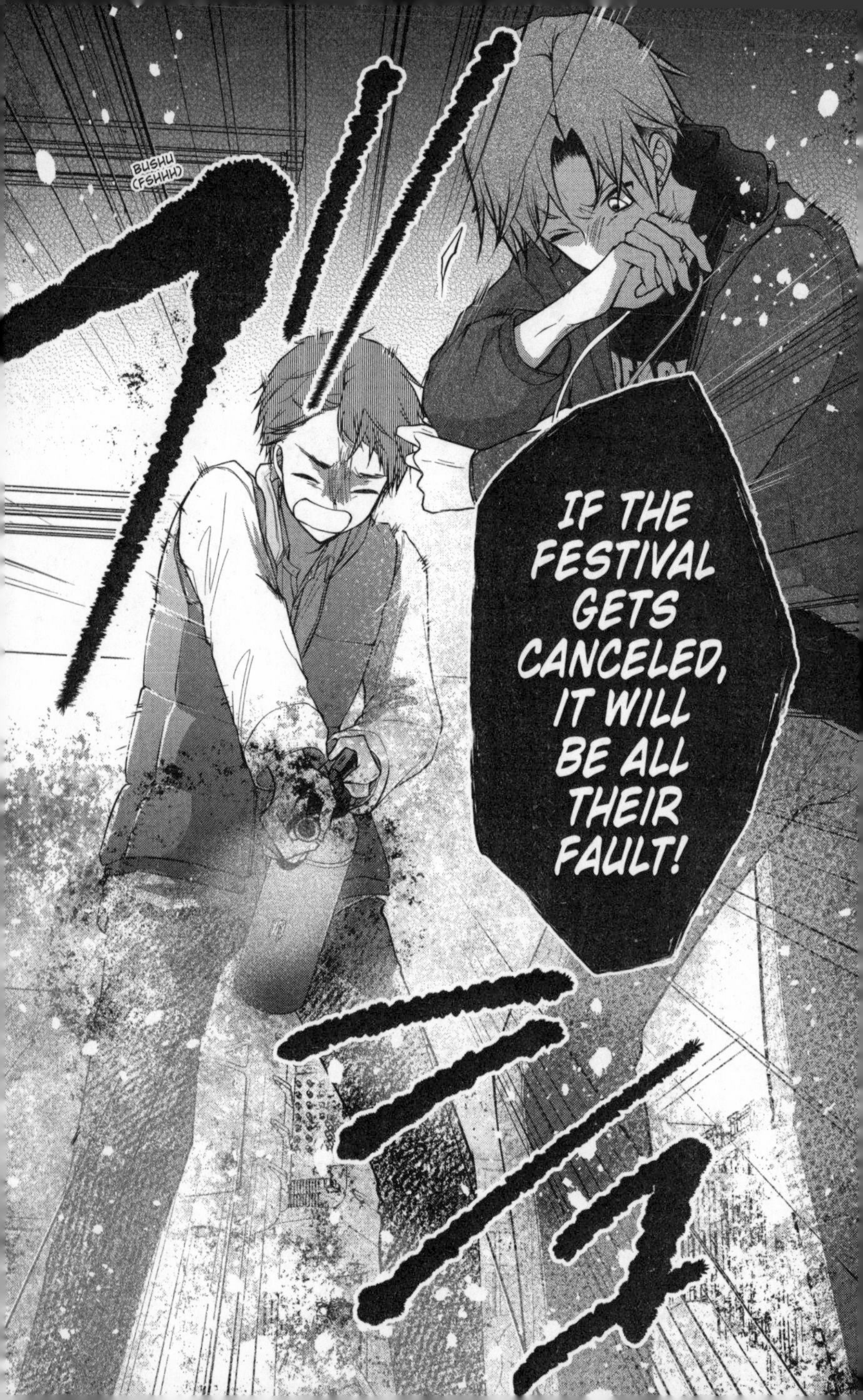
BUSHU (FSHHH)
IF THE FESTIVAL GETS CANCELED, IT WILL BE ALL THEIR FAULT!

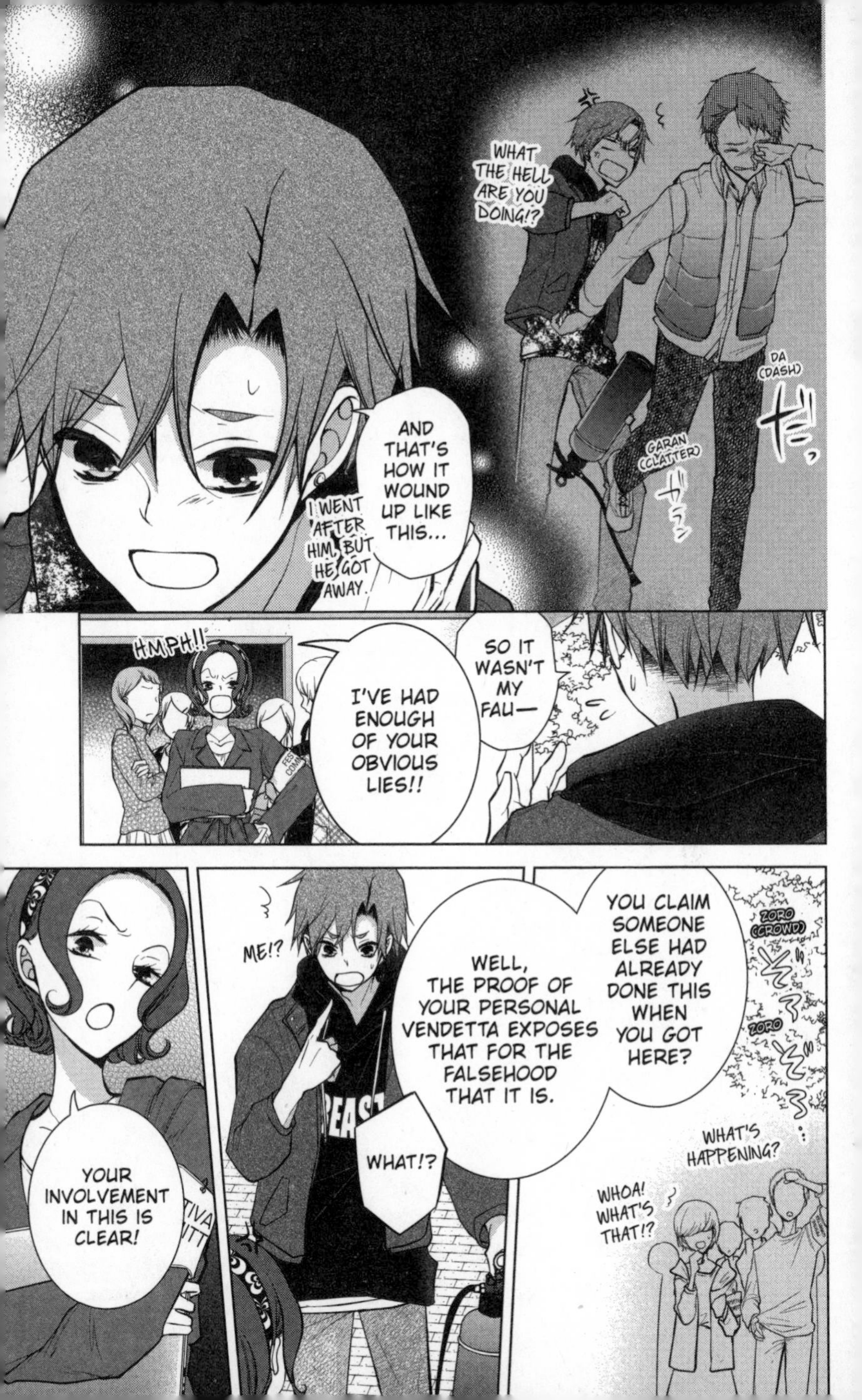
WHAT THE HELL ARE YOU DOING!?
DA (DASH)
GARAN (CLATTER)
AND THAT'S HOW IT WOUND UP LIKE THIS...
I WENT AFTER HIM, BUT HE GOT AWAY.
SO IT WASN'T MY FAU—
I'VE HAD ENOUGH OF YOUR OBVIOUS LIES!!
HMPH!!
ZORO (CROWD)
ZORO
YOU CLAIM SOMEONE ELSE HAD ALREADY DONE THIS WHEN YOU GOT HERE?
WHAT'S HAPPENING?
WHOA! WHAT'S THAT!?
WELL, THE PROOF OF YOUR PERSONAL VENDETTA EXPOSES THAT FOR THE FALSEHOOD THAT IT IS.
ME!?
WHAT!?
YOUR INVOLVEMENT IN THIS IS CLEAR!

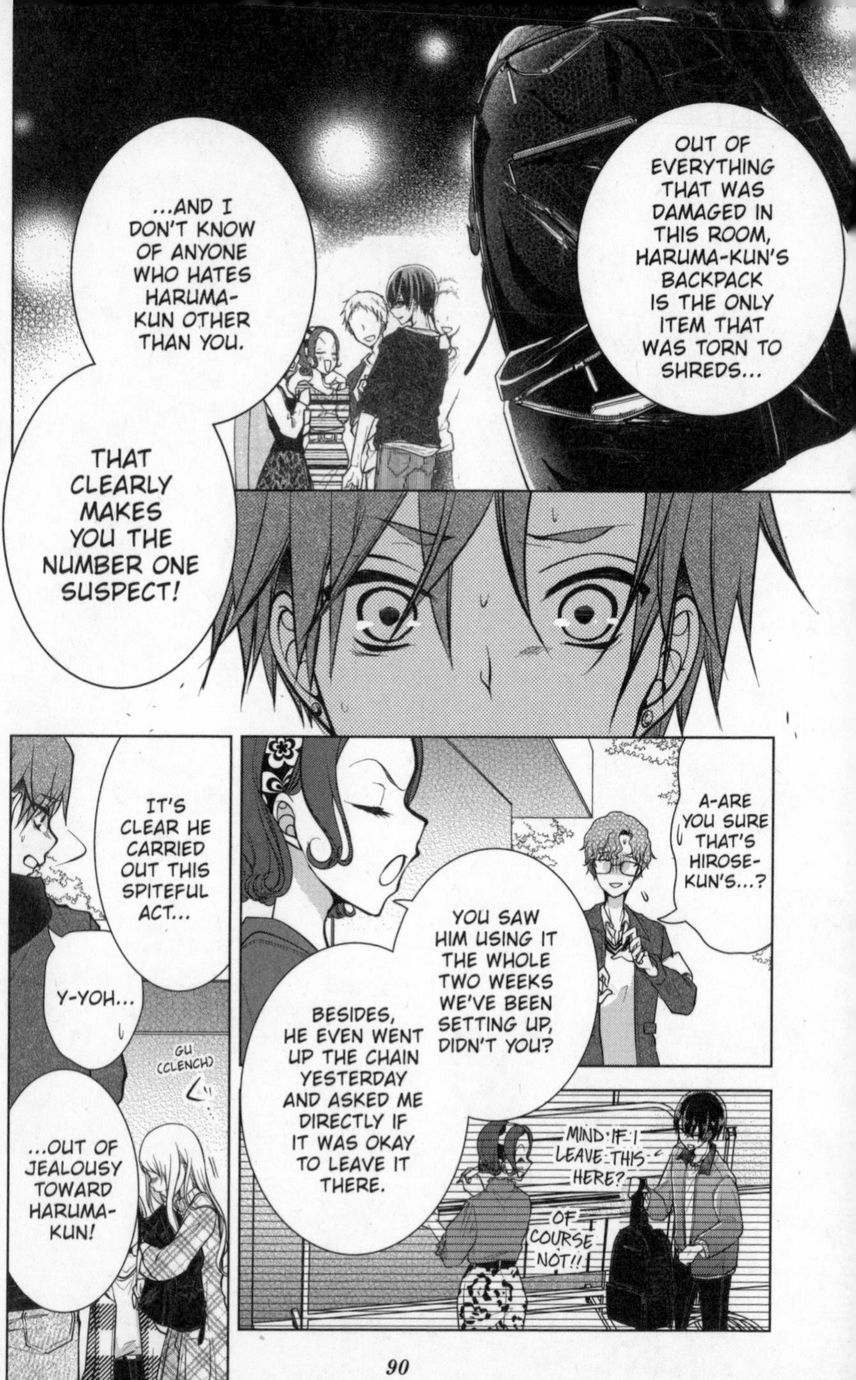
OUT OF EVERYTHING THAT WAS DAMAGED IN THIS ROOM, HARUMA-KUN'S BACKPACK IS THE ONLY ITEM THAT WAS TORN TO SHREDS...
...AND I DON'T KNOW OF ANYONE WHO HATES HARUMA-KUN OTHER THAN YOU.
THAT CLEARLY MAKES YOU THE NUMBER ONE SUSPECT!
A-ARE YOU SURE THAT'S HIROSE-KUN'S...?
YOU SAW HIM USING IT THE WHOLE TWO WEEKS WE'VE BEEN SETTING UP, DIDN'T YOU?
BESIDES, HE EVEN WENT UP THE CHAIN YESTERDAY AND ASKED ME DIRECTLY IF IT WAS OKAY TO LEAVE IT THERE.
MIND IF I LEAVE THIS HERE?
OF COURSE NOT!!
IT'S CLEAR HE CARRIED OUT THIS SPITEFUL ACT...
Y-YOH...
GU (CLENCH)
...OUT OF JEALOUSY TOWARD HARUMA-KUN!

#95

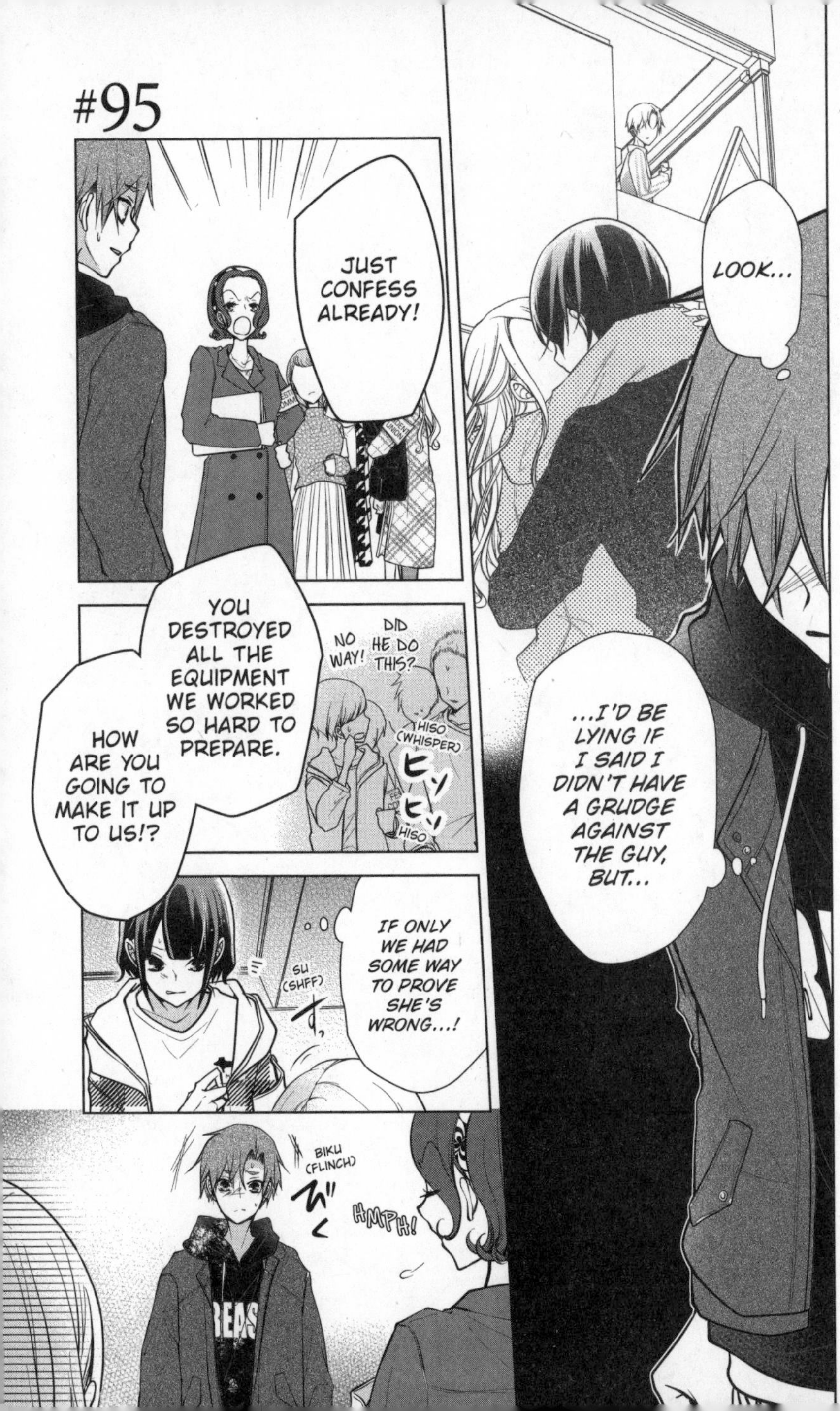

LOOK...
...I'D BE LYING IF I SAID I DIDN'T HAVE A GRUDGE AGAINST THE GUY, BUT...
JUST CONFESS ALREADY!
DID HE DO THIS?
NO WAY!
YOU DESTROYED ALL THE EQUIPMENT WE WORKED SO HARD TO PREPARE.
HISO (WHISPER)
HISO
HOW ARE YOU GOING TO MAKE IT UP TO US!?
IF ONLY WE HAD SOME WAY TO PROVE SHE'S WRONG...!
SU (SHFF)
HMPH!
BIKU (FLINCH)

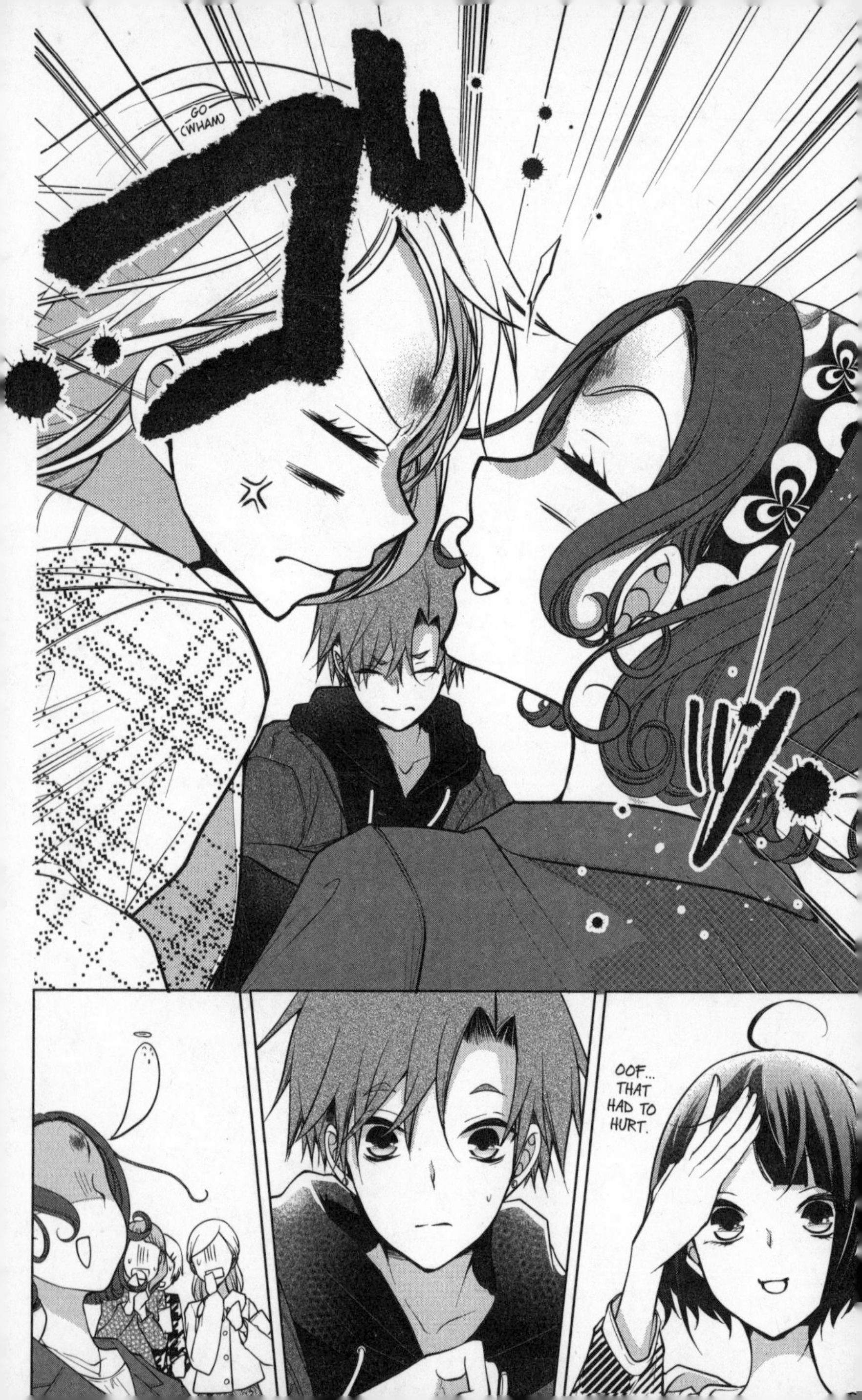
GO (WHAM)
OOF... THAT HAD TO HURT.

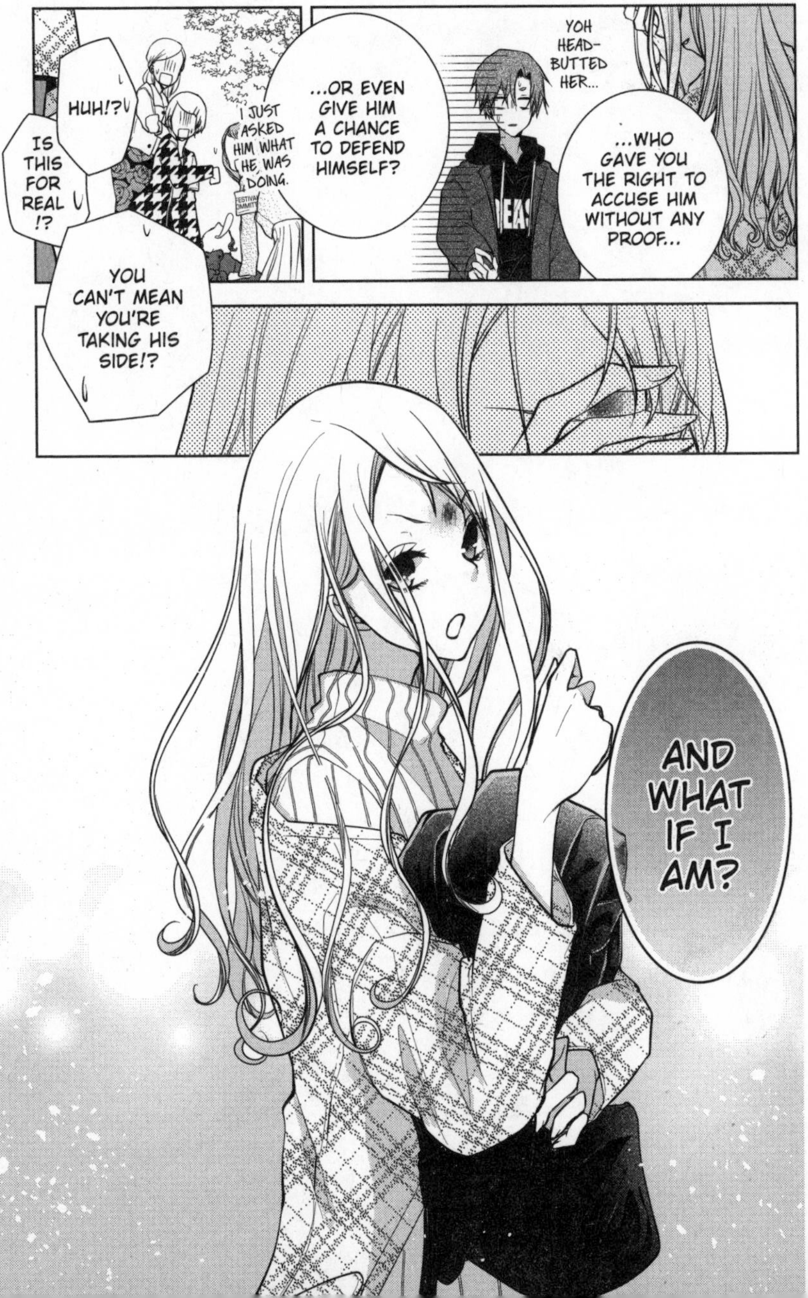
YOH HEAD-BUTTED HER...
...WHO GAVE YOU THE RIGHT TO ACCUSE HIM WITHOUT ANY PROOF...
...OR EVEN GIVE HIM A CHANCE TO DEFEND HIMSELF?
I JUST ASKED HIM WHAT HE WAS DOING.
HUH!?
IS THIS FOR REAL!?
YOU CAN'T MEAN YOU'RE TAKING HIS SIDE!?
AND WHAT IF I AM?

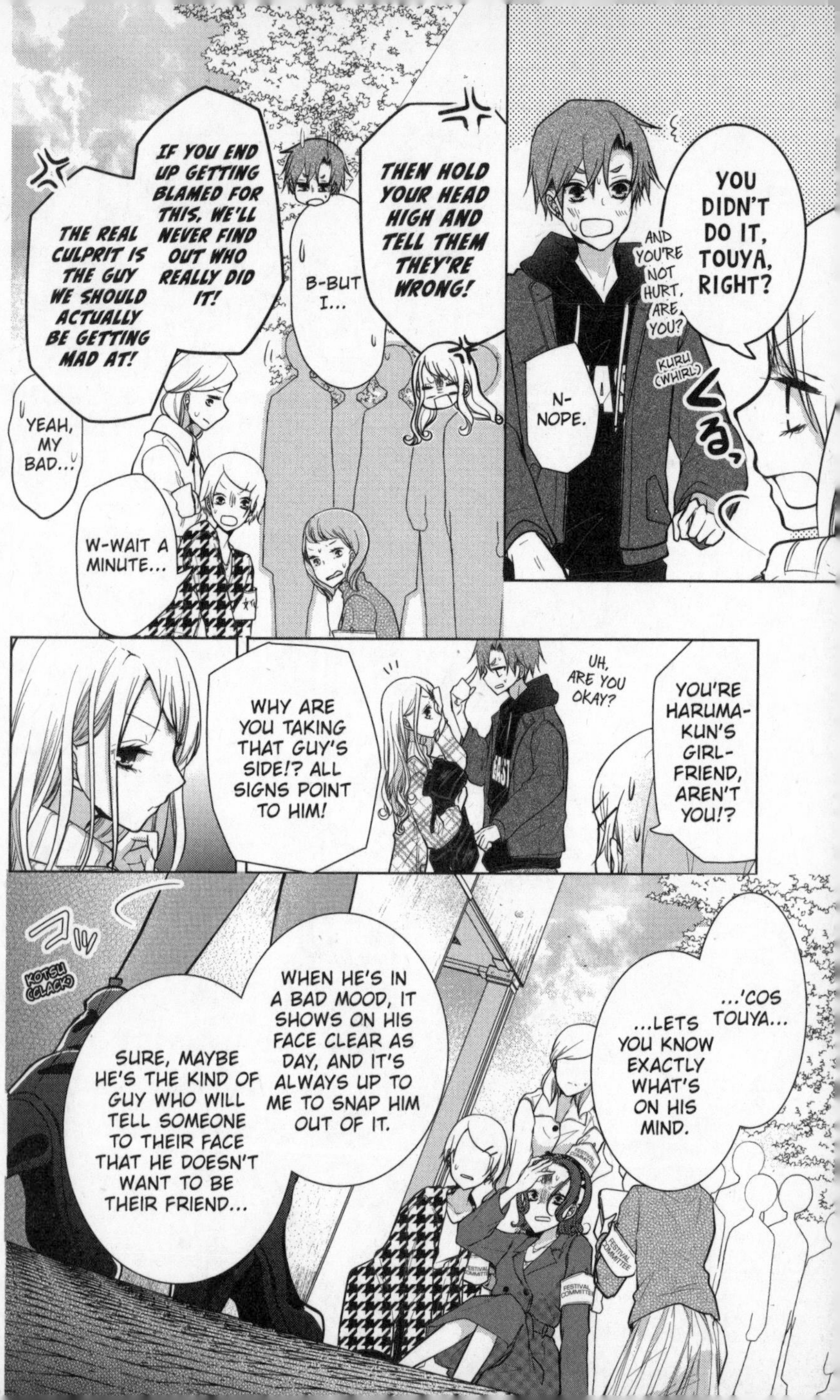
YOU DIDN'T DO IT, TOUYA, RIGHT?
AND YOU'RE NOT HURT, ARE YOU?
KURU (WHIRL)
くる
N-NOPE.
THEN HOLD YOUR HEAD HIGH AND TELL THEM THEY'RE WRONG!
B-BUT I...
IF YOU END UP GETTING BLAMED FOR THIS, WE'LL NEVER FIND OUT WHO REALLY DID IT!
THE REAL CULPRIT IS THE GUY WE SHOULD ACTUALLY BE GETTING MAD AT!
YEAH, MY BAD...
W-WAIT A MINUTE...
YOU'RE HARUMA-KUN'S GIRLFRIEND, AREN'T YOU!?
UH, ARE YOU OKAY?
WHY ARE YOU TAKING THAT GUY'S SIDE!? ALL SIGNS POINT TO HIM!
...'COS TOUYA...
...LETS YOU KNOW EXACTLY WHAT'S ON HIS MIND.
WHEN HE'S IN A BAD MOOD, IT SHOWS ON HIS FACE CLEAR AS DAY, AND IT'S ALWAYS UP TO ME TO SNAP HIM OUT OF IT.
SURE, MAYBE HE'S THE KIND OF GUY WHO WILL TELL SOMEONE TO THEIR FACE THAT HE DOESN'T WANT TO BE THEIR FRIEND...
コツ
KOTSU (CLACK)
FESTIVAL COMMITTEE

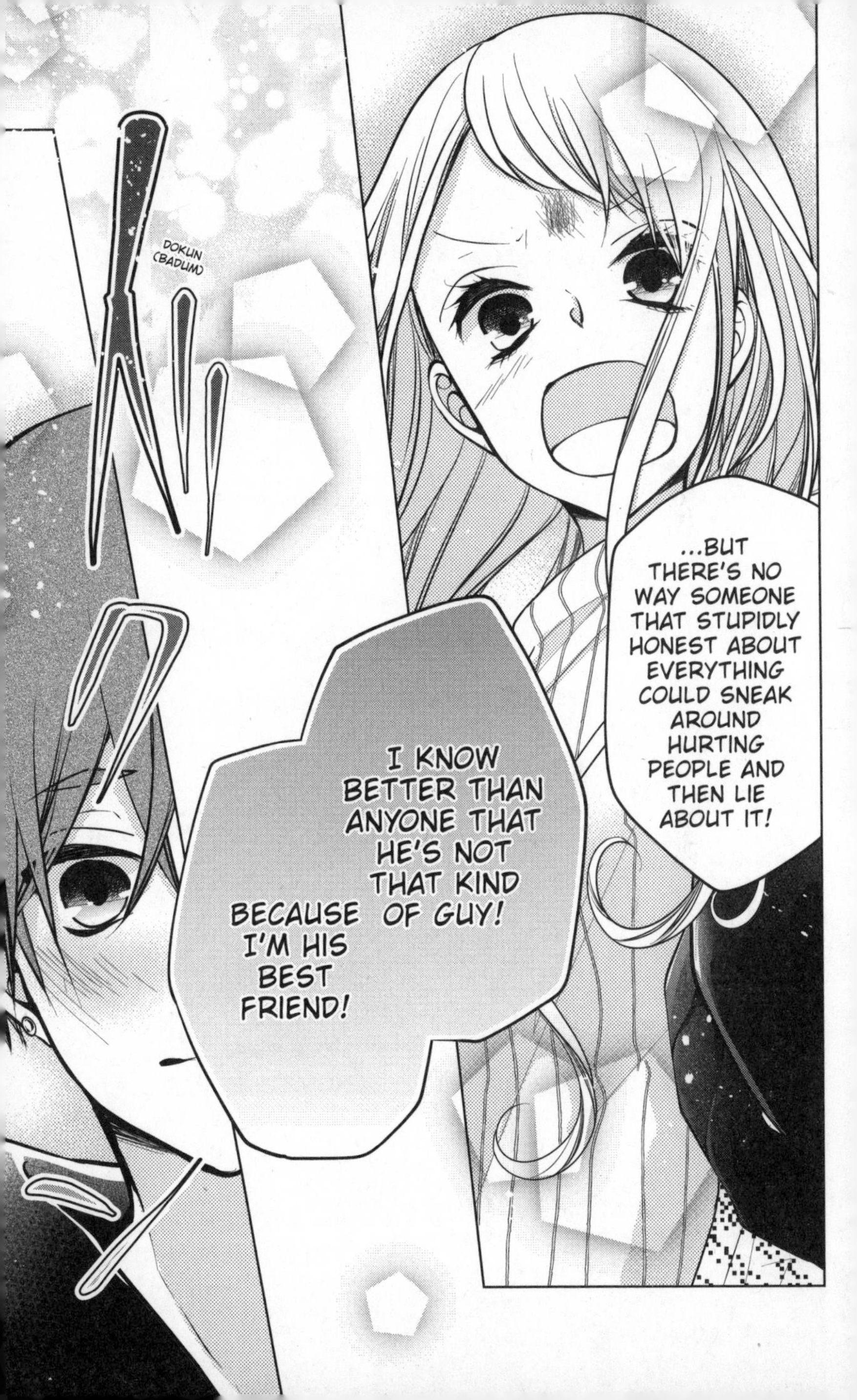
...BUT THERE'S NO WAY SOMEONE THAT STUPIDLY HONEST ABOUT EVERYTHING COULD SNEAK AROUND HURTING PEOPLE AND THEN LIE ABOUT IT!
I KNOW BETTER THAN ANYONE THAT HE'S NOT THAT KIND OF GUY!
BECAUSE I'M HIS BEST FRIEND!
DOKUN (BADUM)

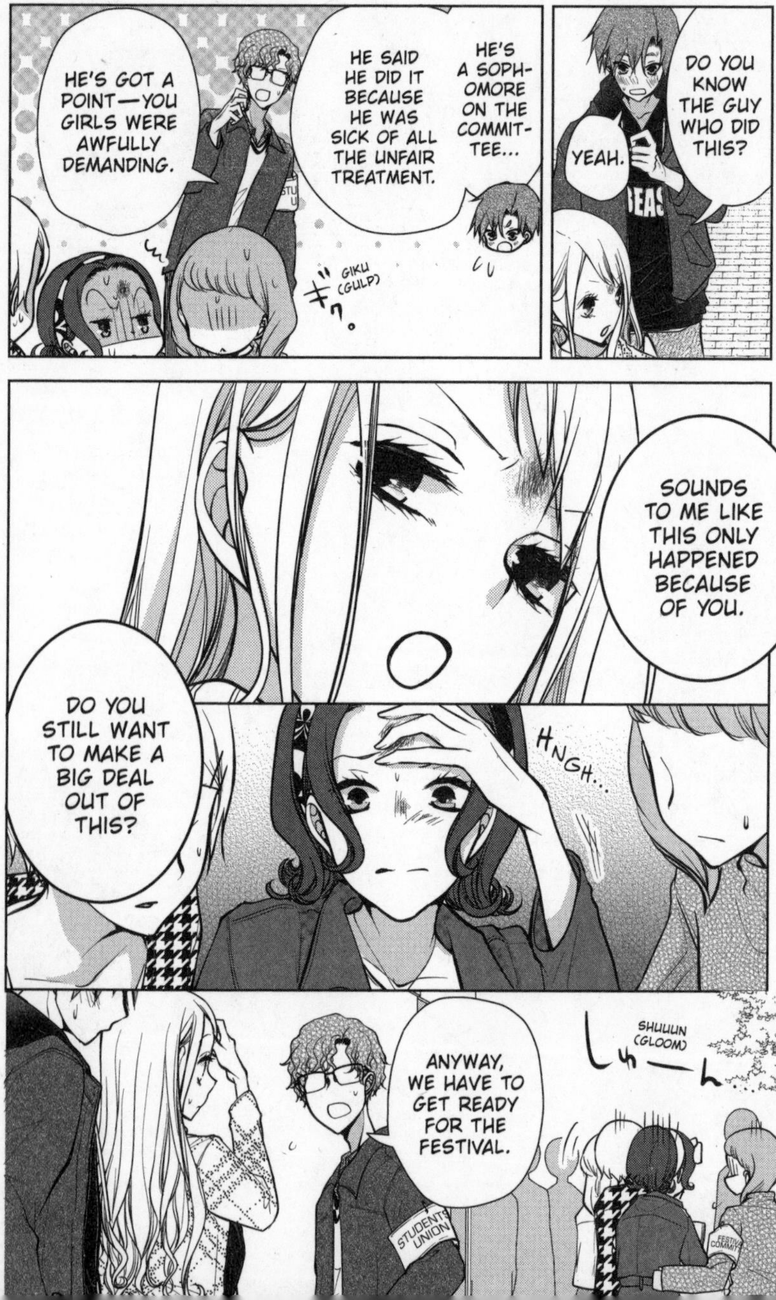
DO YOU KNOW THE GUY WHO DID THIS?
YEAH.
HE'S A SOPHOMORE ON THE COMMITTEE...
HE SAID HE DID IT BECAUSE HE WAS SICK OF ALL THE UNFAIR TREATMENT.
HE'S GOT A POINT—YOU GIRLS WERE AWFULLY DEMANDING.
GIKU (GULP)
SOUNDS TO ME LIKE THIS ONLY HAPPENED BECAUSE OF YOU.
HNGH...
DO YOU STILL WANT TO MAKE A BIG DEAL OUT OF THIS?
SHUUUN (GLOOM)
ANYWAY, WE HAVE TO GET READY FOR THE FESTIVAL.
STUDENTS UNION

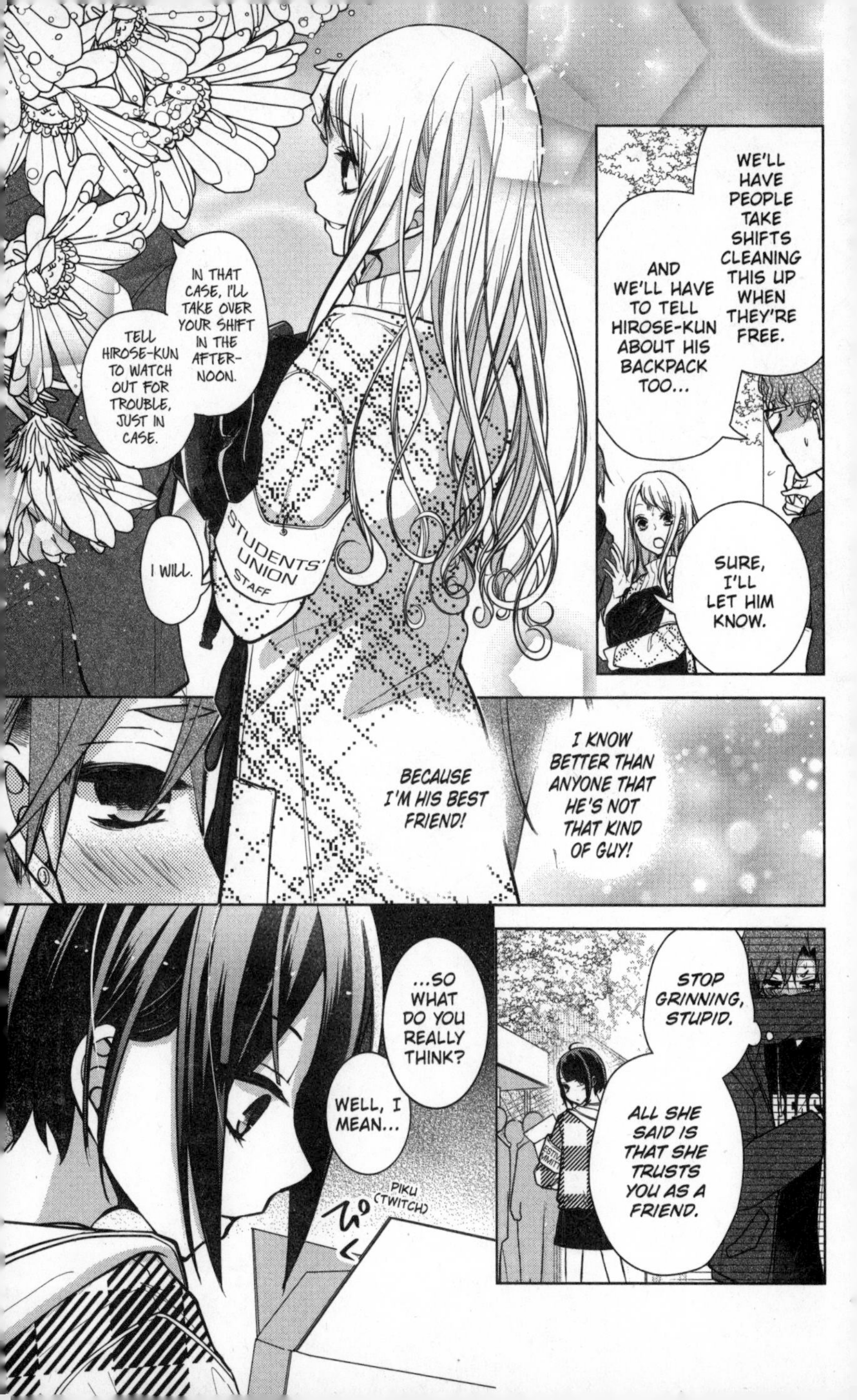
WE'LL HAVE PEOPLE TAKE SHIFTS CLEANING THIS UP WHEN THEY'RE FREE.
AND WE'LL HAVE TO TELL HIROSE-KUN ABOUT HIS BACKPACK TOO...
SURE, I'LL LET HIM KNOW.
IN THAT CASE, I'LL TAKE OVER YOUR SHIFT IN THE AFTER-NOON.
TELL HIROSE-KUN TO WATCH OUT FOR TROUBLE, JUST IN CASE.
STUDENTS' UNION STAFF
I WILL.
I KNOW BETTER THAN ANYONE THAT HE'S NOT THAT KIND OF GUY!
BECAUSE I'M HIS BEST FRIEND!
STOP GRINNING, STUPID.
ALL SHE SAID IS THAT SHE TRUSTS YOU AS A FRIEND.
...SO WHAT DO YOU REALLY THINK?
WELL, I MEAN...
PIKU (TWITCH)

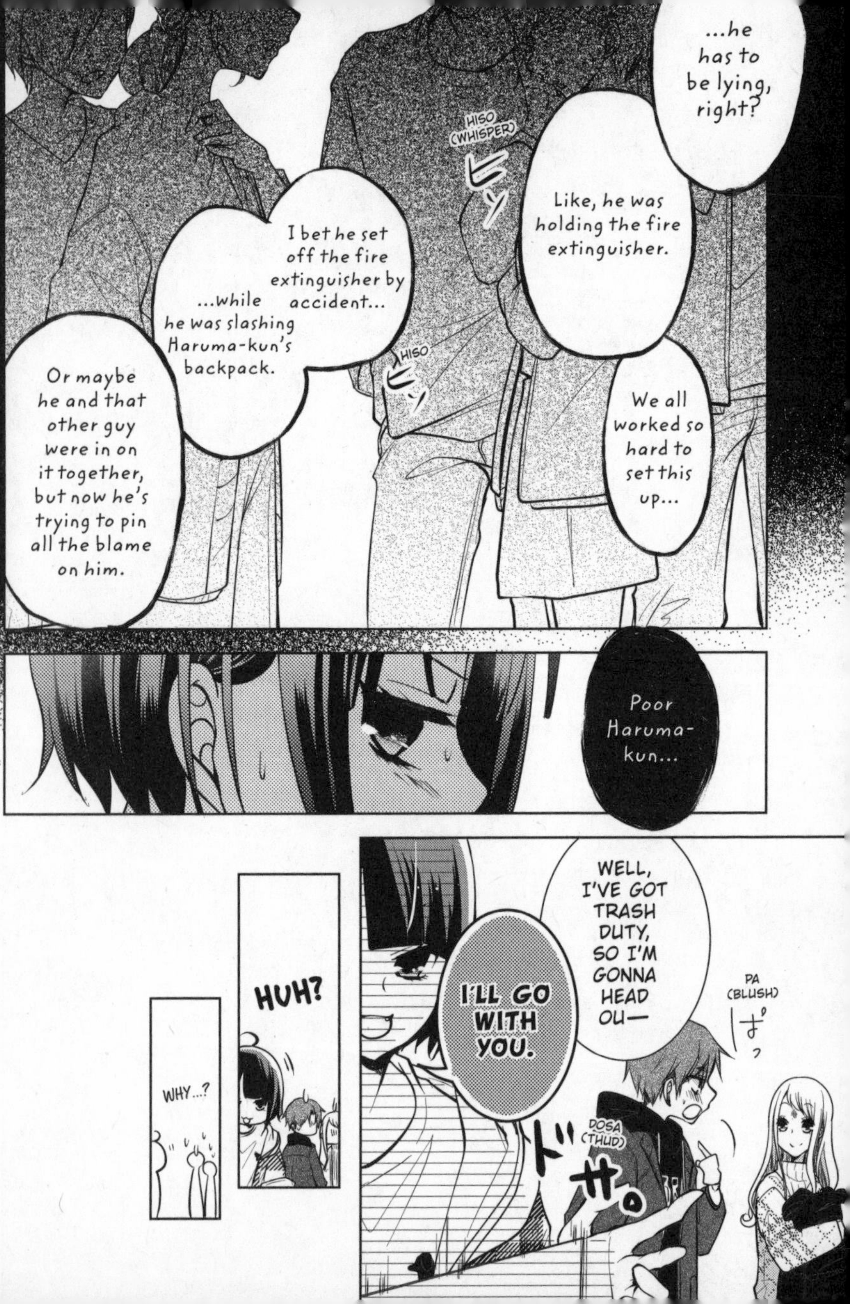
...he has to be lying, right?
HISO (WHISPER)
Like, he was holding the fire extinguisher.
I bet he set off the fire extinguisher by accident...
...while he was slashing Haruma-kun's backpack.
HISO
We all worked so hard to set this up...
Or maybe he and that other guy were in on it together, but now he's trying to pin all the blame on him.
Poor Haruma-kun...
PA (BLUSH)
WELL, I'VE GOT TRASH DUTY, SO I'M GONNA HEAD OU—
DOSA (THUD)
I'LL GO WITH YOU.
HUH?
WHY...?

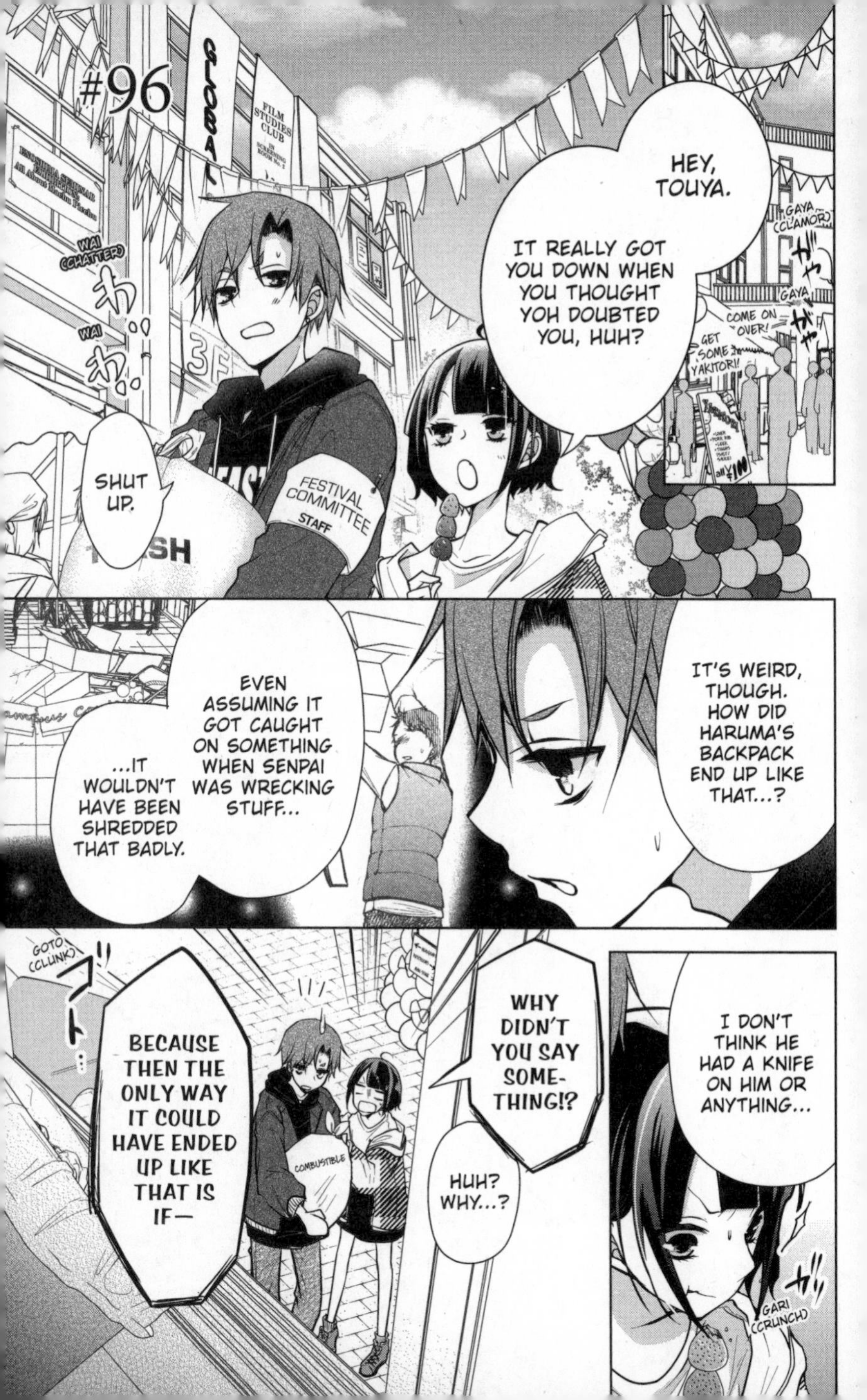
#96
GLOBAL
FILM STUDIES CLUB IN SCREENING ROOM No. 2
HEY, TOUYA.
IT REALLY GOT YOU DOWN WHEN YOU THOUGHT YOH DOUBTED YOU, HUH?
GAYA (CLAMOR)
GAYA
COME ON OVER!
GET SOME YAKITORI!
WAI (CHATTER)
WAI
SHUT UP.
FESTIVAL COMMITTEE STAFF
IT'S WEIRD, THOUGH. HOW DID HARUMA'S BACKPACK END UP LIKE THAT...?
EVEN ASSUMING IT GOT CAUGHT ON SOMETHING WHEN SENPAI WAS WRECKING STUFF...
...IT WOULDN'T HAVE BEEN SHREDDED THAT BADLY.
I DON'T THINK HE HAD A KNIFE ON HIM OR ANYTHING...
GARI (CRUNCH)
WHY DIDN'T YOU SAY SOME-THING!?
HUH? WHY...?
BECAUSE THEN THE ONLY WAY IT COULD HAVE ENDED UP LIKE THAT IS IF—
COMBUSTIBLE
GOTO (CLUNK)

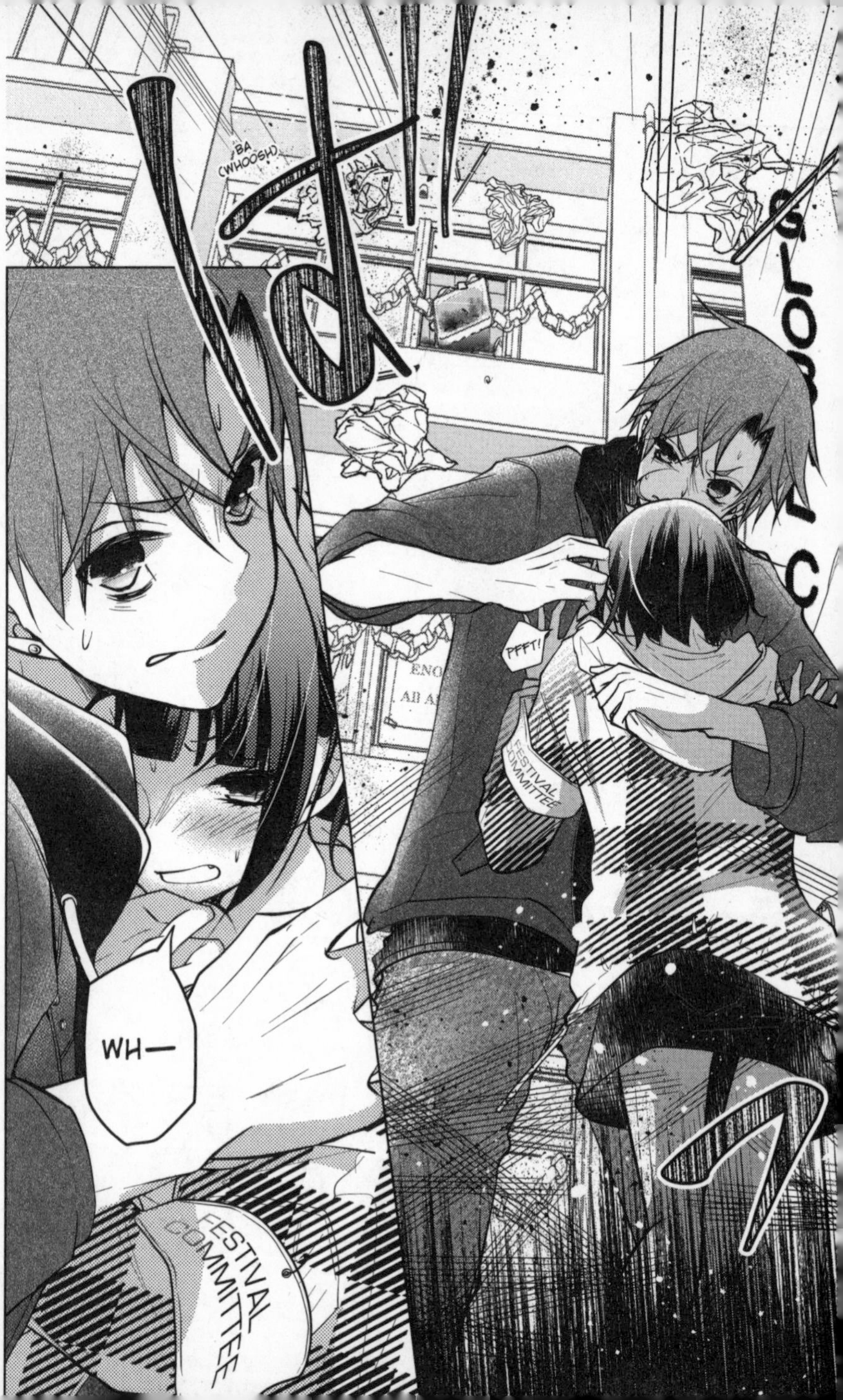
BA (WHOOSH)
PFFT!
FESTIVAL COMMITTEE
WH—
FESTIVAL COMMITTEE

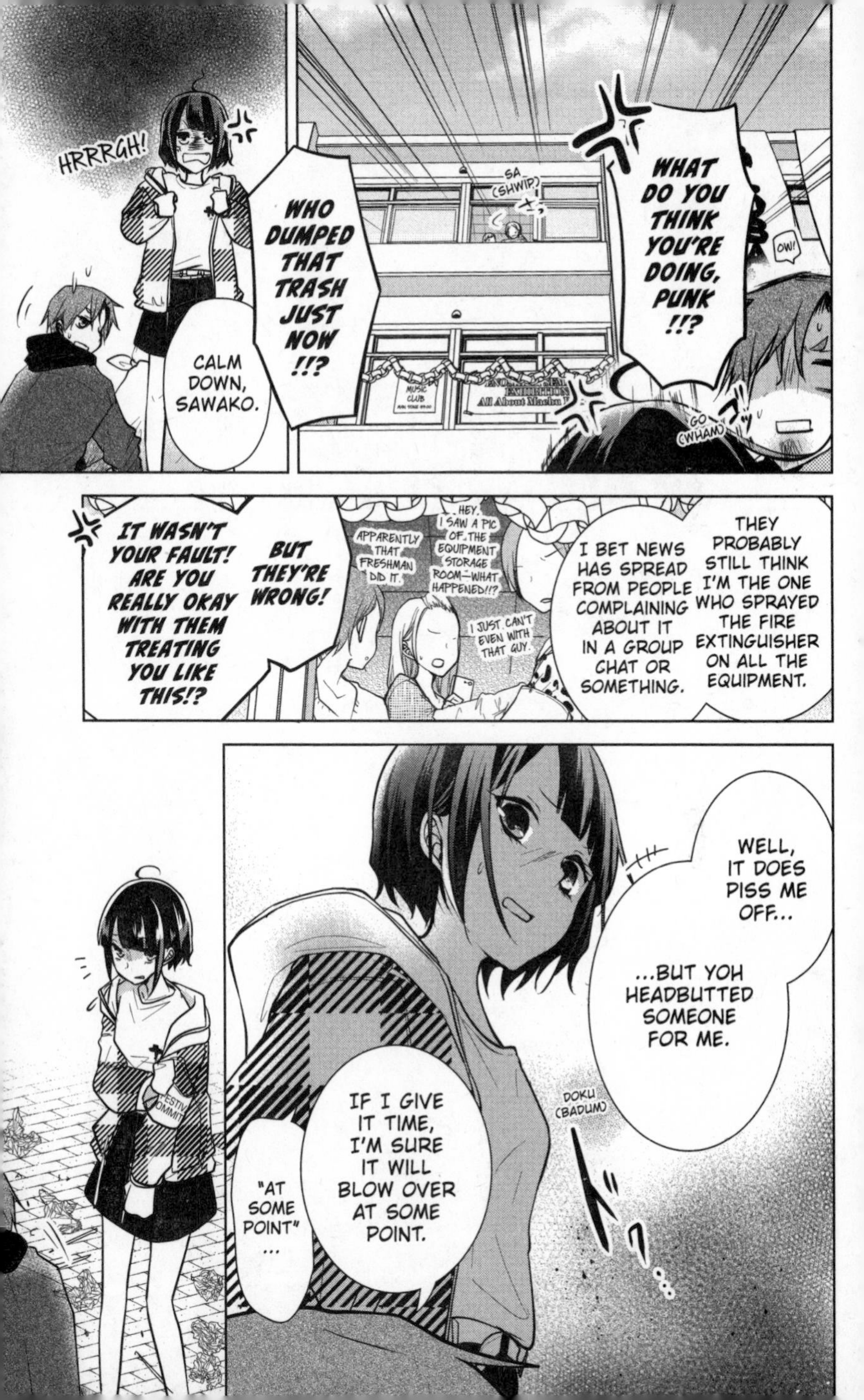
WHAT DO YOU THINK YOU'RE DOING, PUNK!!?
SA (SHWIP)
OW!
MUSIC CLUB
GO (WHAM)
WHO DUMPED THAT TRASH JUST NOW!!?
HRRRGH!
CALM DOWN, SAWAKO.
THEY PROBABLY STILL THINK I'M THE ONE WHO SPRAYED THE FIRE EXTINGUISHER ON ALL THE EQUIPMENT.
I BET NEWS HAS SPREAD FROM PEOPLE COMPLAINING ABOUT IT IN A GROUP CHAT OR SOMETHING.
HEY, I SAW A PIC OF THE EQUIPMENT STORAGE ROOM—WHAT HAPPENED!!?
I JUST CAN'T EVEN WITH THAT GUY.
APPARENTLY THAT FRESHMAN DID IT.
BUT THEY'RE WRONG!
IT WASN'T YOUR FAULT! ARE YOU REALLY OKAY WITH THEM TREATING YOU LIKE THIS!?
WELL, IT DOES PISS ME OFF...
...BUT YOH HEADBUTTED SOMEONE FOR ME.
DOKU (BADUM)
IF I GIVE IT TIME, I'M SURE IT WILL BLOW OVER AT SOME POINT.
"AT SOME POINT" ...

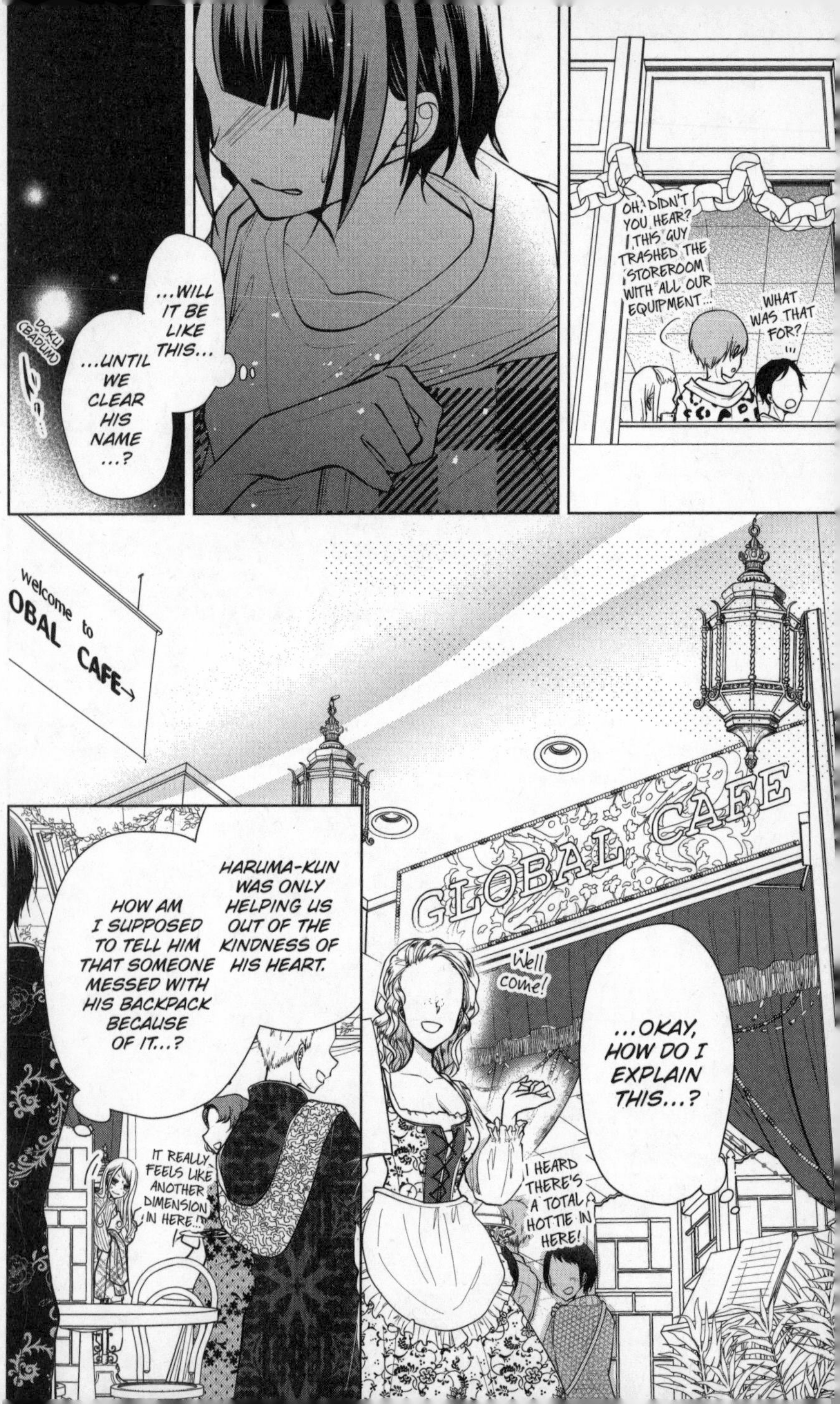
OH, DIDN'T YOU HEAR? THIS GUY TRASHED THE STOREROOM WITH ALL OUR EQUIPMENT...
WHAT WAS THAT FOR?
...WILL IT BE LIKE THIS...
...UNTIL WE CLEAR HIS NAME ...?
DOKU (BADUM)
welcome to OBAL CAFE
GLOBAL CAFE
...OKAY, HOW DO I EXPLAIN THIS...?
Well come!
HARUMA-KUN WAS ONLY HELPING US OUT OF THE KINDNESS OF HIS HEART.
HOW AM I SUPPOSED TO TELL HIM THAT SOMEONE MESSED WITH HIS BACKPACK BECAUSE OF IT...?
I HEARD THERE'S A TOTAL HOTTIE IN HERE!
IT REALLY FEELS LIKE ANOTHER DIMENSION IN HERE...!

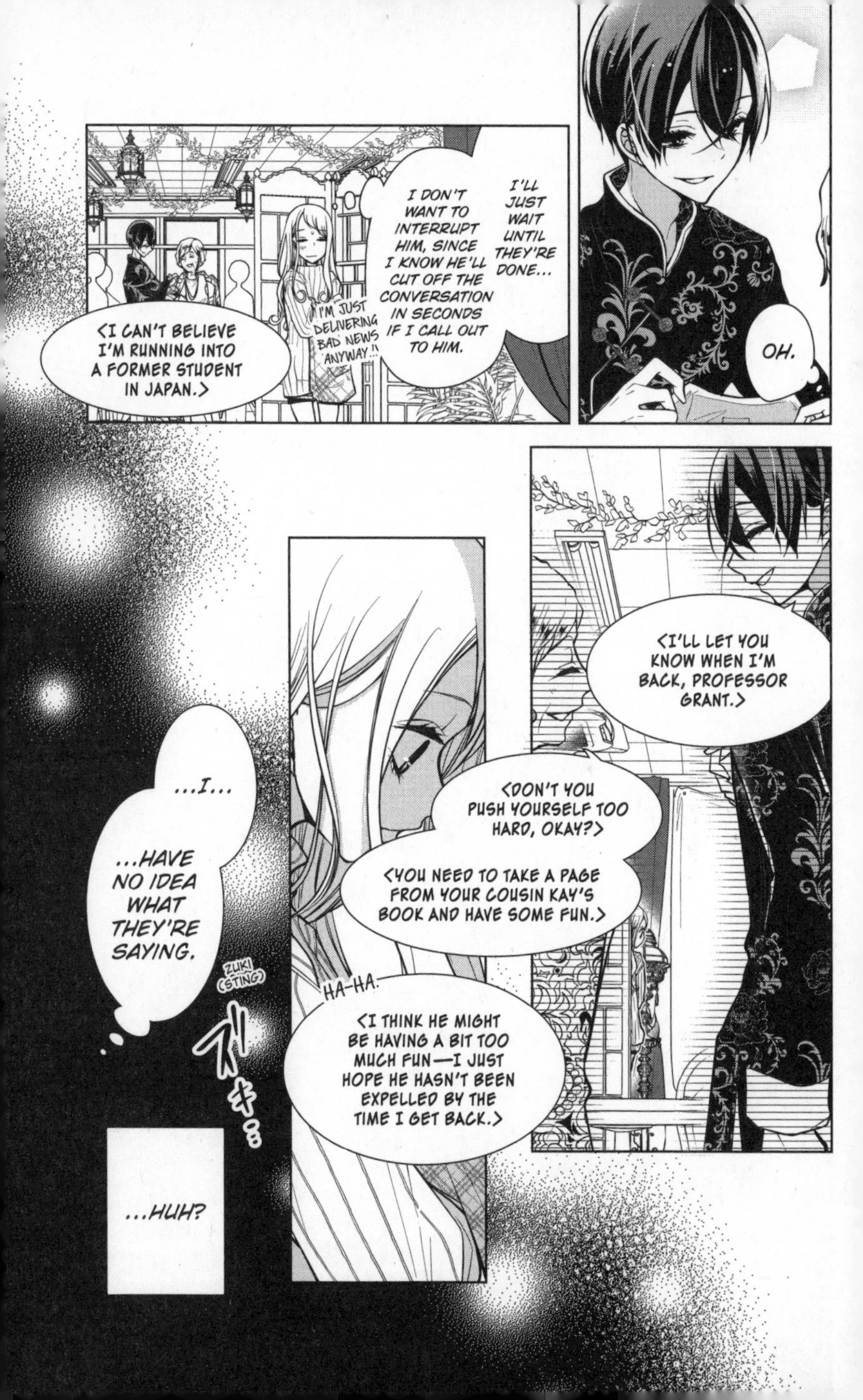
OH.
I'LL JUST WAIT UNTIL THEY'RE DONE...
I DON'T WANT TO INTERRUPT HIM, SINCE I KNOW HE'LL CUT OFF THE CONVERSATION IN SECONDS IF I CALL OUT TO HIM.
I'M JUST DELIVERING BAD NEWS ANYWAY!!
<I CAN'T BELIEVE I'M RUNNING INTO A FORMER STUDENT IN JAPAN.>
<I'LL LET YOU KNOW WHEN I'M BACK, PROFESSOR GRANT.>
<DON'T YOU PUSH YOURSELF TOO HARD, OKAY?>
<YOU NEED TO TAKE A PAGE FROM YOUR COUSIN KAY'S BOOK AND HAVE SOME FUN.>
HA-HA.
<I THINK HE MIGHT BE HAVING A BIT TOO MUCH FUN—I JUST HOPE HE HASN'T BEEN EXPELLED BY THE TIME I GET BACK.>
...I...
...HAVE NO IDEA WHAT THEY'RE SAYING.
ZUKI (STING)
...HUH?

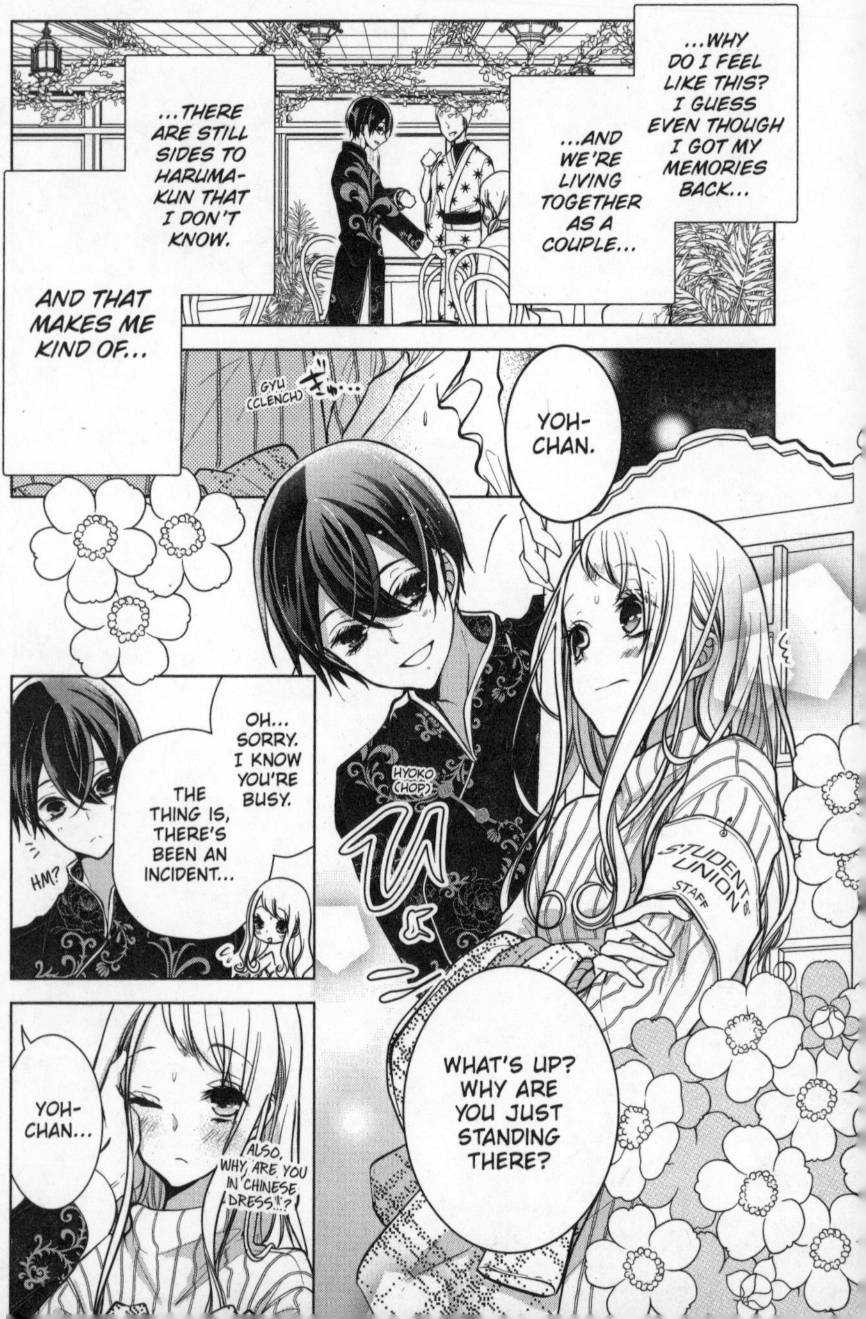
...WHY DO I FEEL LIKE THIS? I GUESS EVEN THOUGH I GOT MY MEMORIES BACK...
...AND WE'RE LIVING TOGETHER AS A COUPLE...
...THERE ARE STILL SIDES TO HARUMA-KUN THAT I DON'T KNOW.
AND THAT MAKES ME KIND OF...
GYU (CLENCH)
YOH-CHAN.
HYOKO (HOP)
WHAT'S UP? WHY ARE YOU JUST STANDING THERE?
STUDENT UNION STAFF
OH... SORRY. I KNOW YOU'RE BUSY.
THE THING IS, THERE'S BEEN AN INCIDENT...
HM?
YOH-CHAN...
ALSO, WHY ARE YOU IN CHINESE DRESS!!?

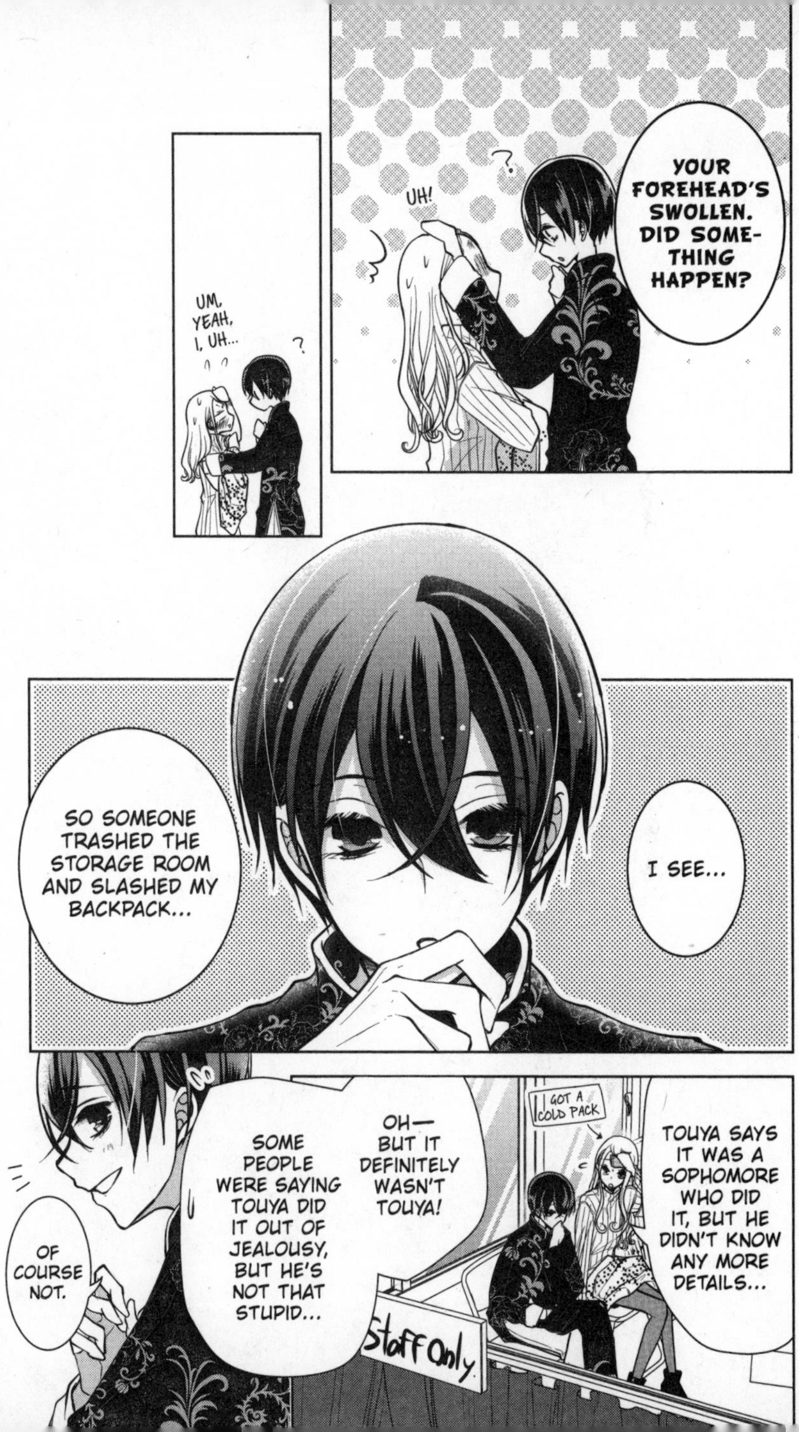
YOUR FOREHEAD'S SWOLLEN. DID SOME-THING HAPPEN?
UH!
?
UM, YEAH, I, UH...
?
SO SOMEONE TRASHED THE STORAGE ROOM AND SLASHED MY BACKPACK...
I SEE...
TOUYA SAYS IT WAS A SOPHOMORE WHO DID IT, BUT HE DIDN'T KNOW ANY MORE DETAILS...
GOT A COLD PACK
OH— BUT IT DEFINITELY WASN'T TOUYA!
SOME PEOPLE WERE SAYING TOUYA DID IT OUT OF JEALOUSY, BUT HE'S NOT THAT STUPID...
Staff Only
OF COURSE NOT.

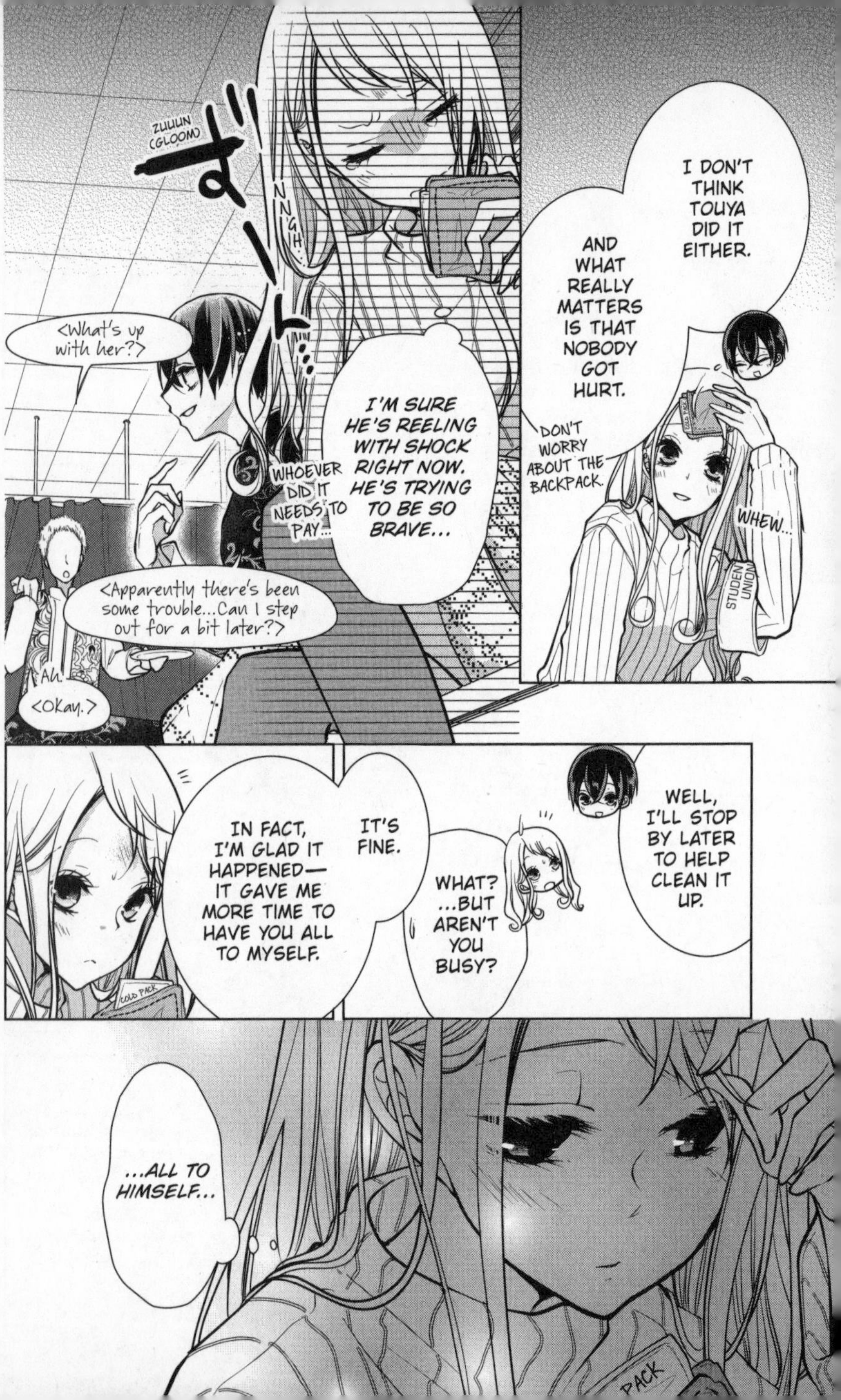
I DON'T THINK TOUYA DID IT EITHER.
AND WHAT REALLY MATTERS IS THAT NOBODY GOT HURT.
DON'T WORRY ABOUT THE BACKPACK.
WHEW...
ZUUUN (GLOOM)
NNNGH...
I'M SURE HE'S REELING WITH SHOCK RIGHT NOW. HE'S TRYING TO BE SO BRAVE...
WHOEVER DID IT NEEDS TO PAY...
<What's up with her?>
<Apparently there's been some trouble...Can I step out for a bit later?>
Ah.
<Okay.>
WELL, I'LL STOP BY LATER TO HELP CLEAN IT UP.
WHAT? ...BUT AREN'T YOU BUSY?
IT'S FINE.
IN FACT, I'M GLAD IT HAPPENED—IT GAVE ME MORE TIME TO HAVE YOU ALL TO MYSELF.
...ALL TO HIMSELF...

#97

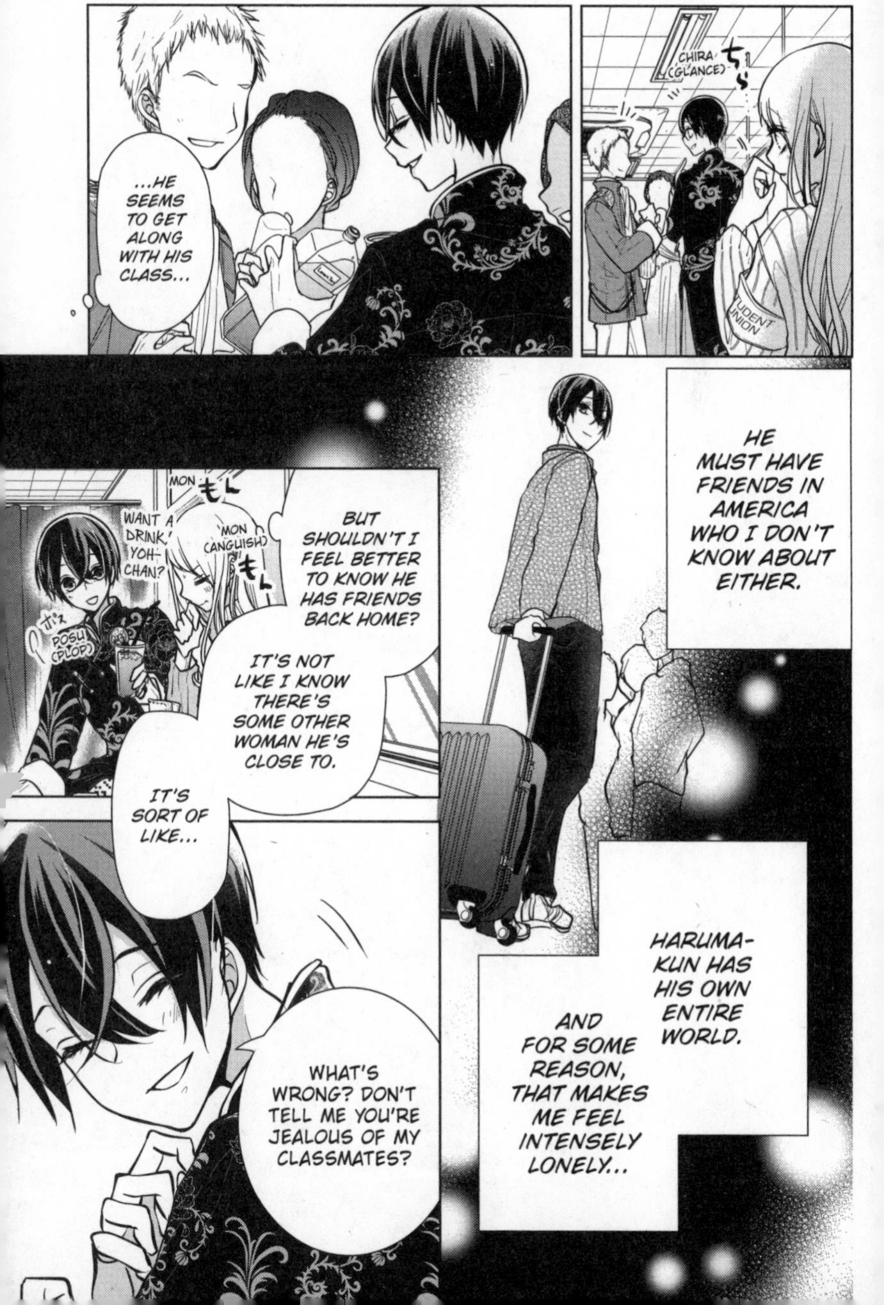
CHIRA (GLANCE)
STUDENT UNION
...HE SEEMS TO GET ALONG WITH HIS CLASS...
HE MUST HAVE FRIENDS IN AMERICA WHO I DON'T KNOW ABOUT EITHER.
HARUMA-KUN HAS HIS OWN ENTIRE WORLD.
AND FOR SOME REASON, THAT MAKES ME FEEL INTENSELY LONELY...
MON
BUT SHOULDN'T I FEEL BETTER TO KNOW HE HAS FRIENDS BACK HOME?
MON (ANGUISH)
WANT A DRINK, YOH-CHAN?
POSU (PLOP)
IT'S NOT LIKE I KNOW THERE'S SOME OTHER WOMAN HE'S CLOSE TO.
IT'S SORT OF LIKE...
WHAT'S WRONG? DON'T TELL ME YOU'RE JEALOUS OF MY CLASSMATES?

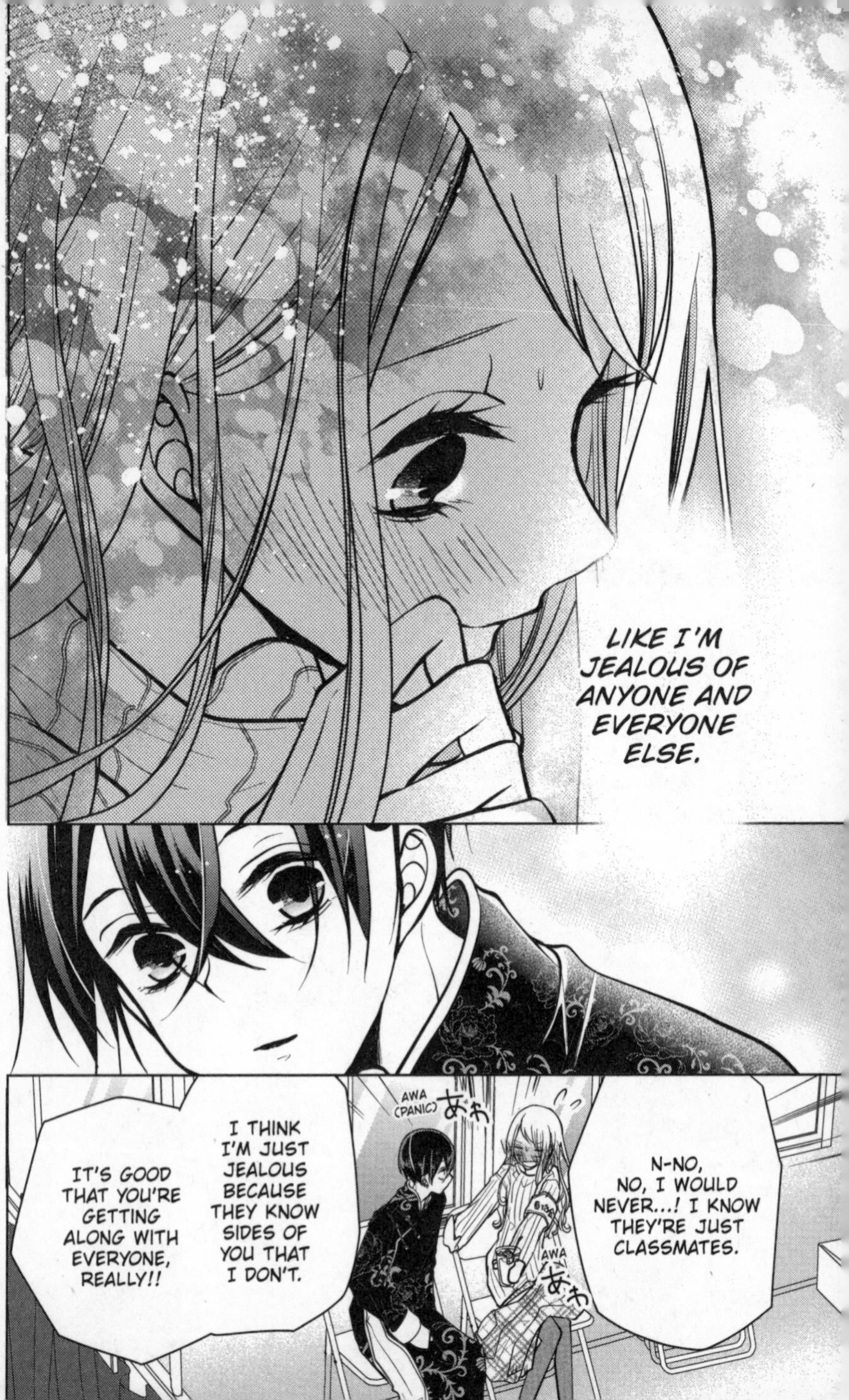
LIKE I'M JEALOUS OF ANYONE AND EVERYONE ELSE.
N-NO, NO, I WOULD NEVER...! I KNOW THEY'RE JUST CLASSMATES.
AWA (PANIC) あわ
AWA あわ
I THINK I'M JUST JEALOUS BECAUSE THEY KNOW SIDES OF YOU THAT I DON'T.
IT'S GOOD THAT YOU'RE GETTING ALONG WITH EVERYONE, REALLY!!

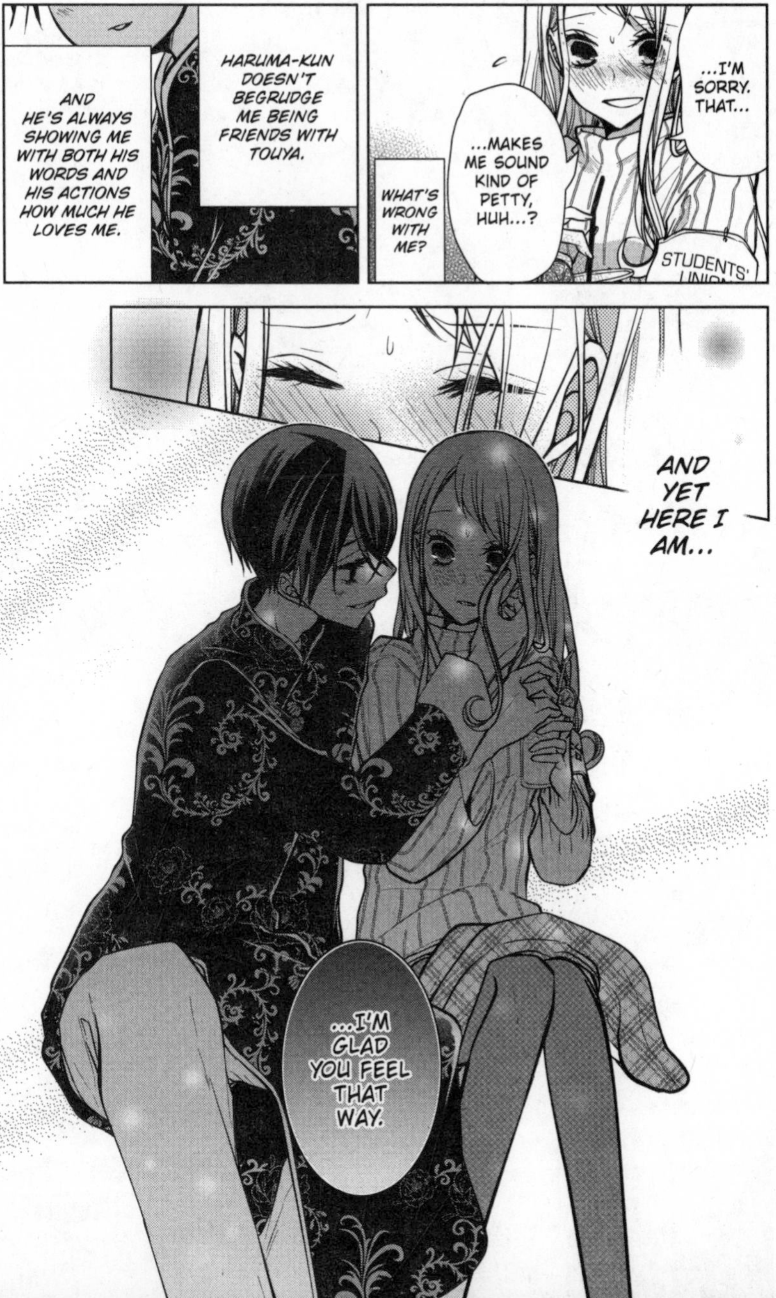
...I'M SORRY. THAT...
...MAKES ME SOUND KIND OF PETTY, HUH...?
WHAT'S WRONG WITH ME?
STUDENTS'
HARUMA-KUN DOESN'T BEGRUDGE ME BEING FRIENDS WITH TOUYA.
AND HE'S ALWAYS SHOWING ME WITH BOTH HIS WORDS AND HIS ACTIONS HOW MUCH HE LOVES ME.
AND YET HERE I AM...
...I'M GLAD YOU FEEL THAT WAY.

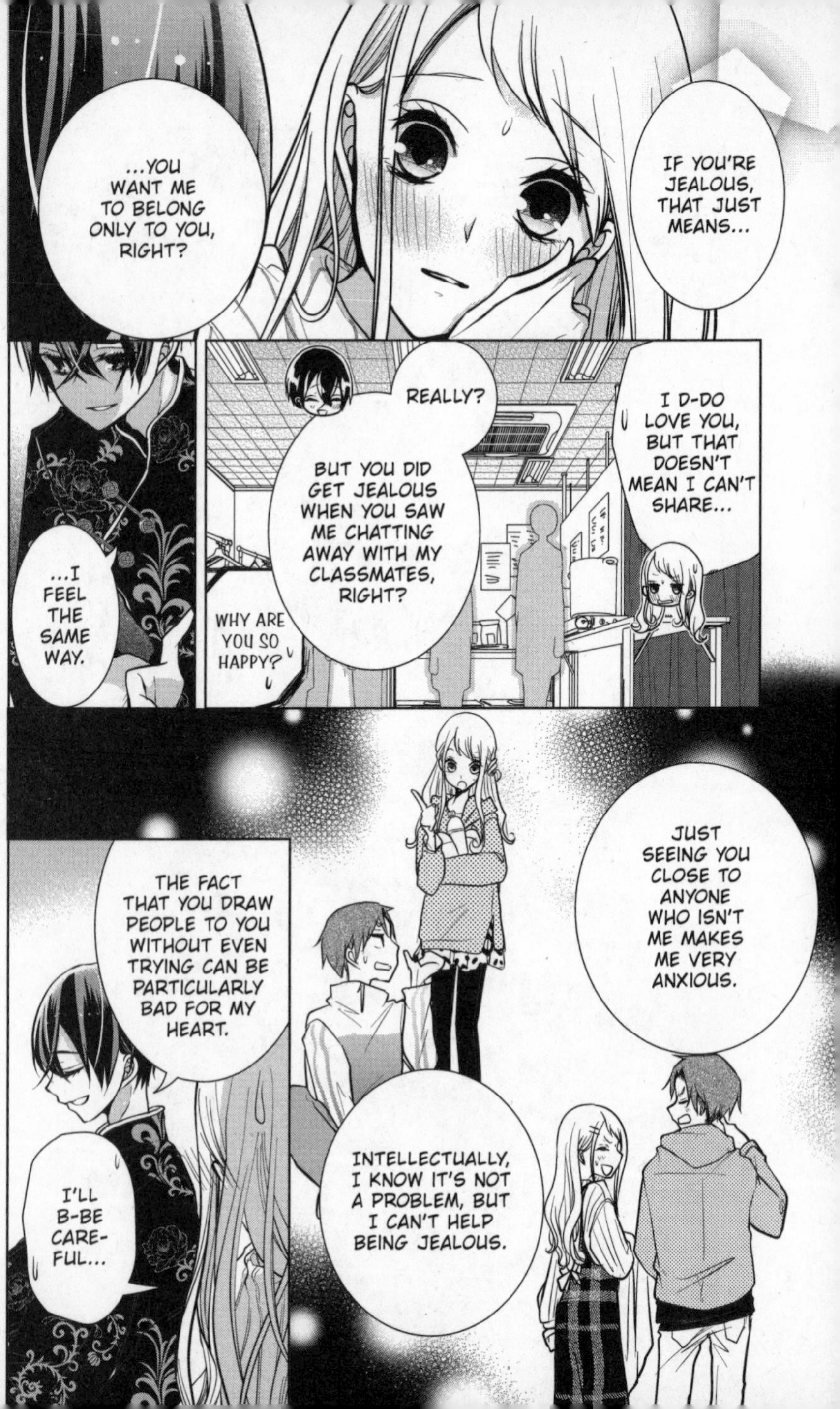

IF YOU'RE JEALOUS, THAT JUST MEANS...
...YOU WANT ME TO BELONG ONLY TO YOU, RIGHT?
I D-DO LOVE YOU, BUT THAT DOESN'T MEAN I CAN'T SHARE...
REALLY?
BUT YOU DID GET JEALOUS WHEN YOU SAW ME CHATTING AWAY WITH MY CLASSMATES, RIGHT?
WHY ARE YOU SO HAPPY?
...I FEEL THE SAME WAY.
JUST SEEING YOU CLOSE TO ANYONE WHO ISN'T ME MAKES ME VERY ANXIOUS.
INTELLECTUALLY, I KNOW IT'S NOT A PROBLEM, BUT I CAN'T HELP BEING JEALOUS.
THE FACT THAT YOU DRAW PEOPLE TO YOU WITHOUT EVEN TRYING CAN BE PARTICULARLY BAD FOR MY HEART.
I'LL B-BE CARE-FUL...

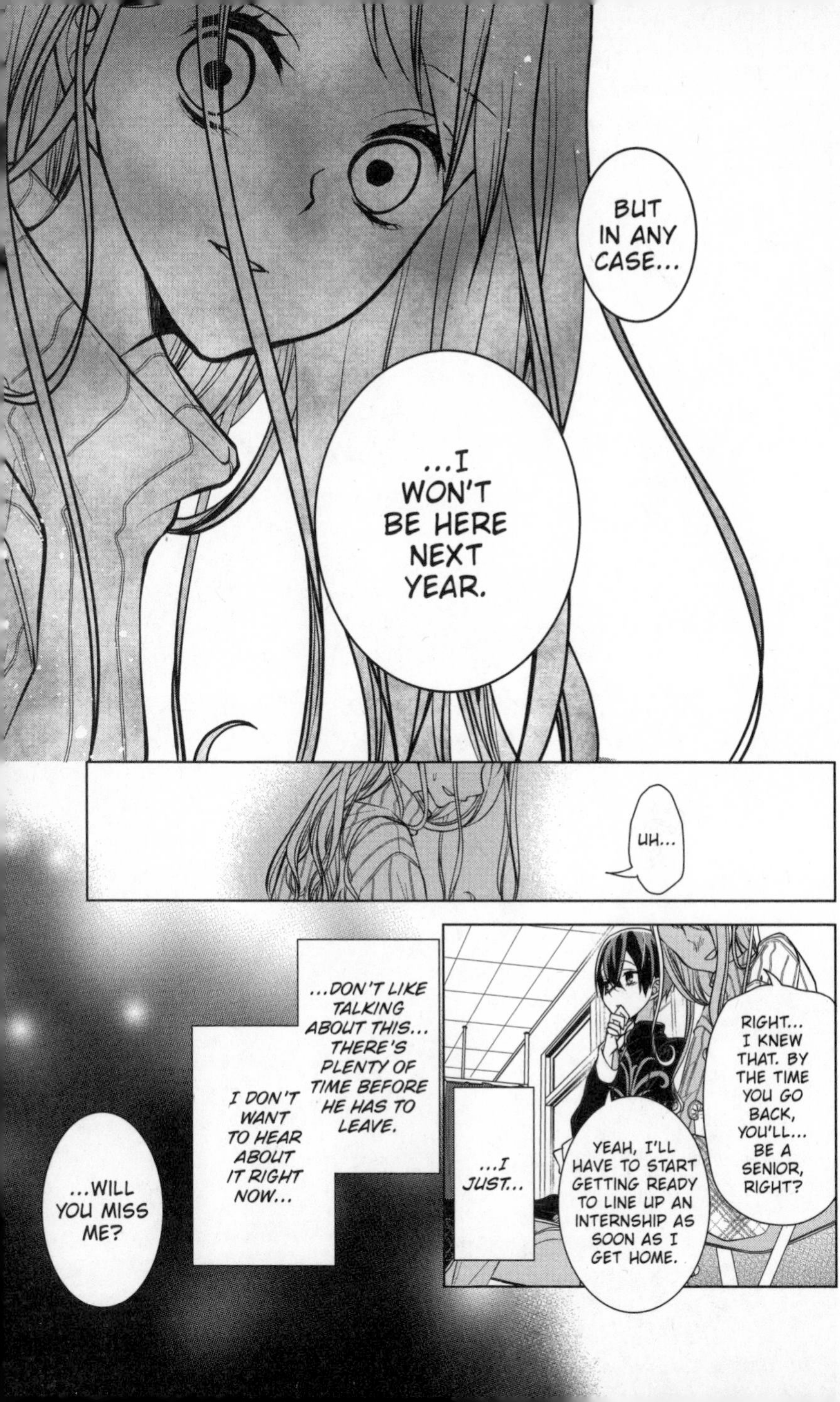
BUT IN ANY CASE...
...I WON'T BE HERE NEXT YEAR.
UH...
RIGHT... I KNEW THAT. BY THE TIME YOU GO BACK, YOU'LL... BE A SENIOR, RIGHT?
YEAH, I'LL HAVE TO START GETTING READY TO LINE UP AN INTERNSHIP AS SOON AS I GET HOME.
...I JUST...
...DON'T LIKE TALKING ABOUT THIS... THERE'S PLENTY OF TIME BEFORE HE HAS TO LEAVE.
I DON'T WANT TO HEAR ABOUT IT RIGHT NOW...
...WILL YOU MISS ME?

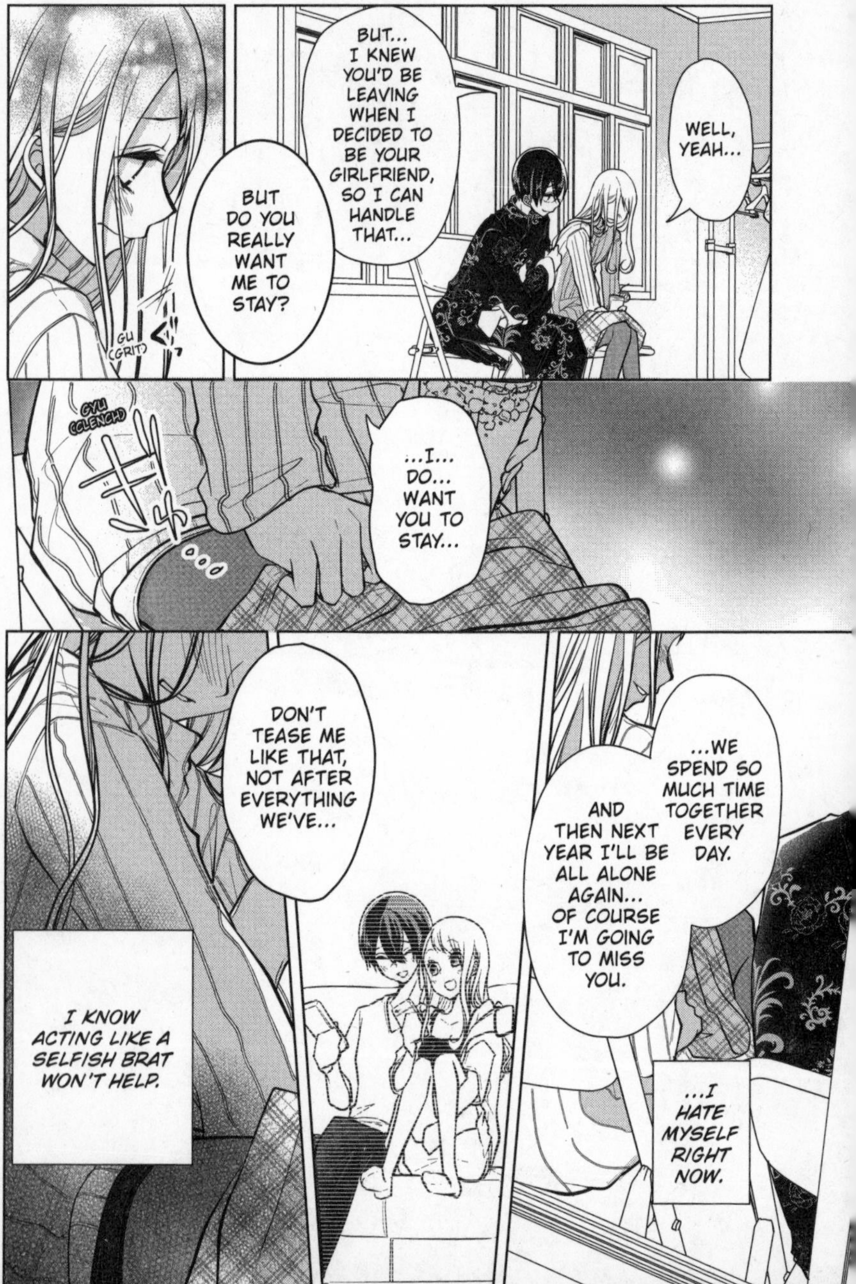
WELL, YEAH...
BUT... I KNEW YOU'D BE LEAVING WHEN I DECIDED TO BE YOUR GIRLFRIEND, SO I CAN HANDLE THAT...
BUT DO YOU REALLY WANT ME TO STAY?
GU (GRIT)
...I... DO... WANT YOU TO STAY...
GYU (CLENCH)
...WE SPEND SO MUCH TIME TOGETHER EVERY DAY.
AND THEN NEXT YEAR I'LL BE ALL ALONE AGAIN... OF COURSE I'M GOING TO MISS YOU.
...I HATE MYSELF RIGHT NOW.
DON'T TEASE ME LIKE THAT, NOT AFTER EVERYTHING WE'VE...
I KNOW ACTING LIKE A SELFISH BRAT WON'T HELP.

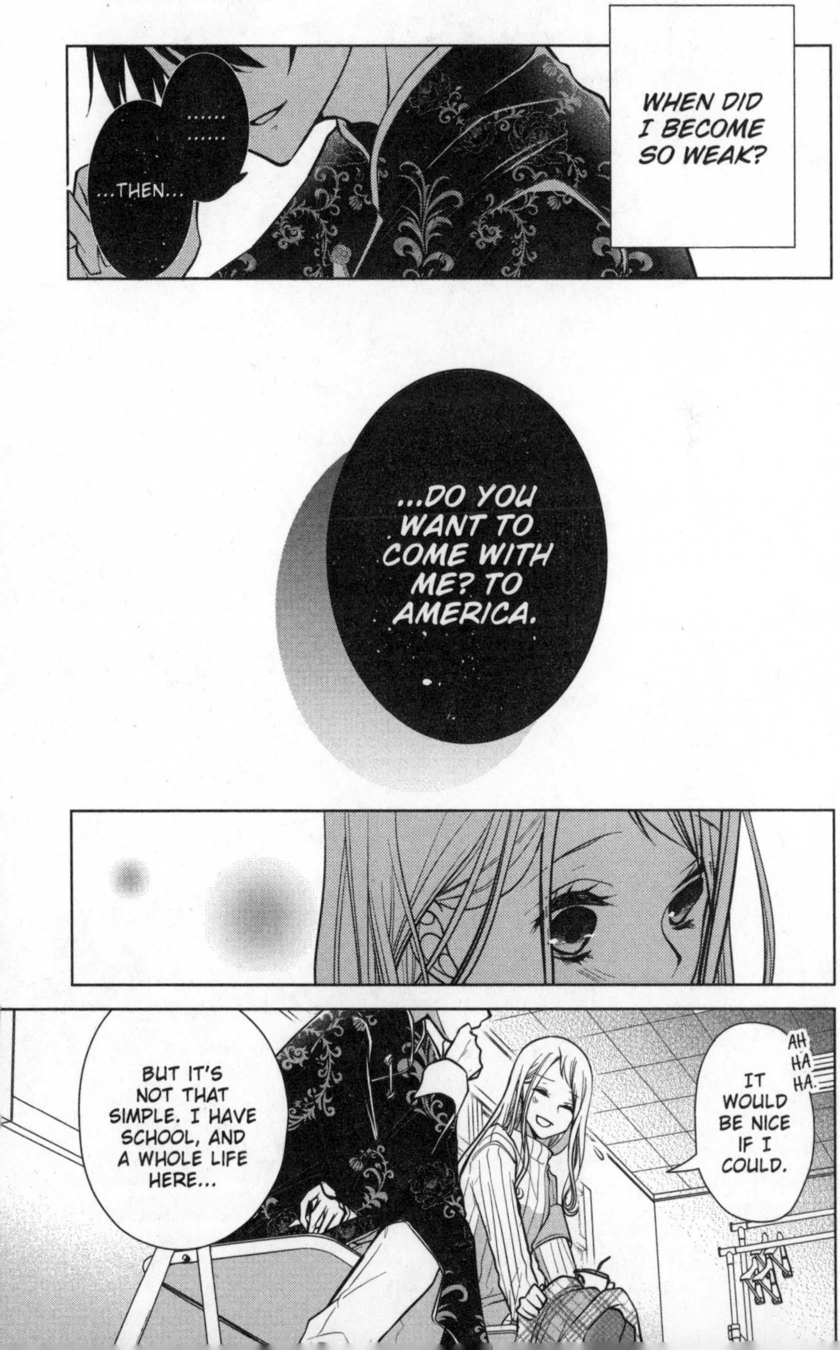
WHEN DID I BECOME SO WEAK?
....THEN...
...DO YOU WANT TO COME WITH ME? TO AMERICA.
AH HA HA.
IT WOULD BE NICE IF I COULD.
BUT IT'S NOT THAT SIMPLE. I HAVE SCHOOL, AND A WHOLE LIFE HERE...

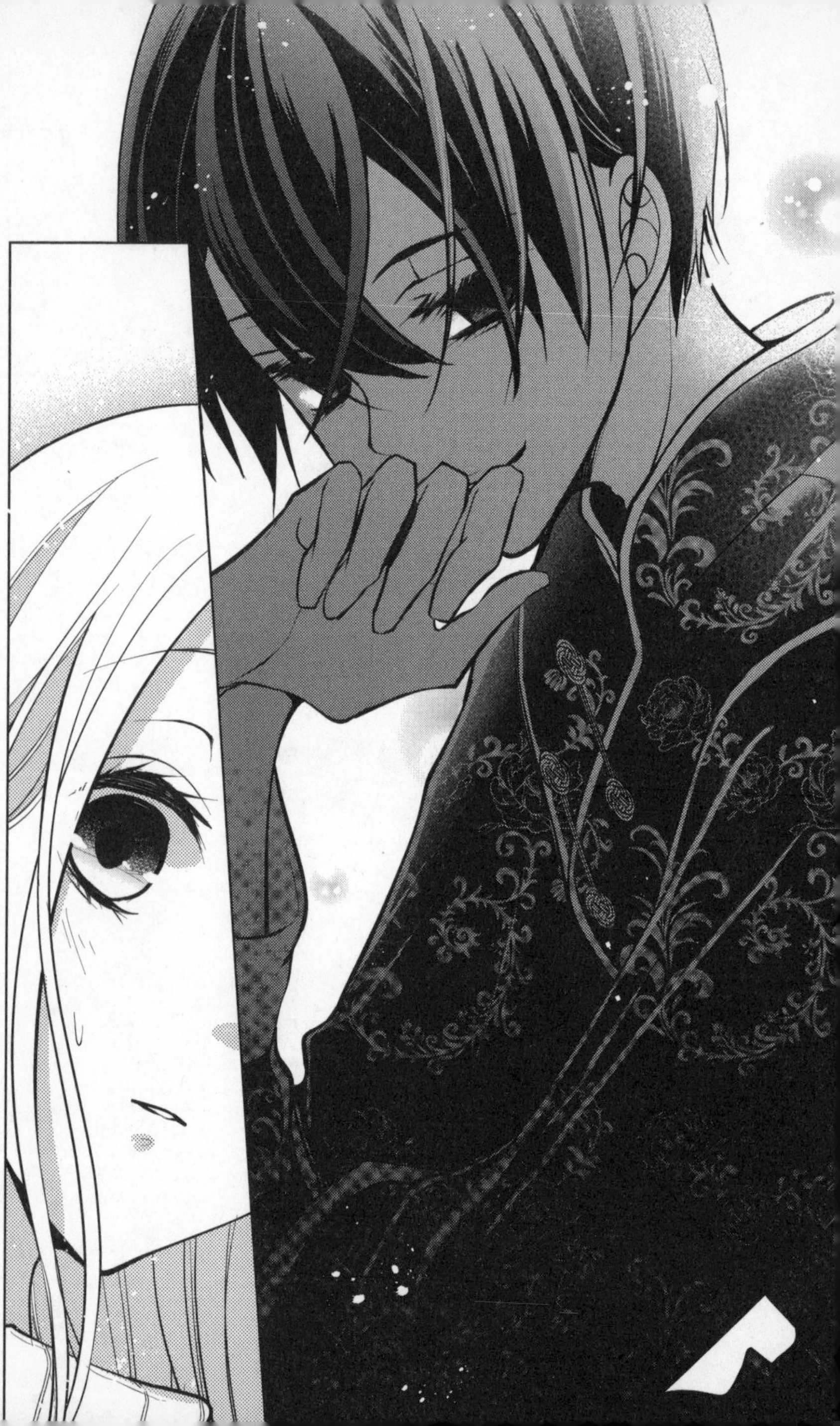

#98

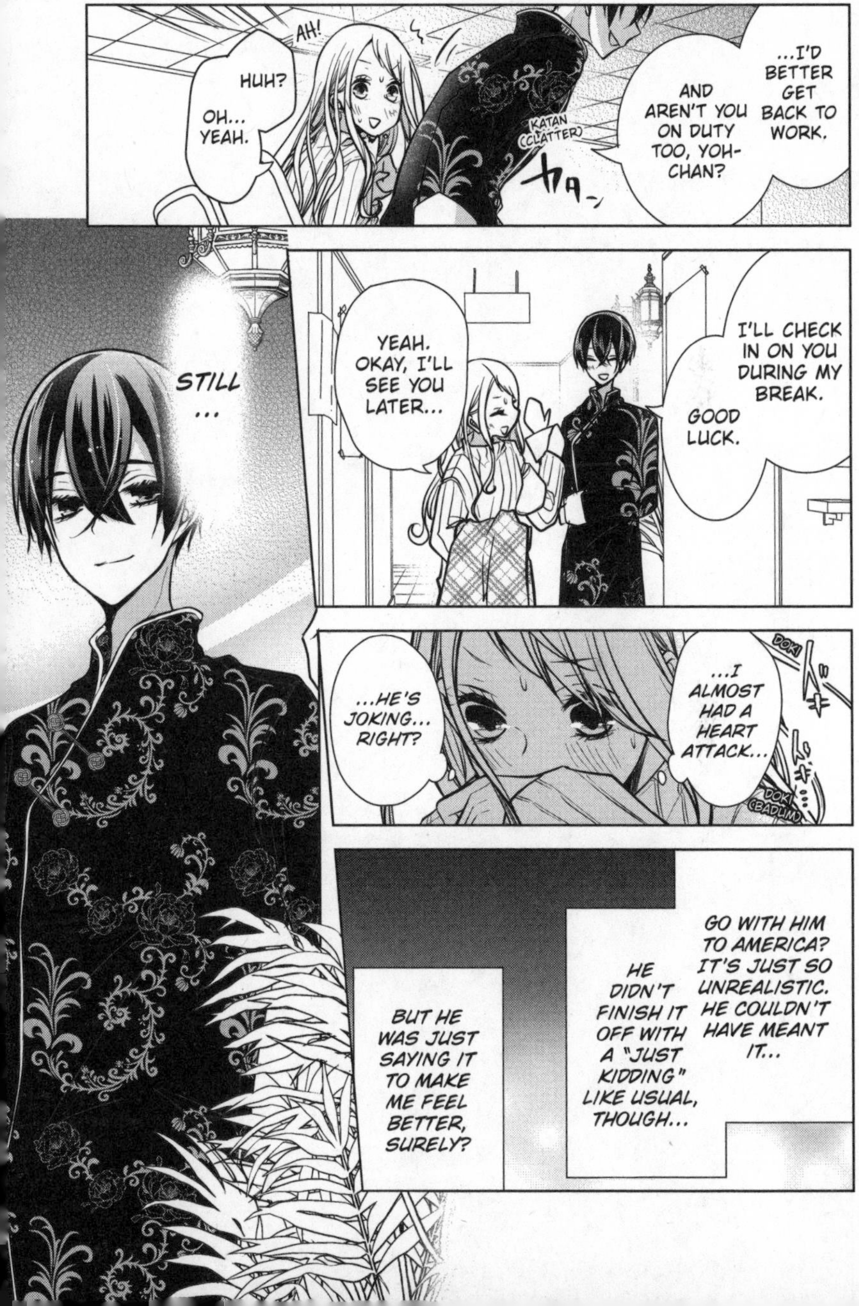
...I'D BETTER GET BACK TO WORK.
AND AREN'T YOU ON DUTY TOO, YOH-CHAN?
KATAN (CLATTER)
AH!
HUH?
OH... YEAH.
I'LL CHECK IN ON YOU DURING MY BREAK.
GOOD LUCK.
YEAH. OKAY, I'LL SEE YOU LATER...
DOKI
...I ALMOST HAD A HEART ATTACK...
DOKI (BADUMP)
...HE'S JOKING... RIGHT?
GO WITH HIM TO AMERICA? IT'S JUST SO UNREALISTIC. HE COULDN'T HAVE MEANT IT...
HE DIDN'T FINISH IT OFF WITH A "JUST KIDDING" LIKE USUAL, THOUGH...
BUT HE WAS JUST SAYING IT TO MAKE ME FEEL BETTER, SURELY?
STILL...

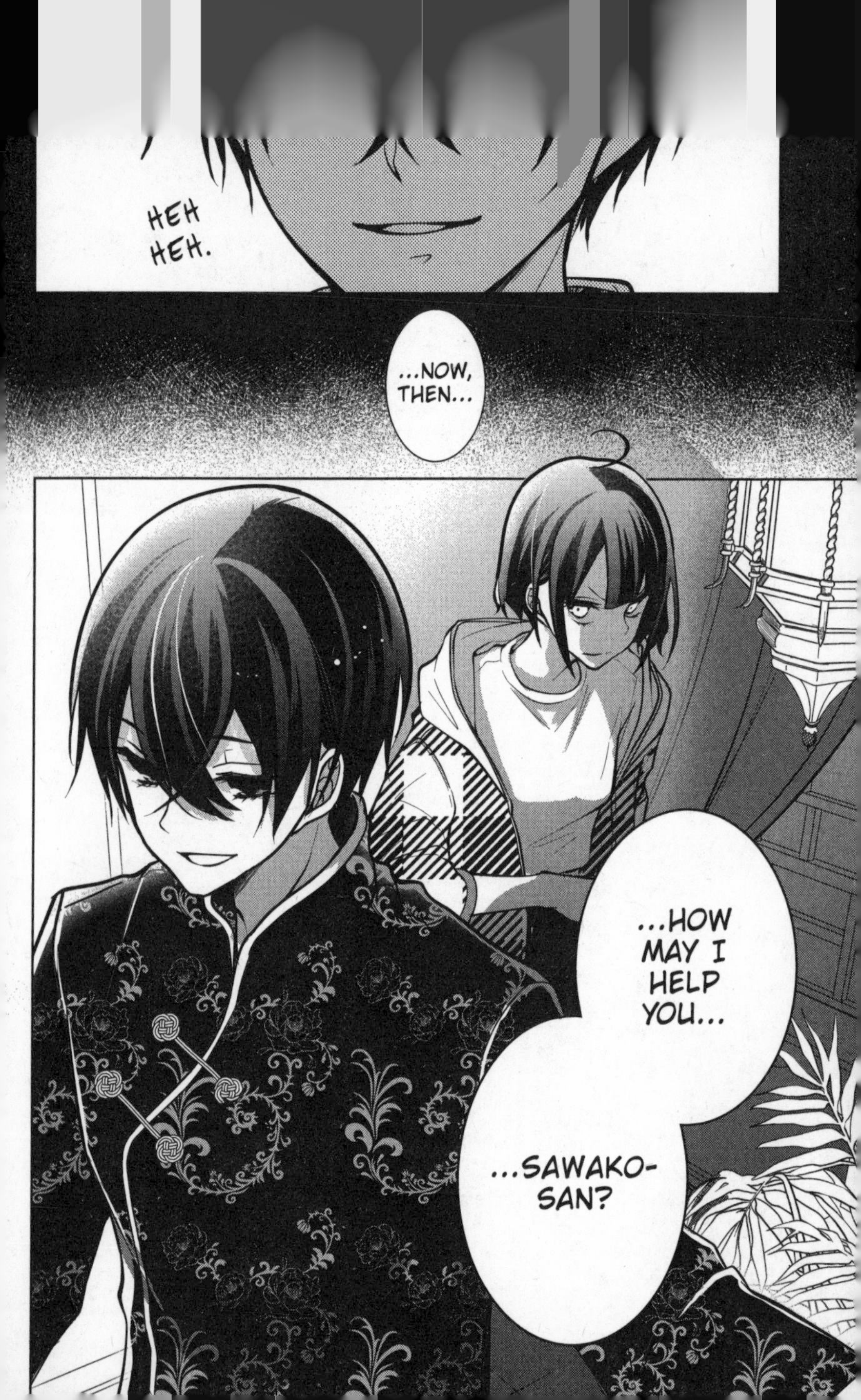
HEH HEH.
...NOW, THEN...
...HOW MAY I HELP YOU...
...SAWAKO-SAN?

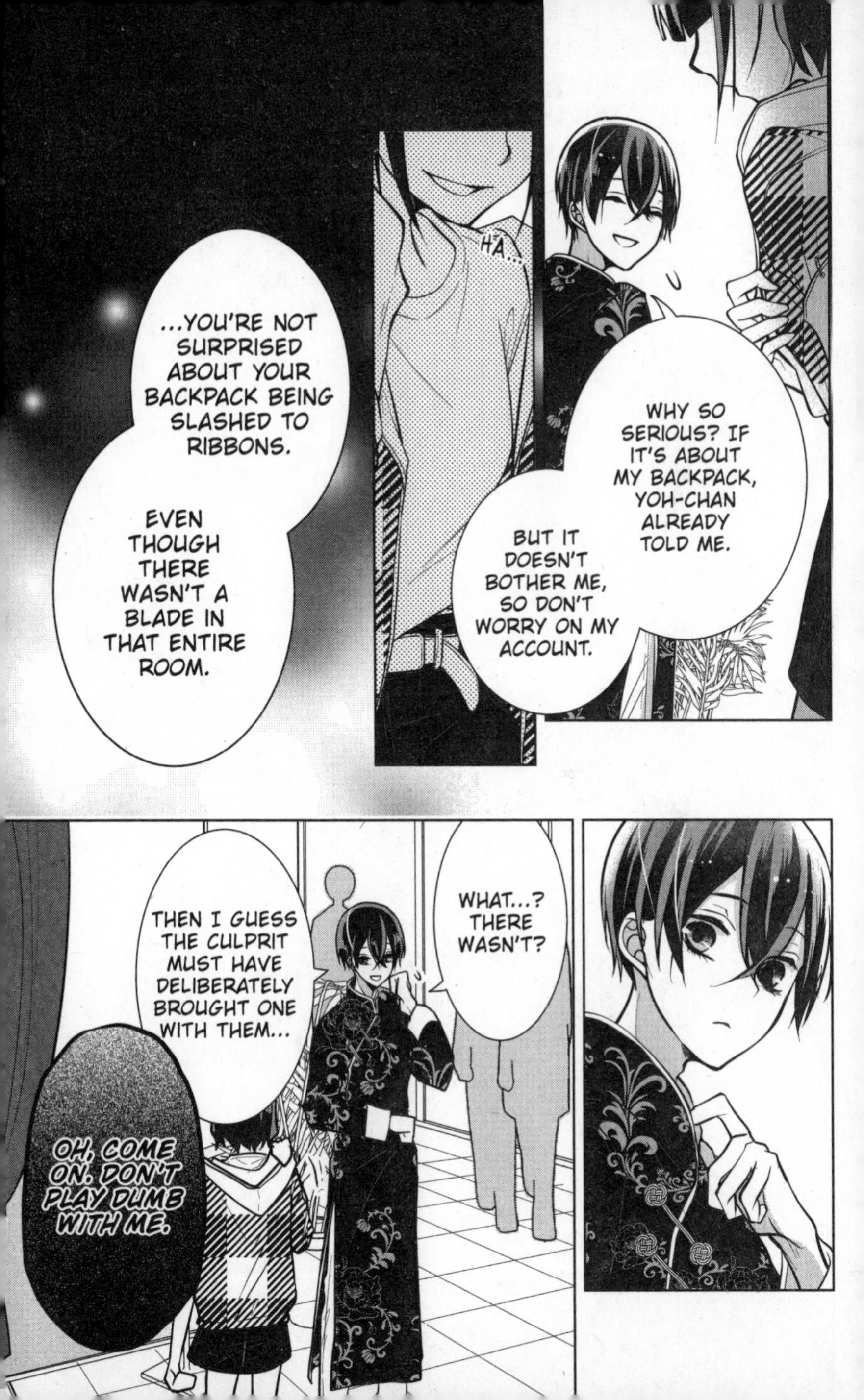
WHY SO SERIOUS? IF IT'S ABOUT MY BACKPACK, YOH-CHAN ALREADY TOLD ME.
BUT IT DOESN'T BOTHER ME, SO DON'T WORRY ON MY ACCOUNT.
HA...
...YOU'RE NOT SURPRISED ABOUT YOUR BACKPACK BEING SLASHED TO RIBBONS.
EVEN THOUGH THERE WASN'T A BLADE IN THAT ENTIRE ROOM.
WHAT...? THERE WASN'T?
THEN I GUESS THE CULPRIT MUST HAVE DELIBERATELY BROUGHT ONE WITH THEM...
OH, COME ON. DON'T PLAY DUMB WITH ME.

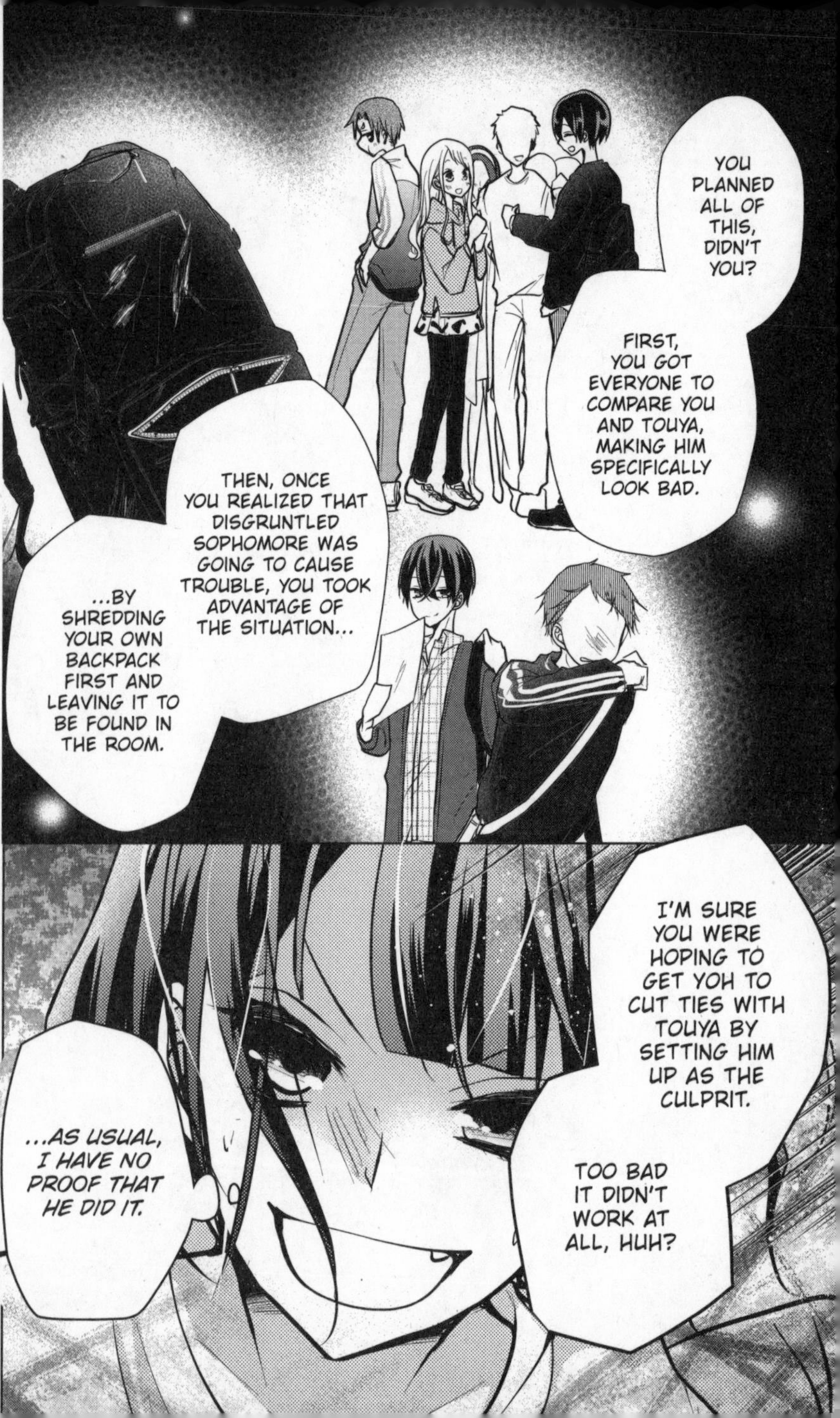
YOU PLANNED ALL OF THIS, DIDN'T YOU?
FIRST, YOU GOT EVERYONE TO COMPARE YOU AND TOUYA, MAKING HIM SPECIFICALLY LOOK BAD.
THEN, ONCE YOU REALIZED THAT DISGRUNTLED SOPHOMORE WAS GOING TO CAUSE TROUBLE, YOU TOOK ADVANTAGE OF THE SITUATION...
...BY SHREDDING YOUR OWN BACKPACK FIRST AND LEAVING IT TO BE FOUND IN THE ROOM.
I'M SURE YOU WERE HOPING TO GET YOH TO CUT TIES WITH TOUYA BY SETTING HIM UP AS THE CULPRIT.
TOO BAD IT DIDN'T WORK AT ALL, HUH?
...AS USUAL, I HAVE NO PROOF THAT HE DID IT.

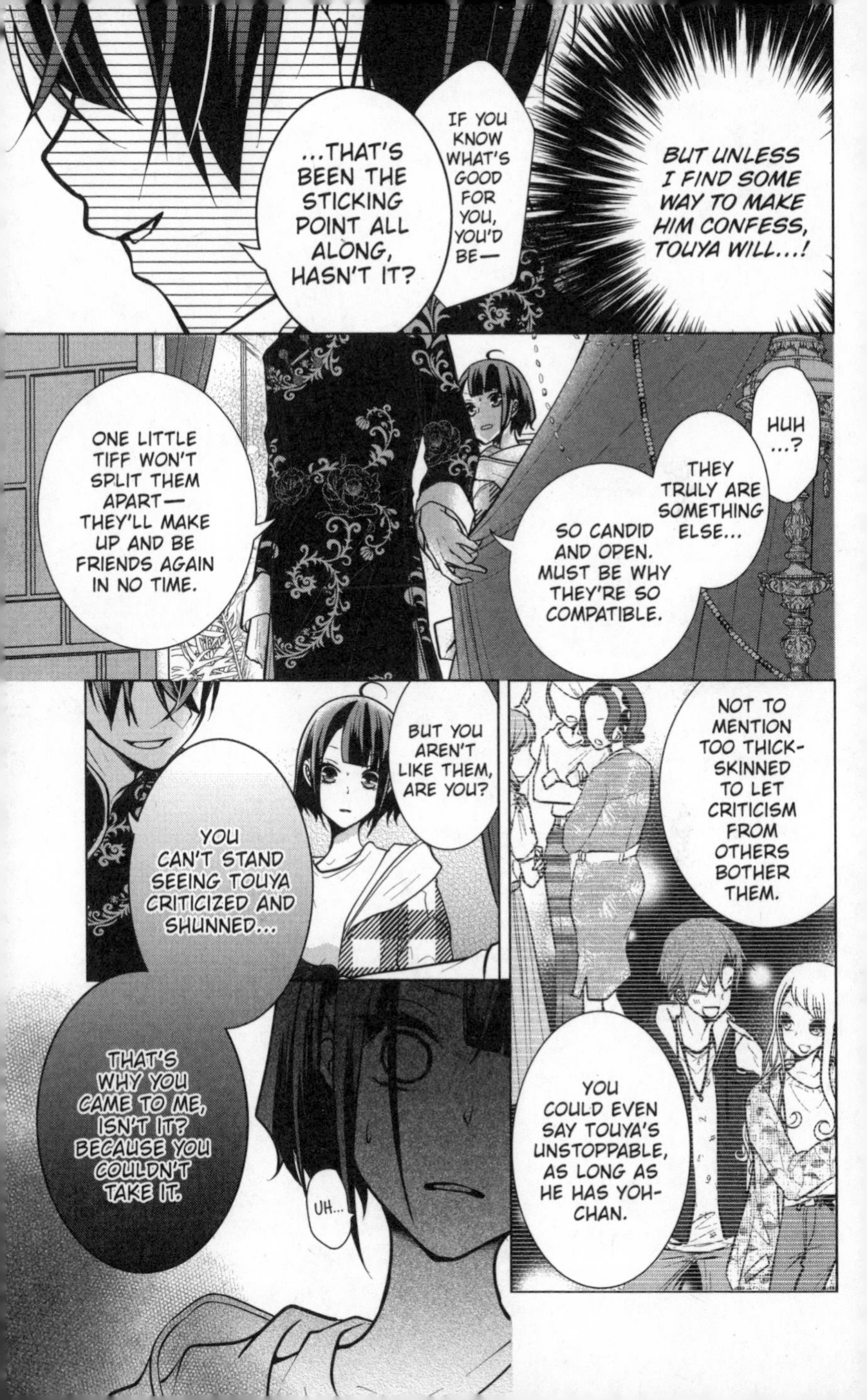
BUT UNLESS I FIND SOME WAY TO MAKE HIM CONFESS, TOUYA WILL...!
IF YOU KNOW WHAT'S GOOD FOR YOU, YOU'D BE—
...THAT'S BEEN THE STICKING POINT ALL ALONG, HASN'T IT?
HUH ...?
THEY TRULY ARE SOMETHING ELSE...
SO CANDID AND OPEN. MUST BE WHY THEY'RE SO COMPATIBLE.
ONE LITTLE TIFF WON'T SPLIT THEM APART— THEY'LL MAKE UP AND BE FRIENDS AGAIN IN NO TIME.
NOT TO MENTION TOO THICK-SKINNED TO LET CRITICISM FROM OTHERS BOTHER THEM.
YOU COULD EVEN SAY TOUYA'S UNSTOPPABLE, AS LONG AS HE HAS YOH-CHAN.
BUT YOU AREN'T LIKE THEM, ARE YOU?
YOU CAN'T STAND SEEING TOUYA CRITICIZED AND SHUNNED...
THAT'S WHY YOU CAME TO ME, ISN'T IT? BECAUSE YOU COULDN'T TAKE IT.
UH...

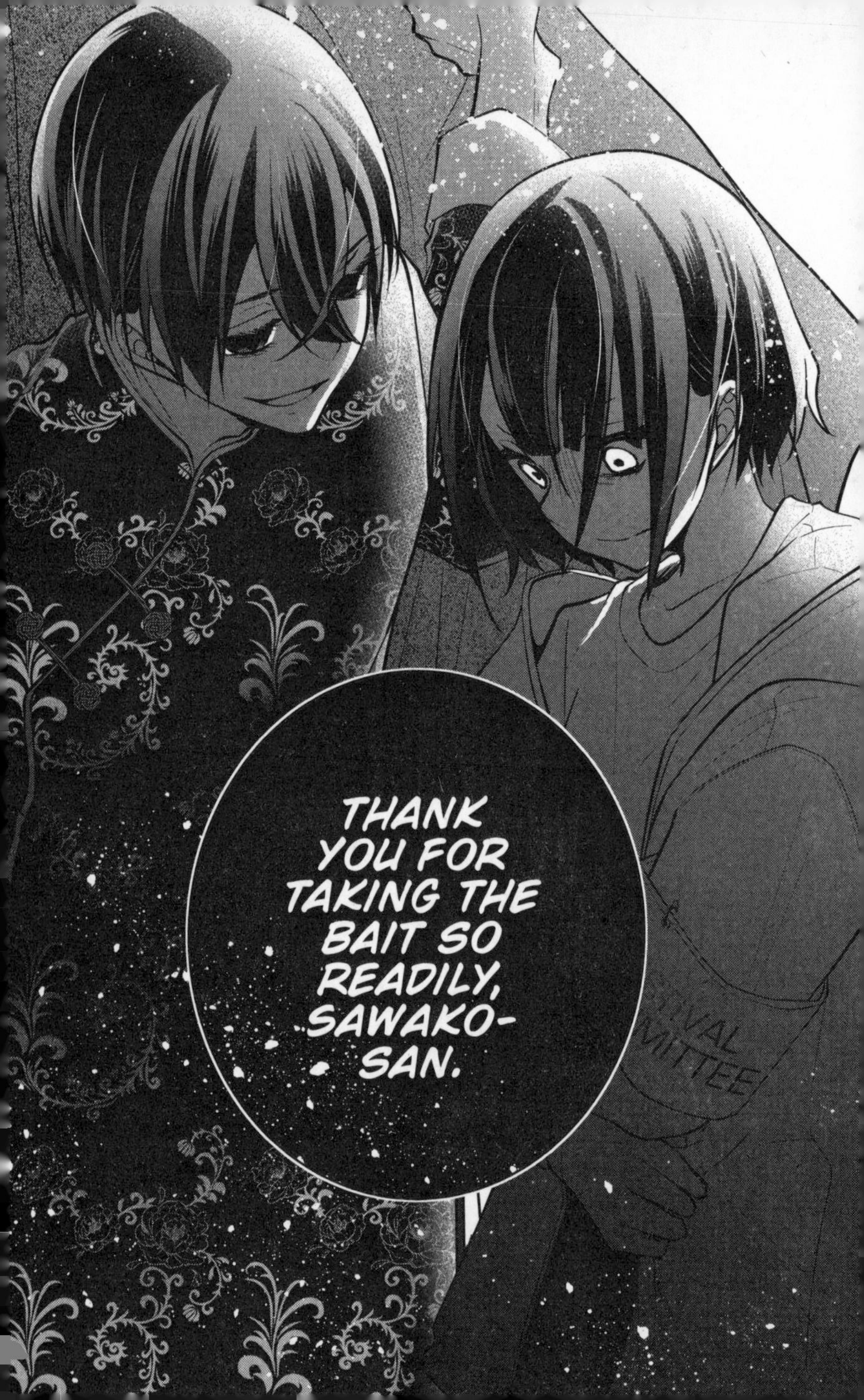
THANK YOU FOR TAKING THE BAIT SO READILY, SAWAKO-SAN.

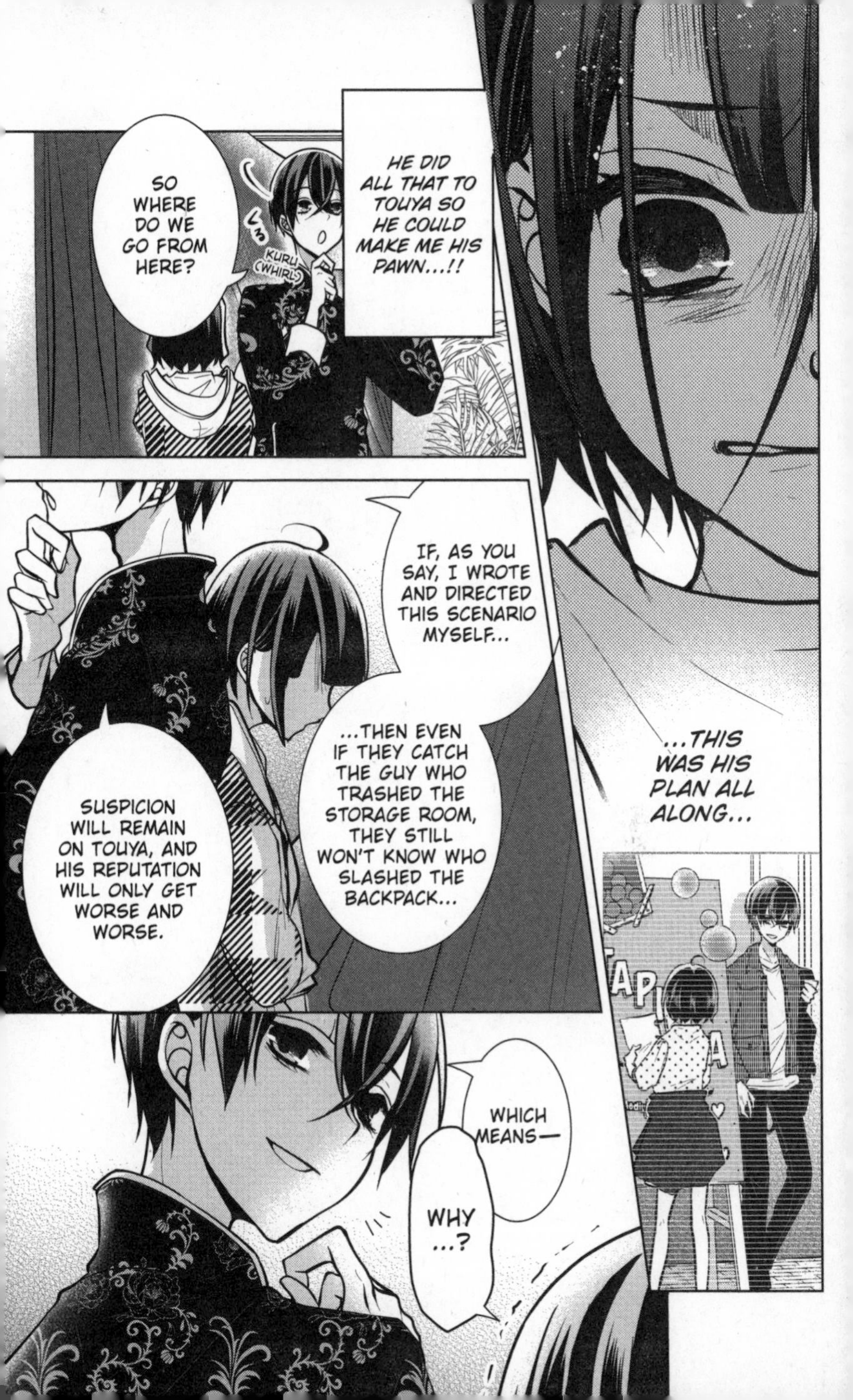

HE DID ALL THAT TO TOUYA SO HE COULD MAKE ME HIS PAWN...!!
...THIS WAS HIS PLAN ALL ALONG...
SO WHERE DO WE GO FROM HERE?
KURU (WHIRL)
IF, AS YOU SAY, I WROTE AND DIRECTED THIS SCENARIO MYSELF...
...THEN EVEN IF THEY CATCH THE GUY WHO TRASHED THE STORAGE ROOM, THEY STILL WON'T KNOW WHO SLASHED THE BACKPACK...
SUSPICION WILL REMAIN ON TOUYA, AND HIS REPUTATION WILL ONLY GET WORSE AND WORSE.
WHICH MEANS—
WHY ...?

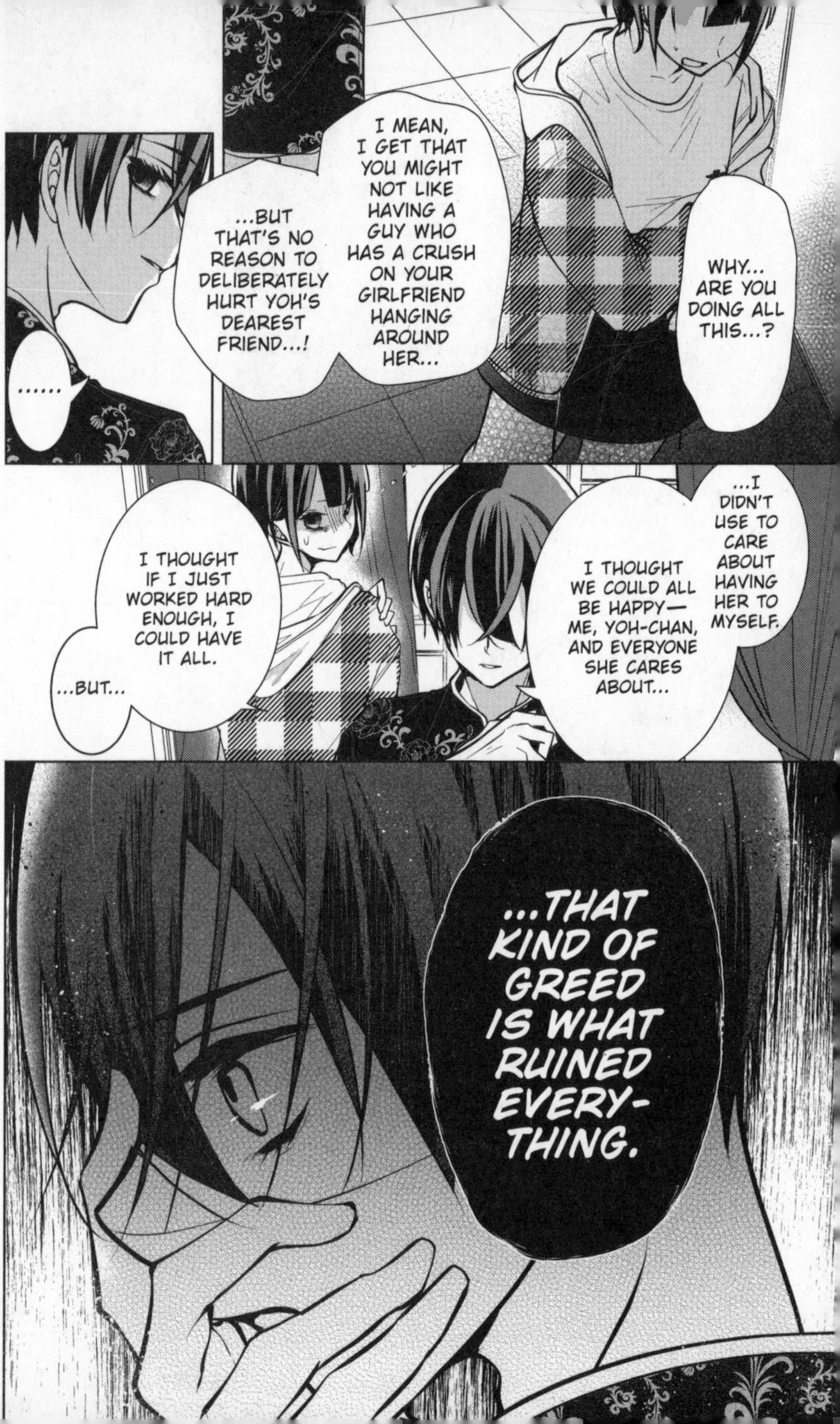
WHY... ARE YOU DOING ALL THIS...?
I MEAN, I GET THAT YOU MIGHT NOT LIKE HAVING A GUY WHO HAS A CRUSH ON YOUR GIRLFRIEND HANGING AROUND HER...
...BUT THAT'S NO REASON TO DELIBERATELY HURT YOH'S DEAREST FRIEND...!
......
...I DIDN'T USE TO CARE ABOUT HAVING HER TO MYSELF.
I THOUGHT WE COULD ALL BE HAPPY— ME, YOH-CHAN, AND EVERYONE SHE CARES ABOUT...
I THOUGHT IF I JUST WORKED HARD ENOUGH, I COULD HAVE IT ALL.
...BUT...
...THAT KIND OF GREED IS WHAT RUINED EVERYTHING.

#99

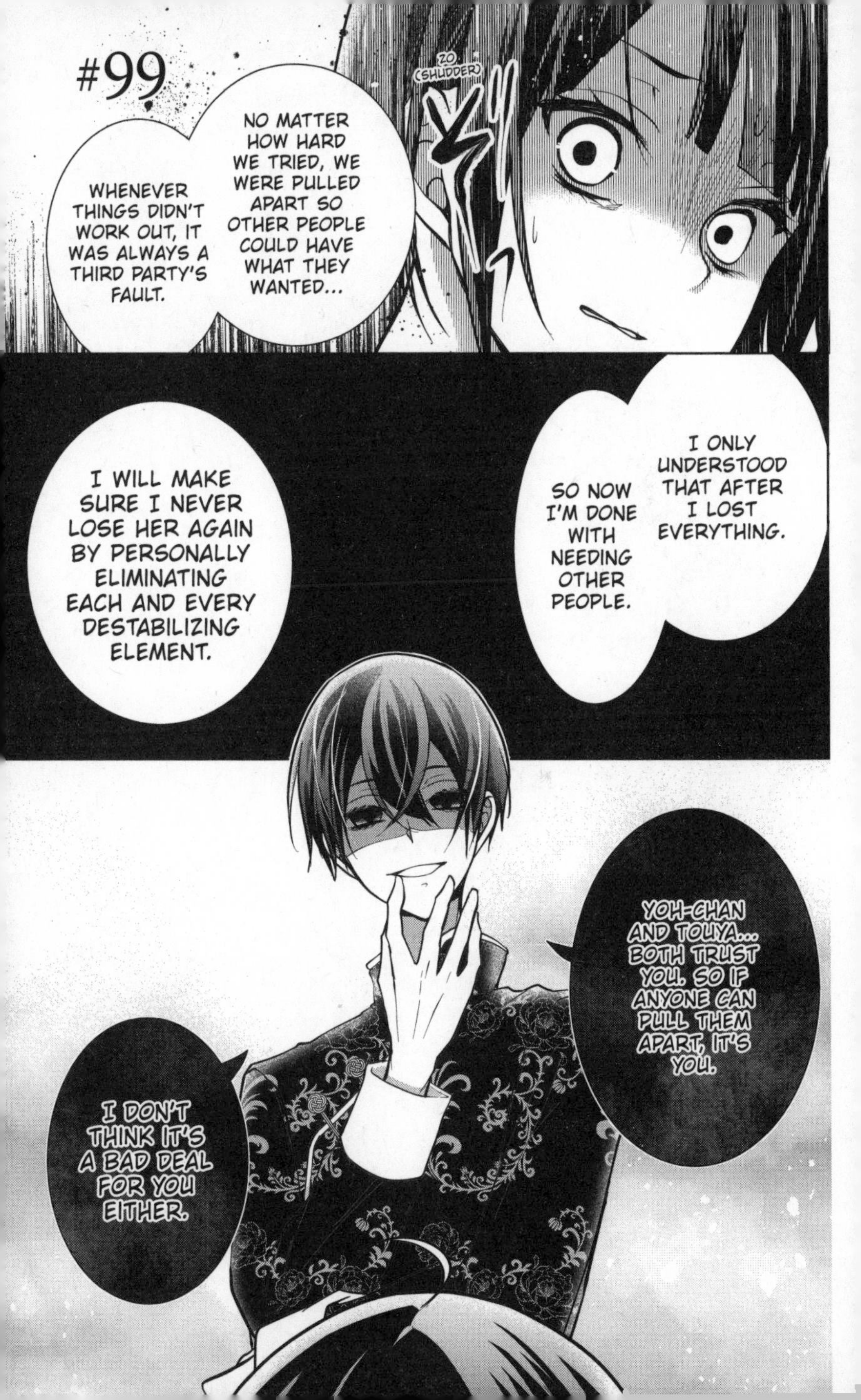
ZO (SHUDDER)
NO MATTER HOW HARD WE TRIED, WE WERE PULLED APART SO OTHER PEOPLE COULD HAVE WHAT THEY WANTED...
WHENEVER THINGS DIDN'T WORK OUT, IT WAS ALWAYS A THIRD PARTY'S FAULT.
I ONLY UNDERSTOOD THAT AFTER I LOST EVERYTHING.
SO NOW I'M DONE WITH NEEDING OTHER PEOPLE.
I WILL MAKE SURE I NEVER LOSE HER AGAIN BY PERSONALLY ELIMINATING EACH AND EVERY DESTABILIZING ELEMENT.
YOH-CHAN AND TOUYA... BOTH TRUST YOU. SO IF ANYONE CAN PULL THEM APART, IT'S YOU.
I DON'T THINK IT'S A BAD DEAL FOR YOU EITHER.

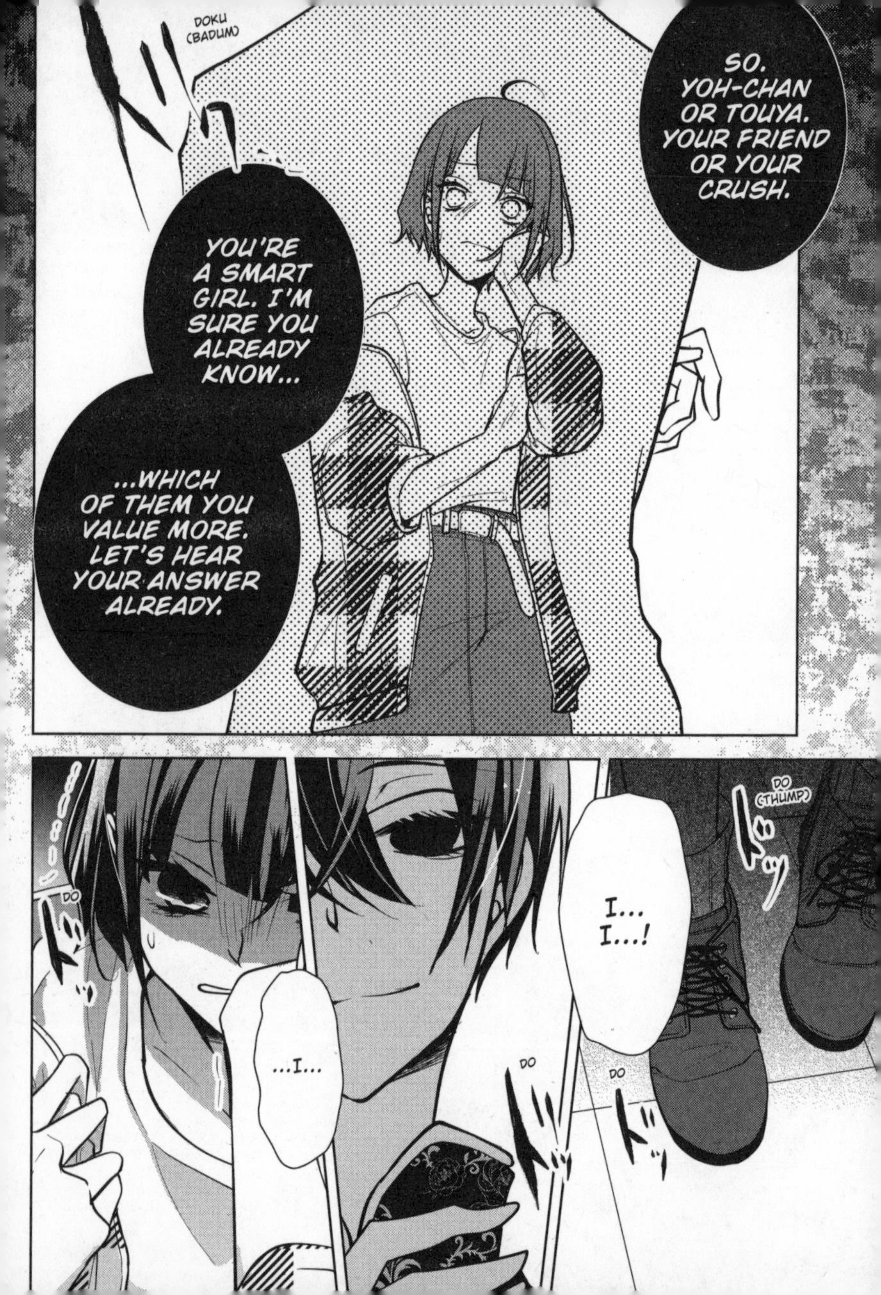
SO. YOH-CHAN OR TOUYA. YOUR FRIEND OR YOUR CRUSH.
DOKU (BADUM)
YOU'RE A SMART GIRL. I'M SURE YOU ALREADY KNOW...
...WHICH OF THEM YOU VALUE MORE. LET'S HEAR YOUR ANSWER ALREADY.
DO (THUMP)
I... I...!
DO
DO
...I...
DO

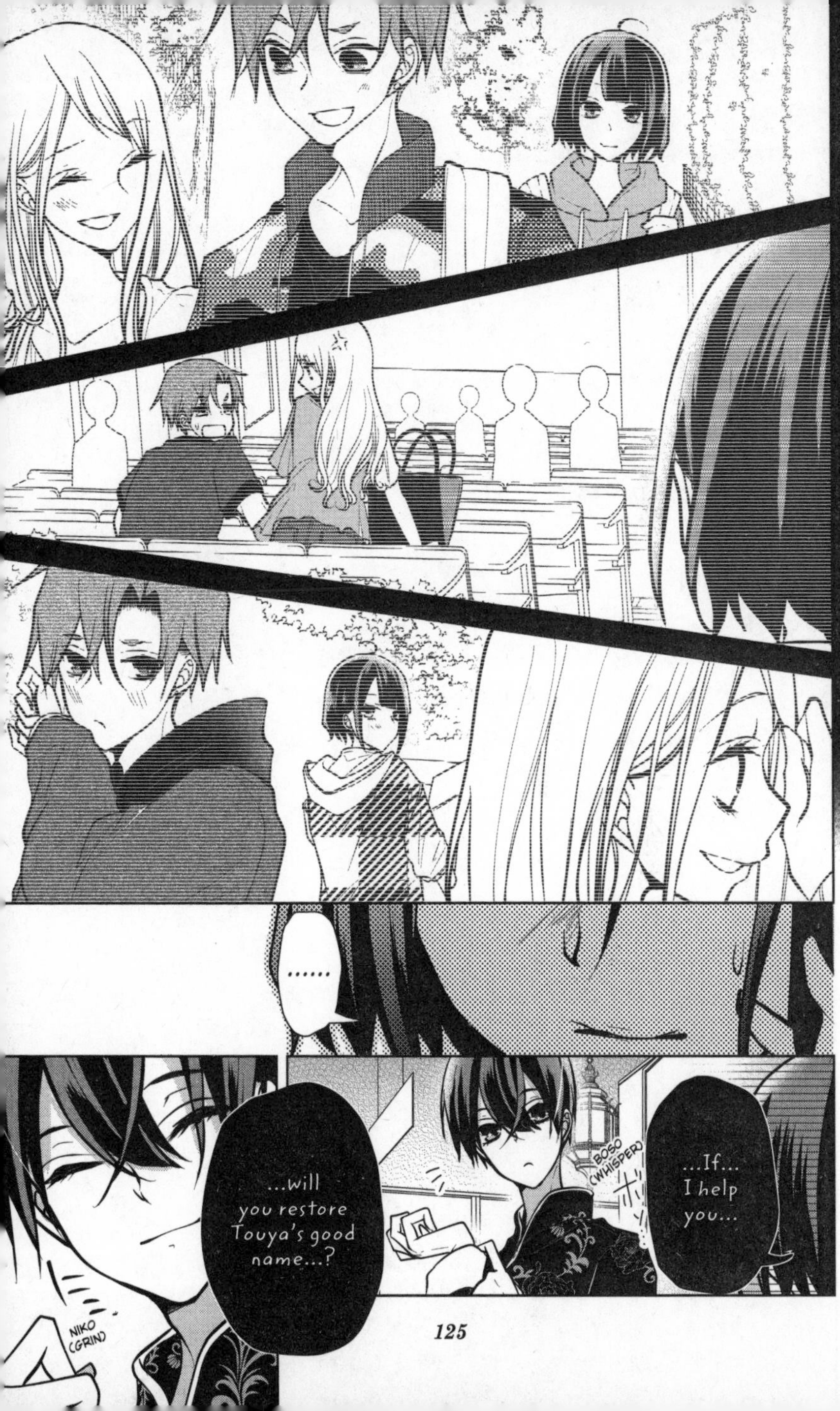
......
...If... I help you...
BOSO (WHISPER)
...will you restore Touya's good name...?
NIKO (GRIN)

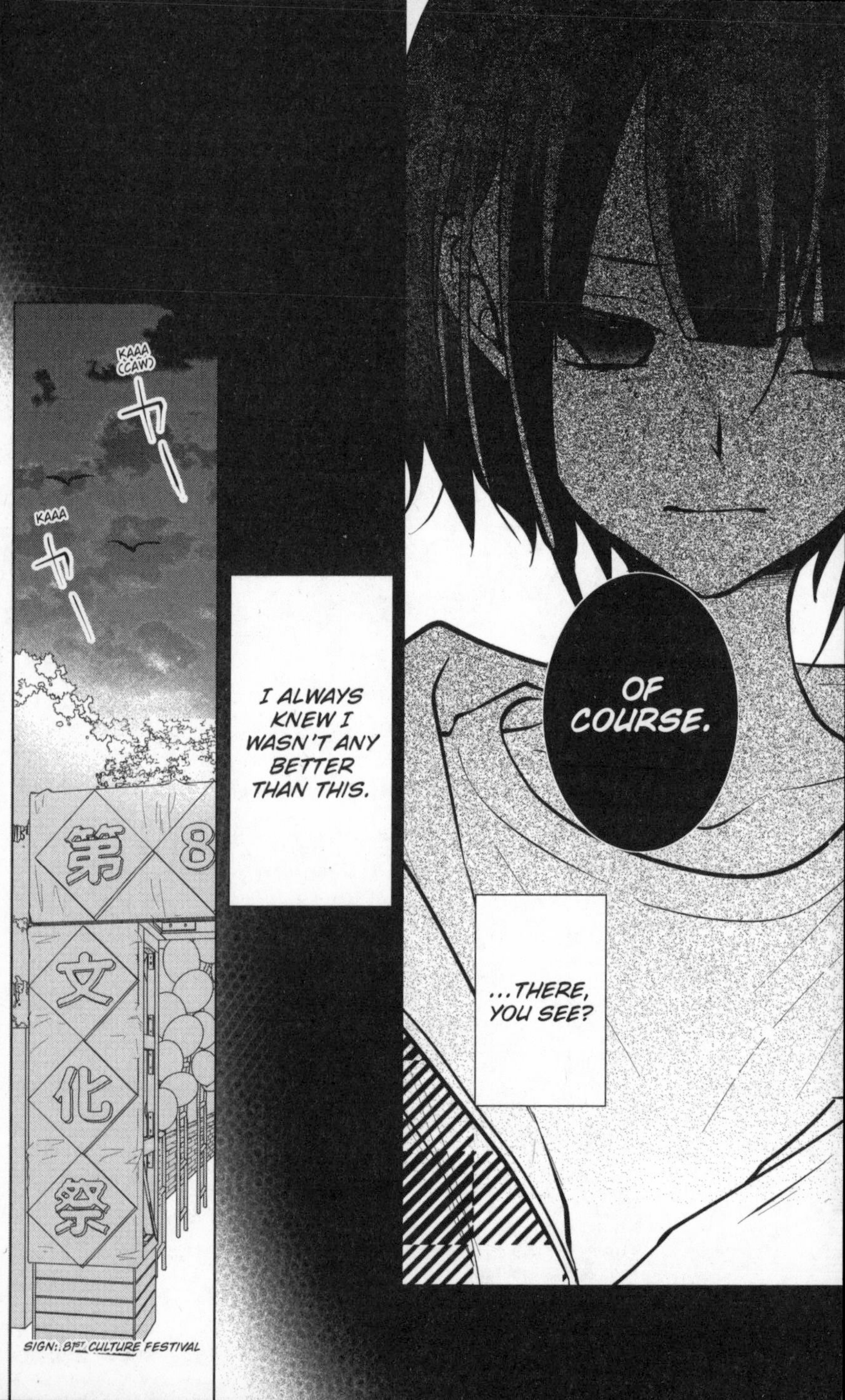
OF COURSE.
...THERE, YOU SEE?
I ALWAYS KNEW I WASN'T ANY BETTER THAN THIS.
KAAA (CAW)
KAAA
SIGN: 81ST CULTURE FESTIVAL

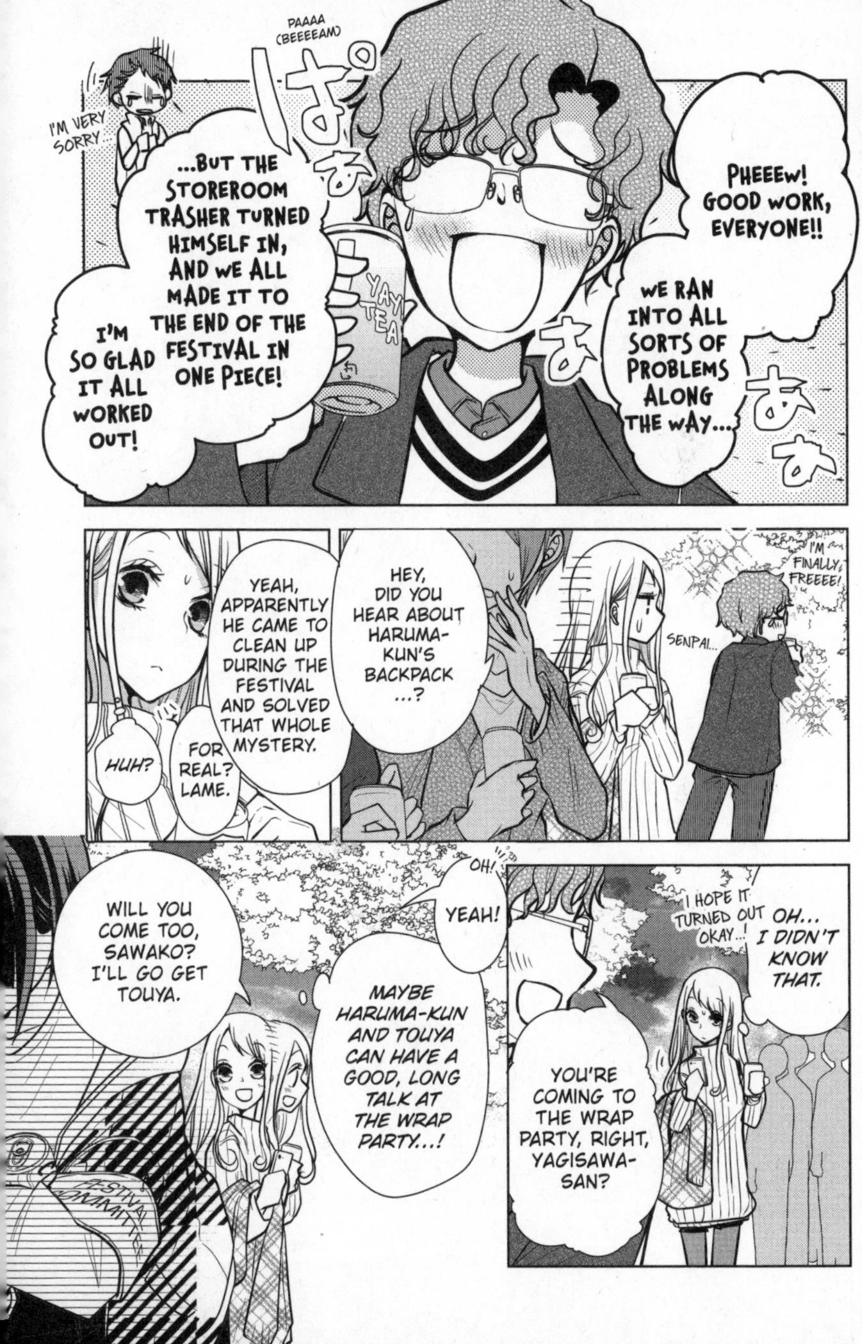
PAAAA (BEEEEAM)
PHEEEW! GOOD WORK, EVERYONE!!
WE RAN INTO ALL SORTS OF PROBLEMS ALONG THE WAY...
YAY! TEA
...BUT THE STOREROOM TRASHER TURNED HIMSELF IN, AND WE ALL MADE IT TO THE END OF THE FESTIVAL IN ONE PIECE!
I'M SO GLAD IT ALL WORKED OUT!
I'M VERY SORRY...
I'M FINALLY FREEEE!
SENPAI...
HEY, DID YOU HEAR ABOUT HARUMA-KUN'S BACKPACK ...?
YEAH, APPARENTLY HE CAME TO CLEAN UP DURING THE FESTIVAL AND SOLVED THAT WHOLE MYSTERY.
FOR REAL? LAME.
HUH?
OH... I DIDN'T KNOW THAT.
I HOPE IT TURNED OUT OKAY...!
YOU'RE COMING TO THE WRAP PARTY, RIGHT, YAGISAWA-SAN?
OH!
YEAH!
WILL YOU COME TOO, SAWAKO? I'LL GO GET TOUYA.
MAYBE HARUMA-KUN AND TOUYA CAN HAVE A GOOD, LONG TALK AT THE WRAP PARTY...!

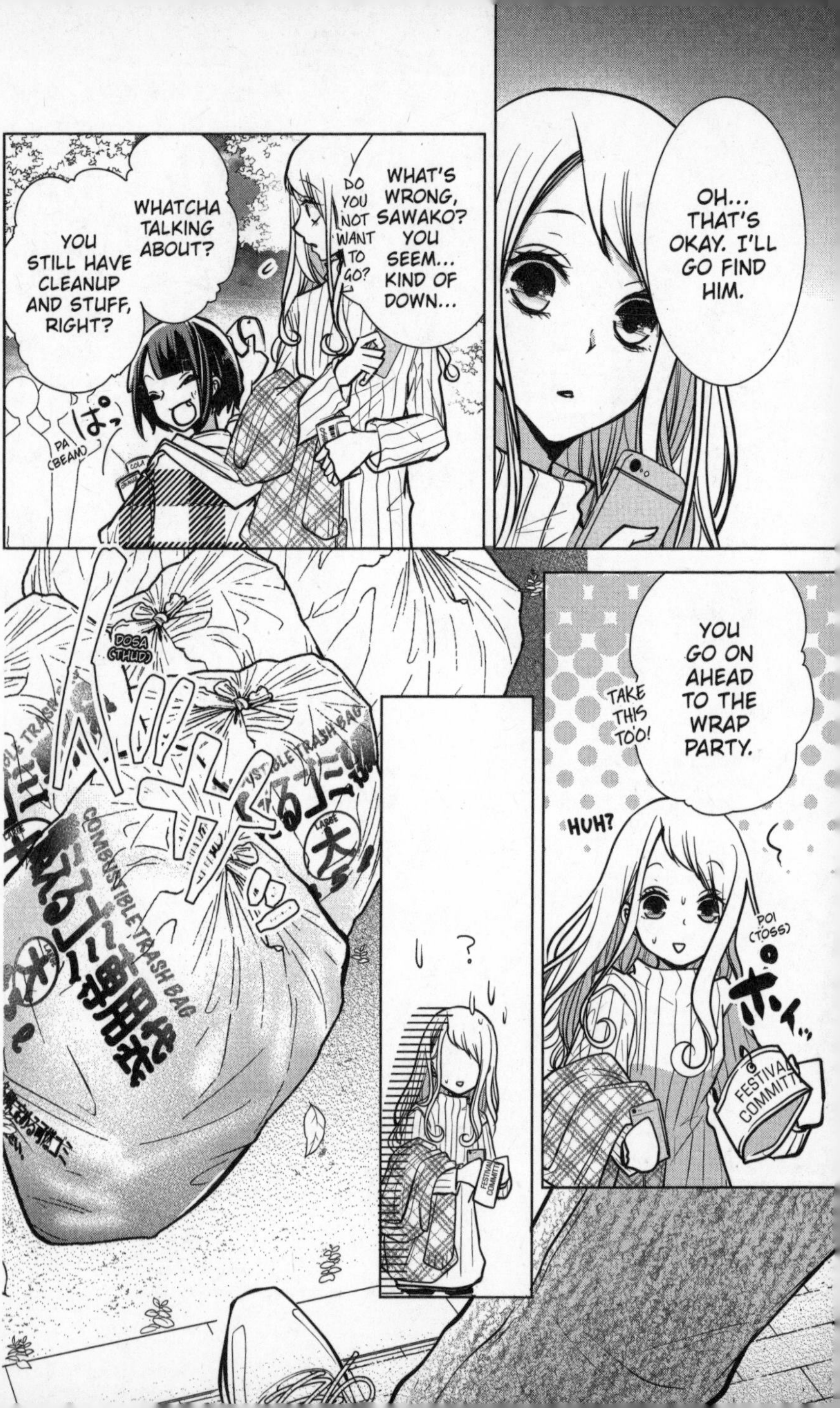
OH... THAT'S OKAY. I'LL GO FIND HIM.
WHAT'S WRONG, SAWAKO? YOU SEEM... KIND OF DOWN...
DO YOU NOT WANT TO GO?
WHATCHA TALKING ABOUT?
YOU STILL HAVE CLEANUP AND STUFF, RIGHT?
PA (BEAM)
YOU GO ON AHEAD TO THE WRAP PARTY.
TAKE THIS TOO!
HUH?
POI (TOSS)
?
DOSA (THUD)

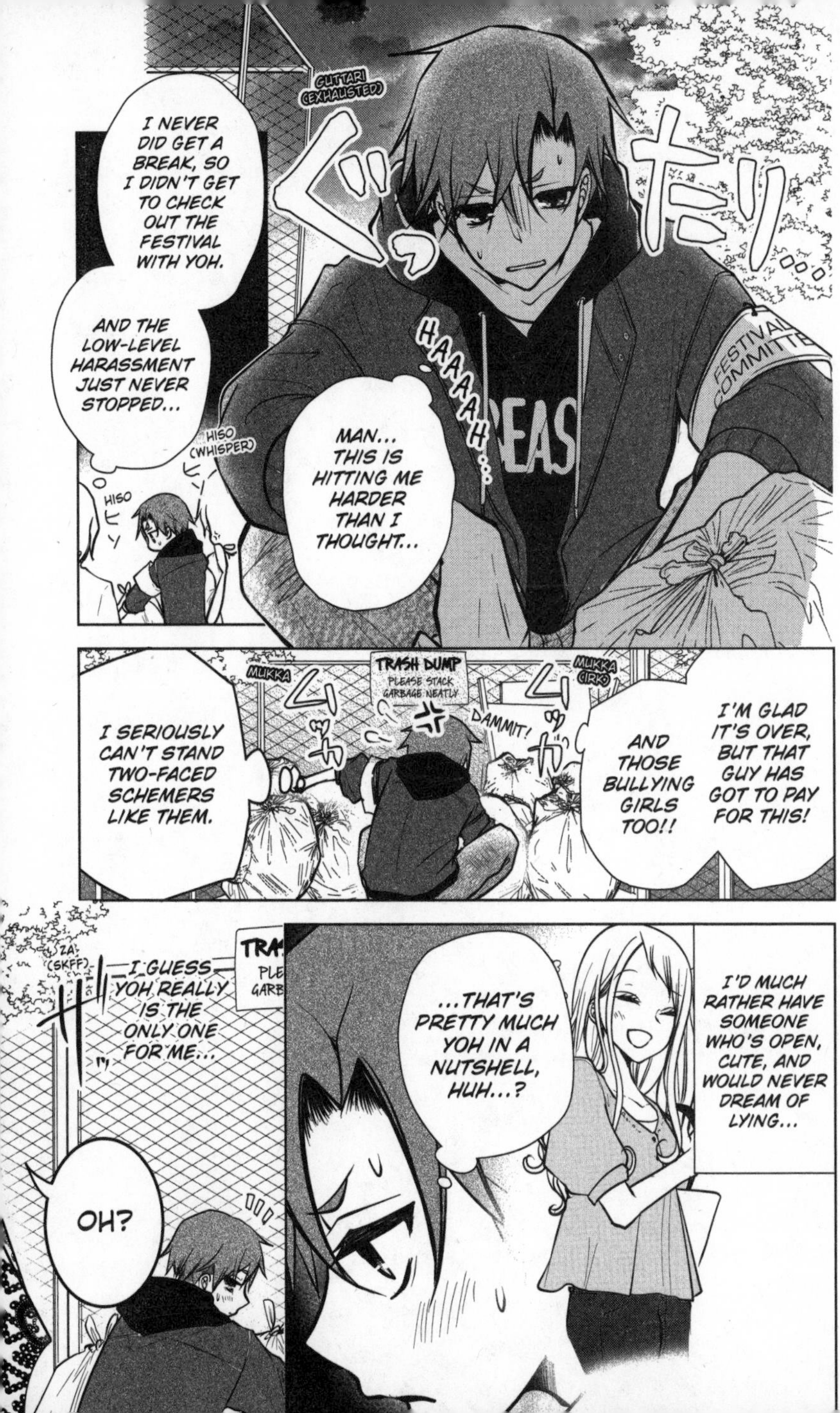
GUTTARI (EXHAUSTED)
I NEVER DID GET A BREAK, SO I DIDN'T GET TO CHECK OUT THE FESTIVAL WITH YOH.
HAAAAAH...
AND THE LOW-LEVEL HARASSMENT JUST NEVER STOPPED...
MAN... THIS IS HITTING ME HARDER THAN I THOUGHT...
HISO (WHISPER)
HISO
I'M GLAD IT'S OVER, BUT THAT GUY HAS GOT TO PAY FOR THIS!
AND THOSE BULLYING GIRLS TOO!!
MUKKA (IRK)
DAMMIT!
TRASH DUMP
PLEASE STACK GARBAGE NEATLY
MUKKA
I SERIOUSLY CAN'T STAND TWO-FACED SCHEMERS LIKE THEM.
I'D MUCH RATHER HAVE SOMEONE WHO'S OPEN, CUTE, AND WOULD NEVER DREAM OF LYING...
...THAT'S PRETTY MUCH YOH IN A NUTSHELL, HUH...?
ZA (SKFF)
I GUESS YOH REALLY IS THE ONLY ONE FOR ME...
OH?

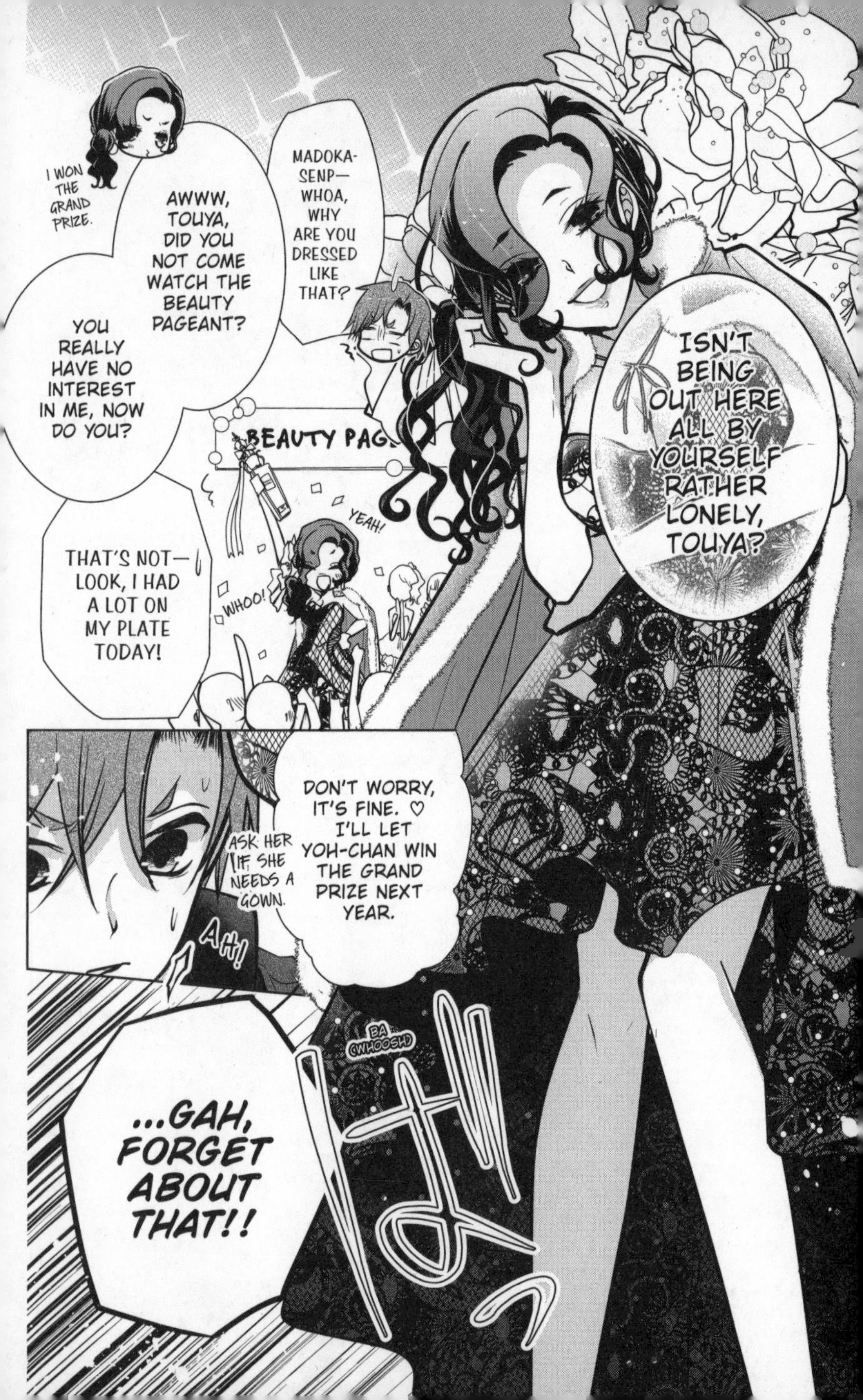
ISN'T BEING OUT HERE ALL BY YOURSELF RATHER LONELY, TOUYA?
MADOKA-SENP— WHOA, WHY ARE YOU DRESSED LIKE THAT?
AWWW, TOUYA, DID YOU NOT COME WATCH THE BEAUTY PAGEANT?
I WON THE GRAND PRIZE.
YOU REALLY HAVE NO INTEREST IN ME, NOW DO YOU?
BEAUTY PAG
YEAH!
WHOO!
THAT'S NOT— LOOK, I HAD A LOT ON MY PLATE TODAY!
DON'T WORRY, IT'S FINE. ♡ I'LL LET YOH-CHAN WIN THE GRAND PRIZE NEXT YEAR.
ASK HER IF SHE NEEDS A GOWN.
AH!
BA (WHOOSH)
...GAH, FORGET ABOUT THAT!!

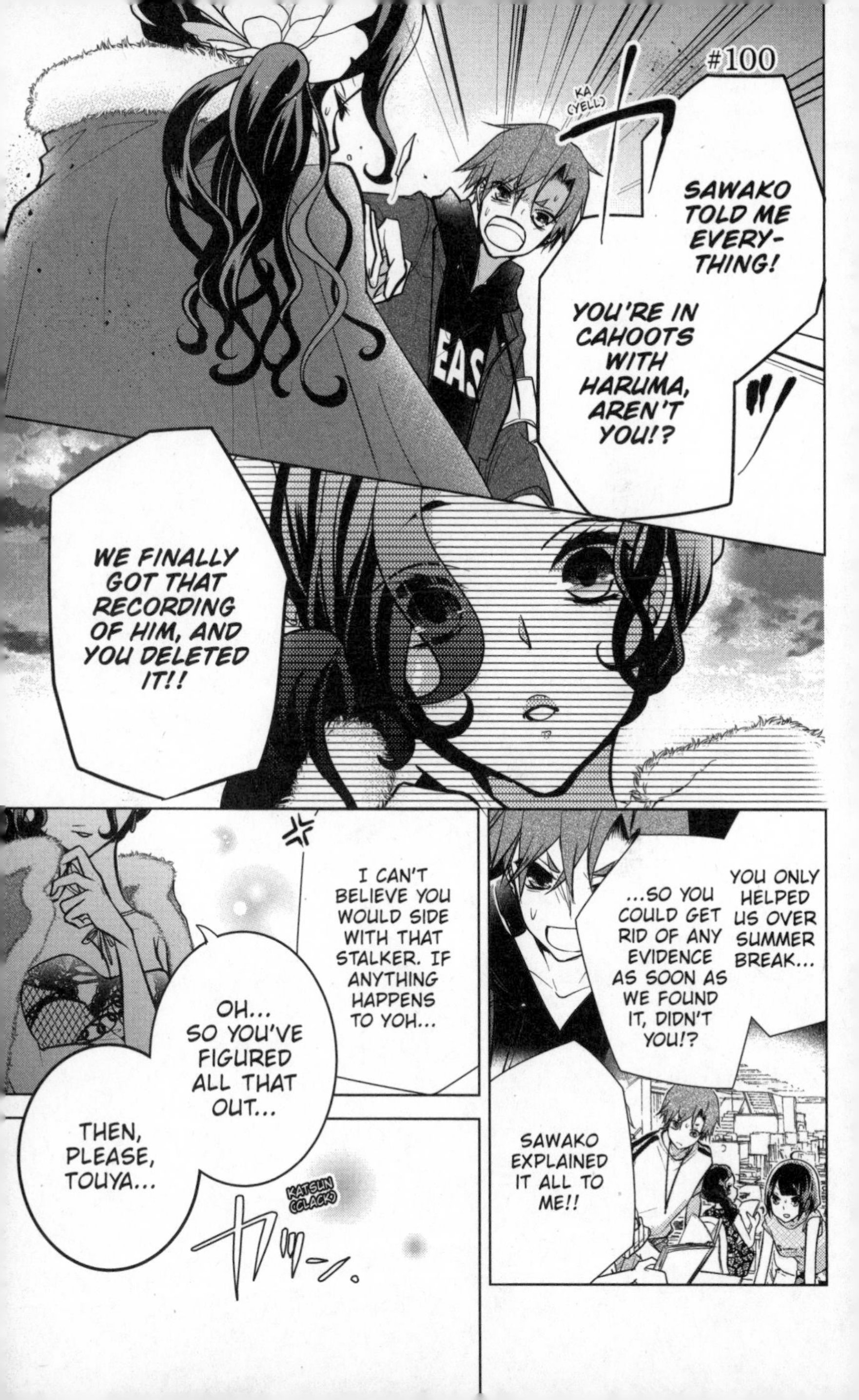
#100
KA (YELL)
SAWAKO TOLD ME EVERY-THING!
YOU'RE IN CAHOOTS WITH HARUMA, AREN'T YOU!?
WE FINALLY GOT THAT RECORDING OF HIM, AND YOU DELETED IT!!
YOU ONLY HELPED US OVER SUMMER BREAK...
...SO YOU COULD GET RID OF ANY EVIDENCE AS SOON AS WE FOUND IT, DIDN'T YOU!?
I CAN'T BELIEVE YOU WOULD SIDE WITH THAT STALKER. IF ANYTHING HAPPENS TO YOH...
SAWAKO EXPLAINED IT ALL TO ME!!
OH... SO YOU'VE FIGURED ALL THAT OUT...
THEN, PLEASE, TOUYA...
KATSUN (CLACK)

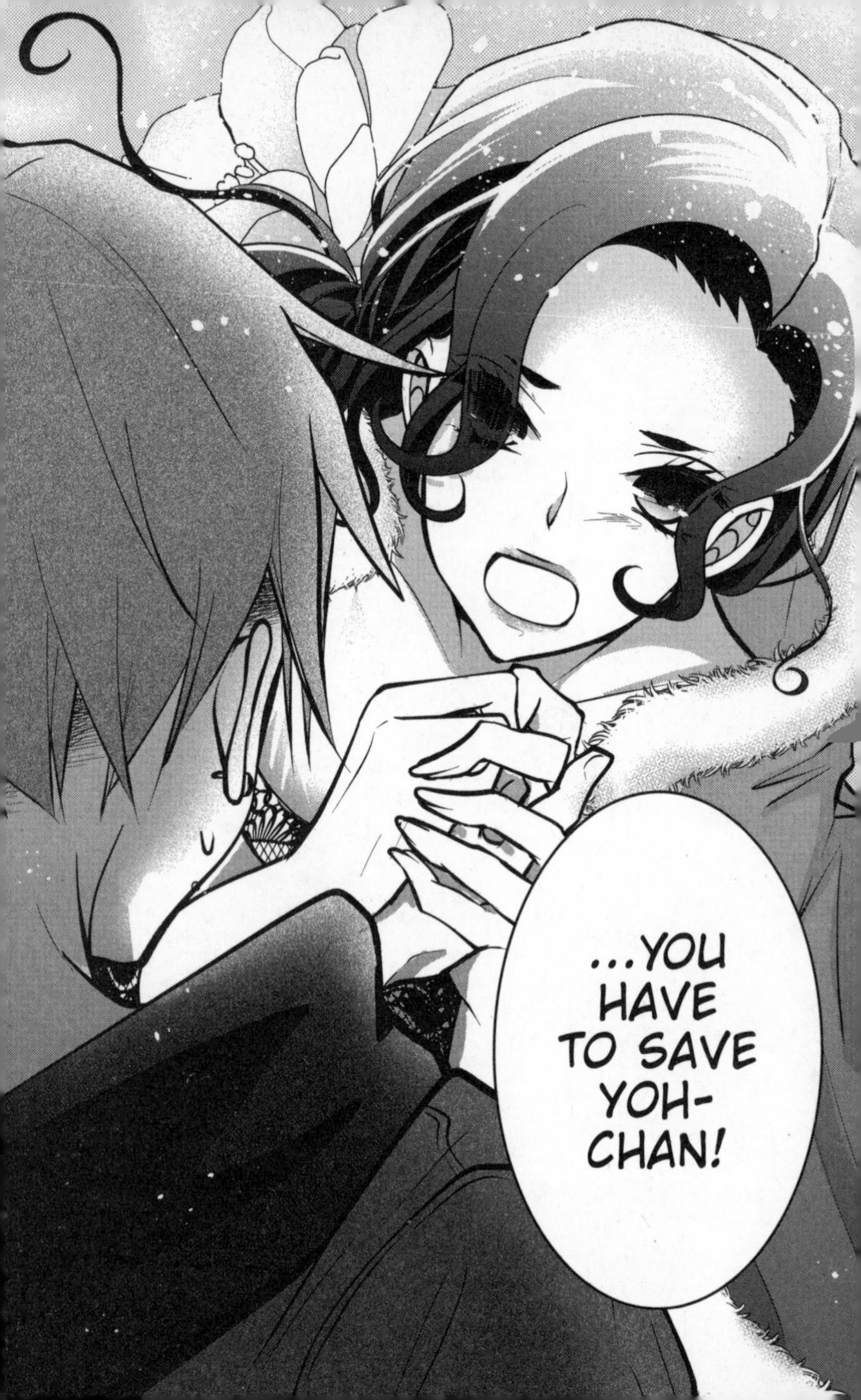
...YOU HAVE TO SAVE YOH-CHAN!

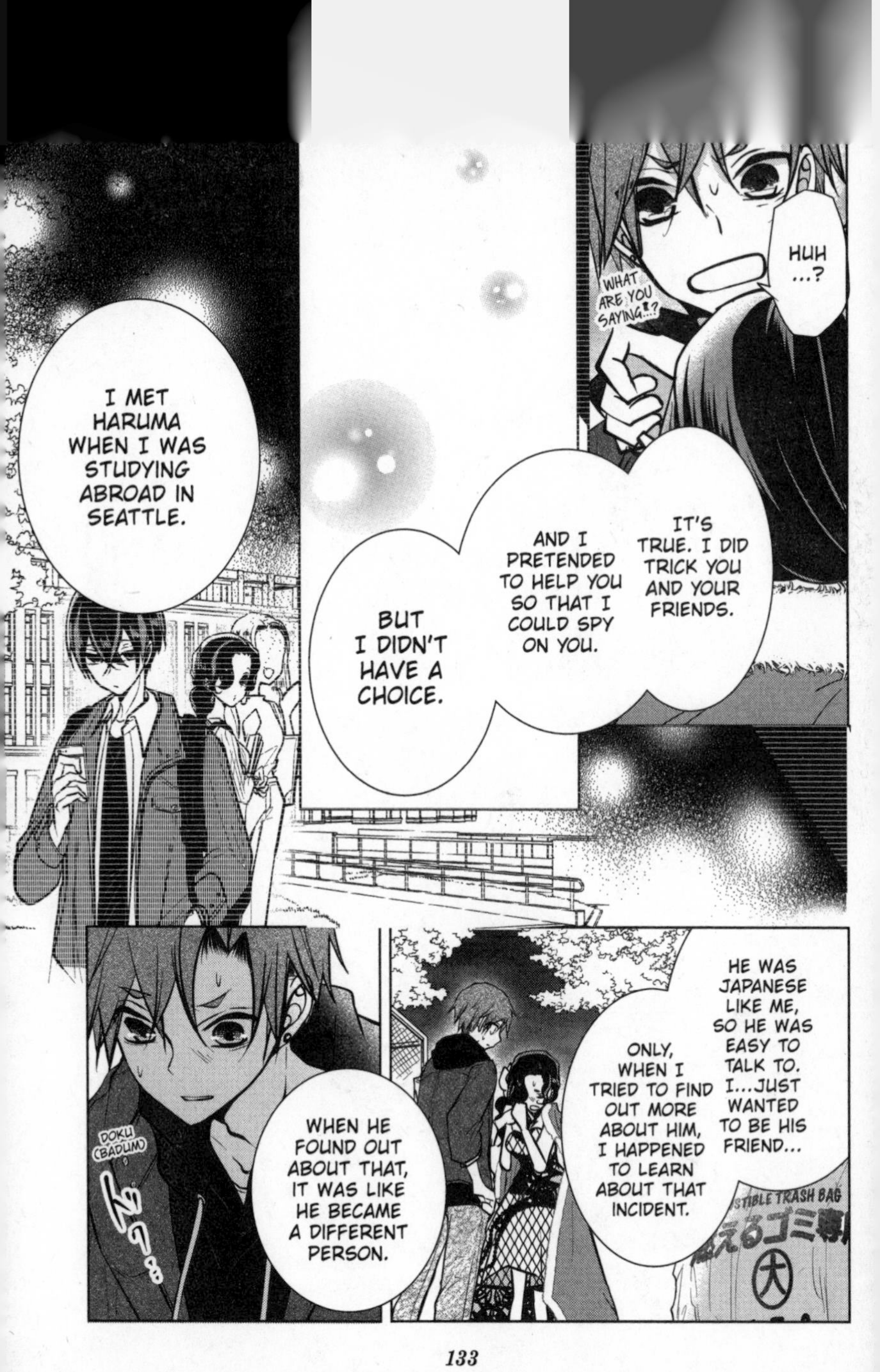
HUH ...?
WHAT ARE YOU SAYING!?
IT'S TRUE. I DID TRICK YOU AND YOUR FRIENDS.
AND I PRETENDED TO HELP YOU SO THAT I COULD SPY ON YOU.
BUT I DIDN'T HAVE A CHOICE.
I MET HARUMA WHEN I WAS STUDYING ABROAD IN SEATTLE.
HE WAS JAPANESE LIKE ME, SO HE WAS EASY TO TALK TO. I...JUST WANTED TO BE HIS FRIEND...
ONLY, WHEN I TRIED TO FIND OUT MORE ABOUT HIM, I HAPPENED TO LEARN ABOUT THAT INCIDENT.
WHEN HE FOUND OUT ABOUT THAT, IT WAS LIKE HE BECAME A DIFFERENT PERSON.
DOKU (BADUM)

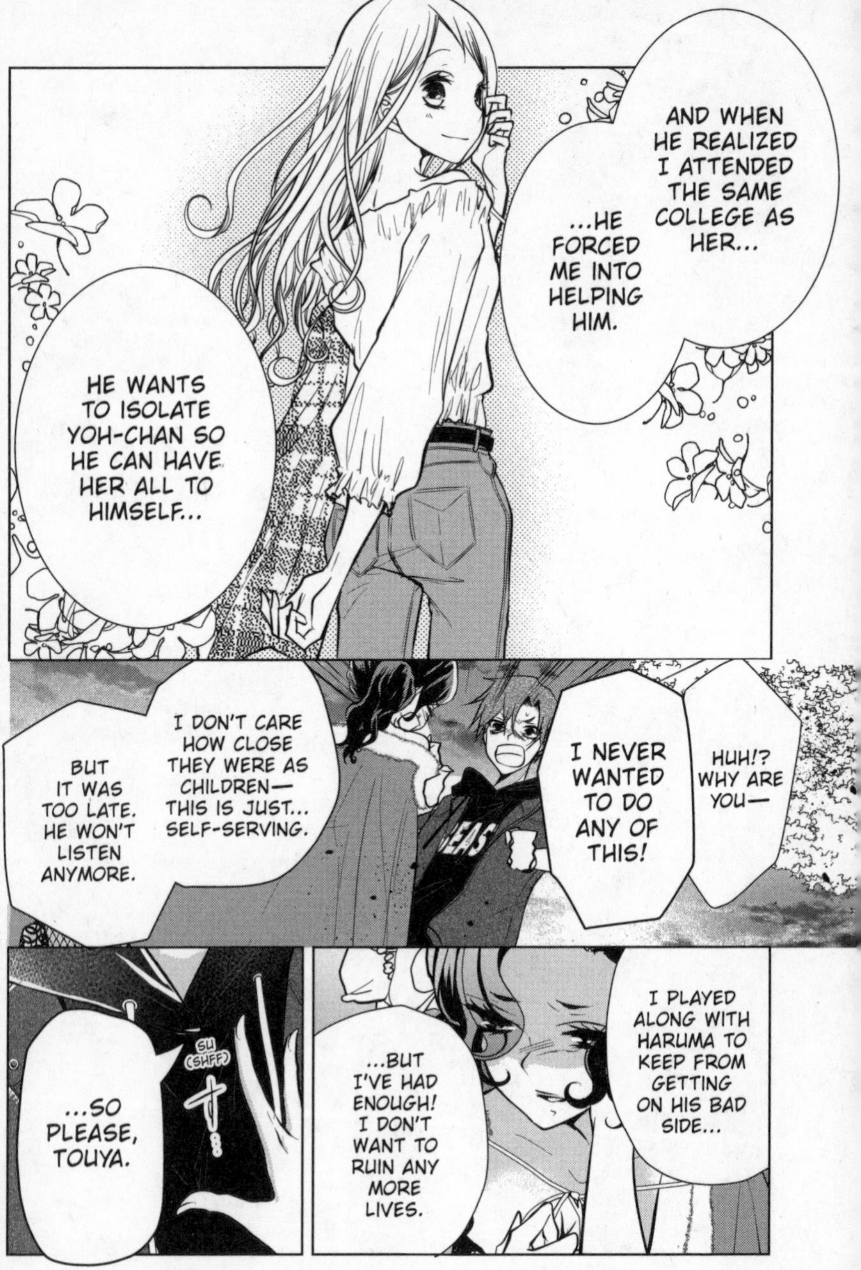
AND WHEN HE REALIZED I ATTENDED THE SAME COLLEGE AS HER...
...HE FORCED ME INTO HELPING HIM.
HE WANTS TO ISOLATE YOH-CHAN SO HE CAN HAVE HER ALL TO HIMSELF...
HUH!? WHY ARE YOU—
I NEVER WANTED TO DO ANY OF THIS!
I DON'T CARE HOW CLOSE THEY WERE AS CHILDREN—THIS IS JUST... SELF-SERVING.
BUT IT WAS TOO LATE. HE WON'T LISTEN ANYMORE.
I PLAYED ALONG WITH HARUMA TO KEEP FROM GETTING ON HIS BAD SIDE...
...BUT I'VE HAD ENOUGH! I DON'T WANT TO RUIN ANY MORE LIVES.
SU (SHFF)
...SO PLEASE, TOUYA.

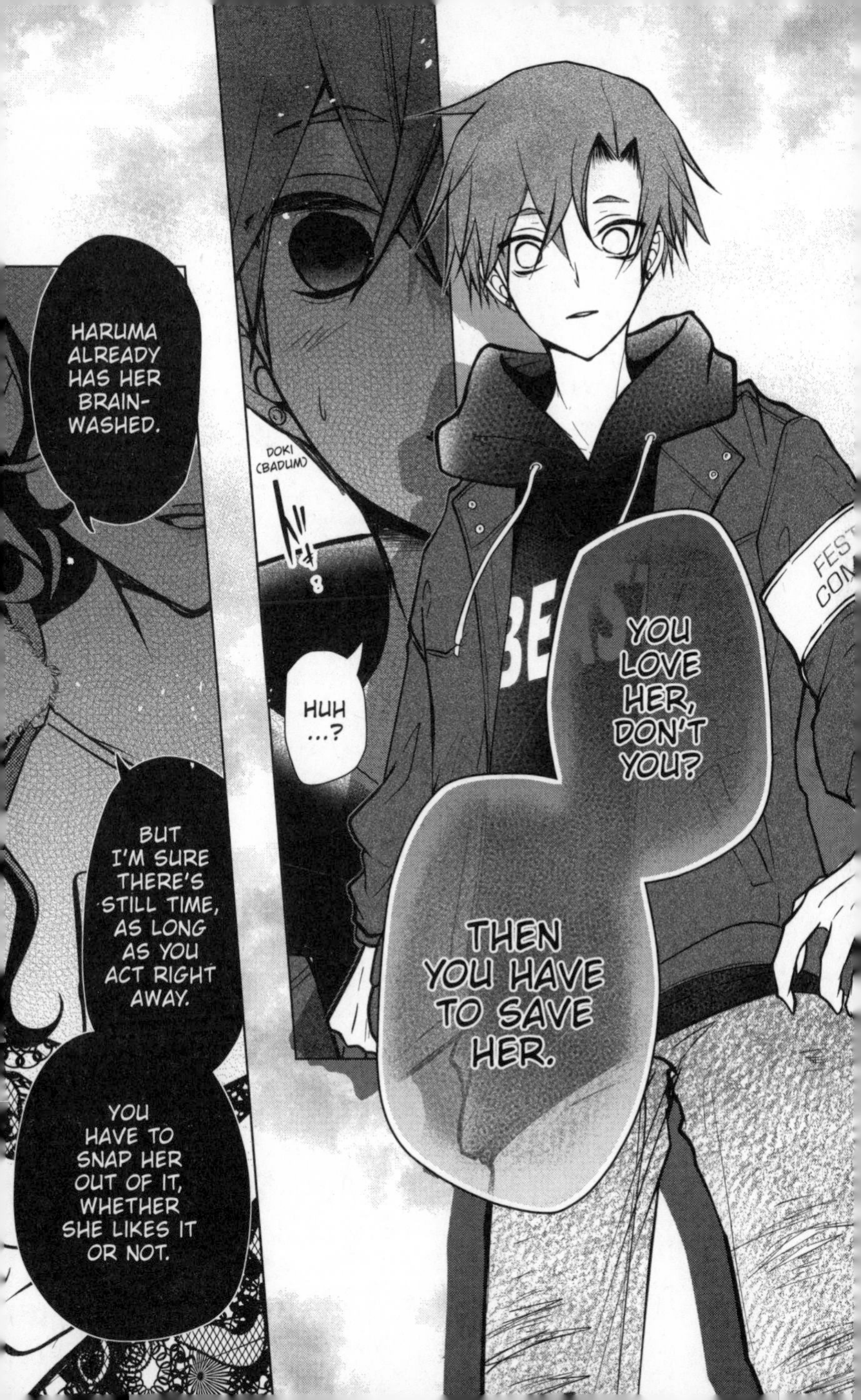

YOU LOVE HER, DON'T YOU?
THEN YOU HAVE TO SAVE HER.
DOKI (BADUM)
HUH ...?
HARUMA ALREADY HAS HER BRAIN-WASHED.
BUT I'M SURE THERE'S STILL TIME, AS LONG AS YOU ACT RIGHT AWAY.
YOU HAVE TO SNAP HER OUT OF IT, WHETHER SHE LIKES IT OR NOT.

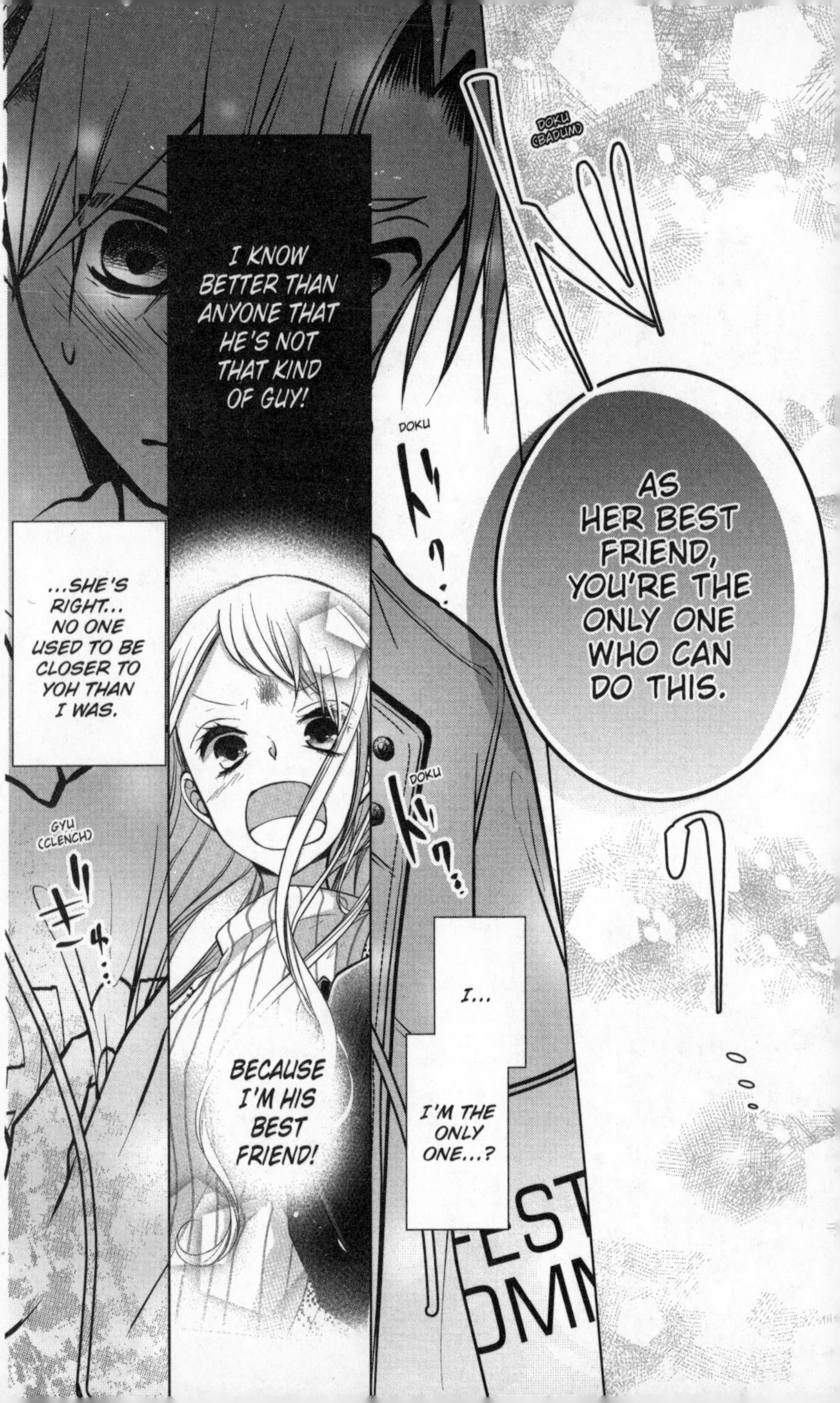
DOKU (BADUM)
AS HER BEST FRIEND, YOU'RE THE ONLY ONE WHO CAN DO THIS.
DOKU
DOKU
I...
I'M THE ONLY ONE...?
I KNOW BETTER THAN ANYONE THAT HE'S NOT THAT KIND OF GUY!
BECAUSE I'M HIS BEST FRIEND!
...SHE'S RIGHT... NO ONE USED TO BE CLOSER TO YOH THAN I WAS.
GYU (CLENCH)

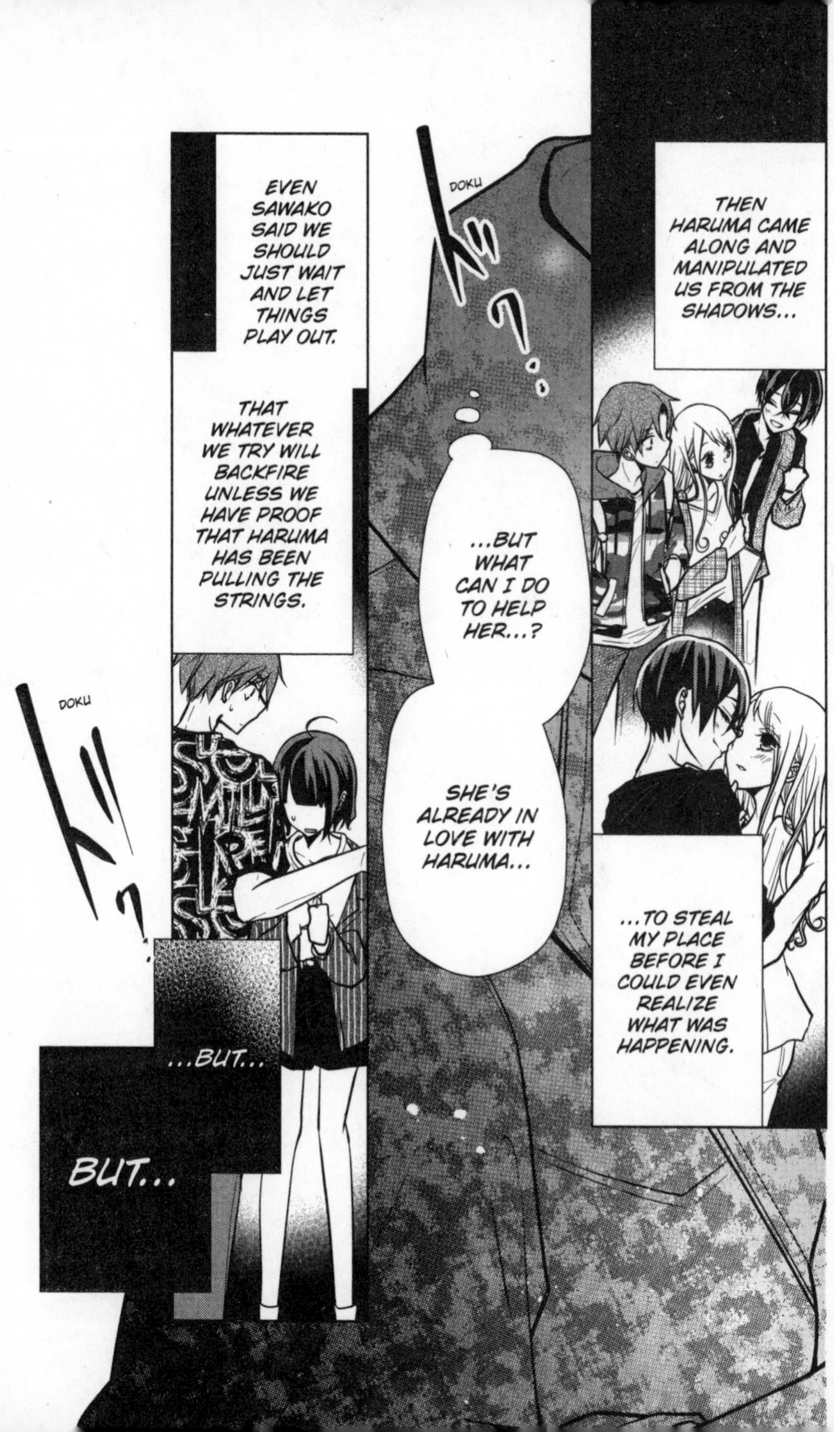
THEN HARUMA CAME ALONG AND MANIPULATED US FROM THE SHADOWS...
...TO STEAL MY PLACE BEFORE I COULD EVEN REALIZE WHAT WAS HAPPENING.
DOKU
...BUT WHAT CAN I DO TO HELP HER...?
SHE'S ALREADY IN LOVE WITH HARUMA...
EVEN SAWAKO SAID WE SHOULD JUST WAIT AND LET THINGS PLAY OUT.
THAT WHATEVER WE TRY WILL BACKFIRE UNLESS WE HAVE PROOF THAT HARUMA HAS BEEN PULLING THE STRINGS.
DOKU
...BUT...
BUT...

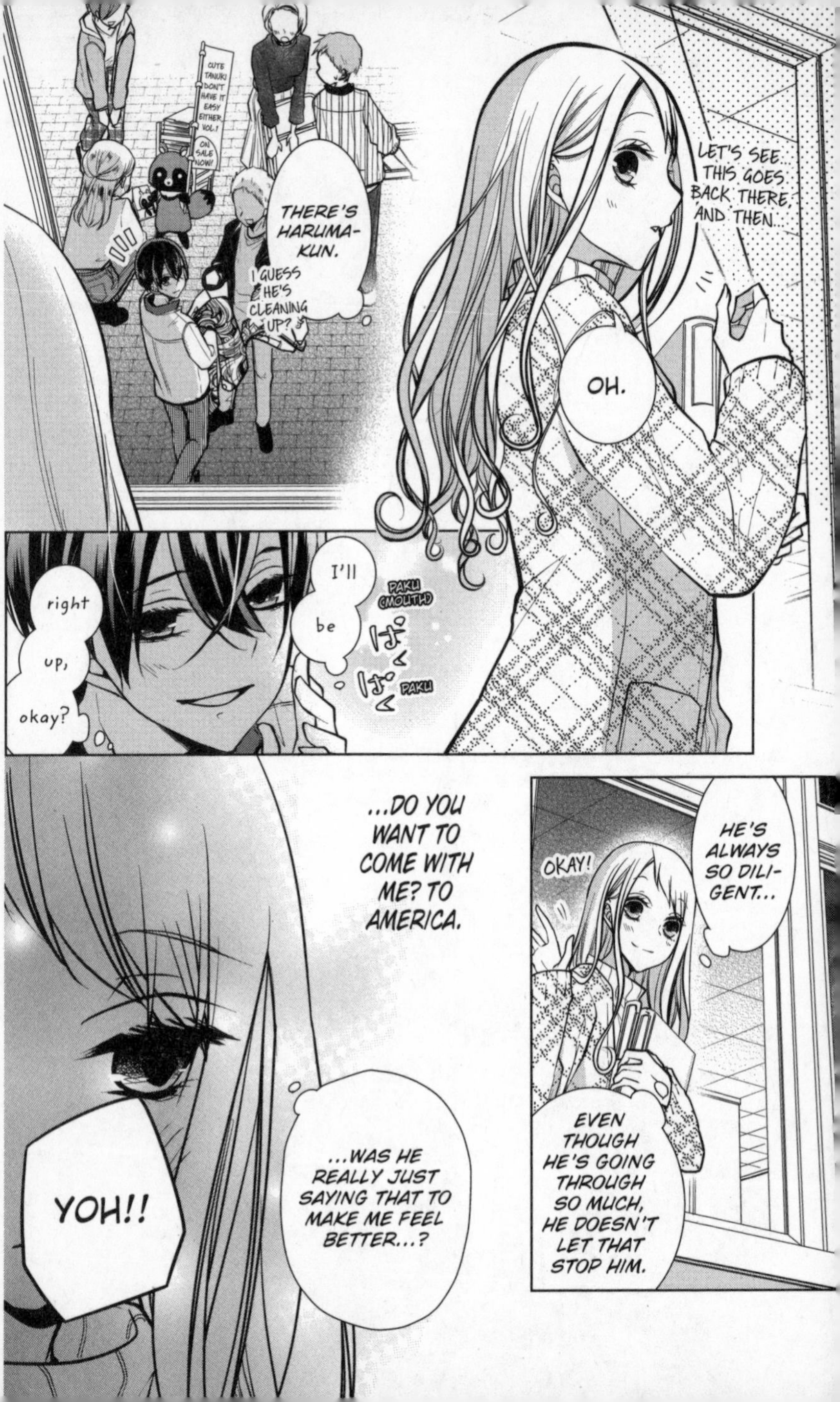
LET'S SEE... THIS GOES BACK THERE, AND THEN...
OH.
CUTE TANUKI DON'T HAVE IT EASY EITHER VOL.1 ON SALE NOW!
THERE'S HARUMA-KUN.
I GUESS HE'S CLEANING UP?
!!!
I'll be right up, okay?
PAKU (MOUTH)
ぱくぱく
PAKU
HE'S ALWAYS SO DILI-GENT...
OKAY!
EVEN THOUGH HE'S GOING THROUGH SO MUCH, HE DOESN'T LET THAT STOP HIM.
...DO YOU WANT TO COME WITH ME? TO AMERICA.
...WAS HE REALLY JUST SAYING THAT TO MAKE ME FEEL BETTER...?
YOH!!

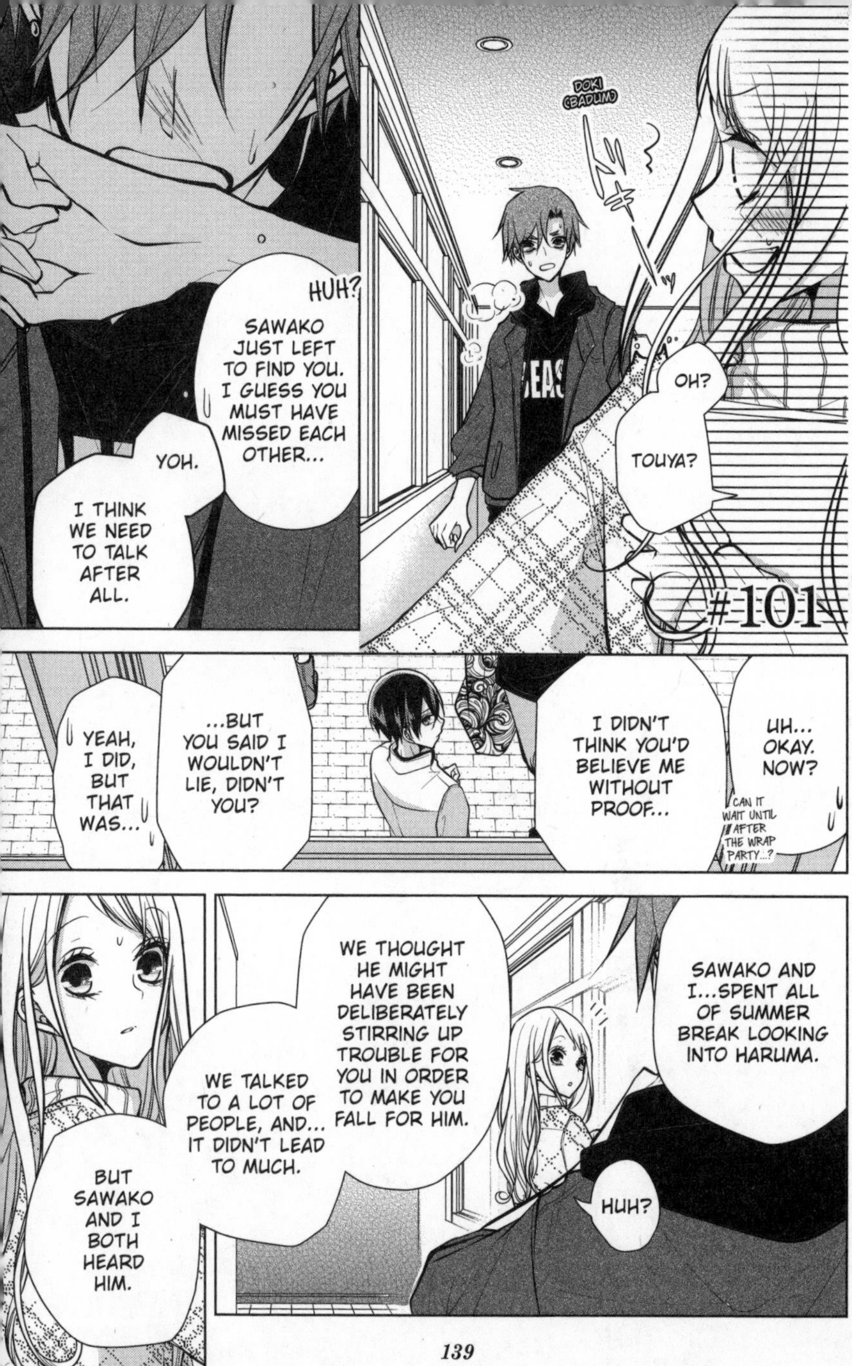
DOKI (BADUM)
OH?
TOUYA?
#101
HUH?
SAWAKO JUST LEFT TO FIND YOU. I GUESS YOU MUST HAVE MISSED EACH OTHER...
YOH.
I THINK WE NEED TO TALK AFTER ALL.
UH... OKAY. NOW?
CAN IT WAIT UNTIL AFTER THE WRAP PARTY...?
I DIDN'T THINK YOU'D BELIEVE ME WITHOUT PROOF...
...BUT YOU SAID I WOULDN'T LIE, DIDN'T YOU?
YEAH, I DID, BUT THAT WAS...
SAWAKO AND I...SPENT ALL OF SUMMER BREAK LOOKING INTO HARUMA.
HUH?
WE THOUGHT HE MIGHT HAVE BEEN DELIBERATELY STIRRING UP TROUBLE FOR YOU IN ORDER TO MAKE YOU FALL FOR HIM.
WE TALKED TO A LOT OF PEOPLE, AND... IT DIDN'T LEAD TO MUCH.
BUT SAWAKO AND I BOTH HEARD HIM.

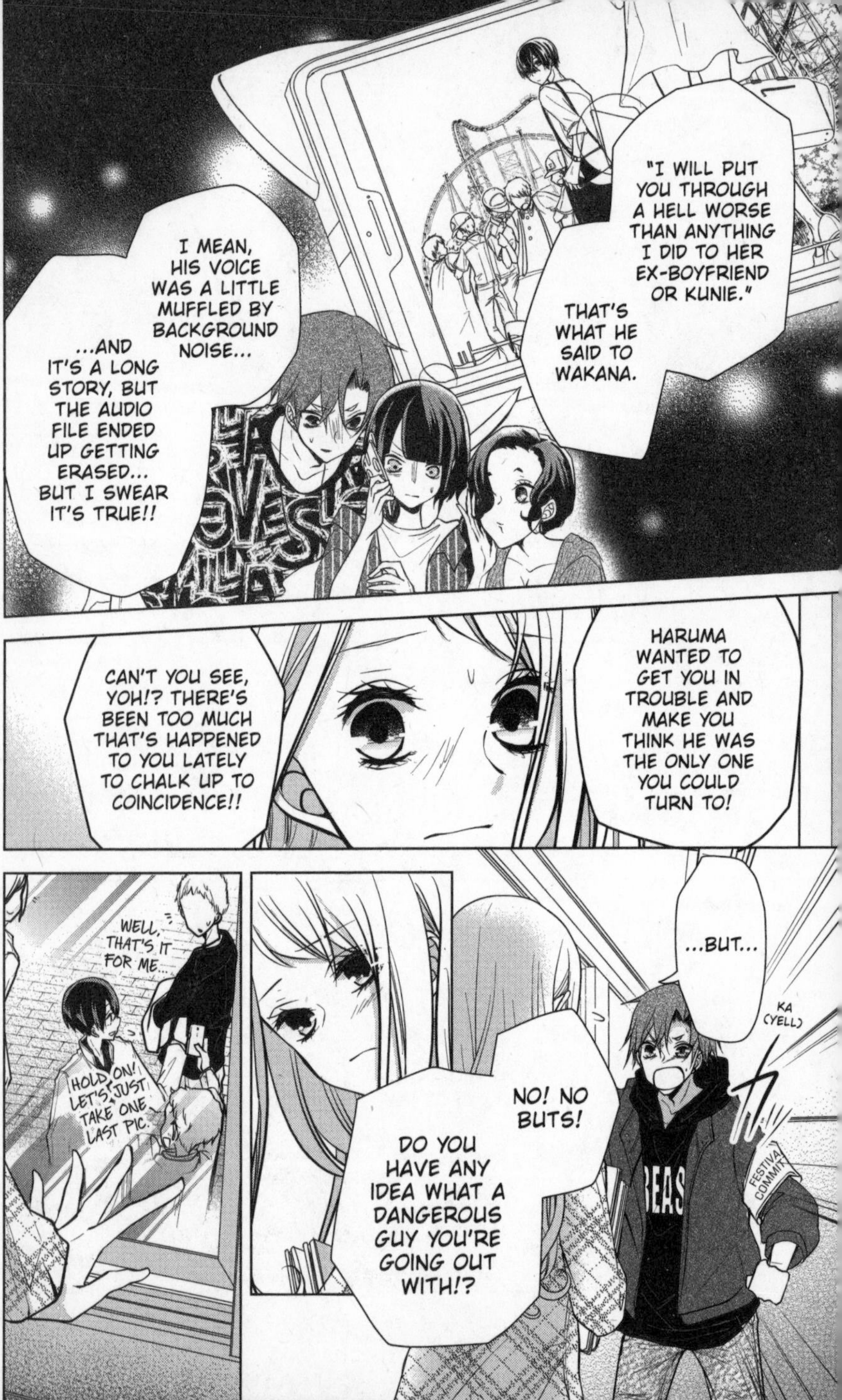
"I WILL PUT YOU THROUGH A HELL WORSE THAN ANYTHING I DID TO HER EX-BOYFRIEND OR KUNIE."
THAT'S WHAT HE SAID TO WAKANA.
I MEAN, HIS VOICE WAS A LITTLE MUFFLED BY BACKGROUND NOISE...
...AND IT'S A LONG STORY, BUT THE AUDIO FILE ENDED UP GETTING ERASED... BUT I SWEAR IT'S TRUE!!
HARUMA WANTED TO GET YOU IN TROUBLE AND MAKE YOU THINK HE WAS THE ONLY ONE YOU COULD TURN TO!
CAN'T YOU SEE, YOH!? THERE'S BEEN TOO MUCH THAT'S HAPPENED TO YOU LATELY TO CHALK UP TO COINCIDENCE!!
...BUT...
KA (YELL)
NO! NO BUTS!
DO YOU HAVE ANY IDEA WHAT A DANGEROUS GUY YOU'RE GOING OUT WITH!?
WELL, THAT'S IT FOR ME...
HOLD ON! LET'S JUST TAKE ONE LAST PIC.

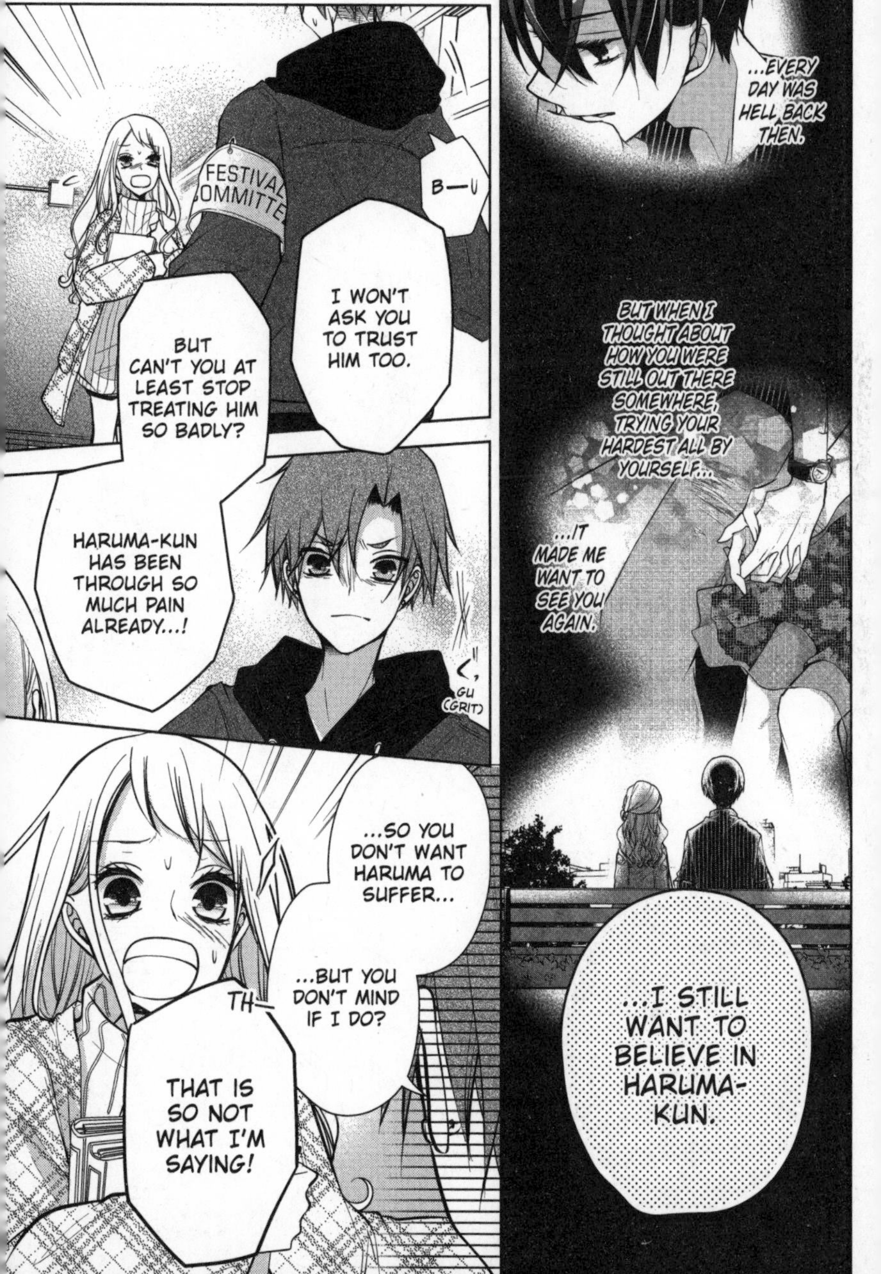
...EVERY DAY WAS HELL BACK THEN.
BUT WHEN I THOUGHT ABOUT HOW YOU WERE STILL OUT THERE SOMEWHERE, TRYING YOUR HARDEST ALL BY YOURSELF...
...IT MADE ME WANT TO SEE YOU AGAIN.
...I STILL WANT TO BELIEVE IN HARUMA-KUN.
FESTIVAL
OMMITTE
B—U
I WON'T ASK YOU TO TRUST HIM TOO.
BUT CAN'T YOU AT LEAST STOP TREATING HIM SO BADLY?
HARUMA-KUN HAS BEEN THROUGH SO MUCH PAIN ALREADY...!
GU (GRIT)
...SO YOU DON'T WANT HARUMA TO SUFFER...
...BUT YOU DON'T MIND IF I DO?
TH—
THAT IS SO NOT WHAT I'M SAYING!

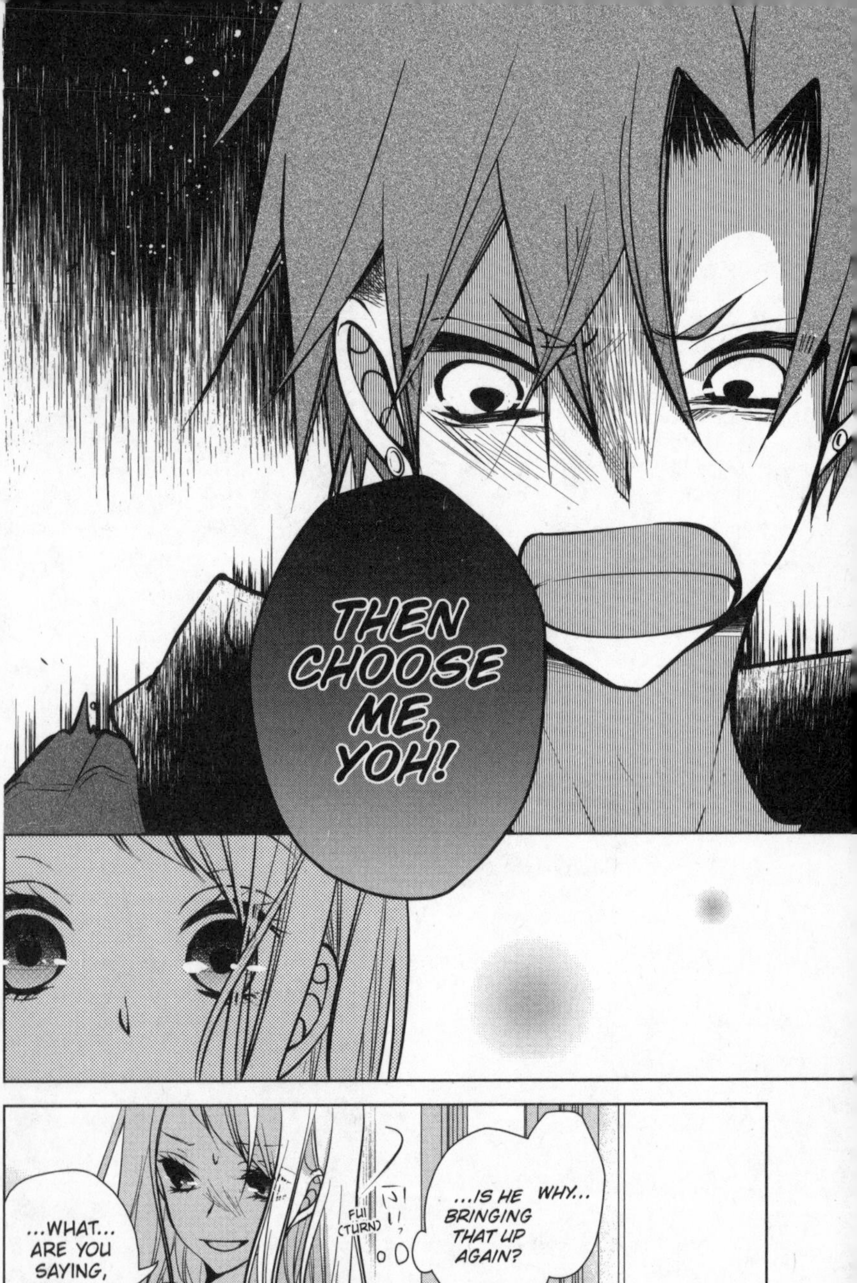
THEN CHOOSE ME, YOH!
WHY...
...IS HE BRINGING THAT UP AGAIN?
FUI (TURN)
...WHAT... ARE YOU SAYING, TOUYA...?

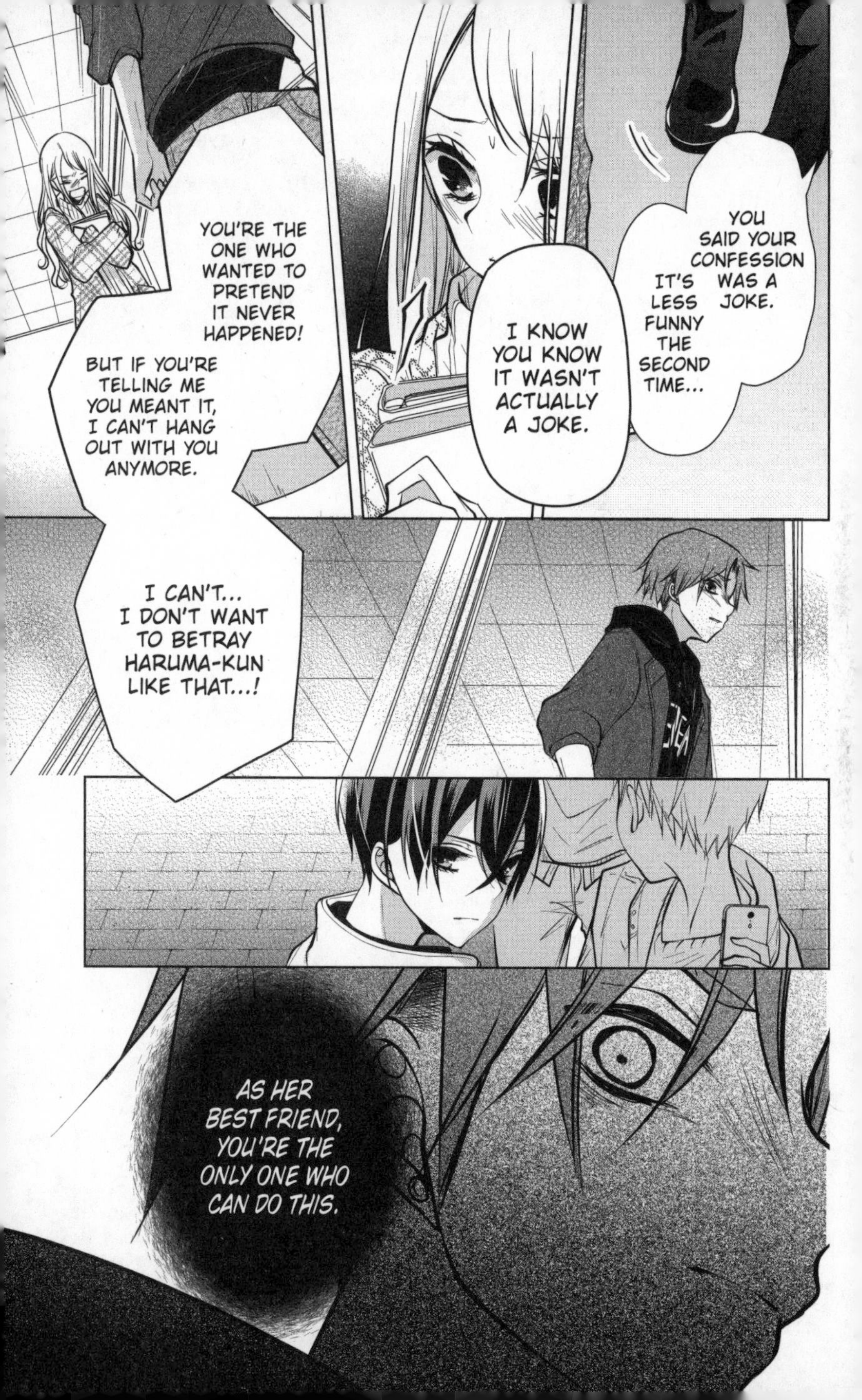
YOU SAID YOUR CONFESSION WAS A JOKE.
IT'S LESS FUNNY THE SECOND TIME...
I KNOW YOU KNOW IT WASN'T ACTUALLY A JOKE.
YOU'RE THE ONE WHO WANTED TO PRETEND IT NEVER HAPPENED!
BUT IF YOU'RE TELLING ME YOU MEANT IT, I CAN'T HANG OUT WITH YOU ANYMORE.
I CAN'T... I DON'T WANT TO BETRAY HARUMA-KUN LIKE THAT...!
AS HER BEST FRIEND, YOU'RE THE ONLY ONE WHO CAN DO THIS.

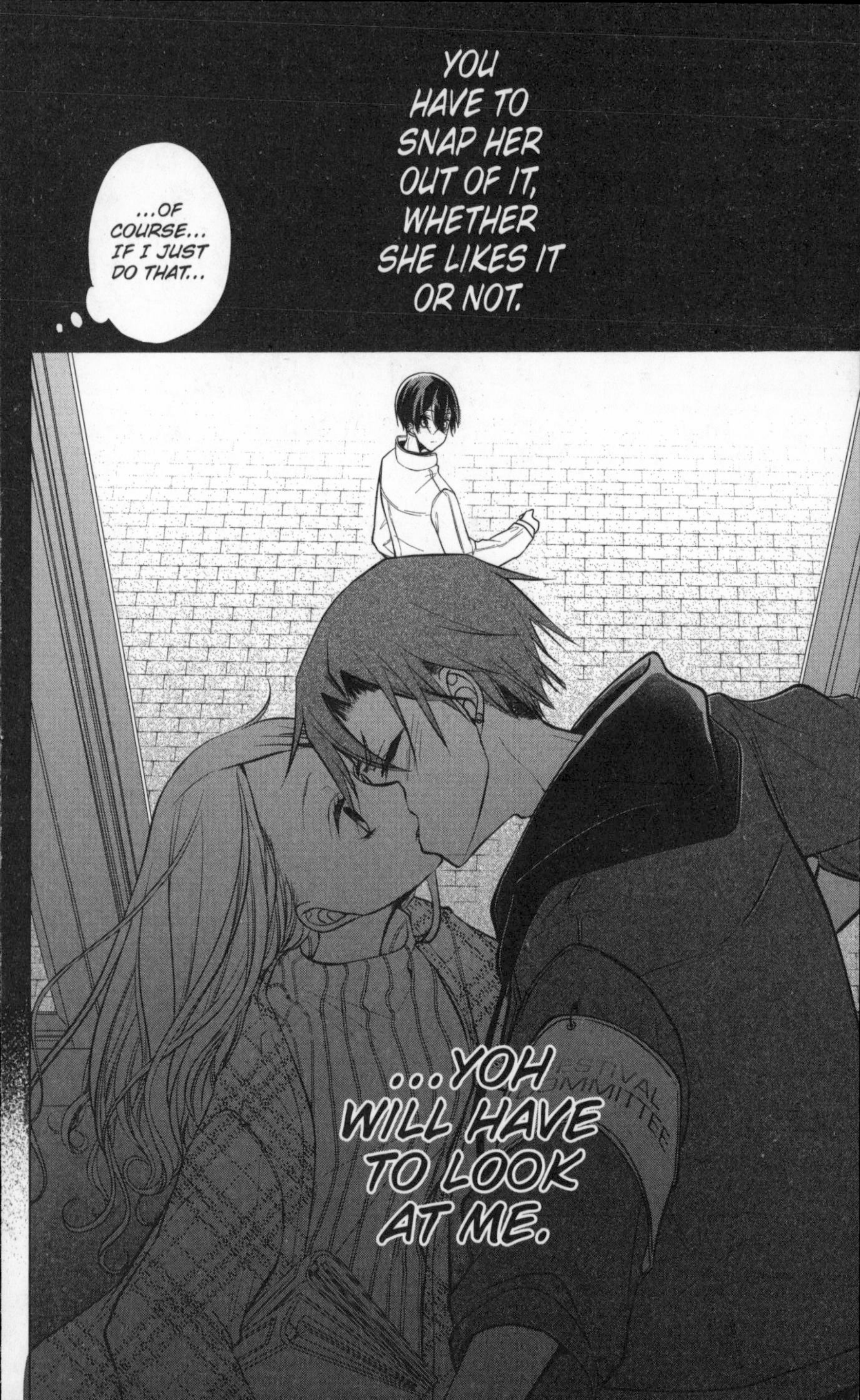
YOU HAVE TO SNAP HER OUT OF IT, WHETHER SHE LIKES IT OR NOT.
...OF COURSE... IF I JUST DO THAT...
...YOH WILL HAVE TO LOOK AT ME.

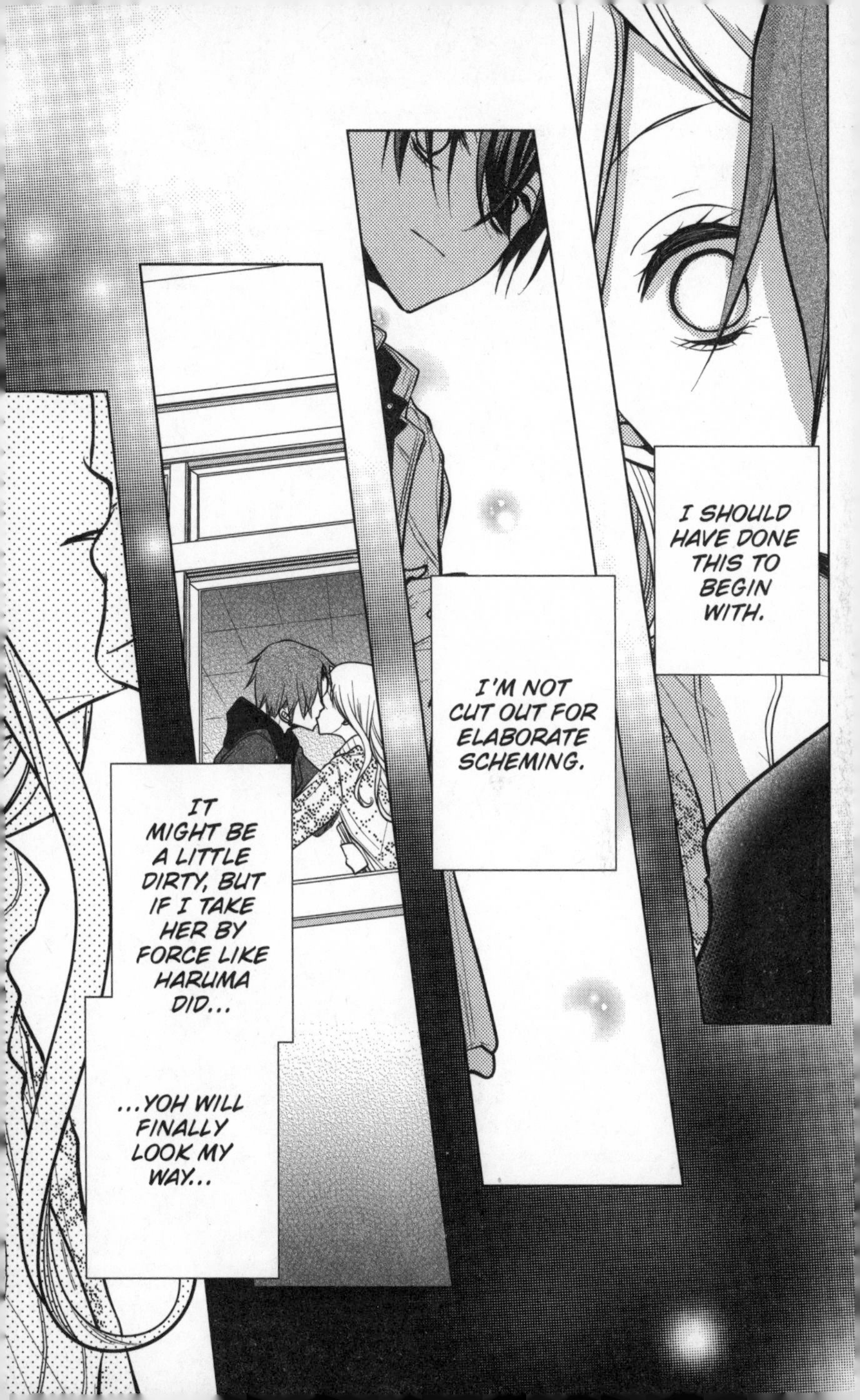
I SHOULD HAVE DONE THIS TO BEGIN WITH.
I'M NOT CUT OUT FOR ELABORATE SCHEMING.
IT MIGHT BE A LITTLE DIRTY, BUT IF I TAKE HER BY FORCE LIKE HARUMA DID...
...YOH WILL FINALLY LOOK MY WAY...

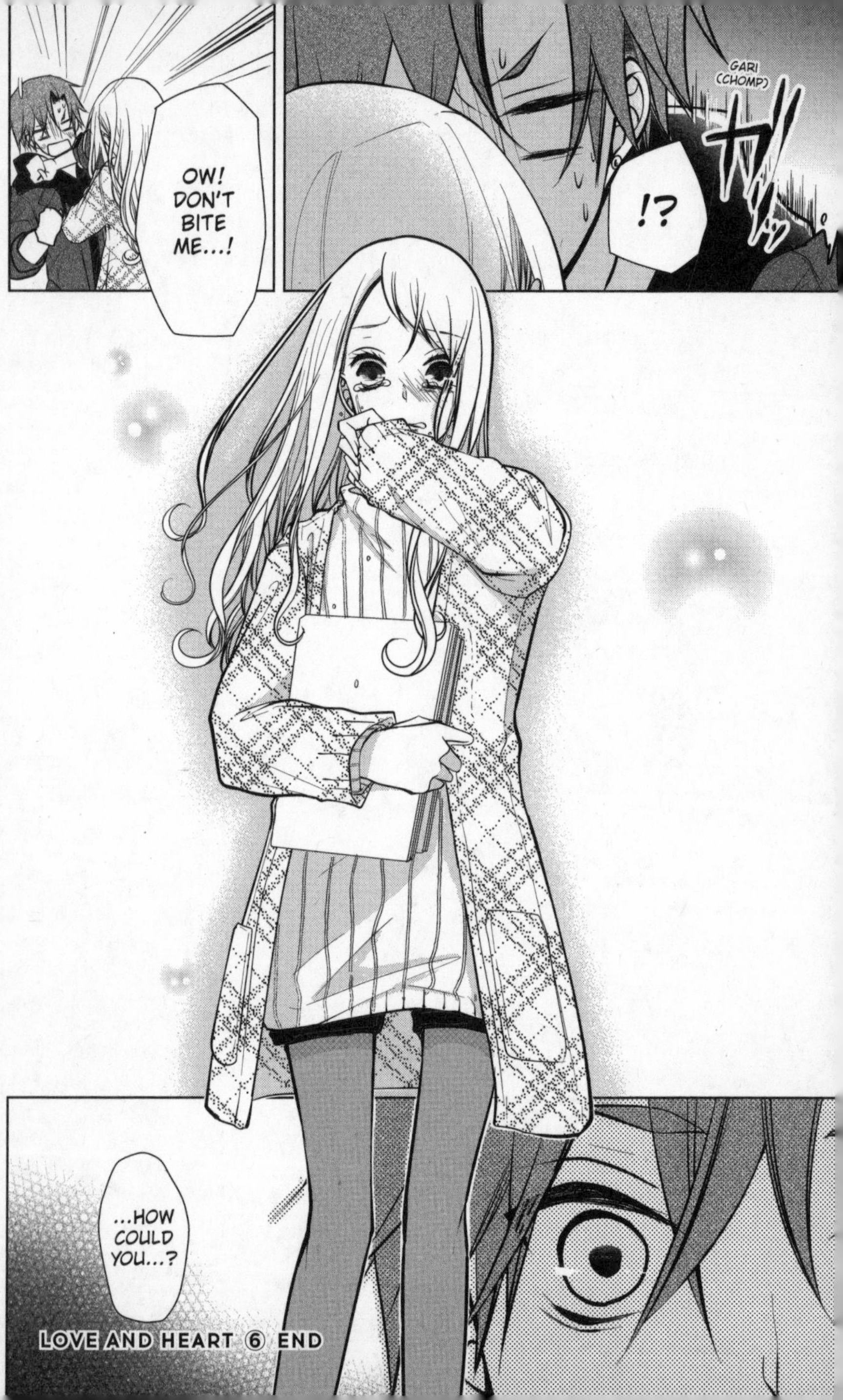
GARI (CHOMP)
!?
OW! DON'T BITE ME...!
...HOW COULD YOU...?
LOVE AND HEART ⑥ END

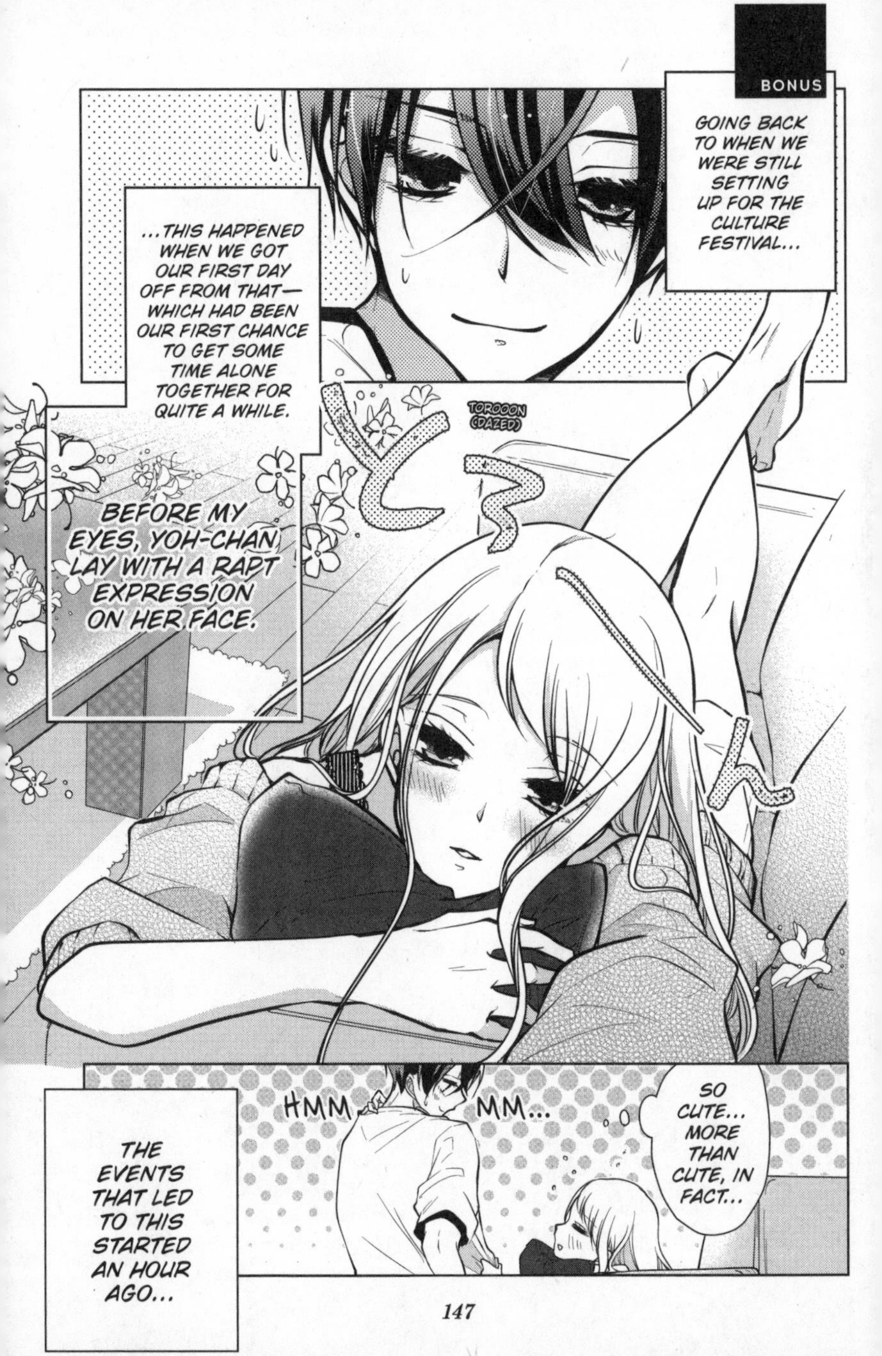
BONUS
GOING BACK TO WHEN WE WERE STILL SETTING UP FOR THE CULTURE FESTIVAL...
...THIS HAPPENED WHEN WE GOT OUR FIRST DAY OFF FROM THAT—WHICH HAD BEEN OUR FIRST CHANCE TO GET SOME TIME ALONE TOGETHER FOR QUITE A WHILE.
TOROOON (DAZED)
BEFORE MY EYES, YOH-CHAN LAY WITH A RAPT EXPRESSION ON HER FACE.
SO CUTE... MORE THAN CUTE, IN FACT...
HMM MM...
THE EVENTS THAT LED TO THIS STARTED AN HOUR AGO...

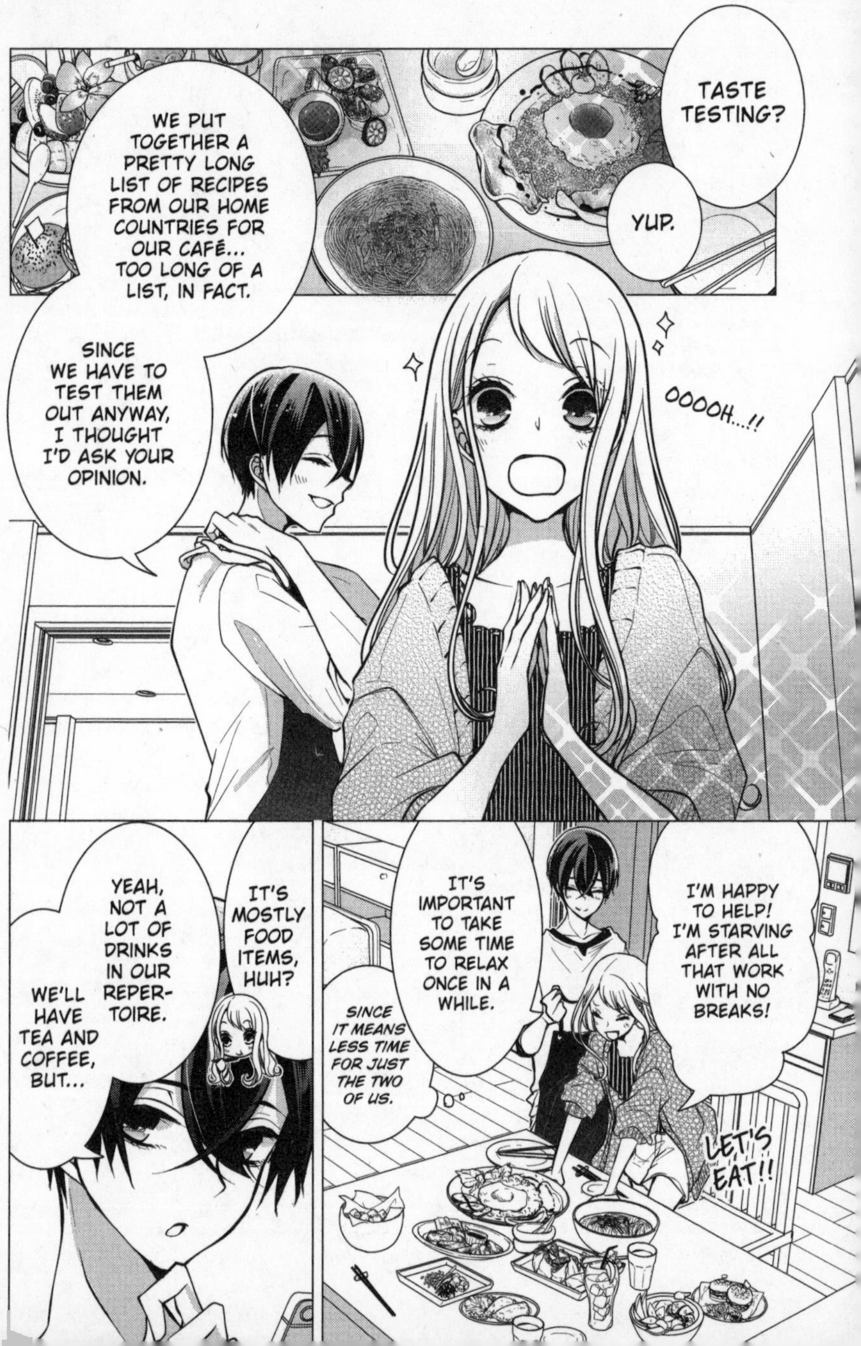
TASTE TESTING?
YUP.
WE PUT TOGETHER A PRETTY LONG LIST OF RECIPES FROM OUR HOME COUNTRIES FOR OUR CAFÉ... TOO LONG OF A LIST, IN FACT.
SINCE WE HAVE TO TEST THEM OUT ANYWAY, I THOUGHT I'D ASK YOUR OPINION.
OOOOH...!!
I'M HAPPY TO HELP! I'M STARVING AFTER ALL THAT WORK WITH NO BREAKS!
LET'S EAT!!
IT'S IMPORTANT TO TAKE SOME TIME TO RELAX ONCE IN A WHILE.
SINCE IT MEANS LESS TIME FOR JUST THE TWO OF US.
IT'S MOSTLY FOOD ITEMS, HUH?
YEAH, NOT A LOT OF DRINKS IN OUR REPERTOIRE.
WE'LL HAVE TEA AND COFFEE, BUT...

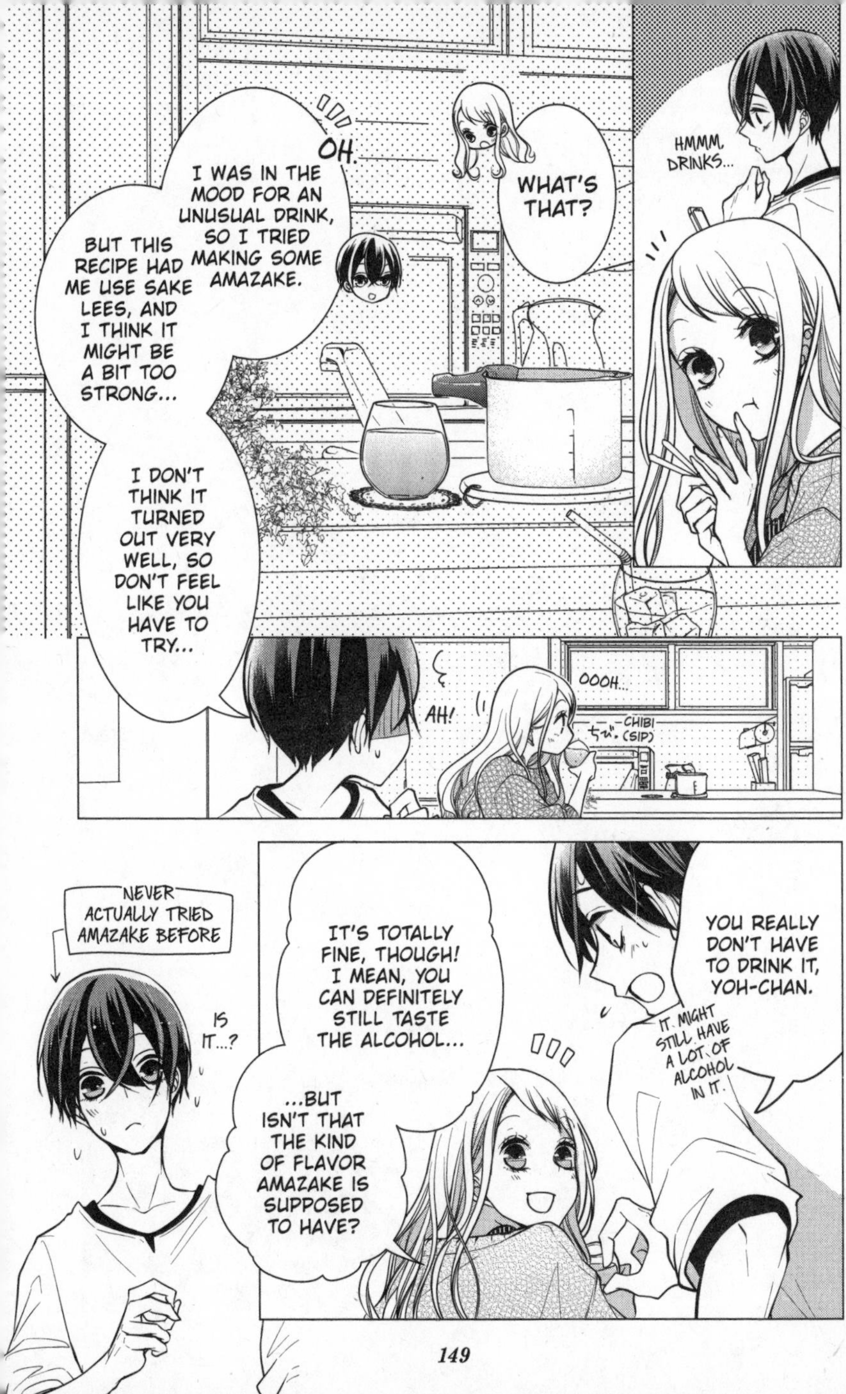
HMMM, DRINKS...
OH.
WHAT'S THAT?
I WAS IN THE MOOD FOR AN UNUSUAL DRINK, SO I TRIED MAKING SOME AMAZAKE.
BUT THIS RECIPE HAD ME USE SAKE LEES, AND I THINK IT MIGHT BE A BIT TOO STRONG...
I DON'T THINK IT TURNED OUT VERY WELL, SO DON'T FEEL LIKE YOU HAVE TO TRY...
AH!
OOOH...
CHIBI
ちび (SIP)
YOU REALLY DON'T HAVE TO DRINK IT, YOH-CHAN.
IT MIGHT STILL HAVE A LOT OF ALCOHOL IN IT.
IT'S TOTALLY FINE, THOUGH! I MEAN, YOU CAN DEFINITELY STILL TASTE THE ALCOHOL...
...BUT ISN'T THAT THE KIND OF FLAVOR AMAZAKE IS SUPPOSED TO HAVE?
NEVER ACTUALLY TRIED AMAZAKE BEFORE
IS IT...?

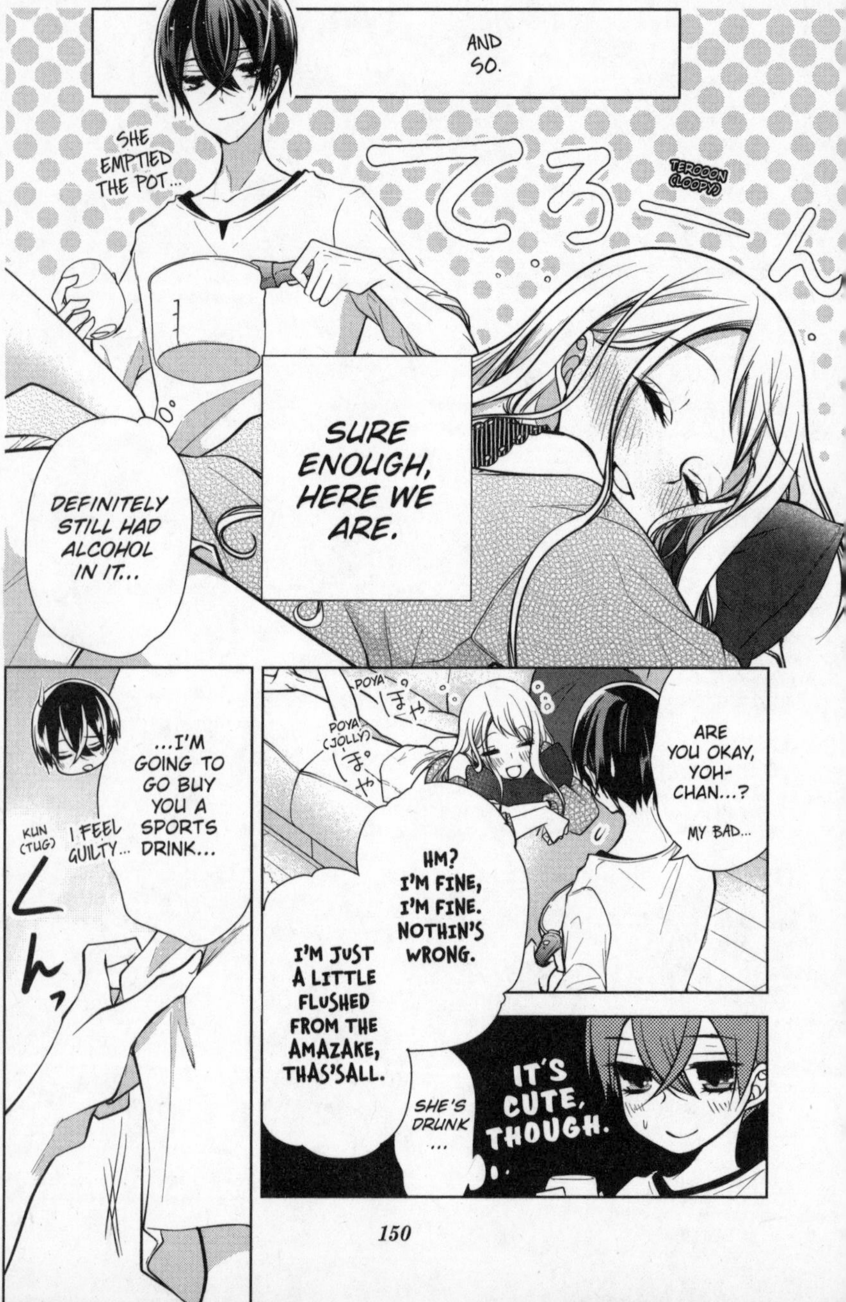
AND SO.
TEROOON (LOOPY)
SHE EMPTIED THE POT...
SURE ENOUGH, HERE WE ARE.
DEFINITELY STILL HAD ALCOHOL IN IT...
ARE YOU OKAY, YOH-CHAN...?
MY BAD...
POYA
POYA (JOLLY)
HM? I'M FINE, I'M FINE. NOTHIN'S WRONG.
I'M JUST A LITTLE FLUSHED FROM THE AMAZAKE, THAS'SALL.
IT'S CUTE, THOUGH.
SHE'S DRUNK...
...I'M GOING TO GO BUY YOU A SPORTS DRINK...
I FEEL GUILTY...
KUN (TUG)

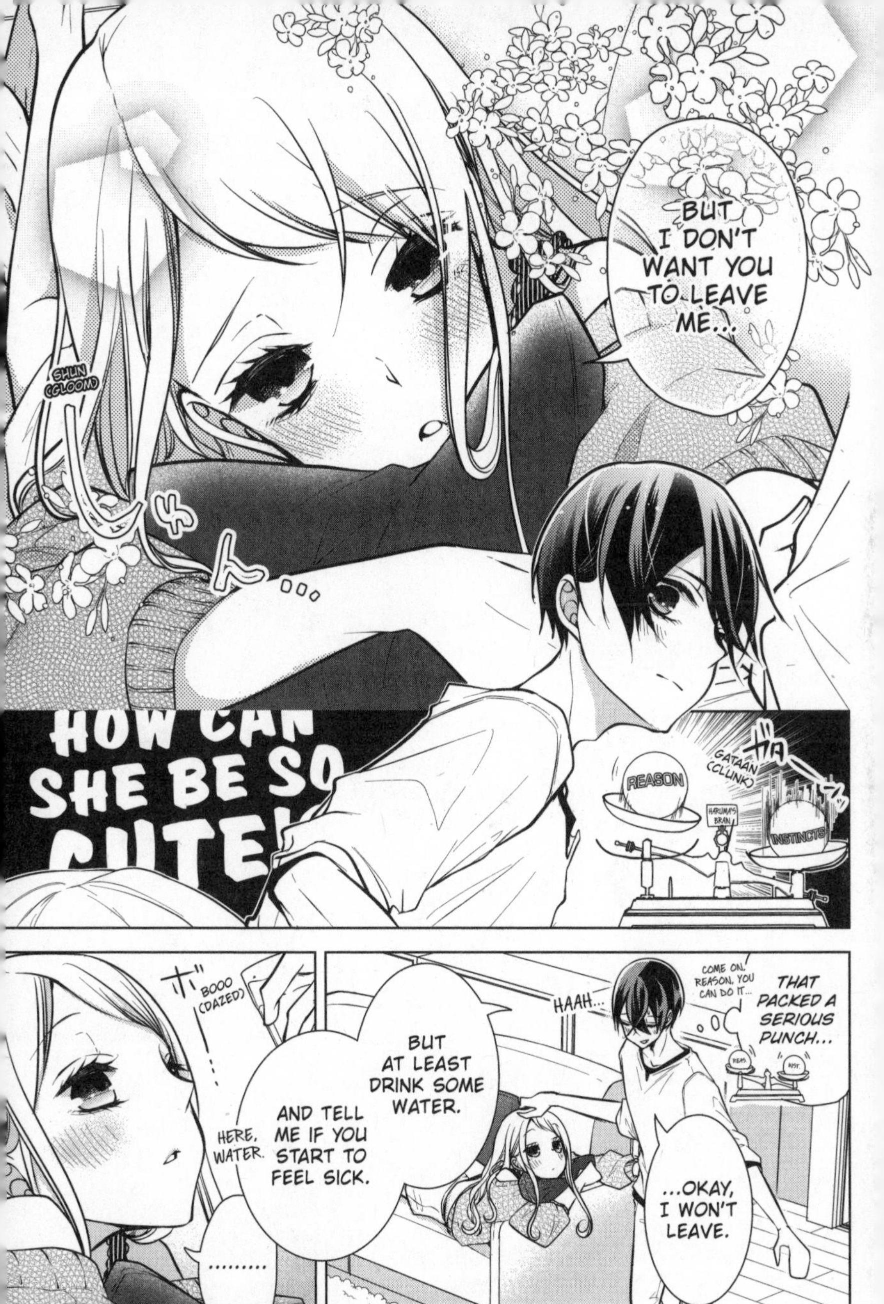
BUT I DON'T WANT YOU TO LEAVE ME...
SHUN (GLOOM)
HOW CAN SHE BE SO CUTE!
GATAAN (CLUNK)
REASON
HARUMA'S BRAIN
INSTINCTS
COME ON! REASON, YOU CAN DO IT...
THAT PACKED A SERIOUS PUNCH...
HAAH...
REAS.
INST.
BUT AT LEAST DRINK SOME WATER.
AND TELL ME IF YOU START TO FEEL SICK.
...OKAY, I WON'T LEAVE.
BOOO (DAZED)
HERE, WATER.
....

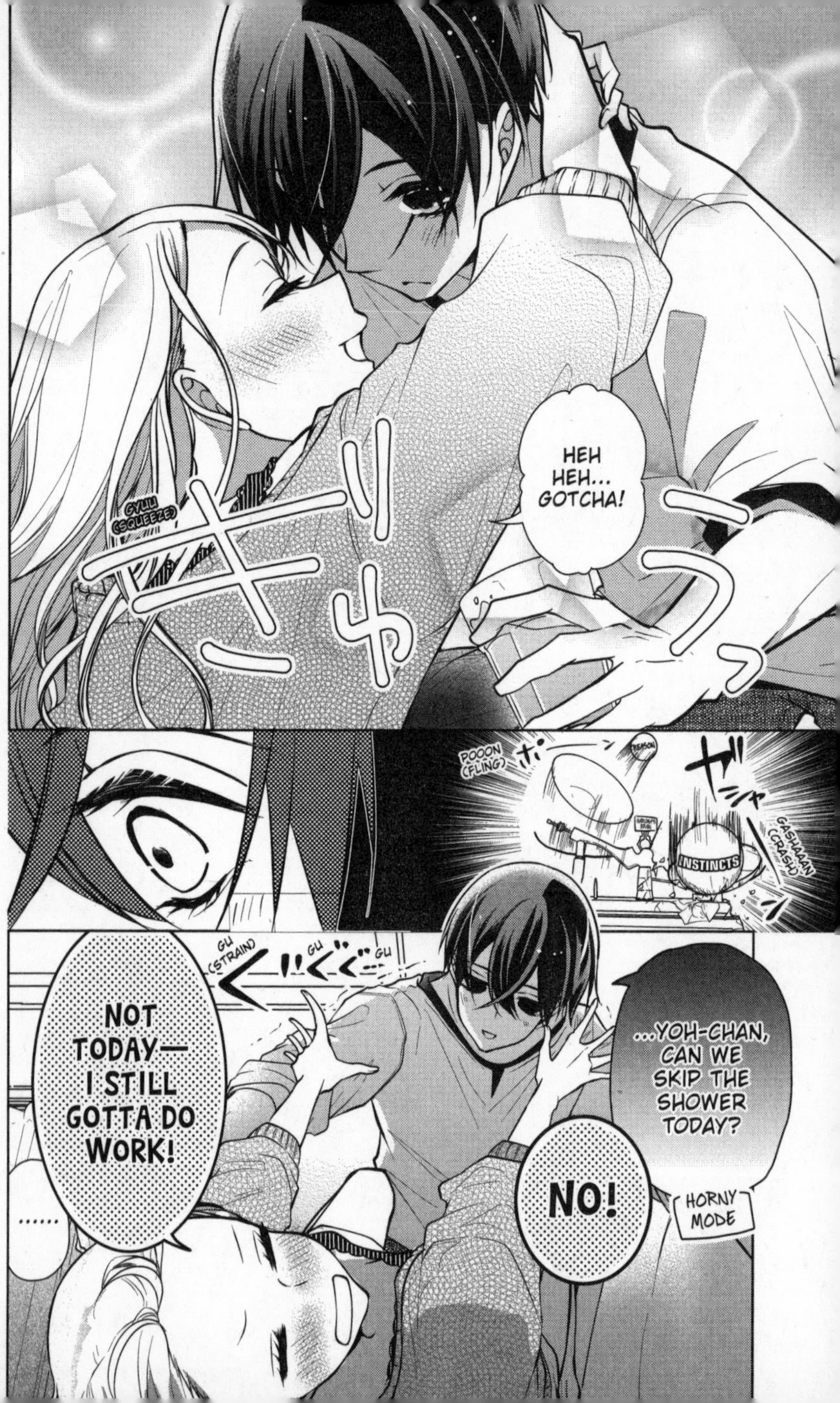
HEH HEH... GOTCHA!
GYUU (SQUEEZE)
REASON
POOON (FLING)
GASHAAAN (CRASH)
INSTINCTS
...YOH-CHAN, CAN WE SKIP THE SHOWER TODAY?
HORNY MODE
NO!
GU GU GU (STRAIN)
NOT TODAY— I STILL GOTTA DO WORK!
......

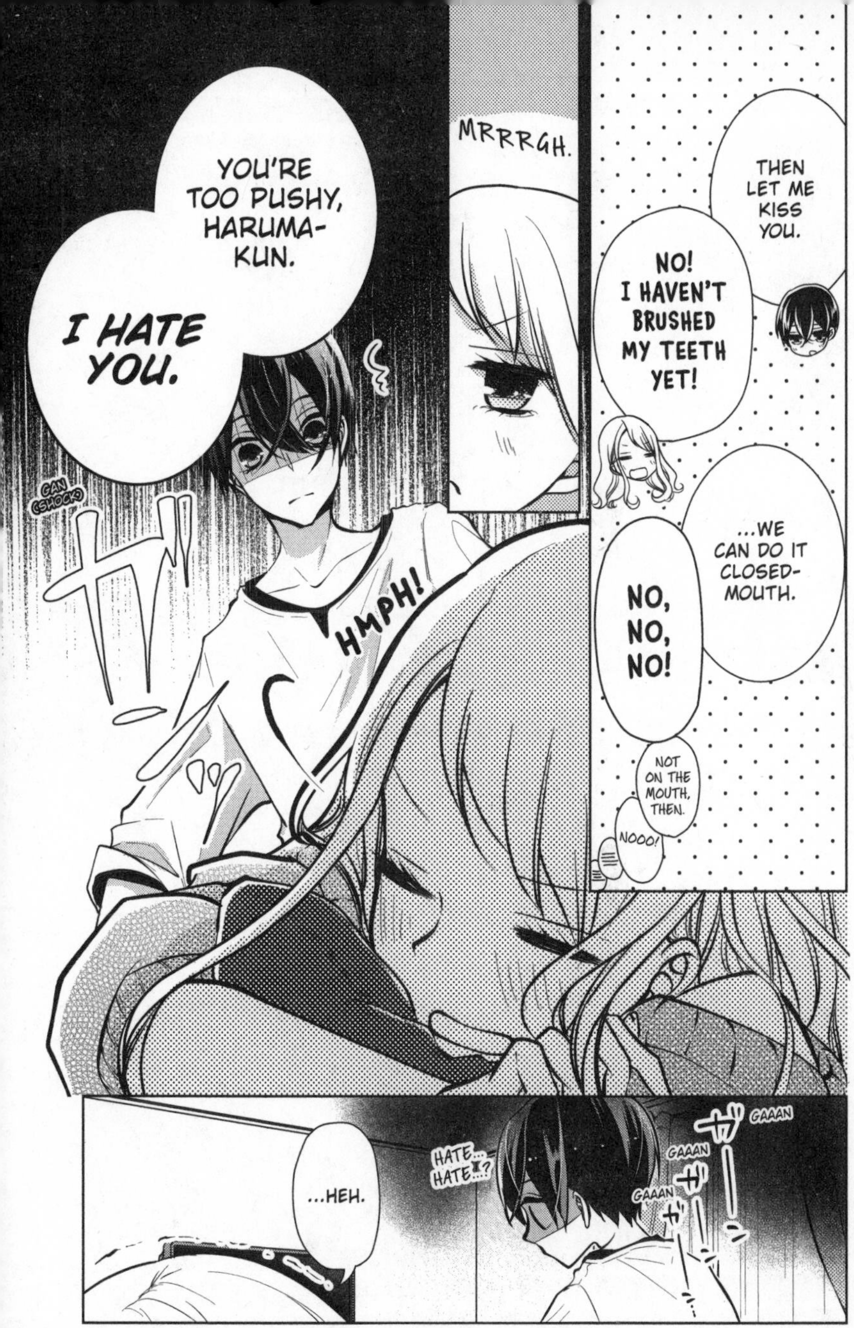
THEN LET ME KISS YOU.
NO! I HAVEN'T BRUSHED MY TEETH YET!
...WE CAN DO IT CLOSED-MOUTH.
NO, NO, NO!
NOT ON THE MOUTH, THEN.
NOOO!
MRRRGH.
YOU'RE TOO PUSHY, HARUMA-KUN.
I HATE YOU.
HMPH!
GAN (SHOCK)
GAAAN
GAAAN
GAAAN
HATE... HATE...?
...HEH.

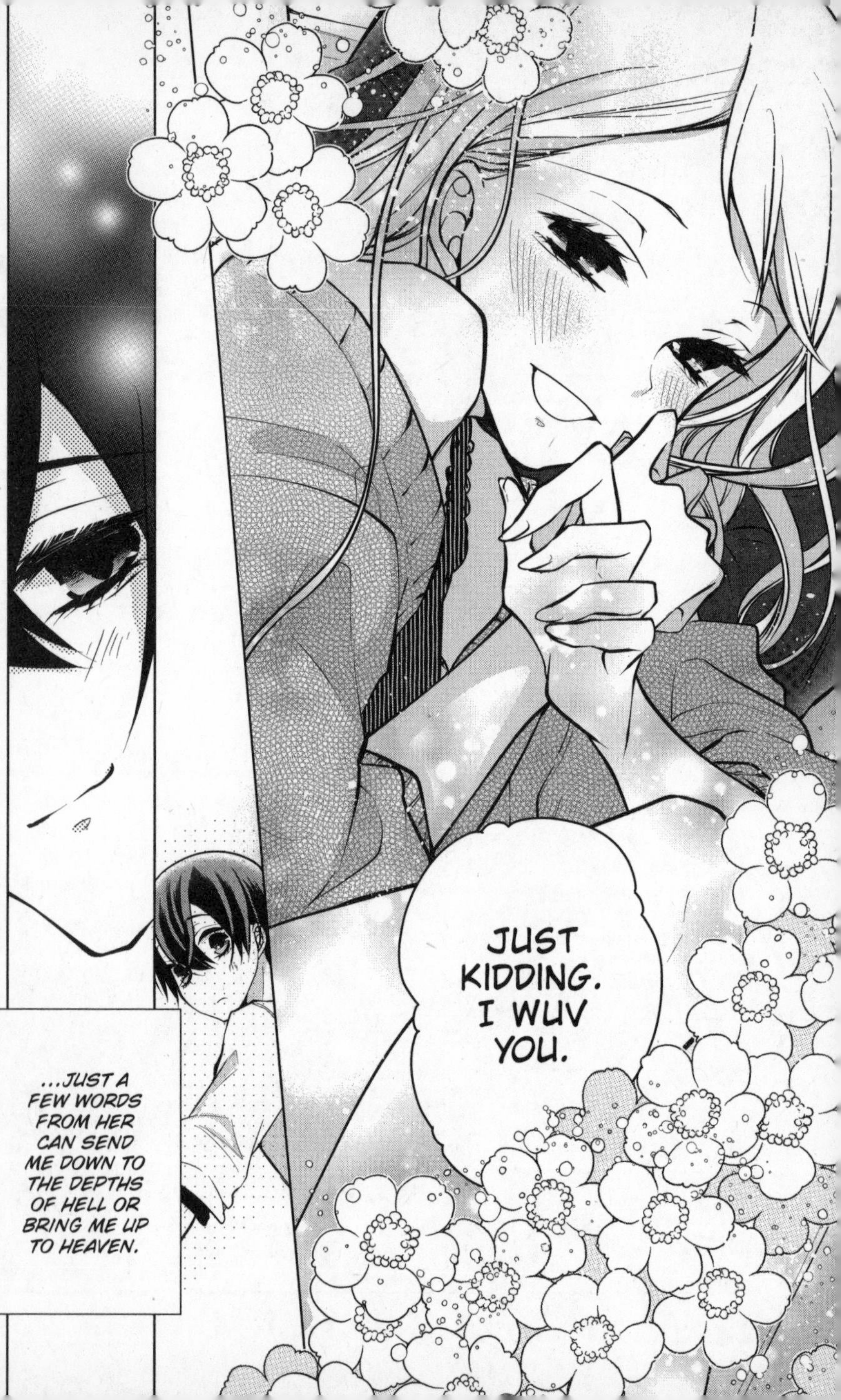
JUST KIDDING. I WUV YOU.
...JUST A FEW WORDS FROM HER CAN SEND ME DOWN TO THE DEPTHS OF HELL OR BRING ME UP TO HEAVEN.

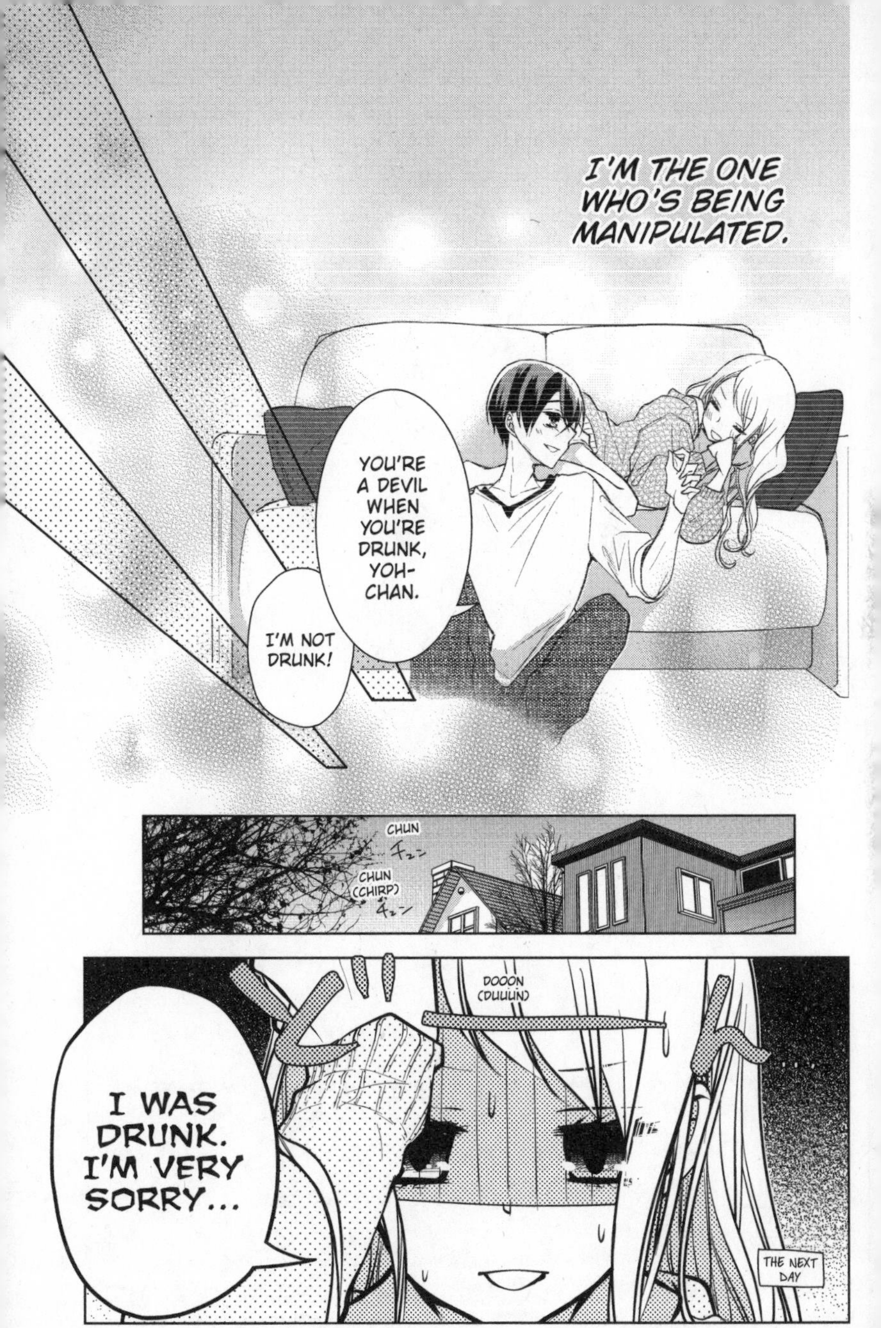
I'M THE ONE WHO'S BEING MANIPULATED.
YOU'RE A DEVIL WHEN YOU'RE DRUNK, YOH-CHAN.
I'M NOT DRUNK!
CHUN
チュン
CHUN (CHIRP)
チュン
DOOON (DUUUN)
THE NEXT DAY
I WAS DRUNK. I'M VERY SORRY...

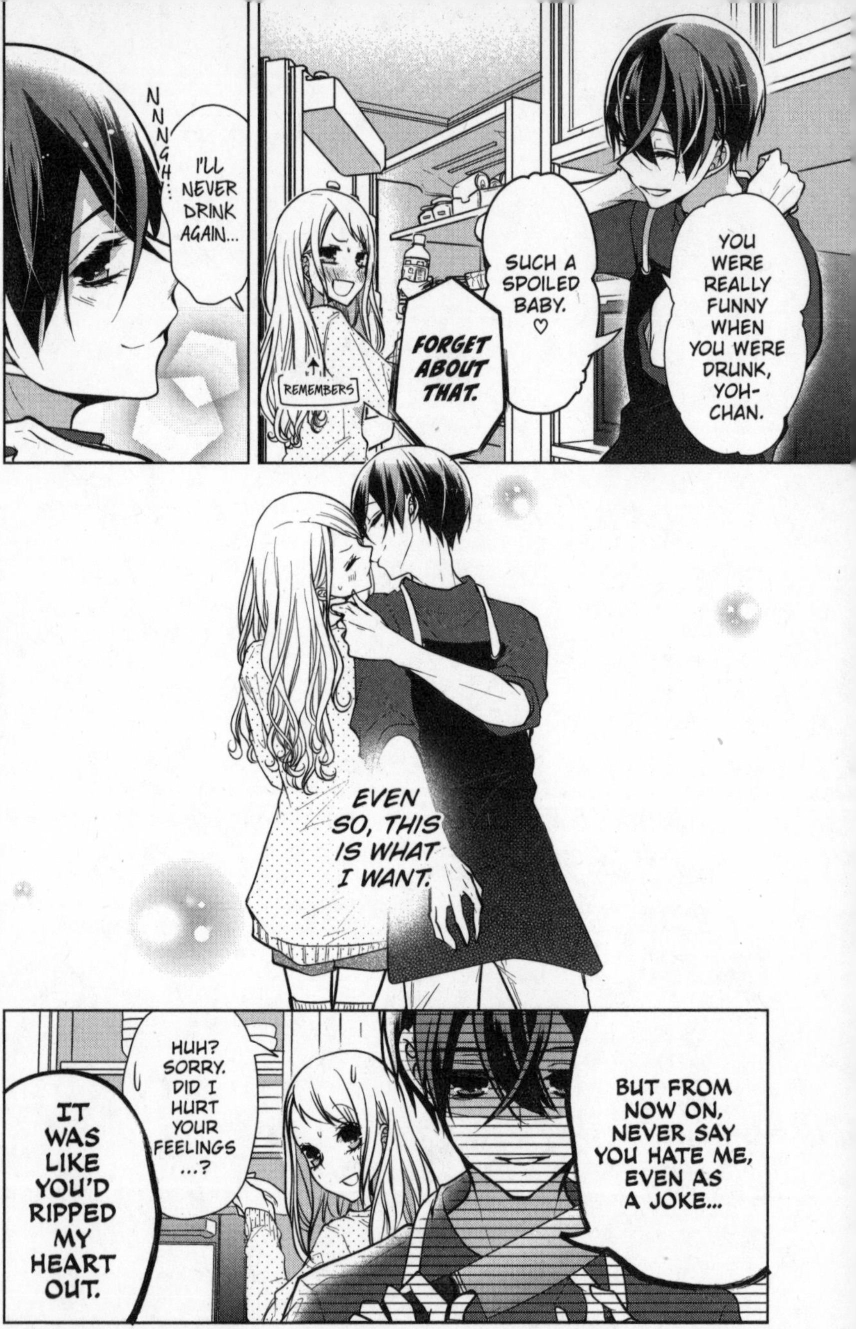
YOU WERE REALLY FUNNY WHEN YOU WERE DRUNK, YOH-CHAN.
SUCH A SPOILED BABY. ♡
FORGET ABOUT THAT.
REMEMBERS
I'LL NEVER DRINK AGAIN...
NNNGH...
EVEN SO, THIS IS WHAT I WANT.
BUT FROM NOW ON, NEVER SAY YOU HATE ME, EVEN AS A JOKE...
HUH? SORRY. DID I HURT YOUR FEELINGS...?
IT WAS LIKE YOU'D RIPPED MY HEART OUT.

BONUS / END

TRANSLATION NOTES

Common Honorifics

no honorific: Indicates familiarity or closeness; if used without permission or reason, addressing someone in this manner would constitute an insult.

-san: The Japanese equivalent of Mr./Mrs./Miss. If a situation calls for politeness, this is the fail-safe honorific.

-kun: Used most often when referring to boys, this indicates affection or familiarity. Occasionally used by older men among their peers, but it may also be used by anyone referring to a person of lower standing.

-chan: An affectionate honorific indicating familiarity used mostly in reference to girls; also used in reference to cute persons or animals of either gender.

-senpai: A term commonly used to respectfully refer to upperclassmen in school or seniors at work. Its antonym, used for underclassmen, is *kouhai*.

Page 27
A **culture festival** is an event where the entire school takes the day off to host booths and attractions that are organized and run by the various clubs and sports teams. They are open to the public and are a popular time for prospective students to visit, which is why the Students' Union's role here revolves around catering to them.

Page 42
Sxxy Zxne is a reference to Sexy Zone, a Japanese boy band. **Clear files** are transparent file folders that also feature opaque artwork of a given pop culture property and are a popular form of merchandise in Japan.

Page 47
White Springs University (*Hakusen Daigaku*) is a reference to the original publisher of *Love and Heart*, Hakusensha.

Page 71
Oshiruko is a sweet, hot, liquidy dessert made of *azuki* beans that is widely available in Japanese vending machines and convenience stores.

Page 102
The exchange student saying **"Well come!"** says "Rasshaimase!" in *katakana* script in the original Japanese version. As she's mispronouncing *irasshaimase* (welcome) and *katakana* can be used to indicate that someone is speaking with an accent, a similar "close, but not quite right" English equivalent has been used here.

Page 127
The symbol on the bottom left corner of Kinoshita's tea is similar to one of Japan's unique **recycling symbols**. Weirdly, even though it seems to be a metal can, the text indicates this is the plastic recycling symbol, and the actual symbol has clockwise arrows with the arrowheads on the top and bottom sides instead of counterclockwise arrows with arrowheads on the left and right sides.

Page 138
Cute Tanuki Don't Have It Easy Either (*Kawaii Tanuki mo Raku janai*) is another real series from *LaLa*, the magazine in which *Love and Heart* was originally published.

Page 149
Amazake (literally "sweet wine") is a drink that typically has low alcohol content. It's usually made from rice and *kouji* mold, but can also be made from combining sake lees (deposits of yeast left behind during the fermentation process) with sugar, a recipe that can apparently pack more of a punch.

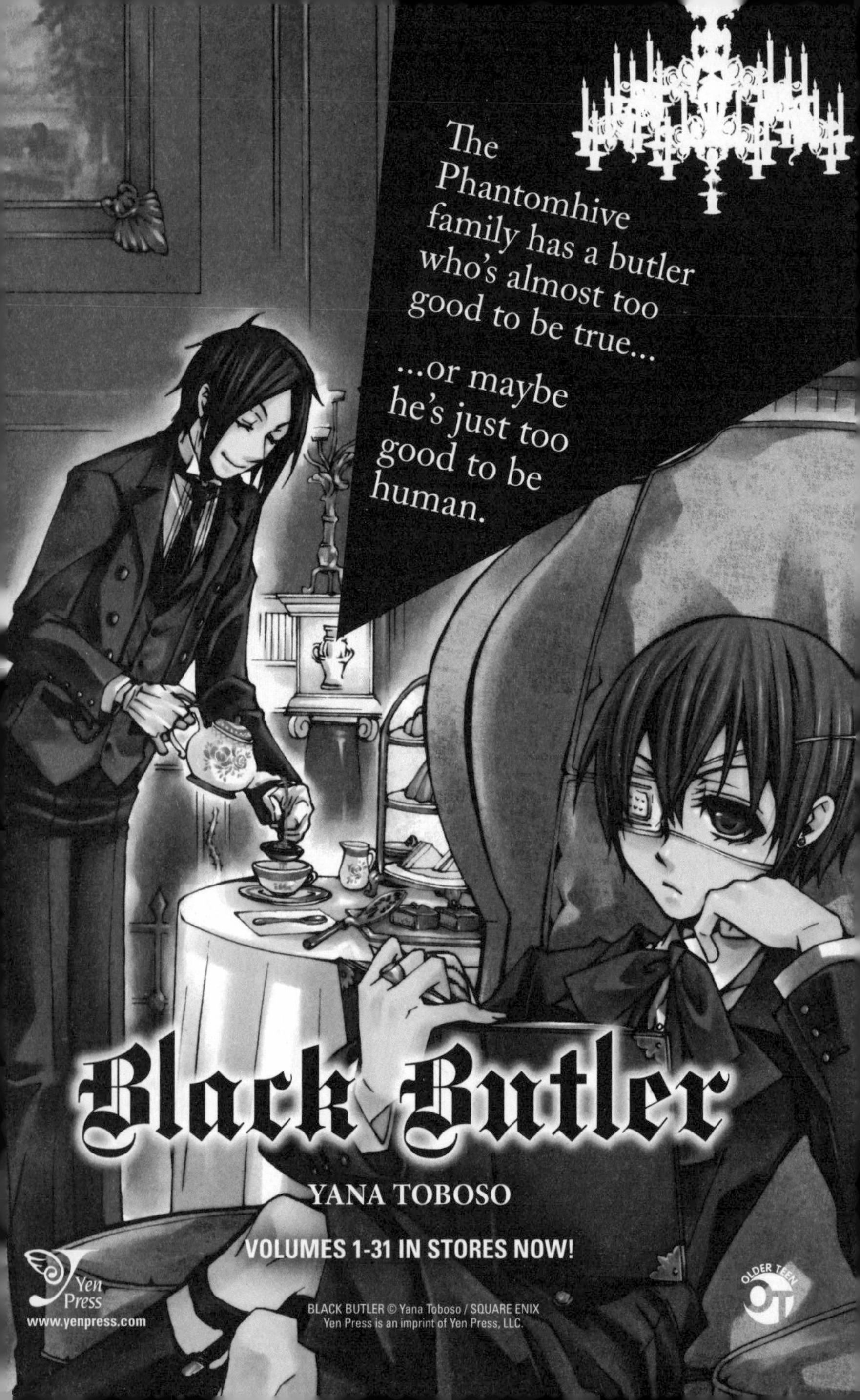

The Phantomhive family has a butler who's almost too good to be true...
...or maybe he's just too good to be human.
Black Butler
YANA TOBOSO
VOLUMES 1-31 IN STORES NOW!
Yen Press
www.yenpress.com
BLACK BUTLER © Yana Toboso / SQUARE ENIX
Yen Press is an imprint of Yen Press, LLC.
OLDER TEEN
OT

©Aidalro/SQUARE ENIX

VOLUMES
1-16 IN STORES
NOW!

VOLUMES 1-17
AVAILABLE DIGITALLY!

Toilet-bound Hanako-Kun

At Kamome Academy, rumors abound about the school's Seven Mysteries, one of which is Hanako-san. Said to occupy the third stall of the third floor girls' bathroom in the old school building, Hanako-san grants any wish when summoned. Nene Yashiro, an occult-loving high school girl who dreams of romance, ventures into this haunted bathroom...but the Hanako-san she meets there is nothing like she imagined! Kamome Academy's Hanako-san...is a boy!

Yen Press

For more information
visit www.yenpress.com

6

CHITOSE KAIDO

Translation: **ALETHEA AND ATHENA NIBLEY**

Lettering: **CHIHO CHRISTIE**

This book is a work of fiction. Names, characters, places, and incidents are the product of the author's imagination or are used fictitiously. Any resemblance to actual events, locales, or persons, living or dead, is coincidental.

KOI TO SHINZO by Chitose Kaido
© Chitose Kaido 2020
All rights reserved.
First published in Japan in 2020 by HAKUSENSHA, INC., Tokyo.
English translation rights in U.S.A., Canada and U.K. arranged with HAKUSENSHA, INC., Tokyo through TUTTLE-MORI AGENCY, INC., Tokyo.

English translation © 2022 by Yen Press, LLC

Yen Press, LLC supports the right to free expression and the value of copyright. The purpose of copyright is to encourage writers and artists to produce the creative works that enrich our culture.

The scanning, uploading, and distribution of this book without permission is a theft of the author's intellectual property. If you would like permission to use material from the book (other than for review purposes), please contact the publisher. Thank you for your support of the author's rights.

Yen Press
150 West 30th Street, 19th Floor
New York, NY 10001

Visit us at yenpress.com
facebook.com/yenpress † twitter.com/yenpress
yenpress.tumblr.com † instagram.com/yenpress

First Yen Press Edition: December 2022
Edited by Yen Press Editorial: Riley Pearsall
Designed by Yen Press Design: Andy Swist

Yen Press is an imprint of Yen Press, LLC.
The Yen Press name and logo are trademarks of Yen Press, LLC.

The publisher is not responsible for websites (or their content) that are not owned by the publisher.

Library of Congress Control Number: 2020950226

ISBNs: 978-1-9753-5022-2 (paperback)
978-1-9753-5023-9 (ebook)

1 3 5 9 10 8 6 4 2

WOR

Printed in the United States of America